Gastropolitics and the Specter of Race

CALIFORNIA STUDIES IN FOOD AND CULTURE

Darra Goldstein, Editor

Gastropolitics and the Specter of Race

STORIES OF CAPITAL, CULTURE, AND COLONIALITY IN PERU

María Elena García

UNIVERSITY OF CALIFORNIA PRESS

University of California Press
Oakland, California

Library of Congress Cataloging-in-Publication Data

Names: García, María Elena, author.
Title: Gastropolitics and the specter of race : stories of capital, culture, and
   coloniality in Peru / María Elena García.
Other titles: California studies in food and culture ; 76.
Description: Oakland, California : University of California Press, [2021] |
   Series: California studies in food and culture ; 76 | Includes bibliographical
   references and index.
Identifiers: LCCN 2020032200 (print) | LCCN 2020032201 (ebook) |
   ISBN 9780520301894 (hardback) | ISBN 9780520301900 (paperback) |
   ISBN 9780520972308 (ebook)
Subjects: LCSH: Food—Social aspects—Peru.
Classification: LCC GT2853.P4 G37 2021 (print) | LCC GT2853.P4 (ebook) |
   DDC 394.1/20985—dc23
LC record available at https://lccn.loc.gov/2020032200
LC ebook record available at https://lccn.loc.gov/2020032201

Manufactured in the United States of America

25   24   23   22   21
10   9   8   7   6   5   4   3   2   1

Para Toño

CONTENTS

ILLUSTRATIONS

PREFACE: UNDERSTORIES

How to stop a story that is always being told? Or, how to change
a story that is always being told?

—AUDRA SIMPSON[1]

Stories are wondrous things. And they are dangerous.

—THOMAS KING[2]

In 2011 PromPerú, the Peruvian state export and tourism agency, launched
a promotional video to mark the international début of Marca Perú (brand
name Peru).[3] In the video, *zampolla* (Andean panpipe) music plays in the
background as a bus with the symbol of Marca Perú and the red-and-white of
the Peruvian flag on its side drives down the open Nebraska plains.[4] The camera pans out across fields as the bus enters the main street of Peru, Nebraska.
As it does, the video's narrator tells us that "every Peruvian, by the mere fact
of being Peruvian, has the right to enjoy how marvelous it is to be Peruvian."[5]
We are then introduced to this small town (population 569), as the narrator
sets the stage. "Peru, Nebraska has a problem," he says. "They are Peruvians,
but they don't know what that means."

The bus stops, the doors open, and the driver—none other than Gastón
Acurio, a leading chef and public figure in Peru—announces their arrival.
As Peruvian chefs, actors, musicians, surfers, and tourism promoters exit the
bus, the narrator explains that their mission is "to be ambassadors of our
country and read them their rights as Peruvians." One of the chefs then picks
up a megaphone and, fist in the air, tells the town in Spanish that they are
Peruvians, and accordingly, they have "the right to eat well." The video, which
went viral almost overnight, goes on to document the power of Peruvian

food and culture. Educating North American Peruvians about their rights *as* Peruvians, these cultural ambassadors perform Peru for their compatriots in multiple ways. Most important, this was a powerful performance of national sovereignty and a reflection of the sentiment expressed in Peru today: Peru is not only in a different place economically, socially, and politically; inverting the common North-South story; Peru is now the one bringing civilization to the world.

This performance is particularly striking when we consider that only eleven years before this video was made, Peru was still reeling from the political violence and economic precarity that engulfed the country in the 1980s and 1990s. As I write in 2020, Peru is enjoying a reputation as one of the world's leading tourist destinations.[6] People are traveling not simply to see Machu Picchu; they are now going to Peru to eat. Indeed, in this story of national resurgence, food has been central as hegemonic narratives emphasize the power of food as a social weapon that can heal the wounds inflicted by long histories of colonial violence, exclusion, and inequality.

This remarkable story of resurgence resonates deeply with many in Peru. Despite ongoing violent conflicts (particularly around extractive industries such as mining), political corruption scandals, and the persistence of strident arguments over who can count as victim (or perpetrator) of the violence and authoritarianism of the late twentieth century, many Peruvians have fervently embraced the hegemonic narrative of a nation transformed "from terror to culinary destination."[7] As I discuss in the pages that follow, this is a story that celebrates what chef Gastón Acurio describes as the "beautiful fusion" of multiple cultural traditions and "races" (*todas las sangres*); of a country that finally recognizes the value of its unique racial, cultural, and culinary blend; and of citizens who, for the first time in decades, are proud to call themselves Peruvian. In other words, this is the story of Peru's "gastronomic revolution."

This book calls into question the celebratory claims of this so-called revolution (also often referred to as Peru's gastronomic boom). I argue that, in fact, hegemonic discourses and performances of inclusion and culinary success obscure ongoing violence, particularly against Indigenous lands and bodies; that the gastronomic boom is simply another expression of the long story that is "the coloniality of power" in Peru.[8] But I make this critique with some hesitation. I must admit that the first time I saw the "Peru, Nebraska" video, I had a rush of nationalist adrenaline that instantly brought a smile to my face. Despite my best efforts to watch critically, and despite the video's problematic representations of cultural and racial difference, I remember a fleeting sense of triumph over the United States, as North Americans were now the targets of a Peruvian civilizational mission. Although I have lived in the United States since I was fourteen years old, I remain closely identified with the country of my birth and tied to Peru by family, friends, and other relations, particularly in Lima and Cusco. I am not above feeling the tugs of nationalist pride, even as I recognize that this is precisely what the Peruvian state, and the makers of this very well-produced video, want me to feel. I know that this glossy and appealing propaganda is just that, and thus must be taken with a few grains of skepticism. This book is driven by that skepticism and my confidence in a critique of what I call the Peruvian gastropolitical complex.

But there are other understories too, understories that weave throughout the pages of this book, perhaps noticeable only to me, though I imagine my grandmother, my parents, my siblings, and others could perhaps also feel them, understand my writing through them. And here too, food is central. As Valérie Loichot notes in her exploration of the works of Haitian American novelist Edwidge Danticat and French novelist Giséle Pineau (whose parents were from Guadeloupe), "[F]ood constitutes the core of Pineau's and Danticat's narratives of childhood and exile . . . a personal experience . . . that ultimately structures their works."[9] For these women, "more than plain survival . . . cooking and eating mend disjointed communities and restore the link to their original land. . . . Food is the original pleasure, food is missed; food is painful, food is shame; food is language, fluid and interrupted, untranslatable yet essential."[10] When I first read Loichot's words, I was struck by how intensely they resonated with my own experience. I can't think of my grandmother, who passed away several years ago, without thinking about (*without smelling*) garlic, sizzling in oil, about to be joined by sliced or chopped onion. This is the base for many Peruvian meals, at least those home-cooked meals many of us grew up with. Rice is not rice without it cooking in a fragrant dollop of garlic browned in oil, a smell and sound ubiquitous to any apartment complex or house in Peru. I remember wanting to learn more about her life, turning on the tape recorder, and her saying, "[L]et's cook. We can talk as we cook."

Earlier still, when we moved to Virginia a few months after I had turned fourteen, food served as that link that Loichot writes about. As I entered high school and my sister began middle school, we were told to study hard, to learn English. We were expected to assimilate, to be grateful to this country for the opportunities it would offer, and to progress as dutiful immigrants. As young Peruvian women, we had to stay away from boys. And, perhaps to avoid such contact, we were to eat lunch only at home, not in school. ("Food is shame, food is language.") We were to sit by our lockers and study while our classmates had lunch in the cafeteria. Once home, we would eat proper food, Peruvian food, food that connected us to our land, to our families, to who we were. Or at least to who we were supposed to be. That connection stayed with me, and for many years after those early moments in this country, and even today, eating Peruvian food, cooking Peruvian food, my family's food, *my food*, says something, and it feels entirely different than anything else I do or eat or smell or feel. The taste of it evokes memories of childhood, family, land, relations, even those I did not know existed.

One of my biggest worries is that this book will upset my family. As I write, my parents, my cousins, my siblings, my aunts and uncles, my godfather, everyone has been excited, supportive, expectant. But many are not fully aware of my critical approach; they do not know that where they might see success, pride, hope, I see dispossession, extraction, appropriation. And yet.

My brother recently opened a Peruvian restaurant in northern Virginia, and it has been wonderfully successful. While he had not finished college, he had done well for himself by working in the restaurant and bar industry. It was in this context of late nights and drunken parties (and Trump-fueled hate crimes) that he was brutally attacked. Five men jumped him, kicking him in the head, breaking every bone in his face. Miraculously, there was no brain damage, and after many surgeries and months of therapy, he recovered. Throughout his recovery, he remained steadfast in his belief that this had happened for a reason. Upon recovering (and despite crippling medical bills and panic attacks), he finished college, got married, found a more stable 9 to 5 job, became a new father, and early in 2019, opened his own Peruvian restaurant. My brother has worked incredibly hard, and he is savvy at marketing. He is also aware that his restaurant's success is in no small part due to the new status of Peruvian cuisine. Indeed, even as they recognize my brother's exacting labor, my family connects his success to the culinary boom associated with chef Gastón Acurio. Without Acurio and other high-profile chefs like him, they might argue, Peruvian food would not have found its rightful place in global gastronomic circles, and Peru would not be recognized as a culinary destination.

Family and friends in Peru (and elsewhere) might ask why, given our backstory of political violence and terror, I don't join others in celebration of this newly branded nation. Why can't I focus on the "good" side of this story about the rise of Peru? To them, and others who might ask similar questions, I can only say that I can't ignore the dark side of this boom, or the fact that this "new" story of resilience, resurgence, and reconciliation is in fact an old story of colonial brutality, representational harm, extraction, and dispossession. I have had many conversations about this work with friends and colleagues. One of those conversations, with Indigenous literary scholar Lydia Heberling (of Yaqui and Apache ancestry), comes directly to mind. Lydia introduced me to the powerful work of Chumash and Ohlone/Costanoan-Esselen writer Deborah Miranda. Part memoir, part tribal history, Miranda's *Bad Indians* is about the experience of California Indians.[11] More specifically, Miranda takes on the tragic story that is California, and in particular, the story of the missionization of California. "Story is the most powerful force in the world—in our world, maybe in all worlds. Story is culture. . . . It exists as truth. As a whole. Even if the whole is in constant change. In fact, because of that constant change."[12] And, she writes, the story of missionization—that story that depicted California Indians as "godless, dirty, stupid, primitive, ugly, passive, drunken, immoral, lazy," and perhaps most significantly, as "disappeared" "has done more damage . . . than any conquistador, any priest . . ., any smallpox, measles, or influenza virus. This story has not just killed us, it has taught us how to kill ourselves and kill each other with alcohol, domestic violence, horizontal racism, internalized hatred. This story is a kind of evil, a kind of witchery. We have to put an end to it now."[13]

This book is an attempt to uncover, explore, and disrupt some of the multiple stories that are Peru: stories about cuisine and hope, race and violence, indigeneity and gender, human and animal. Athabascan literary scholar Dian Million tells us that stories "are a felt knowledge that accumulates and becomes a force that empowers stories that are otherwise separate to become a focus, a potential for movement."[14] Taking inspiration from the fierce Indigenous feminisms of scholars like Million, Miranda, Simpson, and so many others, I want to share some stories that, as Million says, "rock the boat and perhaps the world." "All of this becomes important to . . . our ability to speak to ourselves, to inform ourselves and our generations, to counter and intervene in a constantly morphing colonial system. To 'decolonize' means to understand as fully as possible the forms colonialism takes in our own times."[15] Because colonialism shape-shifts, we must continue to search for it even in projects that seem to shine with beauty, good intentions, and the promise of inclusion.

ACKNOWLEDGMENTS

Since I began research for this book over ten years ago, many people and organizations have offered significant support. There are too many to name here, but I do want to highlight a few who have been central to this project's development. My scholarly exploration of Andean animals began at Sarah Lawrence College and Tufts University alongside others, such as William Lynn, Karen Rader, and students who pushed me to consider more-than-human complexity. Since arriving at the University of Washington, where I began research for this project in earnest, many have encouraged and inspired this work. From conversations in seminars (special shout-out to Amanda, Clara, Dustin, Dylan, Kyle, Meghan, Nienhaus, Quinn, Rae, Sydney, Tahoma, Tessa, and Victoria) and meetings of the Animal Studies Working Group (thank you Annie, Karen, and Katie), to unwavering institutional and collegial support (thanks especially to José Alaniz, Chad Allen, Jennifer Bean, Jean Dennison, Gary Handwerk, Danny Hoffman, Judy Howard, Vicky Lawson, Phillip Thurtle, Kathy Woodward, and Glennys Young), I am lucky to be surrounded by such smart and generous people. Special thanks also to Katie Gillespie, Meghan Jones and Dustin Welch García, who provided significant research assistance.

Some at UW deserve special mention. Louisa Mackenzie was a crucial coconspirator on many projects; Adam Warren shared resources, stories, and contacts in Peru, especially as I began to think more deeply about food; Christian Novetzke encouraged me from the beginning of this work (and he knows I would never have applied for fellowship support were it not for him); Rich Watts offered fierce support and was always there for me, whether I needed a drink or a laugh or a sympathetic ear; Jayadev Athreya, Dian Million, and Chandan Reddy inspired me in countless ways; and Radhika

Govindrajan and Sunila Kale are forces of nature. Their sharp wit and warm friendship sustained me.

Over the years, many colleagues read and offered important feedback on portions of this manuscript at different stages. Neel Ahuja, Cristina Alcalde, Andrew Canessa, Amy Cox Hall (and her students at Amherst), Naisargi Dave, Chris Garces, Shane Greene, Lori Gruen, John Hartigan, Lydia Heberling, Alex Isfahani-Hammond, Claire Kim, Sebastián López Vergara, Bruce Mannheim, Joe Masco, Raúl Matta, Timothy Pachirat, Deborah Thomas, Adam Warren, and Rich Watts, I can't thank you enough for your thoughtful and critical insights. In addition, conversations at workshops at the University of Michigan (thanks to Jason De León for the hospitality), at the Race and Animals Institute at Wesleyan (thanks to Lori Gruen, Claire Kim, and Timothy Pachirat for the invitation), and at the School for Advanced Research seminar, "How Nature Works" (thanks to Sarah Besky, Alex Blanchette, and Naisargi Dave for organizing), shaped this text in important ways. I am also grateful for conversations at the NEH seminar "Urban Environmental Humanities" (thanks Rich and Thaisa), at Cornell (thanks Chris), UC Santa Cruz, the conference Decolonizing Critical Animal Studies at the University of Alberta, and the intellectual community that is the Comparative History of Ideas at UW.

I am especially indebted to Florence Babb, Robert Desjarlais, Radhika Govindrajan, David Greenwood-Sanchez, Bret Gustafson, and José Antonio Lucero for reading entire drafts and offering detailed, generous, and generative comments. If this book is at all compelling, it is because of them.

In Peru, many people made this book possible. Again, there are too many to list, but I do want to offer special thanks to a few: Carlos Camacho, Lilia Chauca, Francesco D'Angelo, Arlette Eulert, Eliana Icochea, José Jimenez, William Lossio, Cecilia Mendiola, Jorge Miyagui, Palmiro Ocampo, Flavio Solórzano, Victor Vich, and Jane Wheeler. Thanks also to Elizabeth Rico Numbela in Bolivia. As with all projects, there are traces left by many who do not often make it into acknowledgment pages. A few who stand out are Aaron, Bobby, Cynthia, Ellika, Jessica, Kate, Kelsey, Laura, Lo, Mark, and Shawn.

This book would not have been possible without the financial support of many institutions. At UW, the Center for American Indian and Indigenous Studies, Center for Global Studies, Comparative History of Ideas Department, Hanauer Honors Professorship, Simpson Center for the Humanities, and Royalty Research Fund offered crucial financial and institutional support. I am also indebted to the National Endowment for the Humanities for support that allowed me to write the majority of this book. Bob, Bret, Christian, Nais, and Radhika, thank you for your support throughout the application process. I am also grateful to Juan Acevedo, José Bedia and José Bedia Jr., Francesco D'Angelo, Elizabeth Lino, Palmiro Ocampo, Jeff Olivet, and Rocío Silva Santisteban for their permission to include their work and words in this book. Thanks to Ben Hibbard at Phaidon Press for his help. The recipes included in the interlude before chapter 2 are reproduced from the book *Central* (by Virgilio Martínez), under license from Phaidon Press Limited © 2016. Thank you also to SAR Press and Duke University Press for permission to reproduce previously published material (chapters 5 and 6). Epigraphs included in the preface are reproduced with permission from Duke University Press (from "Conclusion. Interruptus," in *Mohawk Interruptus*, Audra Simpson, pp. 177–194. Copyright 2014) and University of Minnesota Press (Thomas King, *The Truth about Stories: A Native Narrative*, p. 9. Copyright 2003 Dead Dog Café Productions, Inc. and the Canadian Broadcasting Corporation.)

I could not have asked for a more supportive and accomplished editor than Kate Marshall. She was steadfast in her belief in this project from the beginning and gracefully shepherded this book from beginning to end. Thank you also to Enrique Ochoa-Kaup for stepping in when Kate was on maternity leave. He offered help and much reassurance throughout the production process. Thanks as well to Bob Schwarz, a fabulous indexer.

My family is also present in these pages in multiple ways. From my aunts, uncles, and cousins, who joked and emailed and sent me newspaper and journal clippings, to my godfather Beto and his partner Tom, who engaged seriously with my critiques, to my parents and siblings, who were steadfast in their support, their thoughts and ideas and concerns are part of this book. My grandmother Ana Elena (*mi mamama Ani*) always believed in me. Even before I knew who I would become, even as I made mistake after mistake, she believed in me and found ways to communicate her support. She is always with me. Tony and Toño, I would not be done with this book were it not for you both. Thank you for your love, your patience, your laughter, and the many interruptions. They kept me sane.

Finally, I am grateful to the many companions who reminded me often about the mattering of other-than-human life. Sisa, Micaela, Martín, Fred, Manchay Misi (aka m&m), my Poet, and that beautiful guinea pig tossed out of her enclosure and left to die alone, thank you for the continued reminder to look beyond ourselves.

Introduction

STORIES OF RESURGENCE
AND COLONIALITY

SCENE I—FROM TERROR TO PEACEFUL REVOLUTION

In 2017, PromPerú posted an ad in the New York Times *promoting Peru's culinary revolution and showcasing the country's fourth generation of chefs, the so-called Generación con Causa (Generation with Cause).*[1] *This ad, produced by T Brand Studio, tells the story of Peru's transformation from a place of terror and economic insecurity to a peaceful and culturally vibrant global culinary destination.*[2] *It begins by introducing the most recent generation of chefs, young people in their late twenties and early thirties for whom, the ad states, "cooking is more than just a profession, it is a social revolution." The word* causa *in Spanish means "cause," but in Peru it is also the name of a traditional coastal dish made of mashed potatoes; ají (Peruvian yellow pepper); lime; and a mix of vegetables, seafood, or chicken. Interspersed among colorful photographs of Peruvian cuisine and Native products and shots of coastal Lima and young chefs, and anchored by the socially conscious work of the Generación con Causa, the text tells the story of a remarkable gastronomic revolution.*

This narrative emphasizes the role of chefs as central historical actors in moving Peru away from "chaos" and refashioning the country into a peaceful, modern, cosmopolitan, and socially conscious nation. It weaves through the first generation of chefs, described as the "first ones to honor Peruvian food" and as "pioneers fighting for our dreams in much more difficult times" who "built the conditions . . . [for] what we did later." It then turns to the second generation, including chef Gastón Acurio, who "made Peruvians fall in love again with their country." The third generation is represented by Mitsuharu Tsumura, the owner of Maido, a Japanese Peruvian fusion restaurant, and Virgilio Martínez, owner of Central and Mil; all three restaurants are considered among the best in the world."[3] They are described as elevating Peruvian cuisine to the next level: "The new Peruvian message of food is biodiversity and the unknown. . . . It's not pisco sours, ceviches, and great tasty food anymore. It's at another level" (quoting Martínez).[4] Having presented these three previous generations as paving the way, the ad returns to the particularities that distinguish the fourth and latest generation of chefs and Peruvian food today: a concern for social and environmental causes, such as tackling food waste, hunger, obesity, and deforestation. Keeping its well-educated global audience in mind, the ad foregrounds concepts and key terms familiar in high-end culinary circles, such as sustainability, biodiversity, hyper-locality, and authenticity.

SCENE II—THE BEAUTY QUEEN AND OPEN PIT MINING

The video begins with a smiling beauty queen waving joyfully at the camera. Incongruously, the camera moves from her to a view of the huge Raúl Rojas open pit mine, a void so big it can be seen from space and that has quite literally swallowed much of the city of Cerro de Pasco, Peru. As the big brass sounds of an Andean procession play, a voice-over tells the viewer: "Participate in the election of the Open Pit Mine Raúl Rojas as one of the wonders of Peru," much as Peruvians were asked to vote to make Machu Picchu one of the wonders of the world.[5] This "promotional video" from 2010 encourages tourists to come to Cerro de Pasco and enjoy such activities as "acid rain walks" and "extreme sports" that take place twice a day during the 11:00 a.m. and 3:00 p.m. explosive detonations. The website at which one can view this video introduces viewers to the person behind this audacious idea: La Ultima Reyna (sic), the "Last Queen of Cerro de Pasco," Elizabeth Lino: "I am Miss Cerro de Pasco, the last queen, and from this place I will introduce you to my city and my proposal to declare the Raúl Rojas Open Pit Mine a World Wonder and a National Cultural and Historic Landscape."[6]

In addition to the video, Lino's website provides historical background and links to legal documents, including the text of Peruvian Law 29293, which proposes literally moving the city of Cerro de Pasco somewhere else, given how much of the city has been devastated by mining.[7] Importantly, the historical landscape Lino spells out reminds us of the city's history of Indigenous presence and dispossession, the centrality of mining to its foundation, and the legacies of labor struggles and environmental degradation. Just as important, Lino reminds us that in the early twentieth century, Cerro de Pasco occupied a privileged place in the nation. It was once Peru's second largest city, a place where European dignitaries *strolled the streets and that later contributed to the fortunes of American families with the last names Morgan and Vanderbilt. As the wealth of outsiders grew, so the pit grew larger, swallowing the houses and neighborhoods of local residents.*[8] *Lino, a performance artist who grew up in Cerro de Pasco, explains that this pit devoured her house. She notes that this project was motivated by "the pain that came from seeing the disappearance of this space in which I was born and raised. Put simply, one day you come back and realize that this is not normal, although you had thought it was before. When I was a child, I really thought that all the cities in the world had a giant hole in the middle."*[9]

These two texts—the *New York Times* advertisement and Lino's video— could be read as two distinct performances of Peru's history and future: one hegemonic and officially sanctioned, the other subaltern and unauthorized. The first involves the glossy, high-end, global marketing of Peru's gastronomic revolution, a revolution that, as the story goes, transformed the country from a place of violence to one unified through its cultural and culinary history. The second, Lino's grassroots, radical performance, calls attention to modernity's extractive and destructive force and to the power of art in making such violence visible. Most significantly for our purposes, Lino's performance disrupts the celebratory claims of Peru's culinary revolution and calls attention instead to the revolution's extractive and appropriative dimensions.

As hegemonic discourses celebrate a nation on the way up, Lino refocuses our attention on those sites most distant from (or made invisible by) these celebratory narratives. Significantly, Lino locates the beginning of her project in 2009. As Peru was making headlines for its culinary excellence and economic resurgence, Lino responded to a 2009 Peruvian law that could have emerged from the fiction of Kafka or Borges, declaring that her city would have to move because of the tremendous damage that centuries of mining had done to it. As Cerro de Pasco's days became numbered, Lino declared herself the "last" queen of the city and promised to hand over her sash and tiara to a new "sovereign" once the new city was built. Like other beauty queens, she is a public figure, ubiquitous at inaugurations and parades and often accompanying politicians as they declare the achievements of the nation. However, as Olga Rodríguez-Ulloa notes insightfully, La Ultima Reyna explores the "paradox of mining that goes back to the time of colonial splendour, to prosperity and opulence that nevertheless left misery and contamination in the communities with which it coexists. She is a character that materially embodies her own demise as a representative, head, and body of a territory destroyed."[10]

FIGURE I. *Marca País*. Reproduced with permission from Elizabeth Lino.

La Ultima Reyna, however, is not simply acting. As she tells Peruvian literary critic Victor Vich: "What I am doing is not representation, it is not theater."[11] As Vich writes, Lino "converts her body into an image functional to global capitalism, she . . . fuses herself, obscenely, with the optimistic discourse of contemporary marketing."[12] At a time when there seems to be no space free of the workings of capitalism, Vich suggests that Lino's strategy is not to reject the selling of the nation but to "overidentify" with it. This act of overidentification becomes a new form of "symbolic disobedience" that highlights the obscenity that Vich argues is always present in stories of success.[13] In one of the more telling visuals of the Ultima Reyna's website, Lino superimposes the spiraling Marca Perú logo over the remarkably similar curves of the Raúl Rojas mining pit. The point could not be clearer: Peru, our brand is extraction.

It is worthwhile to consider the paradoxical yet profound theoretical power of Lino's intervention. Through her performance art, she helps call attention to something that does not seem to be hidden: a giant hole in the earth that has literally consumed her home and city. The original narrative of national success, namely the long-standing notion that mining has been the foundation of Peruvian modernity, has managed to obscure the deep ecological and social harm that mining has done to so many parts of the country.[14] By inviting her fellow citizens and even the world to look closely at Cerro de Pasco, Lino asks people to see what they should have seen all along: that stories of success are at the same time stories of destruction. Inspired by Lino's art, I suggest that we might also take a close look at the gastronomic boom and ask what this story of success is hiding in plain sight.

My aim in this book is not to tell *the* story of Peru's spectacular gastronomic revolution, but rather to offer a critical engagement with some of the many gastropolitical stories and performances that produce and reflect contemporary manifestations of capital, culture, and coloniality in Peru.[15] In thinking with these narratives, I explore what I call the Peruvian gastropolitical complex, a network of bodies, institutions, economic relations, knowledge production, and discourses that represents both a hegemonic project and a terrain of struggle wherein alternative stories and political projects can emerge through the cracks and fissures.

BACKSTORIES: LOVE, VIOLENCE, AND COLONIALITY

A central goal of this book is to call into question the cruel optimism that is carried by the term *postconflict*, a designation often given to Peru since the military defeat of Sendero Luminoso (Shining Path) and other leftist insurgencies by the state.[16] *Postconflict* is found in many places, and I wager that in most, as in Peru, it is more aspirational than accurate.

Officially, the war between the Peruvian state and the Shining Path (and MRTA, the Movimiento Revolucionario Túpac Amaru) led to approximately seventy thousand deaths, at least 75 percent of which were of Indigenous peoples.[17] This does not include the countless people who were detained, tortured, displaced, and disappeared. The Peruvian Truth and Reconciliation Commission (Comisión de la Verdad y Reconciliación, or CVR) was tasked with investigating the acts, causes, and implications of this period of violence, officially limited to the twenty years between 1980 (the year the Shining Path declared war against the state) and 2000 (the supposed end of authoritarianism). In its report, the CVR emphasized the impact of the colonial legacies of marginalization and inequality that made Sendero Luminoso possible, and which had to be addressed if Peru was to avoid more violence. Commissioners determined that Sendero was responsible for approximately 54 percent of deaths during this period of violence, while state forces (including military and police forces) were responsible for approximately 37 percent of deaths. This assessment, as well as the commissioners' critical narration of the colonial context in which this conflict unfolded (which implicated sitting presidents), meant that the report fell largely on deaf ears.

To this day, the CVR and the commissioners' report remain controversial, and the politics of memory in Peru are fiercely debated. Discussions over who can count as a "victim" of the violence, who deserves reparations, and who was responsible for the forced sterilization of thousands of Indigenous women and men, for example, continue alongside new corruption scandals at the highest levels of government. My point here is that by reducing conflict and violence to one catastrophic chapter of Peru's history, as horrendous as it was, the postconflict label imposes a periodization that renders almost invisible the many other catastrophes of colonial, structural, and symbolic violence that remain all too present. Here, it is worth remembering the late Patrick Wolfe's oft-cited observation that conquest is a structure, not an event.[18] Lino, too, points to this moment of branding, marketing, and consuming the nation not as an extraordinary moment of success, but rather as only one moment in a history of extraction and dispossession. In other words, we might shift our gaze and see the gastronomic revolution not as a project taking place at a particular postconflict moment (an event), but rather as reflective of the workings of a very old structure of coloniality and power.

To return to gastropolitics and get a sense of how this postconflict sleight of hand can work spectacularly well, let us start with one of the more effective means of neoliberal mystification: the TED talk. In Gastón Acurio's popular TED talk on love and cooking, delivered in New York City in 2018, he makes the seductive argument that cooking at home can change the world.[19] He begins with a love story. The children of Cantonese and Italian families fall in love in the streets of the port city of Callao, Peru. Their families are against their love, so the young couple move far away to make their new home. Romance gives way to disagreement in the kitchen; soy sauce and Parmesan cheese come into conflict. Over time, however, conflict yields to creativity. Old flavors from different worlds mix in new recipes. This, Acurio tells us, is how Peruvian cuisine was born, a product of "500 years of beautiful fusion" and of romantic and harmonious encounters among diverse peoples.[20]

For Acurio, this story—of colonial encounters reframed as tales of love, of differences giving way to not just tolerance but unity—is the story of Peru. Tellingly, he begins his TED talk by positioning himself as a product of such encounters: "I am Limeño, son of all the bloods, as you can see [gestures to his face].[21] My mother, daughter of the coast, aristocratic and viceregal, and my father, a son of the Andes, the Incas, from Cuzco. In my home, the Andes and the coast, historically confrontational, were united thanks to love, as happened to most people from Lima, descendants of the most diverse backgrounds: Africans with Amazonians, Japanese with Andeans, Chinese with

Italians." Here, the sexual violence of colonial encounters is presented as a story of impossible, defiant love. We see this quite explicitly in the tasting menu from spring 2018 for Astrid & Gastón, Acurio's signature restaurant in Lima. The menu, titled "Lima Love," tells the story of contemporary Peru, of a nation "celebrating without fear, thankful for being Limeños, children of all the bloods. Of Andeans with coastal peoples . . . of people from Spain with Africans. Impossible loves that our parents knew how to defend and flower." The first dish on the menu is called *La cama indecente, la del amor prohibido* (The indecent bed, the one of forbidden love). In this formulation, love does not just erase violence. As we shall see, it serves as a powerful affective strategy that *enacts* violence on those bodies that don't conform to the borders of the newly drawn nation and its authorized subjects.[22]

Race and sex haunt Peru's gastronomic revolution. The commonplace descriptions of beautiful fusion, of the love between "races" that flourishes against all odds and, importantly, produces a uniquely Peruvian cuisine, culture, and subject, is nothing more than a rearticulation of mestizaje, that contested national ideology of inclusion prevalent throughout Latin America. As Peter Wade writes, since colonial times, and especially post-independence in the first half of the nineteenth century, "mixture has been seen in most of [Latin America] as constituting the essence of the nation."[23] Multiple scholars have written about the varying configurations, politics, and implications of mestizaje across the region, and in Peru more specifically.[24] What many scholars have emphasized is that the logic of mestizaje has been about state-sanctioned exclusions. Even in the poetic renderings of inclusion, like Vasconcelos's famous idea of a "cosmic race" that upended the Atlantic consensus on White supremacy and racial purity, the project of mestizaje was nation-building homogeneity. If you were not "mixed" enough (i.e., were too Indian or Black), then you were not a proper national subject. As Ronald Stutzman aptly put it for the case of Ecuador, mestizaje was the "all-inclusive ideology of exclusion."[25] In Peru, mestizaje took on even more pessimistic tones, as for many it still carried the baggage of degeneration.[26] Acurio explicitly addresses this, noting that his formulation of mixture and fusion contrasts with older, pejorative understandings of what it meant to be mestizo. Today, he argues, as cultural diversity is embraced by the world, so too must Peru celebrate its diversity. It is significant, though, that often this is coded as cultural and culinary difference. Even though race is mentioned (*todas las razas*), it is a refrain that in fact works to erase race and racial difference; rather, this mixture of races, again, leads to a singular Peruvian subject.

It is worth underlining something about mestizaje that should be obvious but is often passed over in silence: it is inextricably about sex and sexual violence. The tale of conquest, as Andrew Canessa usefully reminds us, was often told as a story of sexual adventure.[27] Amerigo Vespucci's fame had less to do with his cartographic skill than with his accounts of "libidinous" and "lascivious" Native women. In a famous letter in 1504, Vespucci wrote the following about the Native people whom he allegedly encountered during his "first voyage" (which historians doubt ever happened):

> They do not practice matrimony among them, each man taking as many women as he likes, and when he is tired of a woman he repudiates her without either injury to himself or shame to the woman, for in this matter the woman has the same liberty as the man. They are not very jealous, but lascivious beyond measure, the women much more so than the men. I do not further refer to their contrivances for satisfying their inordinate desires, so that I may not offend against modesty. They are very prolific in bearing children, and in their pregnancy they are not excused any work whatever. The parturition is so easy, and accompanied by so little pain, that they are up and about the next day.[28]

Vespucci's letters, riddled with exaggeration and lies, were widely circulated in Europe, and they fueled the sexual imagination of conquest. This becomes especially clear in an engraving by Theodor Galle depicting Vespucci's "discovery" of America.[29] Canessa describes this famous image in the following way:

> European Amerigo Vespucci, erect and holding the tools of rational science (an astrolabe) and his religion finds "America" in her hammock. She is naked but full of wonder rather than fear and appears open to his advances. Europa, the female symbol of Vespucci's continent, is nowhere to be seen in this allegorical encounter; this is not a meeting of equals. Vespucci gives the new continent a feminine version of his name. Indeed the subtitle of the caption reads: "At once he called her; thenceforth she was always aroused." America's response is ambiguous as "excitam" means to rise up as well as to arouse or to excite. It is quite clear that America is doing both.[30]

As many have noted, the tale Canessa revisits is one that shapes colonial encounters across the Americas.[31] Colonialism meant, among many things, that Native women were sexually accessible to White men. Well into the twentieth century, *hacendados* (landowners) practiced the *derecho de pernada*, the "right" to sexually violate a Native woman on the night of her marriage. This was justified as a "civilizing mission" that would whiten populations, what Nancy Leys Stepan calls the ideology of "constructive miscegenation."[32] Mestizaje is never far from the sexual violence of conquest and coloniality.

Chef Acurio's framing of mestizaje, then, is not surprising. His discourse on love, on beautiful and tolerant fusion, is an updated and perhaps more politically correct version of an older (though still common) vision of Peru as a country "integrated" and "reconciled," one that accepts "the encounter" as violent but also, and especially, "mutually beneficial" for Peruvians.[33] In a chapter titled "Columbus's Voyage Continues," Alejandro Miró Quesada Cisneros, an influential lawyer and journalist from an elite Peruvian family, writes that the most significant dimension of Columbus's "discovery" was "having united new human beings, . . . who, voluntarily or involuntarily, initiated an exchange of their advantages and riches."[34] He notes that when analyzing the fruits of Columbus's "discovery" ("which turned America into a continent with a new identity and a new destiny" and is in fact "a voyage that continues") from the perspective of five hundred years, there is no question that "its virtues surpass its defects."[35]

This, again, is not surprising. Many people continue to espouse this ideology, despite its obviously problematic nature. What is worth noting is that this chapter was part of *500 Years Later: The New Face of Peru*, a book published on the occasion of the quincentenary that focused on *hermandad* (brotherhood), on coming to terms with the new Peru, and on emphasizing mestizaje (especially the "mixture" of Spanish and Indigenous peoples) as a positive melding (and erasure) of differences. All the contributors to the volume are men, and the table of contents reads like a list of members of Peru's aristocracy (or oligarchy), with last names such as Vargas Llosa, Roca Rey, and Miró Quesada. These men are an integral part of the gastropolitical complex, either as members of Apega (the Peruvian Society of Gastronomy); as editors (and owners) of *El Comercio*, Peru's newspaper of record; or as cultural or political elites.[36] Bernardo Roca Rey's contribution to the volume includes not only a discussion of his "invention" of *cocina novoandina* (or nouveau Andean cuisine) but also a now familiar refrain about Peruvian cuisine as mestizaje.[37] Mestizaje, for these Peruvian elites, is a beautiful and progressive force.

The amount of work this volume does to ennoble and celebrate mestizaje is perhaps one indicator that the very idea of mestizaje is a site of contention, even as it covers its tracks. As Peruvian sociologist Gonzalo Portocarrero reminds us, "the idea of mestizaje has served to obscure conflict." As he puts it, to deny difference "has been the republican and liberal pact. But denying a fact does not make it disappear. Differences are ignored but they are also reproduced. . . . The dominant notions of mestizaje have not broken free from colonialism."[38] Indeed, the pages of this book call attention to the preoccupation elite White men continue to have with the "Indian problem." For them, Columbus's voyage continues; in other words, the Peruvian civilizational project is not complete.

Similarly, the gastronomic revolution has not broken free from coloniality. On the surface, appearances may seem progressive: chefs, state officials, and entrepreneurs emphasize both fusion and social justice. Largely due to Peru's background of political violence and the disproportionate impact of that violence on Indigenous bodies, gastropolitics emphasizes *both* economic and political resurgence *and* discourses of social inclusion. Gastropolitical elites often underline that the signature dimension of the current gastronomic boom has been the alliances between chefs and producers (wherein chefs buy products directly from producers at fair prices), promoted by Apega and Acurio in particular, and which, they argue, offer evidence of the inclusionary and horizontal nature of this movement.[39] While many Indigenous producers and their families may indeed benefit from new economic opportunities, as I discuss in the first part of this book, this focus on social inclusion (the alliance with producers in particular) is intimately linked to particular gastropolitical understandings of histories of violence and indigeneity in Peru, especially two episodes of violence to which the gastronomic revolution is responding, one explicitly (the years of terror, 1980–2000) and one implicitly (the military government and reforms of General Velasco Alvarado, 1968–75). Emerging from the aftermath of the CVR's report on the terrible years of fear and political violence, gastropolitics seeks to exorcise the ghost of Sendero and its unquestionably ghastly violence, which invited the terrifying brutality of the state. Harder to see, perhaps, is the attempt to exorcise the ghost of the revolutionary presidency of Velasco Alvarado, whose agrarian reform represented a threat to the Peruvian elite. As I argue in chapter 1, gastropolitics in many ways tries to rehabilitate the pre-Velasco order, when Indigenous peasants "knew their place" and worked the land of others, and when landed elites were seen as a source of stability and even paternalistic care.

These histories also have much to do with elite anxieties over what some have called the "Andeanization" of Lima. While the dominant gastropolitical narrative seems to be that cuisine offers a path to reconciliation, to unity in diversity, an alternative reading of this emphasis on tolerance and reconciliation is that gastropolitics responds to the infusion of Andean Indigenous migration in Lima. Eighty percent of Lima's population of over ten million is made up of migrants or the children of migrants.[40] There is a long history of centralism in Peru, where Lima claims to represent the nation, a claim that gained greater demographic credibility over the course of the twentieth century as waves of migrations from the rural countryside Andeanized the coastal capital. As I discuss more fully in chapters 1 and 3, gastropolitics enables a nostalgic vision of Lima, known at its founding as the "City of Kings" and remembered/imagined as emblematic of colonial grandeur. Peruvians often conflate Velasco's rule (particularly his agrarian reform) and the war with Sendero Luminoso with the waves of Andean migration into the capital city. While the military coup that overthrew Velasco tried to undo much of his revolution, that regime was unable to stop a social transformation already underway, as Andean people not only challenged power relations in the countryside but also literally changed the urban landscape as they moved to Lima and created new informal settlements, usually called *invasiones* or invasions.[41] With this rural-to-urban migration came elite fear of angry Indians that fueled upper-class anxieties over Indians as terrorists during the most recent episode of political violence. As shown in the following chapters, twenty-first-century gastropolitical elites rely not on military violence but on practices and discourses that focus on "beautifying" and "cleansing" the city. Gourmet cuisine, gentrification, and "civilizing" others are central components of this culinary project: deploying "hygiene brigades" at culinary festivals, training young men and women from working-class backgrounds to become the labor force for high-end restaurants, and refiguring Indigenous peoples as producers, as key partners in the transformation of Peru through their labor, as long as they remain pliable subjects.

Even as they attend to these historical legacies, gastropolitical framings and stories are also fixed on the future. Narratives about Peru's unique history of fusion, the alliances between chefs and Indigenous producers, and a new generation of chefs working toward a more socially just world almost always emphasize a future of reconciliation. However, this peaceful future is only possible if tolerance is the guiding value, an idea that at its heart is far from progressive, and hardly revolutionary. As political theorist Wendy Brown has helped us understand, this is an example of the "malady of tolerance."[42] That is, far from a virtue, tolerance is at best a conditional acceptance of difference, and at worst it is an enabling condition for violence. In *500 Years Later*, tolerance serves to frame the question of violence in specific ways. All of the contributions in that book note that while terrorism and violence are "awful," we should move away from the description of violence as somehow enabled by the division between rich and poor or by the structural divisions between oppressed and dominating classes. A truly remarkable example is a chapter on violence and modernization by Fernando De Trazegnies. After noting that these binary visions of violence are inadequate, he says "There is no doubt that our ruling classes possess these vices, but so do the 'suffering masses' and those who claim to represent (illegitimately) the neediest classes. There is nothing angelical or diabolical in Society. Such an absurd claim would only affirm the demonic nature of the traditional ruling classes and the angelic nature of the exploited sectors. All are simply men."[43] And he goes on, making arguments that resonate strongly with familiar (and current) narratives about order and civilization: "I want to advance the notion of the permanent existence of violence throughout Peruvian history that is more basic, that consists of a diversity of manifestations and cannot be reduced to just one of them: the injustice of some social groups over others is part of our basic violence, but it does not exhaust or explain it. *Beyond all of this there is a primary form of violence that consists of a general lack of discipline indispensable for living in a civilized manner.*"[44]

This statement is striking for its implicit inversion of who the victims of violence are (civilized, disciplined, elite, Peruvians), if violence is enacted by those who are not living in a civilized manner (subaltern, "undisciplined" subjects). Moreover, this last point resonates with the gastropolitical emphasis, as I note in chapter 3, on teaching Indigenous producers how to "sell correctly," how to relate to their customers appropriately, and how to beautify themselves and present themselves as clean and healthy. Hygiene, race, and civilization have been tightly linked in the Americas for centuries. This has, of course, also been the case in Europe, as the pioneering work of Norbert Elias reveals on the crucial role the practice and pedagogy of manners and cleanliness played in the continent's "civilizing process."[45] However, looking forward, gastropolitical elites understand that this is a new moment, that they can harness the power of "diversity" to entice global capital to Peru and reorganize social hierarchies in ways that are in line with new modes of recognition that in fact reassert colonial domination.

The Generation with Cause does not have the same kind of elite composition or tone. Yet it retains a family resemblance to earlier calls for mestizaje and tolerance. Take the opening lines of its social manifesto, a document that speaks to the urgent problems of hunger and climate change (among others) and to the role of young chefs in solving these social issues: "Causa, emblematic Peruvian dish. A happy encounter between potatoes and chilis of the Andes, with limes and oils from Europe, to bring unity, peace, and happiness to the Peruvian family. *Kausay*, which in Quechua means to give life. Life through a dish that was only made possible in that encounter, that union, and that capacity to overcome any difference. Following that example, today we are here, *Generación con Causa*, giving life to a movement founded in dialogue and unity, to work together in favor of Peruvian cuisine and Peru."[46]

Here again, the emphasis on fusion (the "happy encounter" between the Andes and Europe) and on dialogue, unity, and the ability to "overcome any difference" glosses over the brutality of the colonial encounter and of ongoing experiences of violence, dispossession, and marginalization. In addition, the foregrounding of *generations* of chefs again encodes Peru as forward looking, moving away from the past (chaos, violence, inequality) and toward the future (modern, cosmopolitan, peaceful). The PromPerú ad and the manifesto figure a particular ideal subject—neoliberal, productive, and importantly, happily able to dialogue with fellow compatriots. Moreover, the violence of Peru's birth (Conquest) and the more proximate violence of leftist insurgency (Sendero) are, in this narrative, lodged firmly in the past. Echoing the official periodization of the CVR's report, the future is a time for reconciliation and moving the country beyond the racialized and class-based antagonisms of the past.

However, what troubles this seemingly optimistic reading is that conflicts are hardly gone. What government statistics call "socioenvironmental conflicts" have become a permanent feature of an economic model based on mining and other forms of extractive industry. Yet seen from certain elites' perspectives, those who oppose mining are themselves the new sources of violence. What must be celebrated, therefore, is a prosperous, bountiful, and peaceful future. To make the point even clearer, in March 2019, Peru.com noted that Peru's gastronomy was on full display "at the most important mining event in the world" (the annual meetings of PDAC: The World's Premier Mineral Exploration & Mining Convention).[47] This book, then, explores what is obscured and mystified by narratives that emphasize gastronomy (and mining) as crucial parts of the new story of Peruvian peace and prosperity.

To anticipate some of the arguments to come, let us consider another provocative image that Elizabeth Lino provides on her Ultima Reyna website. Taking from Cerro de Pasco's official repertoire, in particular an image of its open-pit mine and the official slogan that greets visitors upon entering Cerro de Pasco—*Tierra de Machos, No de Muchos* (Land of the machos, not of the many)—Lino reminds us that the violence of modernity is hidden in

FIGURE 2. *Tajo en las venas*. Image reproduced with permission from Elizabeth Lino.

plain sight. By superimposing this on her own body, she invokes Eduardo Galeano's famous phrase that described how transnational corporations have always profited from the "open veins of Latin America."[48] This book explores the dark side of the celebration of Peruvian gastronomy, of contemporary narratives of social inclusion, while leaving room for alternative readings and possibilities opened up by Peru's gastronomic revolution.

A NOTE ON METHOD

When I began thinking about this project, I thought I would be writing mainly about nonhuman animals.[49] Specifically, I thought I would be writing about Andean animals such as guinea pigs (or *cuyes*), alpacas, and llamas, and what I saw as the recent and increasing intensification of their breeding and production. In Peru in the early 2000s, I began to notice a proliferation of dishes that centered these animals, albeit in ways unusual to what I was accustomed. For instance, I remember seeing *carpaccio de alpaca* on the menu of one of the most popular tourist restaurants in Cusco (Inka Grill), a dish that raised questions for me about the changes in the raising of alpacas (traditionally pack animals) used for meat.[50] This dish, and others such as *filet mignon de alpaca*, would mean that this rugged animal's meat had to be tender, not a quality I remembered when I thought back to eating alpaca during dissertation fieldwork in the department of Cusco many years before. I was interested not just in what this shift meant for these animals' experiences of life and death, but also for the impact of this kind of move on the relations between Indigenous families and their animals, since, as others have documented, colonial violence has always affected both human and other-than-human lives and bodies.[51] These concerns prompted me to ask the chef about this dish, and from where the restaurant sourced alpaca and cuy meat, both animals that appeared on their menu regularly.

As I began to ask more questions and pay closer attention to menus and to the marketing of alpaca and cuy in particular, I noticed that the increase in their consumption aligned with the emergence of what I later learned was called *novoandina* cuisine, described as a uniquely Peruvian blend of Indigenous products and European cooking techniques.[52] Bernardo Roca Rey is regularly credited with having "invented" novoandina cuisine, particularly through the creation of the "quinotto," a risotto made with quinoa. The invention and promotion of novoandina cuisine is described by many as one of the key moments in the gastronomic revolution, as the beginning of the transformation of Peruvian food into world-class gastronomy, at least in part by "elevating" Indigenous products through European techniques and artistic culinary presentation.

At the same time, I "followed the meat" and traced how the rise in the inclusion of cuy in restaurant menus was linked to the increase in cuy production in Peru, what would eventually be termed *el boom del cuy*. Guinea pigs, animals used for food in Peru, were domesticated by Indigenous peoples in the Andes centuries ago. In Cusco, cuy has appeared on tourist menus for years, but the recent move has included a shift from serving the animal whole to serving it hidden, such as in the pappardelle with guinea pig ragout dish I tasted recently. More significantly, the animal had very rarely been used in high-end restaurants.[53] Acurio, working closely with Roca Rey and other (primarily) men who are at the center of a network of gastropolitical elites, incorporated cuy in his restaurants in both Lima and Cusco with dishes like cuy ravioli and cuy steak (which, according to a friend who ordered this dish at Astrid & Gastón in 2008, meant fusing the meat of several cuyes together to make one "steak").[54] As I discuss in chapters 5 and 6, cuy researchers and producers noticed, and used this moment to incentivize and promote the intensification of cuy production. As one of the leading researchers of guinea pig breeding and production told me, while work in this field had been ongoing in Peru since the 1960s, it was only now, in the context of the gastronomic revolution, that cuy production could successfully take off.

I became increasingly interested in this context, in the emerging place of Peruvian cuisine in the world, and the need for Native animals to authenticate this cuisine, and by extension, the Peruvian national brand. I was interested in these animals, but also in the ways the recentering of Andean animals and products seemed to reproduce Peruvian historian Cecilia Méndez's oft-cited phrase, "Incas sí, Indios no."[55] In other words, there is a history of appropriation in which the traditions and histories of Native peoples are recruited to give the country a taste of exotic authenticity, while at the same time actually existing Native peoples face continuing discrimination and violence. In addition, the timing for my research was fortuitous. I began research for this project in 2009, as the gastronomic revolution was beginning to make headlines across the globe.[56] In the mid-2000s, articles about Peruvian cuisine began appearing in *Gourmet*, *Bon Appétit*, and *Food & Wine*; Peru was emerging as a surprising new culinary destination.[57] In Acurio's formulation, I began my work at the height of what he and others call the gastronomic revolution's "second phase," a moment when gastropolitical elites were actively working to develop and promote the Peruvian brand, secure Peruvian cuisine's world-class status, and expand culinary tourism, primarily by transforming Lima into a culinary destination for tourists. That revolutionary process has lost some steam. As I write this in January 2020, Mistura, the Lima-based yearly event once considered the most important gastronomic festival in the Americas, has not taken place since 2017.[58] Perhaps even more striking, Apega, the gastronomic association once at the vanguard of this revolution, disbanded in 2019. Without declaring that the gastronomic boom is over (indeed, award-wining restaurants in Lima and Cusco continue to thrive, and there are rumblings of a new organization emerging to take Apega's place), one does have the sense that the energy of the boom has at the very least leveled off.

As is the case for many of us with increasing responsibilities in both the academy and at home, the research I have conducted for this project has not mirrored anthropology's traditional, immersive, long-term field research. Instead, over the past decade I have traveled to Peru regularly to conduct short bursts of research, for weeks or (at best) months at a time. In particular, I have conducted ethnographic research in the cities of Lima and Cusco, two sites that have been central to this culinary revival. As I explore in chapter 1, the gastronomic revolution has in many ways recentered Lima, although as a significant tourist destination, Cusco's culinary landscape has also been an important stage. The importance of Cusco has increased with Virgilio Martínez's opening of Mil, which I discuss in chapter 2. In addition to ethnographic fieldwork that included research at national cuy festivals in Lima, cuy producer conferences, seminars, and workshops, the culinary festival Mistura, many restaurants, farmer's markets, and agro-ecological workshops, as well as a brief visit to a cuy research and production center in Bolivia, I conducted dozens of interviews with chefs, members of Apega, food critics, state bureaucrats, Indigenous producers, Indigenous activists, representatives from women's associations of cuy breeders in Cusco, and cuy producers and researchers in Lima. I also participated in one of several online courses available in cuy production. These ethnographic engagements are in conversation with close readings of various texts, from tasting menus to cuy breeding and production manuals to gastronomic novels, cookbooks, food documentaries, online national and international campaigns, and more.

Finally, I should also note that for me, it has been impossible to escape the gastronomic complex. Much as Kim TallBear writes in her discussion of ethics, accountability, and relationality in Indigenous and feminist research, for many of us, research is about "inhabiting material and virtual worlds"; we do not "just do fieldwork there."[59] As I noted in the preface, my critical engagements with nationalism and cuisine in Peru can't be separated from deep emotional connections to and memories of family, land, and language. Even as I write critically about the commodification of Peru, my brother's Peruvian restaurant is doing so well in part because of precisely the kind of problematic depictions of Peru as the "land of the Incas," what anthropologist Shane Greene calls Peru's "Inca slot."[60] But he is my brother. I want him to succeed, and I want others to not only go to his restaurant, but to know that Peruvian food is delicious. This is to say that part of this book is recognizing and embracing the contradictions that come not only with fieldwork but also with family and other forms of belonging.[61]

My writing about indigeneity, too, is intimately linked to my grandfather, who, I learned late in life, was a Quechua-speaking man from Ayacucho, although he did not self-identify as Indigenous. This is not exceptional. Experiences of erasure loom large in the lives of many and are a constitutive part of colonial histories. As Wolfe reminds us about the workings of what he termed "the settler complex," colonialism is about elimination, erasure, and dispossession, and it is also about affect.[62] As Dakota Sioux historian Phillip Deloria put it, Wolfe's work reveals how "settler colonial binaries hide in plain sight, lodged in the affective structures of feeling that win consent and shape everyday life and that simultaneously offer opportunities for diagnosis, intervention, and resistance."[63]

I find it important to make note of this as it is something that shapes my writing and the affective dimension of this project. I could also say much about my own contradictory engagement with Peruvian food. I love it. It evokes memories; it reminds me of my grandmother and connects me to my ancestors; and it is a central dimension of attempts to connect my son to Peru, in many ways his home, even though he was born in Seattle. But there is also an aesthetic and sensorial dimension to my love of food. I *enjoy* eating, even at those restaurants where I am critical of the blatant appropriative and elitist culinary expression embodied in each dish. This is perhaps what it means to struggle with the gastropolitical complex, to recognize the aesthetic, sensorial, and cultural hold that it has on so many people (myself included), but also to see it as a vast apparatus of power, consumption, and knowledge production that, to borrow from Jodi Melamed, has the ability to "represent and destroy."[64]

OUTLINE OF THE BOOK

This book is divided into two parts. The first, "Structures of Accumulation," considers the workings of gastropolitics from the top down. In particular, I analyze the significance of Gastón Acurio (chapter 1) and Virgilio Martínez (chapter 2), two chefs who figure prominently in the national story of Peru's resurgence, and who offer a window into the workings of racial capitalism in this Andean country. Exploring their political, discursive, and culinary performances, I consider the ways these men engage with, reflect, and reenact histories of race and coloniality in Peru. In this section I also analyze Mistura (chapter 3), considered until recently the most important culinary festival in the Americas, as a central site in the making of the figure of the producer and in the "cleansing" and staging of the cultural and biological diversity that undergirds Peru's gastronomic revolution. This section, then, explores gastropolitics as simultaneously an aesthetic, political, and spatial project that reflects new opportunities for capital accumulation and innovative strategies for managing old anxieties around race. It seeks to repair, or cover up, the tears in the fabric of national sovereignty caused by decades of internal war and racialized inequality. It is a response to disorder, framed as social inclusion, that in fact repositions people and places in familiar racialized arrangements.

The second part of the book, "Narratives from the Edge," explores stories of gastropolitics otherwise; narratives that also reflect long histories of engagement with race and coloniality, albeit from distinct locations. These are alternative tellings from within hegemonic and subaltern spaces that disrupt and reveal the dark sides of success, and that in some cases can even move "beyond" the human-centric dimension of discussions in Peru and elsewhere about cuisine.[65] While Elizabeth Lino's performance art provides a clear example of the various counterhegemonic narratives deployed in Peru today, other alternative stories and performances are less explicitly resisting dominant narratives and hierarchies. Yet they too offer counter-stories that complicate the too-simple story of Peru's transition from terror to tourist destination. As others have noted, hegemonic projects often create the spaces necessary for counterhegemonic possibilities.[66] For instance, I engage with the performative work of emerging chefs and agricultural producers working from within the gastropolitical complex (chapter 4) even as they point to its colonial foundations. In this section I also explore the so-called guinea pig boom that has accompanied the gastronomic revolution, including the development of cuy research, breeding, and production. The cuy is a powerful figure that signals racialized spaces and subjectivities and speaks to racialized histories of internal migration and elite anxieties about difference. The animal can be "cleansed" via high-end culinary techniques, or it can enable subaltern projects that reclaim space and reposition *lo andino*. Examining how researchers at national universities, working-class entrepreneurs, chefs, and others project their hopes and fears onto this animal, I gesture to the importance of multispecies attention to the guinea pig as both figure and flesh (chapters 5 and 6). Cuy production, as an assemblage of human and nonhuman bodies, is in itself a "narrative from the edge." And as chapter 6 tries to convey, cuyes themselves can also narrate stories of pain and anxiety, life and death, if only we are open to listening.

PART ONE

Structures of Accumulation

Hauntings

I REMEMBER THE BLACKOUTS. I remember playing cards by candlelight, never sitting too close to windows, learning to open our mouths when car bombs went off so our ear drums wouldn't burst. I remember the night my brother, maybe three or four at the time, sliced open his face, just above his eye. He had been playing, running, and hit the corner of a coffee table. I remember the flashlights, the panic, the worry of how to get to the hospital during curfew. And I remember the first time I saw Sendero Luminoso's hammer and sickle burning on the side of one of the hills of Lima.

I don't remember the dogs. We were in Mexico City that early morning in December 1980 when people in Lima awoke to the sight of dead dogs hanging from lampposts. But I know that image, the photograph of one of those dogs, still hanging, about to be released by a police officer. That is one of the dozens of photographs included in Yuyanapaq, the photographic exhibit that accompanied the CVR's report. I have seen this image so often that I could say that I do, in fact, remember those dogs. Their deaths can easily become entangled with memories of that time, memories of return despite the violence, and memories of rupture. In 1985, as war hit the streets of Lima more intensely, my parents decided we would not return until that violence ended. We would not return to the arms of my grandmother, to laughter with my cousins, to the smells and sounds and sights of the city I continued to think of as home. That same year, my family moved to the United States, a move I experienced as another rupture, a radical and violent rupture.

I blamed Sendero. My parents, however, blamed Velasco for having had to leave their home in the first place. For them, as for many others in Peru, the Shining Path was an extension of the disorder General Velasco had unleashed in the late 1960s and 1970s. Narratives about Velasco emphasize the expropriation of lands, the redistribution of resources to landless farmers and poor migrants, and the nationalization of Quechua, events that many in Peru remember as the beginning of the end of order, as the moment racial hierarchies were upended. This is a time that is remembered powerfully, violently. Velasco is a ghost who lingers, who continues to haunt a nation. "Velasquismo is a traumatic, repressed phenomenon," writes Gonzalo Portocarrero. "A history that is taboo. A ruin you do not visit. To speak of that period, of that figure, is disturbing and contentious. . . . To return to that moment in time is like descending to a dark and loud underground; a labyrinth populated by ghosts."[1] In late 2019, a Peruvian film about Velasco's agrarian reform unleashed some of those ghosts. Watching *La Revolución y la Tierra* in the theaters, a friend of mine told me, was unlike anything he had experienced. "People yelled, wept, applauded, and angrily stormed out." Very shortly after debuting, the film became the most watched documentary in the history of Peruvian cinema.[2] More than fifty years after his revolution, Velasco's ghost continues to elicit visceral responses: embodied expressions of rage, or vindication, depending on where you stand.

The politics of memory in Peru, as in most places, are fraught. A few years ago, I took a cab to the LUM, the Lugar de la Memoria, la Tolerancia y la Inclusión Social (The Place of Memory, Tolerance and Social Inclusion), a relatively new museum dedicated to archiving memory and sustaining conversation about the times of violence in Peru, meaning the violence of the 1980s and 1990s.[3] The address from the LUM's website did not register on Google maps, and the cab driver was confused and unsure where to go. I had been there once, before the museum's official opening, so I had a sense of where it was located. As we drove, the cab driver suddenly told me he remembered a big square building around the area I was indicating. "That must be it," he said. "I always wondered what that was. But why do we need another museum like that? We should look to the future, not to the past." I was not surprised by the driver's lack of awareness of the existence of this new museum. His emphasis on moving on, looking toward the future and letting go of the past, is a common narrative in Peru, where despite the horrific impact of this violence on tens of thousands of Peruvians, many prefer not to remember. Yuyanapaq ("to remember" in Quechua), the photographic exhibit that accompanied the CVR's report in 2003, has been relegated to the sixth floor of what used to be the Museo de la Nación (now the Ministry of Culture) and is visited mostly by school groups, scholars, and some tourists. And the CVR's report continues to be mired in controversy. This is the historical context in which the LUM operates. The museum was inaugurated in December 2015, but since the beginning of its conceptualization and construction (in 2009), decisions about how to represent this history have been the focus of many debates and discussions.[4] This was even the case among activists and artists, who were divided between challenging state-sanctioned histories of the internal conflict and accommodating exhibits to fit within socially accepted terms and understandings of the conflict.[5] Despite these tensions, there would seem to be more space for discussions about Sendero than about Velasco. Perhaps Velasco's ghost is harder to exorcise for some. Regardless, in the struggle over memory in Peru, there are many who still have little choice in what they can or can't remember.[6]

Andean notions of temporality (in both Quechua and Aymara worldviews) render the past not as something that we have left behind, but as that which lies before us. This is not to say that Andean peoples are somehow "stuck" in the past, but that the temporality of violence in Peru is far from linear.[7] The Quechua term for the past, *ñawpa pacha*, can literally be rendered as the space that we see before us. The Aymara phrase for the past, *nayra*, also refers to what we see in front of us and, like *ñawpa*, etymologically connects with the word for "eye." The past then is literally what we can see, unlike the future, which is spatially behind us. Violence continues to operate, albeit unevenly, over the centuries. The unevenness of violence, like the willingness to think about it, has much to do with race and coloniality and thus has deep implications for understanding the nation and its limits, that is, who counts and who does not.

ONE

Gastropolitics and the Nation

I WALKED THROUGH THE BUSY STREETS of San Isidro, one of the more exclusive districts in Lima, passing high-end boutiques and restaurants and searching for Astrid & Gastón's new locale.[1] Chef Gastón Acurio's renowned restaurant, the first in Peru to be recognized as among the "The World's 50 Best Restaurants," had recently moved from Miraflores (a wealthy neighborhood and popular tourist destination) to this new space in the heart of San Isidro, an even wealthier district.[2] I worried about finding it until I arrived. There was no way to miss it.

The restaurant, housed in the renovated Casa Moreyra, the three-hundred-year-old main house of the old hacienda in San Isidro, was stunning. The house stands on a glamorous avenue between Avenida Los Incas and Avenida Los Conquistadores. It sits majestically across the street from a striking church, La Virgen del Pilar, which originated as the chapel of the old hacienda of the Moreyra Paz Soldán family; the family later gave it to Catholic missionaries, who used the property to create a new convent and rebuild the church in a neocolonial style. The restaurant is also walking distance from one of the more important archaeological sites in Lima, the Huaca Huallamarca, a pyramidal structure used by the Hualla people and other Native peoples since approximately 200 BC.[3] San Isidro pulses with the activity and wealth of a modern financial district, but one cannot help but feel the layers of history upon entering the almost blinding whiteness of the Casa Hacienda Moreyra.

As you walk up the steps into the foyer, you feel as if you are stepping into another moment in time. Quite a deliberate move, taking us back to the time of colonial grandeur, control over production, and perhaps idealized visions of "good" patrones (landowners/bosses) and orderly workers, before the time of Velasco's agrarian reform. As you arrive in the foyer you are greeted by an elegant hostess who asks you graciously to wait while your table is made ready. The tasting experience, which features either seventeen courses or thirty-four, begins with a few cocktails and appetizers on the terrace before you are escorted to the main dining room for what our hostess describes as "a taste of Peru, an embrace from Peru to the world."⁴ For me, the experience was a bringing together of art, alchemy, and gastronomy. I was especially struck by two features. First, you can eat your alcohol. The traditional pisco sour was served on a plate, chilled, with a hint (in the form of a spray) of pisco. And second, the guinea pig, or cuy, arrived hidden, beautiful, never betraying the rodent it once was. The animal appeared in two small circular bits, and when you popped one into your mouth, it dissolved into air, with just a hint of the flavor of cuy meat.

A COUNTRY TRANSFORMED

It is almost impossible to talk about Peru's culinary revolution without talking about Gastón Acurio. He is perhaps the most beloved public figure in Peru today, and he is without a doubt considered the leader of the gastronomic boom. Acurio is credited by most Peruvians with spearheading the success of Peruvian cuisine and transforming the country into a leading global culinary destination.⁵ This process of transformation is narrated as a story of metamorphosis made possible by Gastón (as Peruvians call him). The story goes that he turned Peru from a country torn apart by violence, inequality, and economic precarity into a nation proudly unified by its culinary and cultural history of fusion.⁶ Consider the words of renowned Spanish chef Ferran Adriá:

> In the Gastón phenomenon, we find . . . an innate cooking talent, the good luck of living immersed in a formidable culinary tradition, surely the richest and most varied in all the Americas, a great knowledge of this same gastronomy, the ability to use high cuisine as a platform to make products known . . . and export them. And next to this, a political and social consciousness that... with unusual determination has allowed him to carry out a project that seems as if it were from a novel (*parece casi de novela*). It is a magical realism story, or a fable from Italian neorealism, but without jokes or fictions. This is the most serious thing I have seen in my entire life.⁷

But this story, of the chef turned national savior and hero, is itself a product of the gastropolitical machine. As much as it is about power and political economy, gastropolitics in Peru today is also a set of stories and performances.

It generates narratives—about enlightened and patriotic chefs, about the expansion of economic opportunity, about racial tolerance and beautiful mixture—that in turn enable the strategic cultivation of a fierce nationalism.

Despite claims to include all of Peru, this is a vision of the nation that centers the capital city of Lima and, I argue, tries to reestablish dominant hierarchies.[8] Gastropolitics crafts stories that loudly celebrate difference and diversity (or "fusion") as central to repositioning Peru as an exemplary (and marketable) nation. Through online campaigns (like the Peru, Nebraska, video) and initiatives such as alliances between Indigenous producers and (mostly White, mestizo, and male) chefs, the promotion of iconic Peruvian products from the Andes and Amazon, and social development projects targeting marginalized youth, Acurio and other gastropolitical elites call attention to difference and inequality in order to, paradoxically, make it harder to see. The gastronomic revolution, in other words, can be read as yet another settler colonial strategy to eliminate the other; gastropolitics manages, cleanses, and beautifies difference.[9] Astrid & Gastón's move to Casa Moreyra is significant here. By reclaiming, restoring, and rewriting this old hacienda's history, Acurio and his collaborators carefully craft a story of return: a return to the imagined colonial grandeur of the "City of Kings," to the time before waves of rural migration "stained" the city and "destroyed Lima's monumental patrimony."[10] Most important, this is a return to the time before the agrarian reform of the late 1960s that, at least in theory, ended feudal rule in Peru by expropriating land holdings and redistributing these to campesinos. If, as Peruvian anthropologist Enrique Mayer suggests, the agrarian reform is made up of "ugly stories," gastropolitics offers instead beautiful stories of Peruvian success.[11] Two of the most important are the intertwined stories about the rise of a chef and the rebuilding of a nation.

THE CHEF

Acurio's origin story—at least the one he shares widely—is by now well known. His father, Gastón Acurio Velarde, a prominent politician, expected his son to follow in his footsteps. He enrolled Acurio at one of the most prestigious universities in Lima, the Catholic University of Peru (Pontificia Universidad Católica del Perú), to study law, but the violence of the 1980s pushed the family to send their only son to study in Spain instead. Acurio hated law school, and away from his father's gaze, he took the money he had been given and enrolled instead in Le Cordon Bleu in France to study culinary arts and follow his dream of becoming a chef.[12] There he met his wife, German-born pastry chef Astrid Gutsche, with whom he eventually returned to Peru (in 1994) to open their eponymous restaurant, Astrid & Gastón.[13]

Importantly, when Acurio relates this story he emphasizes that the reason for returning to Peru was his sense of patriotism, of giving something back to the country that had given him so many opportunities. Acurio credits his father for this sensibility, noting in many interviews that his father had inculcated in him this sense of responsibility and obligation to his country. This is a significant detail, one that is highlighted in documentaries and news articles about the chef and that has been taken up by the gastropolitical machine in Peru to single Acurio out. It is a crucial moment in the telling of his story and the making of the figure of the hero chef. Why return to Peru? And why return in the mid-1990s, when the country was still reeling from the violence of political conflict and an authoritarian regime? Given his social position, Acurio easily could have stayed in Europe, but he chose to return to his city and country, with hopes of doing good. He is wildly successful, yet also humble. He is a national hero, but an approachable one, and is often described as *muy sencillo* (down-to-earth) despite his wealth and celebrity status. While this may sound like a stretch, in its broad outlines, Acurio's story is formally identical to many origin stories of superheroes. As psychologist Robin Rosenberg writes, whether they involve trauma, destiny, or chance, "origin stories show us not how to become *super* but how to be *heroes*, choosing altruism over the pursuit of wealth and power."[14] Like Batman in Gotham, Superman in Metropolis, or Spider-Man in New York, Acurio returns to his polis and patria with grand and seemingly selfless ambitions.

I don't want to push the origin story analogy too far, but I do want to say a word about how we should think about this as a "story." Stories about extraordinary individuals are important because they are never about just one person; rather, they point to broader narratives of a world that has gone wrong and must be righted. Whatever the actual motivation of the chef, the point of his story is to construct a figure who can serve, as Rosenberg suggests, as an example for other Peruvians to follow. Consider for instance the following passage from an interview with Acurio in which he describes his initial return to Peru in 1994:

The Peru I returned to was not the Peru of today. Terrorism was coming to an end, but not fear. Peruvian elites of that time still looked to Europe or North

America as their point of reference.... They yearned for Paris and then, in more recent times, Miami. The moment we are living now, of building a society that finds itself and moves together toward an objective, had not yet arrived. That was the Peru I left, and the one I returned to.... Very few people even considered that behind a potato or a lime, there was someone who harvested that product. The diner would go to their small isolated worlds [e.g. French restaurants, weddings at the *Palacio de Gobierno*], without realizing that these were bubbles in the midst of a society with enormous inequality.... That was Peru then. But fortunately, Peru has changed, it is changing, and it is clearly changing for the better.... Today, Peruvians celebrate our differences and those earlier times will never return.[15]

What Acurio does not say explicitly here, but what both his colleague Ferran Adriá and food writer and journalist Ignacio Medina note explicitly in the interview, is that the person largely responsible for this change is Acurio himself. His is the example other Peruvians must follow in order to sustain the tolerant multicultural society Acurio has made possible.

Acurio also writes and talks frequently about the process of "rediscovery" that his return to Peru entailed. He describes arriving in the country in the mid-1990s with his wife Astrid, "penniless" (though clearly rich in the cultural, symbolic, and social capital that came from belonging to a prominent family) and with the conviction (with other elites) that French cuisine was the only high-end cuisine in the world. With help from their friends and family, Astrid and Gastón opened their restaurant: a French bistro in the upscale Miraflores neighborhood. Over the years they moved from traditional, high-end, Parisian cuisine to a "refined" version of Peruvian cuisine. Acurio describes this as a gradual process, informed by a process of globalization that "while it implied the uniformity of many practices, was also opening up space for difference and diversity ... and this generated a sense of contradiction between what we were doing at the restaurant every day, and what we lived everyday as Peruvians."[16] He describes the process of including on the menu "street plates that everyone loved but that no one could imagine in a high-end restaurant," a practice that by the year 2000 reflected their main proposal: "the rediscovery of our identity."[17]

This rediscovery of identity—of looking inward toward Peru rather than outward toward France or the United States—is central, and among the principal messages conveyed by the gastropolitical complex of which Acurio is a crucial part. It is also an important marketing strategy. As Acurio tells Mirko Lauer, one of the principal storytellers of the Peruvian gastronomic revolution, "[Peruvian] authenticity is today a traditional value.... [B]efore it was a threat, something we needed to control. Today, he who is afraid to showcase our heritage is already at a disadvantage. The more authentic one is, the more possibilities he has to seduce and promote in today's modern tourism."[18] This story of return and rediscovery, however, is more often told as a tale about forbidden love: falling in love with Peru, moving past old prohibitions, embracing diversity, and using that diversity to renarrate the nation as one that reflects a beautiful and peaceful fusion of culinary and cultural traditions. Take for instance the message that pops up when you make a reservation at Astrid & Gastón at its website: "Have we arrived? Maybe. It's true, we fought for a long time, but here are our young people, dreaming in peace. Celebrating without fear, grateful to be from Lima, children of all bloods. From Andean to coastal, from Chinese to Japanese, from Italians to Arabs, from Spaniards to Africans. Impossible love that our parents knew how to defend and make flourish. And here we are today, seeking to be free at last, telling everyone, among chili peppers and dressings, that you do not have to build walls but bridges."[19]

The emphasis on peace, forbidden love, and flourishing fusion echoes Acurio's recent TED talk and is clearly central in narrating the story of a nation united through food and strengthened by histories of immigration and mestizaje. It has allowed gastropolitical elites to tell a story of striking transformation, a story of going from "being less" to "being more," from racial hatred and inequality to "beautiful and tolerant fusion," from an image of Peruvians as lazy (or *vivos*) to an image of Peruvians as entrepreneurial, creative, and socially responsible.[20] And yet Acurio is by no means the first to try to tap into the power of food and culture. There are others who have been studying and writing about food and its cultural and political significance for years.[21] Moreover, restaurants have been promoting high-end Peruvian cuisine since at least the 1980s.[22] What, then, explains Acurio's prominence? In some ways, Acurio's story is less about food than about business and marketing.

Indeed, Acurio's story about transforming the nation would not be possible without the tremendous commercial success he enjoyed as a savvy businessman who saw an opportunity to market Peruvian cuisine. He has created an empire that includes dozens of restaurants in Peru and around the world.[23] He starred in his own television show (*Aventura Culinaria*) and in several documentary films.[24] He is also the author of many books about Peruvian cuisine, gastronomy, and nationalism, all mobilizing his message—now the Peruvian state's message—of food as a social weapon, a uniting force, and a path toward social development and global culinary domination.[25] While

Acurio may be genuinely committed to improving the lives of Peruvians through the dissemination of Peruvian cuisine, he is also a successful entrepreneur deeply embedded in Peru's neoliberal turn.

Acurio's return to Peru coincided with the rise of another figure aspiring to save the nation: Alberto Fujimori. Those familiar with Peru will already know about the dramatic rise and fall of Fujimori, a Japanese Peruvian agronomist who went from being a powerful and popular president to a convicted criminal.[26] For the purpose of this chapter, it suffices to focus on the moment during which Acurio returned to Peru, in 1994. This was toward the end of Alberto Fujimori's first term as president, just a few years after this previously unheralded university professor and political outsider had beaten renowned novelist Mario Vargas Llosa. Although Fujimori had campaigned as a populist against Vargas Llosa's neoliberal plans, Fujimori went on to enact an austerity program that was even more severe than Vargas Llosa's proposed adjustment program. The costs of austerity, what many called the "Fujishock," were disproportionately shouldered by the poor. Nevertheless, Fujimori enjoyed high approval ratings due in part to what was perceived as his success in prosecuting the war against the Shining Path. Invoking the logic of national security, Fujimori closed congress in April 1992, suspended constitutional guarantees, and purged the military. In September of the same year, Peruvian security forces captured the head of the Shining Path, Abimael Guzmán. Although the capture of Guzmán had more to do with the work of local police than the authoritarian measures of the president, Fujimori was able to use Guzmán's capture and Sendero's military defeat to consolidate his increasingly authoritarian rule.

Acurio arrived during this moment of aggressive neoliberal reform and authoritarianism. This is where his social position made a significant difference. While most Peruvians were heavily impacted by Fujimori's economic and social policies, Acurio was advantageously positioned. Not only did he come from an elite family that afforded him many political and business connections, his whiteness, and European pedigree, provided him high status within the context of Peruvian racial formations that are characterized by enduring colonial legacies and histories of racial marginalization.

The political context, however, changed once Fujimori was accused (and ultimately convicted) of a variety of criminal corruption and human rights violations and fled the country in disgrace in 2000. With the transition to democracy, there was an increasing awareness of the need for promoting economic development and also an agenda of inclusion. In 2001 Alejandro

Toledo was elected president and promised a democratic opening. Toledo himself had a compelling origin story, from shoeshine boy to Stanford PhD. He also made much of his Andean ancestry to suggest that he embodied the promise of greater social inclusion for *todas las sangres*, the famous phrase José María Arguedas used to describe the multiracial Peruvian nation.[27]

After years of war and dictatorship, Toledo sought to promote a new vision of Peru to the world. A particularly notable example was his participation in the *The Royal Tour* series on the Travel Channel, in which a head of state takes a week from his presidential obligations to take a US television crew around the country in the hopes of inviting global tourism. Toledo's "tour" emphasized the "magical and mystical" dimension of Peru, reflected by the tremendous cultural and biological diversity of the country.[28] In other words, the timing was perfect for others to follow Toledo's lead in selling a new, postwar image of Peru to the world, and no one was better positioned than Acurio.[29] Improving upon Toledo's *Royal Tour*, precisely by making it less "royal," Acurio's television program *Aventura Culinaria*, across various seasons and episodes, told the story of everyday people who were making Peru the gastronomic envy of the world. With his celebration of popular markets, local chefs, and producers across the country, Gastón Acurio brilliantly converted his own celebrity status into something of a collective phenomenon. Through this television show (and with his many cookbooks), Acurio seemed to be suggesting that without understanding the local stories of ceviche, *guiso*, or chicharrón, one could not understand the national story of Peruvian cuisine or its most successful practitioner.[30] On television sets around the country (and now on Facebook, Twitter, and Instagram), Acurio provided recipes for remembering the nation, one meal at a time.

CONQUERING AND CRAFTING A NATION

This quest to rediscover Peru, to celebrate its culinary diversity and unite the country through food, is part of a strategy to commodify and market the nation. Acurio has been explicit about this. "Our mission isn't just making restaurants," he told *Food & Wine* magazine during an interview in 2008. "What we are doing, really, is selling a country."[31] This is in line with the Peruvian state's work to promote tourism and investment since 2001. However, while these early efforts looked outward, enticing foreign tourists to travel to Peru to visit iconic sites such as Cusco, Machu Picchu, and the Nazca Lines,

Acurio also focused on looking inward. With a growing network of state, public, and private entities, he emphasized the importance of selling Peru *to Peruvians*. In order to conquer globally, he seemed to be saying, you must also conquer locally.

This sentiment is evident in a statement Acurio made during an interview for a documentary about Mistura, for many years the most important culinary festival in Peru (arguably in the Americas), and a site that, according to the executive director of Apega at that time, "best represents Peruvianness":[32]

> Perhaps Mistura is the fiesta we have been waiting for; where our emotional independence finally has arrived and together we can celebrate our ability to conquer the world. May the campesino be lauded much more than the chef that is featured in the famous magazine. May the most famous restaurant have a smaller clientele than the man on the street corner selling *anticuchos*.[33] And may no one be bothered by the other, but instead may all help all, may all celebrate all, may all embrace all. From Peru we are helping demonstrate that our cuisine contains weapons more powerful and, of course, less bloody, that can contribute to a world where justice and pleasure, ethics and aesthetics always go hand in hand. The dreams of Mistura are large. History is just beginning.[34]

There is much to unpack here. But let's pause on the language of conquest and empire. Acurio has repeatedly stated that Peru is "conquering the world" through food, "expanding its empire one restaurant at a time." The metaphor of military victory is mobilized by Acurio's rhetorical flourishes in which chefs are the nation's "soldiers of peace," and food is "a social weapon."[35] The "Peru, Nebraska" video offers an interesting reflection of this as Peruvians from the global South take over the town of Peru, Nebraska, in the global North.[36] Afro-Peruvian dancers displace two-stepping regulars at a local bar, mustard and ketchup are replaced with *ají amarillo* and *rocoto*, and the town's sheriff agrees (reluctantly) to trade his donuts for *picarones*.[37] Most significantly, at the end of the video one representative from each "Peru" joins the other to raise the Peruvian national flag, and one of the Peruvian guests paints on the accent over the "u" in Peru, written on the side of a large water tank.

This video was wildly successful among Peruvian audiences, both within and outside of Peru. It can be read as both a narrative of invasion and a document of liberation. Peru is no longer the colonized, but rather the colonizer. In the arc of the narrative, the video also tells the story of a kind of cross-cultural courtship, which moves from initial suspicion and resistance, to tentative acceptance, to, finally, a warm embrace. With great skill and humor, the video takes us from a tense encounter with a small-town sheriff (whom a Peruvian trickster calls "Tony Curtis" as he swaps Peruvian *picarones* for the officer's donuts), to a scene of North Americans traveling to Peru to continue their cultural exchange and connection. Visually, it reflects the dream articulated by Acurio: "May no one be bothered by the other, but instead may all embrace all." This is the story Acurio and others want to tell for Peru, a nation that while once fragmented, is now one in which people come together despite differences and embrace one another as compatriots. As well as this text works as a promotional video directed at audiences in the global North, the real audience, especially at the time it was released, was Peruvians themselves. The story of Peruvian culinary conquest is always already a global and local one.

Once again, it is worth slowing down to think about the discourse of "conquest" even when it takes playful and humorous forms as in this video. Importantly, in Spanish the term *conquest* also has a sexual connotation. According to the Royal Academy of the Spanish Language, *conquistar* has four principal meanings:[38]

1. tr. To win a territory, population, position, etc. through military operation.

2. tr. To win or obtain something, ordinarily through effort, ability, or the overcoming of adversity.

3. tr. In regard to another person: To win over someone [*ganar la voluntad*], to bring them to one's party or position.

4. tr. To win the love of another, to capture their affection.

That final meaning of conquest, with its affective and even sexual notion of winning someone's affection and will (*voluntad*), reminds us of the unmistakably gendered dimension of the gastropolitical imaginary. Overwhelmingly, male chefs are the ones exerting their agency over other territories and bodies. Through the power of aesthetics, domination is euphemized but is clearly in operation as the masculinist march of progress, capital accumulation, and success makes its way in the world.

Indeed, this centering of masculine expertise and agency is by now a familiar feature of a gastropolitical project that reproduces heteronormative visions of the nation.[39] A few years ago Bernardo Roca Rey, then president of Apega, made a statement about Peru's participation in Madrid Fusión, an important global culinary event, that is worth quoting at length:

Peruvian gastronomy is no longer seen as something exotic.... It has everything necessary to become part of the select club of the most important culinary traditions in the world.... We saw this in action in the last iteration of the elite gastronomic conference, Madrid Fusión.... There the audience participates in order to discover and fall in love. *They are like princes in search of a princess....* Among the candidates ... there are some that are already married, others that are already out of fashion.... And among them there is a new princess, well dressed and even better put together, elegant and mysterious at the same time. They have heard and read about her, but they don't know her well. That girl has a lot to say. *Peru is this new girl, still unexplored, ready to make herself known and to fill with excitement all those ... in search of constant inspiration.*[40]

The gendered language here is striking. The framing of Peruvian gastronomy as a girl (not a woman—an important distinction), "still unexplored, ready to make herself known," is disturbingly familiar, and speaks to the androcentric dimension of this culinary revolution. This is not surprising given the severely patriarchal society that is Peru. Indeed, the ways in which gastropolitics reinforces dominant gender norms are remarkably similar to the ways in which it also reinforces existing racial orders, with White Peruvians at the center, making the generous decision of which subalterns to include and how.

Gastropolitics, then, is an artifact of the patriarchal and authoritarian context from which it emerged. Despite the democratic opening of 2000 and 2001, Peru was still a country torn apart, precariously held together by hopes of reconstruction and reconciliation. Peru was also characterized by anxieties that, as always, were inflected by gender and race. For many middle- and upper-class residents of Lima, the Andean highlands continued to represent zones of danger, and that danger was intimately related to the way that highland (and lowland) regions were racialized as home to potentially dangerous "Indians," territories one had to enter with care and certainly a guide. Let me offer an example from my own family. My grandfather was a Quechua-speaking man from Ayacucho, the region in Peru that was hardest hit during the war. Like many others, he eventually moved to Lima to raise his family. Decades later, in the mid-1990s, the idea that I, as a young woman, would travel to and live in the Andes alone to conduct dissertation research was seen as dangerous and improper by some of my family members.[41]

While geography in Peru has always been racialized, this was heightened during the last thirty years of the twentieth century, particularly after the conflict of the 1980s and 1990s. Violence in the Andes and Amazon displaced many communities and fueled migration to the large cities, especially Lima, where newcomers would create new informal settlements that were, without irony, called *invasiones* by Limeños.[42] One of the many impacts of the recent political conflict, then, was the projection of an image of Peru as a place of violence, poverty, and inequality. Tourism dropped significantly during these years, and if tourists arrived it was primarily to visit Machu Picchu and Cusco, rarely Lima. Moreover, the war with Sendero Luminoso had challenged the nation's sovereignty. In the late 1980s, half of Peru was considered an emergency zone (*zona roja*), which meant that the Shining Path had control of a significant part of the country.[43] Peruvians—particularly the middle and upper classes in Lima—were keenly aware of Peru's image in the world. They also continued to associate most highland and lowland regions of the country with terrorism and drug trafficking. Thus, gastropolitical elites had to craft a new image and tell a different story, one of national resurgence, of a nation rediscovering and celebrating its multicultural identity, and a story of food as a social weapon: *the* weapon, in fact, that made possible Peru's reemergence as a peaceful, beautiful, tolerant, culturally sophisticated, and economically successful nation. The culinary boom would finally win the peace for the nation that the military could not.

A COUNTRY FOR SALE

Acurio is arguably the leader of what we might call a gastropolitical complex that includes state, private, not-for-profit, and academic organizations, all working toward the promotion of tourism and increased economic investment in the country. This has translated into the savvy, creative, and relentless publicity of Marca Perú, particularly through the promotion of Peruvian cuisine. PromPerú, the Commission for the Promotion of Peru for Export and Tourism, is one of the principal actors in this network. It is an agency of the Ministry of Foreign Trade and Tourism, which as its name suggests, is tasked with promoting Peru's image, specifically through tourism and export. Its mission, as described on its website, is "to position Peru in the global scene by promoting the nation's image as a tourist destination and producer of value-added products, thus contributing to the nation's sustainable and decentralized development."[44] PromPerú is perhaps best known as the agency that developed Marca Perú, and it has generated countless publicity campaigns, promoted on multiple media and social media platforms in Peru and throughout the world.[45] Importantly, PromPerú was created in 1993 under

Fujimori, one year after his self-coup, and one year before Gastón Acurio's return to Peru. Its original purpose was to "develop the country's informational policies and centralize decision-making regarding the dissemination of the Image and Reality of Peru."[46] One might be forgiven for reading some Orwellian intention behind this communication strategy to shape Reality (with a capital R).

Here too, Acurio played a central role. In 2006, five years before PromPerú's official launch of Marca Perú, Peruvian economist Felipe Ortiz de Zevallos, then head of the elite Universidad del Pacífico, invited Acurio to deliver the inaugural speech for that academic year. The decision to invite a chef to speak to a group of students in economics and administration was, according to some, met with skepticism from faculty. But that talk has become among the most important declarations of Peruvian nationalism. Now referred to simply as "Gastón's speech" (*el discurso de Gastón*), it was quickly reprinted in its entirety in one of Peru's most important newspapers (*Peru 21*) and shared widely via email by Peruvians inside the country and out.[47] The political moment is significant. This was March 2006, just before presidential elections in April that determined the runoff between born-again conservative Alan García and the ostensibly left-leaning Ollanta Humala. As Lucero and I have noted elsewhere, this election was racially charged, as Humala, a former military official with Andean roots, was seen as a threat to the comfortable classes in Lima.[48] There were even rumors that the rich were confiscating the DNIs (national identification documents) of their domestic servants so they could not vote for this dangerous "Other." Alan García won in a very close election, using the campaign slogan "Responsible Change." Change indeed was on the minds of many Peruvians, including Acurio.

In his talk, Acurio foregrounded the need for national branding—for a Peruvian national brand—and made a powerful, emotional plea for the importance of branding as key to marketing the nation.[49] The implication, of course, is that Peruvian success means the ability to commodify and sell the nation. How, asks Acurio in this speech, can we accomplish this? What could be Peru's comparative advantage? Economists might have been tempted to say that it was the rich minerals in the ground or the cheap labor in the fields and factories. However, Acurio had what seemed like a different answer that took the country beyond the boom and bust cycles that had worked to undermine democracy and empower authoritarians: "While we might think the natural resources our country relies on have been a blessing, history has always taught us the opposite. Before it was rubber, then guano;

today it is minerals. However, when these are depleted, the cycle of economic bonanza ends and in its place appears that odious debacle and uncertainty that destroys democracies and gives rise to false leaders."[50]

What distinguished successful industrialized nations, he argued, was not resources, but the intellectual and conceptual work of marketing that could serve as a strategy to export Peruvian products and services around the globe. Gastronomy could be the key. Peruvian gastronomy was more than a great resource; it was "the sum of kitchens and concepts that in many cases still obscure the great potential" that with the elaboration of new frames of representation and dissemination could be "exported around the world."[51] To make it clearer to his business school audience with some numbers, Acurio noted that "in the last ten years, more [Peruvian] cookbooks have been published than in the entire history of [Peruvian] publishing... [and] over the past five years, 22 culinary schools have opened." Moreover, he noted that in 2006, "30% of tourists visiting Peru stayed in Lima to eat." This last point had been one of the key goals of gastropolitical elites, and as he noted in his speech, was "nothing short of a culinary revolution." But importantly, this culinary revolution would only work if people knew about it. The story of the revolution must be told. "The most important journalists of the world" must be dispatched "to cover this culinary revolution and publish articles and produce television programs that reveal their astonishment over the imminent global invasion of Peruvian flavors."[52] But beyond media attention, Acurio's point was also about property, especially intellectual property. "What we are lacking" he stated clearly, is "a national brand."

One of the striking features of this text from 2006 is how it follows another key text of Peru's neoliberal turn, Hernando De Soto's *The Mystery of Capital* (2000). De Soto anticipated Acurio's trajectory in remarkable ways. A generation before Acurio, De Soto also had a great "return" from a successful career in Europe. In 1979, De Soto returned to a Peru that would soon enter into its worst economic and political crisis. As Sendero advanced its bloody revolution, De Soto wrote about what he called El Otro Sendero (The Other Path), which was about providing property rights to the country's informal sector.[53] The poor, he argued, especially Andean immigrants in Lima, were working incredibly hard, but their settlements and work in informal markets lacked the protection and promise of property rights. He returned to this theme in *The Mystery of Capital*. If his first book was an attempt to bring Milton Friedman's economics into Peru's shantytowns, the 2000 book added Jacques Derrida and Michel Foucault to the neighborhood. Inflecting his neoliberal message with a postmodernist sensibility, De Soto declared that the solution to the "mystery" of why some nations are poor while others are rich lies in the power of representation. "And so formal property is this extraordinary thing, much bigger than simple ownership. Unlike tigers and wolves, who bare their teeth to protect their territory, man, physically a much weaker animal, has used his mind to create a legal environment—property—to protect his territory. Without anyone fully realizing it, the representational system the West created to settle territorial claims took on a life of its own, providing the knowledge base and rules necessary to fix and realize capital."[54] Representation is indeed an extraordinary thing. It can transform simple material objects into capital. For Acurio, gastronomy can involve a similar kind of transformation. If we can get the story and branding right, Peruvian cuisine can itself be the path to prosperity and inclusion.

THE POWER OF FUSION

While De Soto turns to economics and philosophy for his vision of Peruvian prosperity, Acurio finds interesting inspiration in a reading of Peruvian history and society, most notably his understanding of mestizaje, or racial mixture. As noted in the introduction, mestizaje was adopted as a nation-building ideology by many Latin American elites in the early twentieth century as a way to counter North Atlantic notions of White supremacy. Theorists of mestizaje declared that racial mixture was an evolutionary step forward for humankind.[55] In the combination of people of "all bloods," Latin America represented the strength of mixture and the folly of discourse around purity. But some Peruvian theorists of mestizaje approached things slightly differently and instead saw deformity in mixture.[56] Aware of these histories, Acurio has worked to resignify mestizaje. In countless writings and interviews, he emphasizes the importance of recognizing the uniqueness and beauty of Peru, a nation shaped by "centuries of racial and cultural fusion" and "harmonious dialogue between nature and man."[57] Take for example the description of some of his dishes, such as "Las causas cinco razas," featured in his book *500 Years of Fusion: The History, the Ingredients, and Peruvian Cuisine's New Proposals*:[58] "Five bloods run through the veins of the Peruvian of today, five great influences make up our cuisine. The Andes, with all its different cultures. Europe, that since the arrival of Pizarro has not stopped sending Spanish, Italian or French migrations. Africa, with its rhythm and seasoning. China, with its woks and ancient gastronomic taste. Japan, with its maritime vocation and great stylization. Five cultures perfectly assembled: may five *causas* pay them homage."[59]

Perhaps one should not read too much into the incredibly reductive language of Andean, European, African, Chinese, and Japanese "bloods." Nevertheless, it is worth noting how this view of "cultures" flattens and caricatures centuries of imperialism, violence, indentured servitude, slavery, and conquest. In their place, one finds the smooth language of integration and fusion. Similarly, in the introduction to one of his cookbooks (titled simply *Peru: The Cookbook*), Acurio writes:

> We are convinced that our cuisine is the fruit of a long, tolerant relationship among people and a treasure trove of ingredients that is the result of centuries of dialogue between our ancestors and nature.... It is also the cuisine of a country to which different peoples, immigrants from Japan, China, Africa, Spain, Italy and the Arab world, migrated over the last 500 years. All brought with them their nostalgia, customs, and products, which were beautifully assimilated into an example of unique tolerance. The result is a Peruvian cuisine that infuses a little of each of those peoples into each bite, transforming it into something new, something Peruvian.[60]

Similarly emphasizing inclusion and tolerance, Mirko Lauer and Vera Lauer write that Peru's gastronomic revolution has been particularly multiregional, has included "multiple classes" (*ha sido pluriclasista*), and "could not be nicer and less demanding.... [I]t is a joyful mobilization of resources in which all of us, in one form or other, participate."[61] Returning to Acurio's resignification of mestizaje, it matters that this is a history of racial *and* cultural mixture; it evokes the colonial encounter and also histories of immigration. Of course this formulation necessarily relies on a selective vision of history and inclusion.

The resignification of mestizaje allows Acurio and other gastropolitical elites to make a case for the greatness of Latin American, and specifically Peruvian, cuisine:

> The key is in understanding that we are a great nation, with a great live culture born out of centuries of mestizaje and that it is precisely that mixture that has allowed our cuisine to offer a variety of dishes that has captivated the international public, and that it is in that mixture where Peruvians must find the inspiration not only to generate wealth, but also, above all else, to accept and love ourselves as a nation, and only then, from that place of love and acceptance, find from within all those ideas that will then transform themselves into products and brands that will conquer the world.... Having these

[Peruvian] concepts and brands throughout the world would give Marca Perú the power of seduction that would ... bring other Peruvian offerings ... to the world's attention.[62]

Elsewhere, Acurio makes his understanding and reframing of mestizaje even more explicit: "When I was a child, the word mestizo was pejorative; today it is our worth [*nuestro valor*]."[63] The use of the word *valor* signals not only strength and courage, but also something's market value, suggesting, as he does in the preceding quote, that the promise of national fusion is linked to the marketability of Peruvianness. In other words, what mestizaje requires now is a new kind of representation, or more simply put, better branding. Acurio's message found a receptive audience in many elites, who quickly found a way to help through the formation of a gastronomic society that could be the vanguard of the culinary revolution, or perhaps more accurately, its advertising agency.

Until its demise in 2019, Apega, the Peruvian Society of Gastronomy, was the organization most focused on promoting the products of the gastronomic boom and the process by which it was happening.[64] Apega emerged in 2007, just one year after Acurio's *discurso*. On its website, following the spirit (and letter) of Acurio's speech, the organization notes that Apega was "born in 2007, due to the need to articulate efforts to give Peruvian gastronomy the place it deserves in the world, and to transform it into a source of identity, innovation, and sustainable development for Peruvians."[65] Over its twelve years in existence, Apega supported culinary and agricultural research, publishing texts on gastronomy, development, and cultural identity, and worked to promote "inclusive gastronomy," primarily through work with small-scale producers across the nation and the much-touted chef-producer alliances.[66] Perhaps most important, Apega was the principal organizer of Mistura, the culinary festival that in its heyday hosted almost half a million visitors. As I discuss in chapter 3, Mistura celebrated a "beautiful fusion" that could also be understood critically as less inclusive than it may have seemed at first blush. The festival could be read as a stage for the exhibition and managing of difference; a dimension of the gastronomic revolution's civilizing project. Yet for Acurio, Apega, and others, this was a crucial site for showcasing chef-producer alliances; for celebrating the accomplishments of emerging cooks, the development of artisanal beer, coffee, chocolate, or the innovative techniques of world-class chefs; and for exploring (through its Gran Mercado or Grand Market) the pantry (*la despensa*) full of exotic and authentic ingredients that is Peru. And while this is the stuff of glossy English-language promotional materials, this is just as much about marketing Peru to Peruvians as it is to tourists. As Apega's then executive director, Mariano Valderrama, told me during an interview in 2012, Apega worked hard to "show Peru to Peruvians. We need to revalorize our identity," he continued, "by rediscovering Peru's beauty and diversity."[67]

In order to succeed, then, Peruvians need to love and accept themselves as Peruvians; they need to re-member the nation, to move away from racial antagonisms and recognize each other as fellow Peruvians. Despite persistent poverty, acute social conflict, gentrification, blatant racism, and class hierarchies, for Acurio and many others, this is the promise of Peruvian cuisine. If Peruvians could just taste their nation anew, if they could recognize the unique fusion of cultures in each of their beloved dishes, then perhaps that recognition could extend beyond the plate. And for many, this promise has in fact become a reality, at least in the ways nation is imagined in Peru. Filmmaker Ernesto Cabellos captures this beautifully at the start of his documentary *Cooking Up Dreams*: "Over two centuries of racial mixture, of encounters and evasions, Peruvian cuisine has constructed a deliciously integrative experience. In the kitchen and in the pot, tastes, aromas and colors struggle, contest, negotiate and reconcile. Each one searches for its place and coexists with the other."[68] The mention of reconciliation is especially notable coming only a few years after the formal end of political violence between the state and leftist forces and the completion of the CVR's final report. To be Peruvian, then, entails recognizing our place in the pot, our own particular contribution that allows us to coexist with the other.

TOWARD A SOCIALLY JUST CUISINE: NARRATING PERU'S FUTURE

These are indeed revolutionary ideals in the context of Peru, scarred by centuries of racism and inequality, and as many would argue, still living through what the late Peruvian sociologist Anibal Quijano famously termed the "coloniality of power."[69] Acurio and others claim to recognize the limits of these ideals, which is why alongside fusion, another key part of the national story of culinary excellence is the significance of thinking about both aesthetics and ethics. Acurio has been vocal about promoting "a culinary ethics that goes beyond mere pleasure."[70] He insists that this culinary movement must also be guided by ethical principles that account for where food comes from and who benefits from its consumption. "Gastronomy and hunger simply do not go together. It is immoral to enjoy good food and lavish meals when you know that the fisherman who caught your divinely-cooked seafood lives in a shabby hut and must survive on next to nothing."[71]

Acurio's work with Native producers, and especially in training young cooks from poor socioeconomic backgrounds, is of particular note. One of Acurio's best known projects is the Pachacutec Institute of Culinary Arts, a cooking school located in a "slum" north of Lima where young people without resources to attend other institutes can train to become chefs.[72] Acurio and many others insist on the crucial role chefs play in promoting peace and social inclusion. Acurio writes: "We never imagined . . . that a cook would become a messenger of peace and solidarity among people, a spokesperson for educational, nutritional, and environmental issues, and above all, a bridge to happiness for many people in the country, at sea, and in cities. . . . We, the chefs of Peru, are precisely today's messengers. With honor and humility, we are the ambassadors of our cuisine in the world."[73] Peru's gastronomic revolution has served as a powerful response to recent episodes of violence precisely by placing that violence firmly in the past. Chefs are "messengers of peace," and gastropolitics, like state narratives about the years of terror, is invested in moving Peru "forward," toward visions of the future. In a recent book by (and about) Acurio (whose title translates as, appropriately enough, *Seasoning in Action: Some Recipes for the Peru We Want*), the editors write: "Gastón Acurio has developed a vision not only of Peruvian gastronomy, but of Peru, our nation. And this vision . . . has always looked to the future. If there is one thing to note about Gastón, it is that he is one of the few voices that speak to us more about the promises of the future, than the difficulties of the present, or the misfortunes of the past."[74]

The focus on the future may not seem all that remarkable given how often political and market rhetoric invokes a better tomorrow. Yet when the acknowledgment of "misfortunes of the past" (understood to be the war between the state and Shining Path, though perhaps more obliquely also evoking Velasco) is juxtaposed with Acurio's claims about Peruvian fusion being the product of five hundred years of "balanced, reflexive and consensual" mixture, a curious conception of Peruvian history becomes apparent.[75] For example, let's consider the historical narrative gastropolitical elites have crafted about the gastronomic revolution. This story looks to the future even in its retelling of the past. Strikingly, references to violence are all but removed in this narrative of the years of terror. In a way, the armed conflict is a kind of public secret. Without ever being explicitly invoked, Sendero haunts the story of the nation. Peruvians know (and feel) this violent backstory, which is why it does not need to be mentioned. It remains firmly lodged in the background, allowing elites to write Peru's history anew, foreground their aspirations, and disseminate them to local and global audiences.

Acurio himself, in the remarks quoted earlier, points to the importance of telling this story far and wide by emphasizing the recent history of publishing on Peruvian gastronomy. The proliferation of such books is not just an indication of the commercial success of gastronomy. It is itself a powerful mechanism of the remaking of the nation. As Benedict Anderson famously noted, print media is a crucial dimension in the making of an imagined community.[76] Moreover, Appadurai's influential work on gastropolitics in India cites the importance of cookbooks in the making of a national cuisine, and of nationhood.[77] In Peru, books about gastronomy—including high-end coffee-table cookbooks published in English; cookbooks and texts about cuisine and the culinary revolution, published with a Peruvian middle-class in mind; and regular supplements about cooking and gastronomy published by *El Comercio*—are important mediums through which to disseminate a vision of the nation, one that renarrates recent history with little or no reference to what many have called "the time of fear."[78] Except for minimal and obscure references to "difficult times," they have brilliantly reconfigured a once dominant historical narrative about the decades of violence. Prior to 2006, references to the 1980s and 1990s inevitably had to do with political and economic turmoil. Since the rise of the gastronomic boom, along with these texts, as well as other academic and journalistic works about Peruvian cuisine, those decades are not about crisis and death, but rather described as ones of initial experiments in fusion cuisine that set the stage for what was to come.[79]

Based on the periods that gastropolitical elites have themselves emphasized, the historical narrative of Peru since the 1980s goes something like this:

- Setting the Stage. 1986–1996. Roca Rey coins the term *cocina novoandina*, and the first experiments in fusion cuisine begin. Acurio returns to Peru after studying and living in Europe, and with his German wife, Astrid Gutsche, opens the now renowned Astrid & Gastón. This is also the moment when culinary "pioneers" set the stage for the second generation of chefs, including Acurio and Rafael Osterling.

- Phase 1, 1996–2006. Described by Acurio as the first phase of the gastronomic revolution, these are the years in which he brings his expertise in international gourmet cuisine to Peru, works with others to develop and disseminate nouveau Andean cuisine, and works toward achieving Peru's world-class status in global gastronomic circles. Acurio also works to develop excitement among Peruvian elites about Peruvian fusion cuisine, a challenging move in the context of a community looking outward (to Europe and the United States) for what is deemed worthy or valuable.

- Phase 2, 2006–2016. In March 2006 Acurio delivers the convocation address at the elite Universidad del Pacífico in Lima. The second phase of the gastronomic revolution, again using Acurio's periodization, begins with a focus on manufacturing national pride by cementing Peruvian cuisine's world-class status and working hand in hand with state tourism and export agencies to brand the nation and expand culinary tourism. A central goal is transforming Lima into a culinary destination for tourists.[80]

- Phase 3, 2016–2026. At Yuntémonos, a one-day gathering (November 26, 2016) of gastropolitical elites, university students, chefs, journalists, academics, and politicians at the prestigious Pontificia Universidad Católica del Peru, Acurio calls for the beginning of the third ten-year phase of the gastronomic revolution. This phase invites the academy and public sectors to join hands with private industry in an effort to utilize Peruvian gastronomy as "a weapon" against poverty, malnutrition, obesity, climate change, and for the protection of Peru's biodiversity. The midpoint of this phase, the year 2021, is of particular import as it will mark what Apega has termed Peru's "second independence," two hundred years after Peru's original independence from Spain (July 28, 1821).

While the third phase is ostensibly about socially and environmentally just causes, this moment is still very much about continuing to work toward culinary dominance and wealth. PromPerú's recent international marketing campaign, "Peru, the richest country in the world," is a great example. The campaign was unveiled in 2017 at the World Travel Market, the United Kingdom's most prominent tourism trade exhibition.[81] It is worth reproducing the ad's language here:

Nowadays, they say that being rich isn't about having the most, it's about experiencing the most unforgettable moments, moments that can only be found in one country, Peru. A country blessed with the most valuable wealth of all, wealth that is measured in terms of harmony with nature; wealth that you feel when savoring a meal that feeds both body and soul. Or when the sun sinks below the horizon, but its glow lingers in your heart. Today, Peru invites you to experience true wealth, the kind of wealth that you keep, on the inside. Welcome to Peru, the richest country in the world.[82]

Note the reframing of wealth: being rich is not about having things, but experiencing life, including through travel and novel sensory experiences. But this is clearly a story for global elites, a story for those who can travel, who can experience, who can eat at the world's best restaurants. Peruvians of "all the bloods" who will never eat in these elite spaces can at least observe the spectacle of this national success and bask in the glow of these riches.

Gastropolitics, then, celebrates the fact that Peru "has arrived." And interestingly, it is in this moment—with Peru clearly positioned as the world's leading culinary destination, and with three of the best fifty restaurants in the world located in Lima—that we begin to see the violence of the 1980s and 1990s mentioned more directly, and as clearly in the past. This is evident in the Generación con Causa campaign, and in the recent *Chef's Table* episode about chef Virgilio Martínez (see chapter 2). The present and future of Peru, in this story, promises a move away from this violence and toward peace and prosperity. This is a particularly important point of inflection as Peru approaches its "second independence" in 2021.[83] It is also an important move because it makes Peru's story of national resurgence even more remarkable. This periodization does important work; it marks the violence of the internal conflict as exceptional, glossing over ongoing racial, settler colonial, and gendered harm. Curiously, though, the one episode of Peruvian history that gastropolitics does invoke is the impact of the Revolutionary Government of the Armed Forces (RGAF; 1968–80), and particularly Velasco Alvarado's policies, including his program of agrarian reform. While references to Velasco might be difficult to detect for those outside of Peru, the very language used by Apega, Acurio, and others to announce Peru's "second independence" has unmistakable echoes that older generations in Peru have no trouble hearing.

FROM UGLY TO BEAUTIFUL STORIES

One of the main arguments of this book is that the gastronomic revolution tells a particular story about Peruvian history. This is a story that uses the violence of the 1980s and 1990s as background in order to prop up a vision of a peaceful and socially inclusive future, while glossing over centuries of violence involving conquest, slavery, and indentured labor. Emphasizing fusion as the product of love, tolerance, and even consent, gastropolitical discourses erase long histories of sexual, racial, and gendered violence that undergird the making of the Peruvian nation. These erasures usually take the form of sweeping characterizations of Peruvian history, but in some instances the historical vision is remarkably specific. This is precisely the case in the gastronomic revolution's engagement with the RGAF, and particularly the legacy of the reforms of general Juan Velasco Alvarado (1968–75).

That "Peruvian revolution" radically transformed society.[84] Going against the grain of the right-wing, anti-Communist military dictatorships emerging throughout Latin America at this time, Velasco's was a leftist military government. As historians Carlos Aguirre and Paulo Drinot describe it, the message of the revolution was clear: "[Velasco] was leading a nationalist project aimed at radically transforming Peruvian society, eliminating social injustice, breaking the cycle of foreign domination, redistributing land and wealth, and placing the destiny of Peruvians into their own hands."[85] As I argue in this book, the specter of this other, earlier revolution haunts gastropolitical discourse. Proclaiming a "second independence"—something Velasco did decades ago—simultaneously evokes, challenges, and erases Velasco, without having to mention his name. Velasco's ghost is also evident in statements such as Acurio's description of the culinary revolution as "a revolution without blood, *that does not take from anyone*, but rather shares," or Mirko Lauer and Vera Lauer's insistence that this is a "nice" revolution that "does not make demands."[86] Mirko Lauer's role in narrating Peru's gastronomic revolution is particularly interesting, as he was also a member of the RGAF's Agrarian Reform Diffusion Center, a team charged with mobilizing propaganda about the agrarian reform.[87] His use of the term *revolution* in the title of his first book about Peru's culinary boom is quite deliberate. In it, he explicitly contrasts Velasco's revolution as a process that "closed Peru to the world," while describing Peru's contemporary culinary revolution as "open, modern, forward-looking, neoliberal, and libertarian," reflecting his own political shift from Left to Right.[88]

Gastropolitical elites look selectively and romantically to a feudal past, before Velasco and agrarian reform, to imagine a neoliberal future. If gastropolitics promises a "second independence" in 2021, it is a vision of a renewed nation that celebrates beautiful mixture and social inclusion, premised on a (symbolic) return to pre-Velasco racial and gendered orders. The nation may be beautifully mixed and socially inclusive, but there is little doubt about who is including whom.

Peruvian anthropologist Enrique Mayer writes that the RGAF "was the first government [in Peru] ever to execute significant income redistribution in a society of great inequalities. It completed the abolition of all forms of servitude in rural estates, a momentous shift in the history of the Andes, akin to the abolition of slavery in the Americas."[89] The comparison with the abolition of slavery illustrates the momentous impact this government had on Peruvian society. During Velasco Alvarado's rule in particular, the RGAF implemented education and labor reform programs, nationalized foreign-owned companies, and implemented a radically ambitious land reform project that led to the expropriation of tens of thousands of properties, including millions of hectares. As Portocarrero puts it, Velasco's rule was "the most audacious attempt in the history of Peru to contain social antagonisms."[90] Velasco developed a wide network of state propaganda (including print, radio, television, posters, and festivals) through which he disseminated a nationalistic rhetoric that deliberately incorporated those who had previously been most marginalized. Moreover, as Mayer writes, he "clipped the wings of the elites, breaking up their self-assurance and the privileges they had taken for granted, partly by ridicule and partly by imposing new, more popular horizontal forms of treatment for everyone."[91]

Mayer's book is titled *Ugly Stories of the Peruvian Agrarian Reform*. While he seeks to equally represent "the good, the bad, and the ugly" dimensions of the revolution, the "ugliness" of the memories from this period is what is most emphasized.[92] As he notes, throughout his years of research and interviews, he found "not one person who wanted to tell me that he or she was happy with the way the agrarian reform worked itself out."[93] In an attempt to offer a more nuanced and comprehensive history of this period, however, Mayer brings together stories told by a range of actors involved in or impacted by the reform, such as landowners, bureaucrats, academics, peasants, veterinarians, and agricultural experts. "Because Velasco's revolution has been deliberately placed in the category of things best forgotten," he tells us in the conclusion, "I have in this book endeavored to bring it back to the consciousness of today's readers."[94]

But if the rhetoric of gastropolitical elites is any guide, this history has not been forgotten. As Mayer himself notes, "the current neoliberal atmosphere has satanized the Velasco government for every evil that befell Peru and which needs to be repaired."[95] Peruvian historian Paulo Drinot also provides evidence of the lingering power of the memory of the RGAF and of Velasco and his reforms.[96] He offers important insights into the collective (and contested) memories of the Velasco regime through an analysis of comments attached to three YouTube videos about Velasco, one promoting a positive image of the general and his policies and the other two offering a clearly negative portrait. Much like Mayer's and Portocarrero's findings, Drinot's analysis shows that while there are many positive memories about Velasco—as the leader who liberated Indigenous peasants, providing them with land and dignity, for example—there are just as many violently negative ones.

In direct contrast to supporters of the regime who credit Velasco with the liberation of Indigenous Peruvians, many claim that Velasco's agrarian reform in fact impoverished the peasantry further. By expropriating land from "entrepreneurial *hacendados*" and giving it to "uneducated," "untrained," or "lazy" Indians, agricultural production suffered, and poverty increased. "The only thing they achieved was to fuck up productivity in the country. After 40 years since the [agrarian] reform . . . we know what results it has produced: more poor peasants."[97] This theme is common, and some of the comments Drinot cites make clear the paternalism and racism that accompany this sentiment. One post, for instance, notes that "it wasn't the right time to redeem the peasants. . . . Today, the poor peasant, although he enjoys freedom to think and make his own decisions, this freedom is of no use to him because he is still poor and poorer than he was before the reform, because at least he had something to eat under the gamonal [the hacienda landlord] . . . but now he does not know how to produce or how to eat."[98]

Others speak even more directly to the ways race and indigeneity in Peru are deeply embedded within racial capitalist and neoliberal ideologies. A few examples of posts make the point quite forcefully:

[M]any people who, with great effort, had haciendas, land . . . etc., lost them. He is not the general of the poor of Peru, he is the general of the lazy, because the poor are provided with opportunities to make a living and the lazy are given everything for free.[99]

They took my grandmother's hacienda because of this idiot who believes in giving the same to everyone . . . instead of giving opportunities so that everyone can achieve their goals by virtue of their effort and hard work. [It was a mistake] to give land to so many ignorant Indians who don't even know how to manage an hacienda.[100]

Velasco gave them machinery and seeds, land, etc., and what did the Indians do? They sat on their arses and let the machinery and seeds go to waste. . . . They went back to their mountains, to their coca, and continued to breed more children and more poverty.[101]

With eerie similarity these posts echo comments I have heard many times in Peru. The "rhetoric of reaction," as Albert Hirschman usefully described it, has some fairly sturdy tropes.[102] Beyond the familiar "bootstraps" of liberal individualism and the racist images of "backward" Indians, these comments converge with the theses of conservative critique that Hirschman calls futility (reforms won't work), perversity (they just make things worse), and jeopardy (they create new dangers). Versions of these theses continue to circulate in Peru and especially in middle- and upper-class Lima, where the "invasions" of Andean migrants have transformed the Peruvian capital.

As Drinot notes, many Peruvians understand the agrarian reform "in terms of its supposed consequences for the social and racial makeup of Lima, arguing that it contributed to the wave of migration from the highlands to the capital, which, in turn, radically transformed what was until then a largely criollo, or white, city."[103] Take just two of the comments Drinot analyzes:[104]

[Velasco] was a fucking Indian, a cholo, because of him the cholos fucked up Lima, the city was made 100% by Europeans and now it's a disaster full of combis [public transport vans], filthy markets, Indians begging in the streets and other shit. . . .

Velazco [sic] . . . stole your parents' land with that agrarian reform bullshit, as a consequence of that your forefathers (antepasados) migrated to Lima, that is to say, they invaded Lima to work as servants and that is why we need to put up with this invasion of darkies (cobrizos) that we see now in Lima with all their delinquency, thefts, gangs, and corruption.

These are responses that make clear the affective legacies that accompany memories about this time, generations after the reform. Even for those too young to have experienced Velasco directly, the reproduction of the rage of the propertied classes has, for many, become something of a family tradition.

Growing up, I heard many negative comments about Velasco. We had to leave the country during this time (in 1976), after my father—as the story goes—spoke back to a general and was told by a friend that, for his safety and the safety of his family, he should leave Peru. We moved to Venezuela when I was only five years old, and when I began to ask questions about why we had left, the answer was always Velasco. Like many of the Peruvians quoted here, family members spoke about Velasco as a resentido social who took land and property away from those who knew how to manage it; turned the country into a backward, underdeveloped nation; and most significantly, upended clear social orders. A *resentido social* is not only one who carries a "chip on their shoulder" (as Mayer translates the term) but someone who resents the entire system and hopes to disrupt the established order of things.

There is an obvious class (and racial) dimension to this, as those deemed *resentidos sociales* are generally also from marginalized populations. According to many I have spoken with in Lima, after Velasco, "maids thought they could talk back"; "uneducated people" thought they were qualified to manage multinational companies and run the country; and most important, Velasco "fueled resentment among the lower classes." This last statement was often followed by a deeply held belief that it was because of Velasco, and because of this "new" resentment, that Sendero Luminoso emerged. This speaks directly to elite fears of Indigenous revenge, akin to fears of slave uprisings that have haunted the Atlantic world since the Indigenous uprising of Túpac Amaru in the 1780s and the Haitian Revolution in the 1790s.[105] Mayer details a conversation with one landowner in Piura (in the north of Peru) who, like many others, was contemptuous of Velasco and particularly of his agrarian reform. "Velasco was a *resentido social*. It was not our fault that he was born poor, no?" He continues: "Here in Piura there is a saying about the three worst evils: 'A poor white, a black with money, an *indio* with power.' That general, he gave power to the Indians and they avenged themselves."[106] Again, this speaks to the common assumption during the early years of the internal conflict that Sendero Luminoso was an "Indian rebellion." During the years of political violence, many in Lima would speak of their fear of maids and the inevitability of Indians being terrorists. Mayer notes that Velasco's reforms meant in practice that peasants were freed from living in slave-like conditions; that they "woke up" and learned about their rights. For many in Peru, this was precisely the problem.

The specter of Velasco—and by association, socialism—was evoked during the 2006 elections between García and Humala, and again in 2011 when Humala won the presidency. And as noted earlier, Velasco is also often blamed for setting the stage for the war with the Shining Path and driving Peru to economic ruin.[107] While contemporary rhetoric emphasizes forgetting and moving forward, Velasco's revolution remains an obstacle precisely because it led directly to the upending of social orders. While elites can't advocate a return to the hacienda system and feudal orders explicitly, they can promote a "new order" brought forth by gastropolitics, which though masked in the language of inclusion and alliances is really a return to old hierarchies, with a clear ruling class (successful, benevolent patrones who provide for "their" campesino producers) and in which people know "their place," a theme to which I return in chapter 3.

RETURN TO CASA MOREYRA

Casa Hacienda Moreyra, the main house of what used to be the Hacienda de San Isidro, was designed and built in the mid-seventeenth century by Catalán architect Pedro de Noguera. The Paz Soldán family, a cornerstone of Lima's aristocracy, bought the hacienda in the mid-1800s and remained in control of the property until Velasco's agrarian reform.[108] It was declared a historical monument by the state in 1972. As noted at the beginning of this chapter, Acurio's decision to move his flagship restaurant to this specific space speaks volumes. This is a project of reclaiming ownership, restoring order, and rewriting history.[109]

For one thing, Acurio has literally inhabited a national monument of Peru's pre-Velasco glory, a significant symbolic move. What Mayer says about haciendas in general applies well to Casa Moreyra in particular: it "evokes not only the land but also a world of refined privilege. It associates a family surname with a place. . . . The memory is also fused with a building, the casa hacienda, constructed on an imposing place as the exclusive domain of the family and guests."[110] Haciendas were one of the key institutions of Spanish colonialism. They were vital not only for their political economic role but also for reproducing a colonial social order. As Mayer puts it: "The hacienda was a place where traditions were kept, continuity with the past was affirmed, privilege was underlined, and refinement was cultivated. It was an intensely private world with sharply defined boundaries and rigidly enforced patterns of exclusivity."[111] It is one of the striking features of the coloniality of Latin America that haciendas are unapologetically aestheticized and even romanticized today.[112] Astrid & Gastón's web page is illustrative of the Peruvian and arguably hemispheric fascination with the grandeur of colonial times. The website provides a description not far from Mayer's: "Casa Moreyra was always more than a place of residence. Its significance in history is linked to its original rural role rather than to its current palatial beauty. It was a center where all types of activities came together and took place: first the economic ones and then the social, cultural and religious ones."

The house is more than a house. And while the house serves various functions, the economic role is the one most emphasized. The website recalls that the hacienda's eight thousand hectares of cropland formed part of "the great pantry of Lima." Those days of rural glory, however, came to an end. And while he is never mentioned, the ghost of General Velasco Alvarado haunts this history as well. "During the twentieth century," the site tells us, "due to urban expansion, these properties were divided and they eventually disappeared. Lima began to rely on distant pantries and the few hacienda houses that remained were removed from their original role, and they started to be confused with common houses or urban mansions." Even if there is no direct mention of agrarian reform or expropriation, Peruvians reading this history are well aware of what is meant by "the eventual disappearance of these properties."

Moreover, Acurio is clearly positioned as the figure of *el buen patrón*, that feudal figure who laid down the law, and the benevolent patriarch who took care of "his" workers. In interviews, both Apega functionaries and small producers have referred to Acurio as "el patrón." And in his role as one of the principal proponents of the alliances between chefs and producers, he too positions himself in this way, even if implicitly. I return to this point in chapter 3, but it is worth noting here one more echo of Velasco's moment that can be heard in Acurio's revolution. Velasco's speech on June 24, 1969, announcing his agrarian reform, is perhaps one of the most famous speeches in Peruvian history. It ends with a sentence that, as Drinot notes, has come to define not only the agrarian reform but the whole Velasco government: "We can now say to the man who works the land [*hombre de la tierra*], using the immortal and liberating words of Túpac Amaru: 'Peasant, the landlord will no longer eat from your poverty!'"[113]

Acurio turns this on its head. In reworking this idea, he seems to be saying that feeding the "landlord" (the globalized elites of today rather than the feudal elites of the past) will in fact bring prosperity, and the ability to produce, to rural farmers. With only a bit of exaggeration, one might say that the new revolutionary message is: *Hombre de la tierra*: Feed the landlord, feed yourself. This is the idea behind the chef-producer alliances: chefs in Lima commit to buying directly from producers in rural regions of Peru, and in that way not only support farmers economically but showcase them and their products as the protagonists and engine necessary to keep the revolution moving and to keep world-class restaurants operating. Of course, the caveat is that producers are expected to be grateful for the support of their new patrón. Thus, the gastronomic revolution—not Velasco's revolution—is in fact what will liberate them, by anchoring them to working the land and returning to the imagined benevolent relations of the feudal past. Actual market relations may be very different, but discursively, the imaginary of the present moment is one that turns Velasco's revolution upside down.

Finally, the historical narration of Casa Moreyra, and the website more generally, also does important work in recentering and revisioning Lima.[114] After a brief introduction to the significance of the Casa Hacienda, Acurio notes that its history begins even before its construction, and the website then takes one to a timeline that begins in AD 1000 (when the "lands that were part of the Hacienda de San Isidro were irrigated by the Huatica irrigation canal, what is now Avenida Camino Real") and goes directly from that moment to 1538, three years after the founding of Lima.[115] With only a few stops along the way, the history of Casa Moreyra ends in 2014, with the arrival of Astrid & Gastón.

Without spending too much time on this periodization, a few observations are warranted. First, in a thousand years of history Native peoples simply never appear. Even before the arrival of the Spanish, the only historical fact that merits attention is the fact that there existed an "irrigation canal." Who designed and built the canal is rendered unimportant and irrelevant. Similarly, while the catacombs at Casa Moreyra would seem to signal the presence of slaves on the hacienda, there is no mention of the entangled histories of slavery and haciendas in Peru. Second, the entire decade of the 1980s, when the war between the state and leftist insurgents was terrorizing large parts of the country including Lima, is avoided completely. The late twentieth century events include the declaration of the house as a national monument (ironically in 1972, during Velasco's government) and the fact that the house was the site of an important continental gathering of architects and designers in 1999. The house is a time capsule that emerges effortlessly in the sixteenth century, passes through several aristocratic hands, is a witness to the founding of Lima and Peru, and is untouched by the violence of the centuries. The house is literally a monument to the glory of an agrarian and elite world that gave birth to the City of Kings, Lima. It is a bridge between feudal and neoliberal worlds.

CONCLUDING REFLECTIONS

The future is also haunted, then, and clearly linked to affective memories of what used to be: of a Lima before racialized urbanization, before order was upended. The gastronomic revolution is anchored in these visions of the past and offers a path forward through civilizing projects that are racialized and aestheticized. Despite and through the language of "revolution," gastropolitics is in fact a restoration: it reestablishes racial orders. As shown in the following chapters, the discourse of a peaceful revolution obscures ongoing violence against those who don't conform to contemporary norms of beautiful mixture and tolerant relations. At a time when Indigenous and environmental movements are violently criminalized for their opposition to the increasing presence of mining and other forms of extractive industry, what can be a more effective way of changing the subject from violence against Native bodies and lands than inviting the world to a beautiful feast of "tolerance and inclusion."

Moreover, a gendered reading of the discourse of beautiful mixture that permeates Peru today also reminds us of the all-too-common erasure of the sexual violence and violation that was, and remains, a central part of colonial encounters and relations.[116] It ignores the deployment of sexual violence and torture—in the form of rape, forced sterilization, and more—as a weapon of war during the recent internal conflict in the country, as well as the rising rates of femicide in Peru.[117] Responding to the daily murders of women and the lenient sentences (if any) men receive for killing or other acts of violence against women, in 2016 activists in Peru organized a march to protest this violence. This march followed others throughout Latin America under the banner #NiUnaMenos (Not One Less), inspired by the words of murdered Mexican activist and poet Susana Chavez Castillo: "Ni una mujer menos, ni una muerte más" ("Not one woman less, not one more death").

In response, Cardinal Juan Luis Cipriani, the Opus Dei archbishop of Lima (and former bishop of Ayacucho), stated during mass that "campaigns to damage the dignity of women in their being mothers and wives, and wanting to impose the so-called 'gender ideology,' are inhuman."[118] The next week, during his weekly radio program, which is broadcast nationally, he expanded on those comments: "Women often cause a scene which provokes men [to violence]. Statistics tell us about girls having abortions but not being abused. It's like that because girls cause a scene and provoke men. This is what will occur in the next march with #NiUnaMenos."[119] These threatening words underscore a fierce defense of patriarchal order. Women have a particular place in Peruvian society: they are wives or mothers, not activists or people challenging conservative gender norms. In this context, Roca Rey's description (cited earlier in this chapter) of Peruvian cuisine as an "elegant and mysterious princess," a girl "still unexplored, ready to make herself known," and who is there to fill with excitement all those (presumably men) in search of inspiration, takes on perhaps a more sinister tone, and certainly it links up with a heteronormative and patriarchal view of the nation, reasserting and sustaining a particular gendered (and racial) order of things.

After a leisurely lunch at Astrid & Gastón in January 2020, a friend and I took a brief tour of Casa Moreyra. I wanted to see if and how restaurant staff acknowledged the entangled histories of the house with slavery, so I asked about the catacombs. As soon as I mentioned them, our guide shook her head and said "Oh no. We don't go in there. One of my colleagues heard screams coming from there, the screams of a little girl." I asked how they knew it was a girl. "We saw her," she whispered.

The echoes of slavery and colonialism, it seems, remain firmly lodged in the recesses of this renovated casa hacienda. The little girl's ghostly presence invites reconsideration of such decorative details as the words libres seamos *(let us be free), inscribed on the walls of Astrid & Gastón in gentrified, colorful chicha lettering, or Acurio's description of the gastronomic revolution as one that "began . . . as a kind of cry for freedom (grito de libertad)."[120] The ghosts of the past resist being forgotten, insist on being heard, and insinuate themselves, disrupting (perhaps purposefully) Acurio's beautiful fusion. As we will see, the specter of coloniality also infuses the culinary artistry of chef Virgilio Martínez.*

Eating the Nation

Diversity of Quinoas (Diversidad de Quinoas)

We create our own diversity of quinoas, less related to ecotype than their different colors.[1] We continue the tradition of using natural dyes, seen in the textiles of the pre-Inca cultures of Peru, in our food. We never realized these dyes were something that could be so diverse and delicious. It's also a way to help us paint a Peruvian aesthetic—one that links the dish to the multitude of colors found naturally around us.

Serves 6

Quinoa leaves, 20 g

White quinoa, 300 g

Black quinoa, 100 g

Flaxseed oil, 40 ml

Airampo Dye, 10 g

Quinoa sprouts, 100 g

Llama and Chlorophyll

- Run the quinoa leaves through a juicer to extract the chlorophyll and set aside.

- Working with one color of quinoa at a time, toast the white and black quinoa in a dry saucepan, then cover with 1 L water, bring to a boil and cook for 15 minutes. Remove from heat and let stand, covered, for 30 minutes. Drain in a sieve and let cool.

- Divide the white quinoa into thirds. Mix one-third of the white quinoa with the chlorophyll and 10 ml of the flaxseed oil. Mix another one-third of the white quinoa with the airampo dye and 5 ml of the flaxseed oil. Leave the remaining white quinoa and mix with 10 ml of the flaxseed oil.

- Mix all of the black quinoa with 10 ml of the flaxseed oil.
- Spread the fresh quinoa sprouts and mix them with the remaining 5 ml of the flaxseed oil.
- Serve alongside the llama & chlorophyll in small mounds separated by color.

Alpaca & Amaranth (Alpaca y Kiwicha)

One of the most common images of the high Andes is alpaca grazing on fields amid a backdrop of mountain peaks. You'll find countless postcards depicting the scene. This dish returns the alpaca to this landscape, a place of wild herbs and grains.

Serves 4
Alpaca neck, 400 g
Annatto oil, 20 ml
Maras salt
Alpaca milk, 1 L
Kiwicha leaves, 500 g
Kiwicha grains, 100 g
Coffee beans, 20 g

- Remove the fat from the alpaca neck and finely dice. Combine the meat with the fat. Dress with oil and salt to taste.
- Line a dehydrator tray with a silicone mat. Bring the alpaca milk to a boil and, using an immersion blender, whip the milk for 2 minutes until there is a lot of foam. Spread the milk foam carefully over the lined tray and dehydrate at 70 degrees C for 15 hours.
- To extract the chlorophyll, pass the kiwicha leaves through a juicer.
- In a saucepan with boiling water, cook the kiwicha grains for 5 minutes. Drain the kiwicha, let cool completely, and mix with the kiwicha chlorophyll.

Grate the coffee beans on top of the plate and place the alpaca neck in the center of the plate. Top with the milk crust and green kiwicha.

TWO

Cooking Ecosystems

THE BEAUTIFUL COLONIALITY
OF VIRGILIO MARTÍNEZ

THE LAST EPISODE of season 3 of *Chef's Table*, the polished and global Netflix tour of high-end gastronomy, features Virgilio Martínez. Martínez is the owner of several restaurants in Peru and London, including Central, listed among the world's top ten best restaurants. Writing in 2019, I can say that he is undoubtedly the new face of Peruvian high cuisine. Unlike other chefs, Martínez organizes Central's menu according to Peru's elevations and ecosystems. Highlighting the chef's ecological approach, the episode begins with a close-up of Amazonian flowers (from Tambopata, at 210 meters altitude), then pans across a range of Amazonian trees before abruptly stopping at the sound, then image, of an ax hacking a tree. We see hands collecting tree sap, hands writing in notebooks, and then Martínez. The background music moves from evoking beauty to something slightly more sinister, and then the chef speaks. "In Peru," he tells us, "we always have this sense of the unknown. An unknown territory; the unknown Amazonia. There are lots of things just waiting for us to discover [as he tastes plants, mushrooms], discovering these new things that people have never seen before. That is my obsession."[1]

The Amazon, in this formulation, is conveniently empty of people. Martínez can thus "discover new things people have never seen before."[2] This is obviously not the case, as local people are showing him the plants, seeds, and mushrooms he is "discovering" and tasting. In the familiar imaginary of colonial "discoveries," he has in mind particular subjects: elite Limeños, high-end tourists, and always someone from outside of these Native spaces.[3] Moreover, this is a particular understanding of Peru as a repository of "products" that will be studied, classified, and eventually transformed into ingredients that make up the stunning dishes that, in Martínez's view, allow global elites to feel, understand, and consume Peru.

Martínez has been particularly "obsessed" with *Andean* Peru, and with the "ancestral knowledge" (as he calls it) he can obtain from Indigenous Peruvians in Andean communities.[4] Later in the *Chef's Table* episode, Martínez elaborates on this obsession with the unknown. He tells viewers that as he was traveling the country looking for culinary inspiration, he spent a week with a family in the Andes near the archaeological site of Moray (near the city of Cusco). Moray is made up of circular terraces that, archaeologists theorize, were part of an experimental farm where the Incas tested diverse crops to understand how plants grow differently at different altitudes. "After seeing these terraces," he tells us, "I was so obsessed." He continues: "And then we started to talk to people and I learned some Andean philosophy of life. While most people see the world in a horizontal way, people in the Andes see the world in different levels and altitudes, they see the world in a vertical way, not in a flat, horizontal way. That was it for me, it changed the way I was thinking about Peru."

That visit changed not just how Martínez thought about Peru but how he thought about what was possible in his kitchen and in the global world of gastronomy. Moray, and the Andeanist scholarship in which he immersed himself after that visit, inspired the chef's reconceptualization of the menu at Central, now known globally for its innovative and ecological approach to Peruvian cuisine. In short, he moved from cooking high-end Peruvian cuisine that "made people feel like they were in London or New York" to creating dishes meant to offer diners a literal taste of Peru and the experience of being in (and consuming) the various regions of the country.[5] Using the Andean idea of verticality, made famous decades ago by anthropologist John Murra, he organized the menu by altitudes and ecosystems, starting at ten meters below sea level and continuing through the Andes and Amazon.[6] As he puts it, "At Central we cook ecosystems."[7]

Moray inspired a personal reinvention of sorts, a "rediscovery of identity" (akin to Acurio's) and a rethinking of his vision as a *Peruvian* chef. Martínez narrates this moment of epiphany as one that led him to understand the importance of Peruvian "authenticity," and that put into relief his responsibility to discover, study, and make known the myriad indigenous plants and tubers and other "new things" that would otherwise be lost to deforestation and neglect. It led to the creation of Mater Iniciativa, a research institute led by his sister, Malena Martínez.[8] The institute's name comes from the Latin word for mother and signals his connection with a long line of European efforts to discover and name the world, efforts that go back at least to Linnaeus. This obsession with Peruvian biodiversity led eventually to the opening of his dream project, Mil (described as a restaurant, an interpretation center, a food lab, and a community cooperative), situated at 3,680 meters above sea level and just next to Moray.[9]

Martínez represents a new moment in Peru's gastronomic revolution. His project offers a vision of the nation (and of cuisine itself) quite distinct from the one Acurio celebrates. For Acurio, Peruvian cuisine proudly represents the diversity of his nation; it reflects the beautiful fusion of *todas las razas*. Moreover, food is a social weapon, a force that can unite all Peruvians in a vision of peace and hope and equality. Martínez, through his culinary and exploratory work, tells a different story, a story that foregrounds authenticity, indigeneity, biology. Moreover, his dishes aspire to be more than representations of Peruvian diversity. They *are* Peru. At Central, for instance, Martínez invites you to literally consume the nation by "experiencing" ecosystems from varying altitudes, which includes eating tree bark or algae or clay. While Acurio highlights the importance of producers and their agricultural *labor*, Martínez foregrounds "unknown" *products*—plants, seeds, tubers—and the significance of the "ancestral knowledge" necessary to uncover these products' potential. In other words, producers matter because they can offer knowledge about and context for understanding unusual products. However, he stops short of crediting this knowledge as Indigenous intellectual labor or recognizing it as Indigenous intellectual property. Instead, Indigenous knowledge must be validated by the science of his Mater Iniciativa—by scientific exploration, discovery, classification—and finally, by the artistic expression of Martínez's culinary work. Science and art provide the ways to access the real forms of Peru.

Thinking about both Acurio and Martínez as artists provides another way to think about their difference. One might consider Acurio's relationship with food to be comparable in form, but different in ideology, to the work of Latin American artists like Diego Rivera or Oswaldo Guayasamín. Like Rivera and Guayasamín, Acurio sees the nation through its connection with its past and its constituent political-economic sectors and classes. And like the master muralists, these connections should be displayed publicly. He does not paint on walls, but he provides access through television shows, cookbooks, and franchises. Martínez, on the other hand, might be more like Henri Matisse, master of both impressionism and primitivism. Less concerned with the messy materiality of the social or political conditions of the nation, he is nevertheless aspiring to something more fundamental. As Fagioli puts it,

"[T]hrough his paintings and his sculptures, in a dense web of allusions that privileged the aspiration to a pure and essential form, Matisse definitively undermined the conception of art as 'representation' and laid the foundations... for art as pure and absolute expression of forms."[10] Similarly, for Martínez, food is about much more than food.

In a recent gastronomic forum, Martínez stated: "Two decades ago, we talked about fusion or a mixture of cuisines (*mestizaje de cocinas*), about how the table united us. But today the world expects much more from gastronomy."[11] One could read Martínez here as marking a clear distinction between his project and Acurio's. Arguably, Martínez's culinary work is less about preparing food or promoting national cuisine than it is about staging the nation through gastronomic artistry. For Acurio food *matters*. The dishes he serves in his myriad restaurants must be tasty and satisfying. And importantly, food must be accessible. Even if Acurio, as a high-end chef, may not be as inclusionary as he would like to think, he nonetheless seeks to speak to a broad, national audience. Martínez's project, by contrast, is unapologetically elitist. He is concerned with the *experiences* his dishes can offer diners; at Mil, for instance, the menu includes eight distinct "moments," not courses. And he is concerned with showcasing specific Native products, with uncovering and translating "deep Peru" for his patrons through his staging of "edible nature."[12] In other words, Martínez presents global (high-end, culinary) consumption as a practice that must be concerned with discovering, selecting, classifying, and transforming local, "unknown," Indigenous knowledge and ingredients.

The performance is masterly. As his multiple international awards suggest, Martínez is an artist at the height of his power. And yet his art may obscure a more problematic political operation. His culinary performance attempts to reframe extractive, neocolonial acts into what appears to be a radically local and decolonial project. As such, his masterful work may be another version of what we might call the settler-colonial sublime, art that conceals and obscures the erasure and appropriation of specific Indigenous peoples and practices.

THE NATION CONSUMED

Martínez, considered among the best chefs in Peru, is seen by many as the successor to Gastón Acurio. Acurio remains firmly anchored in the hearts of Peruvians as the father of Peruvian gastronomy and the reason for Peru's success in recent years. He is an outspoken public figure, appearing at most important social or political events in the country, organizing conferences and culinary festivals, and urging industry and the state to invest in Peruvian gastronomy as a way to invest in Peruvian nationalism and economic success. Martínez travels the world (recent visits include Hong Kong, Singapore, London, Thailand, Lummi Island, Ireland, and New York), brilliantly marketing Peruvian cuisine as "young, colorful, exciting, healthy, and above all, delicious."[13] This is sometimes the way Martínez himself is represented. He has been described as "magnetic" and as "slight, and suave, . . . [with a] thick mop of glossy dark hair and defined beard [that] frame his chocolate-brown eyes."[14] One food blogger wrote about her experience at Central, and meeting Martínez: "I flew across an ocean and a continent to eat at Central. . . . The experience was worth every single penny and every single minute of my journey. . . . Virgilio came to greet me at my table, I turned into a blithering mess, hardly able to talk. . . . His looks reminded me of Mexican actor Gael García Bernal, which made me even more weak at the knees. Never have I met a chef so approachable, so open."[15] These descriptions are woven into many articles about Martínez. He simultaneously embodies and sells the beauty of authenticity, the mix between tradition and modernity. Much like the cuisine he showcases for the world, he projects the sophistication of a cosmopolitan gourmet, *and* the authenticity of Peru *profundo*. Moreover, at least in some cases, guests arrive at Central not just to consume his food, but to consume Martínez himself. Even Acurio seems to suggest this: "If you want to discover Peru and its treasures in its most modern version, to feel our unique biodiversity, . . . to taste the soul of young Peruvians proud of their culture, [Central] is the perfect way to do it."[16]

So, how did Martínez arrive at this moment? Like Acurio, he has crafted a compelling story of return, describing his journey almost as a decolonizing discovery that wove through the kitchens of Europe and the United States, to the high cuisine of Andean fusion, to the realization that his restaurant, although unquestionably high-end, should not make its patrons feel like they were in New York or London or any other cosmopolitan city. They should "feel like they are in Peru."

While Acurio longed to cook, Martínez longed to skateboard. He dreamed of being a professional skateboarder, but his family pushed him in a more traditional direction. His father and brother are both lawyers, so Martínez too enrolled in law school. As he describes it, the law did not provide "the sense of freedom I really wanted," freedom he felt when he was skateboarding, or surfing.[17] Surfing introduced him to the "life of the sea;" to eating ceviche with fishermen, "shucking oysters, sea urchins, and clams, and eating them raw. I appreciated food and seeing where it came from, but even more than that, I appreciated the freedom I had then.... I wasn't ... particularly passionate about cooking. I just wanted to get away."[18] It was this need for freedom that pushed him to quit law school and, with his family's support, enroll in Le Cordon Bleu culinary school in Ottawa, Canada. "Ottawa was new to me," writes Martínez, "so it felt good to be there. It was clean and secure, much different than Lima during that time."[19] But again, he notes that cooking was still not his primary passion. He was restless and decided to transfer to Le Cordon Bleu in London, a more exciting city in his estimation.

From there, the story goes, Martínez worked in several well-known restaurants in New York, London, and Spain, when he began to notice the rise of Peruvian cuisine and of Gastón Acurio. In *Chef's Table*, he tells viewers that he was in London when he began to hear about Acurio's work. "Acurio is a revolutionary, in a global way. He was the best Peruvian chef, he started to become a huge inspiration to me. I knew I wanted to learn from him. So I asked him for a job."[20] It was then, in the early 2000s that Martínez returned to Peru to work with Acurio, shortly thereafter becoming executive chef at Astrid & Gastón in Bogotá, Colombia, and Madrid, Spain.[21] But after several years of working for Acurio, Martínez notes, he wanted to cook something new and creative. "I was dreaming about creating a new Peruvian cuisine, and I could not do this in his restaurants." And Acurio agreed. "There is a moment when you need to play the game," he says, "and there is a moment when you need to play *your* game, and clearly it was time for Virgilio to play his game."[22] Martínez returned to Peru, opened Central in 2009, and then his restaurant Lima in London in 2012.

During the early stages of his career as a restauranteur, Martínez's approach to Peruvian cuisine aligned more directly with Acurio's vision of culinary fusion. In *Lima: The Cookbook*, Martínez writes that "modern Peruvian cuisine is the result of a crosscultural culinary exchange between foreign immigrants and native Peruvians, resulting in new flavors and new dishes."[23] Moreover, in these early days, Lima figured centrally: "Lima is a city where all the native Peruvian culture and its immigrant influences meet, and where that cultural diversity is translated into hearty food. It's a fascinating, intriguing place, both modern and ancient, cosmopolitan and provincial, luxurious and humble, all at the same time. Bursting with restaurants and vibrant authentic markets, it is the gastronomic heart of Peru and the central reference point for Latin American cuisine today."[24]

Much like Acurio's, Martínez's story of return also describes a gradual transition toward his love of Peru. For instance, he describes working with Acurio at Astrid & Gastón at the transitional moment when the chef "started to Peruvianize everything": "I didn't completely understand it at the time, [but] I could appreciate that Gastón was building something different. I'm very grateful to this day to have witnessed that process from the beginning and to have been able to watch an empire being built as he rallied the entire country around our food."[25]

This last point makes clear the role of marketability and the promise of wealth in the discovery of "new" Peruvian ingredients. But in the early moments of this gradual embrace of Peru, the focus was on cosmopolitan Lima. He was not thinking about indigeneity or the Andes, yet. In *Chef's Table*, he describes the process that leads him to rethinking his approach:

> I had to grow in my own country, with my own dreams. I wanted to create the next step for Peruvian cuisine. I wanted to communicate Peru in a way that people had never seen before. [But] I was confused about the kind of food I wanted to serve; I was doing European cuisine with a Peruvian touch. There was something missing, this lack of identity. I was looking for inspiration. [Here he is shown traveling the country, hiking through the Amazon in the rain.] I started feeling some connection; I started to realize that Peru is so much more than Lima.[26]

This is the moment when he tells viewers that he discovered Moray and became "obsessed" with Andean ways of seeing the world, and specifically the idea of verticality. Martínez thus returns to Central with a new vision for his restaurant, organizing it around such vertical thinking, and moving patrons from an altitude of minus 25 meters, sampling seaweed and octopus, to the heights of 2,875 meters to discover the wonders of kiwicha. As he tells viewers of *Chef's Table*:

> At Central we want to show you Peru in a vertical way. You are here in the restaurant, and you are eating a dish that comes from 4000 meters above sea level, and you are experiencing the Andes. And then, you will go down to the sea, going to the valleys, then cross to the Amazonia, you are going to 17 ecosystems in one experience. At one point, you can be a bit dizzy, but that is very important, just not to see one ingredient, one landscape, one region of Peru... For us to understand Peru, you have to see the whole thing.[27]

"You have to see the whole thing." One might reasonably ask: Who is the "you"? And what is "the whole thing"? We already know the answer, of course. Martínez offers the whole of Peru to those diners who can afford to eat at his restaurant. That is to say, this is for elites who can to fly to Lima from various points of privilege, not unlike the travelers who can afford to visit the Louvre, Guggenheim, or other repositories of high art.[28] In this case, Martínez is the cultural agent who has taken up the task to curate the nation: "It is not just about seeing the landscape, it goes to a different level; I want people to *feel* these different parts of Peru."[29]

At Central, Martínez argues, one can feel the entirety of Peru without having to travel beyond Lima.[30] One could read him as saying that there is no need to see the landscape when you can feel it as you consume it. Moreover, Martínez is described as uniquely positioned to do this work. During the *Chef's Table* episode, Nicholas Gill, editor and publisher of *New World Review* (whose very name reminds us that the language of discovery and colonialism, again, is never hard to find), and cofounder of newworlder.com (an online source focused on food and travel in the Americas), describes the menu at Central, noting that "no one had ever laid out Peru in quite this way ever before." He continues: "In 2013 Central enters the 50 Best List. . . . [P]eople from around the world started to come to Central to experience Peru, to experience his menu. Central became more than just a restaurant."

As in the case of Acurio, there is a fascination with the figure of the singularly talented chef. The great man theory of culinary history is not new, nor is the larger history of heroic explorers who break new ground. And like many of these stories that center the heroic, masculine subject as he tames nature and makes possible civilizational progress, Indigenous knowledge and Indigenous people recede into the background and even out of view. Martínez, and supporters like Gill, recognize Indigenous innovation (he spent time with an Andean family, learning about terraces and verticality) while simultaneously invisibilizing and colonizing that knowledge ("no one had ever laid out Peru in quite this way ever before"). Toward the end of *Chef's Table*, Martínez states: "[S]ince I came up with the idea of the altitude menu, we have been discovering these new things, and after four years, I have realized we know nothing; well, we know a little, and I'm still learning a lot. This is a work in progress. This is just the beginning."[31]

In this story, Martínez is a dreamer, a visionary, an explorer. Describing dining at Central, Acurio tells viewers that "Virgilio's menu makes you feel, makes you discover in areas that you thought you already discovered everything. . . . You don't go just to eat, but to experience something new." And Nicholas Gill tells viewers that Martínez's work can't be pinned down. "It isn't so much *avant-garde* as it is about understanding what exactly is Peru." He continues: "What Virgilio is doing, [going] into these remote places, seeing all these ingredients within ecosystems, and then [figuring] out a way to put them all together. That dish becomes a painting of that landscape. Through these plates we get the sensation of being there, in that part of Peru. Virgilio is a dreamer, he is dreaming of the potential of what Peruvian food can be."[32]

Discovering, dreaming, painting. These are descriptions of the chef as artist and as pioneer and guide to places that most of us will never know. The recipes included in the interlude preceding this chapter, for example, describe a quite ambitious relationship between food and nation. These recipes invite people not only to taste but also to reconstitute the landscape ("this dish *returns* the alpaca to this landscape, a place of wild herbs and grains"); they invite us to taste the deep (and importantly, *Indigenous*) history and tradition of Peru ("we continue the tradition . . . seen in the textiles of the pre-Inca cultures of Peru"). In other words, they invite us to literally consume Peru, to experience authenticity, to experience what some scholars have called *el Perú profundo*, or deep Peru.[33] Martínez is quite explicit about this. In one interview with CNN's food program *Culinary Journeys*, he tells the interviewer that "people are looking for authenticity, and this [my restaurant and project] *is* Peru."[34]

It is remarkable to see how Martínez positions himself. He is the one continuing the tradition of "pre-Inca cultures." In this stunning, yet familiar, deployment of settler-colonial logic, Martínez has a clear sense of the importance of his own exploration in revealing what the "real Peru" is. And actually existing Native peoples are often missing in that formulation. The landscape to which the alpaca is returned is empty of people; it is "a place of *wild* herbs and grains"—wildness, emptiness, but holding long histories of authentic Indigenous tradition that only he can recover and reproduce. Moreover, the emphasis on the "sensation of being there" (in the previous quote) points to a family resemblance with the work of travel books, as theorized by Mary Louise Pratt in relation to the workings of imperialism. As she notes, "[T]ravel books gave European reading publics a sense of ownership, entitlement, and familiarity with respect to the distant parts of the world that were being explored, invaded, invested in and colonized."[35] In this case, wealthy consumers, sitting in the capital city of Lima, can taste all of Peru, parts of the country being explored, invaded, and invested in by the colonialism of global capital.

And yet Martínez understands that Lima is not Peru. And as much as Central achieves in reassembling the country's landscapes and ecosystems one dish at a time, the experience of tasting and consuming the nation seems to require new explorations in the land and new opportunities for fellow elites to travel that path with him. This is especially clear in the opening of his restaurant Mil in the region of Cusco, the heart of the Inca Empire, and in the expansion of Mater Iniciativa, Martínez's "biological and cultural research center," without which, he claims, his restaurants would not work.

THE CHEF AS EXPLORER

I arrived at Kjolle, Pia León's new restaurant, on a cool afternoon in October 2018. León is Martínez's wife and culinary partner. The restaurant, in a complex housing Central, Kjolle, Mayo Bar, and Mater Iniciativa, is situated in a nondescript corner of Avenida Pedro de Osma in Barranco, a hip neighborhood known for its vibrant nightlife, art galleries, and bohemian sensibility. As I walked in through the gate surrounding the entire complex, I was struck by the beautiful garden and clean lines of the buildings. There was one guard, and there were two people at the door, one in charge of checking for reservations, the other to walk me to the restaurant. As I walked toward Kjolle, I noticed the "mater box" (caja mater), much like the one I had seen in Mil just a few days prior. The long glass box, nestled in a lovely garden, was pyramidal in shape, slightly raised, and had four vitrines showcasing several plant specimens. As I walked toward the building, I noticed a drawing of the Mil logo on the glass wall by the entrance. It was a representation of Moray's circular terraces, with "Mil" written in the center.

I entered the building and noticed the offices of Mater Iniciativa, where researchers were at work. The offices, two large rooms made of glass walls, were displayed prominently, clearly designed for all to see. Whether one was going to Central, Mayo, or Kjolle, Mater's researchers could not be missed. I remember thinking this was a clever move, showcasing and staging the significance of research, and of the products—mostly plant specimens hanging on the wall and throughout the complex—so central to Martínez's project. This centering of research and exploration also marked a clear shift from the earlier instantiation of Mater Iniciativa, a small room located inside and upstairs at Central's previous location in Miraflores. As Martínez's empire grows, it seems, so does the need to foreground exploration, discovery, research, and science.

Pia León was head chef at Central for ten years before opening her own restaurant, Kjolle, timed to coincide with Central's move to Barranco in 2018.

FIGURE 3. Screenshot of Virgilio Martínez from the "About Central" section of Central's website. Accessed October 11, 2018.

That same year, she was awarded Best Female Chef in Latin America.[36] León has been a crucial part of Martínez's culinary and research team since the beginning. They met when she was twenty-one (he is ten years older); she walked to the construction site that was to become Central to ask Martínez for a job.[37] Since then (the couple married in 2013), León has been the driving force in Central's kitchen, even as Martínez has been the one in the spotlight, showcasing his creative genius. During the *Chef's Table* episode, Nicholas Gill tells viewers that "[Martínez] has Malena and Pia to bring structure into the restaurant, so he can be the dreamer, and explorer." This is a striking comment, one that reveals the masculinist dimension of this culinary performance.

There is one image from Central's website that pairs well with such a statement, and that reminded me of Mary Louise Pratt's "seeing-man," that "white male subject of European landscape discourse—he whose imperial eyes passively look out and possess."[38] In this photograph, Martínez stands in his restaurant, arms crossed, wearing his chef's apron, gazing out into the distance. There is a figure in the background who looks like León, partly hidden but visibly cooking in the kitchen.

Martínez here is clearly the man, the one in charge, the leader of this space and of his team. This image, and the accompanying text, evoke Gill's description of him as a visionary dreamer and explorer:

The team at Central, with its ally Mater Iniciativa, is made up of a group of expeditionaries, full of curiosity about Peru. Aware of our lack of connection, we humbly assumed the great challenge of getting to know ... this beautiful country replete with unique ingredients, landscapes, culture, tradition, and history, but above all, with those who live and narrate these [traditions, cultures, and histories]. Our collaborative team works hard to ... make visible those elements that in daily life not everyone can see. The expedition we undertake has no destination or end, but centers on constant movement, on observation and on respect for the temporality and the seasonality that Earth dictates.

Note the self-presentation as "humbly curious" and "respectful," but also the clear need to discover Peru and to translate for those who "live and narrate" Peruvian histories, traditions, and cultures. This framing not only centers the noble explorer but also describes him (and it is almost always a "him" in these tales of discovery) with the familiar language of settler innocence. Moreover, the idea that there is no destination or end to exploration speaks to the unending availability of land and the innumerable possibilities, again reinscribing settler colonial tropes of openness and discovery.

There are a few additional remarkable things about the "seeing-man." While Martínez seems to be looking out into the distance, he is looking into a glass door that acts like a mirror, and in effect appears to be looking at himself. During this moment of self-contemplation, Pia León is working in the kitchen. It is hard not to read this, almost too easily, as yet one more representation of gendered labor. Indeed, in some interviews, León describes the relationship with Martínez in ways that seem to reaffirm dominant understandings of gendered divisions of labor. For example, she has noted that "she's a little more 'crazy' in the kitchen compared with Martínez, while he is more calm and controlled," and that she "credits Martínez for teaching her discipline and perseverance."[39] In a different interview she is quoted as saying that "[Martínez] is a more calm person and I am speedier. I'm quick with decisions and Virgilio is more intellectual. We complement each other."[40] Perhaps. Their styles may indeed be complementary, and we might leave it at that. Yet there is no doubt that, intentional or not, these descriptions of women's work are part of the web of discourses and practices that uphold patriarchy. Even the recognition that León has received as "best *female* chef award" serves to diminish women as they, literally, can't be compared to men.

Some, including León, might disagree with this gendered reading. In a recent interview, for instance, León notes that Martínez always encouraged her to step into the limelight and accept the well-deserved attention she received as head chef of Central, but that it was she who preferred to stay in the background. "Virgilio always encouraged me to go outside but it was my own decision to remain in the kitchen," she is quoted as saying. "I'm . . . not a person who loves being in the spotlight. . . . But time has passed and now it's my turn and I'm very happy to be in the spotlight. It's my responsibility."[41] This last point about the responsibility of stepping outside into the spotlight is interesting. In most interviews with León (as opposed to interviews with Martínez or Acurio), there is always a question about gender, and some even point implicitly to the significance of her, as a woman, establishing herself as a chef in her own right. And yet León herself seems to reproduce gendered narratives and ideologies and to push back against any kind of feminist inclination. Every time she is asked a question about the fact that approximately half of the cooks in her kitchen are women, for instance, she notes that this was not intentional: "I don't tend to focus on whether cooks are men or women; it's simply about the fact that they do a great job."[42]

León does not seem to want to disrupt gendered orders, so clearly spelled out in Peru. Importantly, she notes in various interviews that she was determined to be a mother—and she now is one. Their son, Cristobal, features prominently in many interviews with León. The couple live above their restaurant complex in Barranco, and she has noted that this was a decision they made in order to be better able to balance caring for their son with the everyday workings of the restaurant and their frequent research trips to the Andes and Amazon. While this is laudable, my point is that she performs a particular kind of femininity, one in which professional achievement must also always be accompanied by public declarations about her work as a devoted mother and supportive wife. Her efforts to bring more women into the workplace must be justified as the workings of the "invisible hand" of the market. In other words, León is deeply invested in this gastropolitical project, a project that is as much about ideology and knowledge production as it is about the economics or aesthetics of food.

UNEARTHING THE UNKNOWN

Mater Iniciativa is often described as central to Martínez's project. As one person told me, Mater is "the spirit of and engine for Martínez's work. Without Mater there would be no Central, Mil or Kjolle." As noted earlier, Mater's Lima offices are located in the same complex as Central and Kjolle, right at the center of the building, between Central and Mayo Bar, the swanky tapas bar also part of their new complex. A variety of dried plant specimens hang on walls, and lists of plant names are written in black and red ink on the glass walls. I was especially struck, though, by the fact that while at dinner at Central, one can see members of the Mater team working away, typing on computers or talking on the phone. They too, much like the plants displayed in the Caja Mater in the garden outside, are in vitrines, dutifully performing research and innovation. This is clearly part of what one consumes when dining at Central. I am unable to evaluate the science that takes place behind the glass walls of Mater, but there is no question that the performativity of this scientific space is intended to be an important part of the Central experience.

It is worth noting the shift that took place in the presentation of Mater with the move to Barranco. In the earlier version of Central, while the restaurant was still in Miraflores, Mater was housed in a small office above the restaurant's dining room. Diners could certainly ask for a tour of Central, including Mater and Martínez's garden, but the research conducted was not displayed as prominently as it is now.[43] The first time I spoke with someone from the Mater team (I will call him Javier) was in Miraflores. I remember being surprised by the smallness of the space, especially given the emphasis placed on the significance of products discovered by the chef. It was during that conversation with Javier that I learned about Mater's expeditions. According to him, at that time team members and other collaborators (including chefs, nutritionists, anthropologists, forest engineers, and entrepreneurs) traveled each month to different regions of Peru in search of new products they might be able to use at the restaurant. They hosted interdisciplinary workshops, each focused on a particular product, to learn as much as possible about that product's history, culture, and biology. This was especially important as part of their mission was to classify these products, documenting what they learned from these expeditions before determining which product had the potential to be used in Central's kitchen. Javier's emphasis was on the significance of both discovery and, as I return to later, recovery.

This link between cuisine and research has intensified greatly with the opening of Mil in Moray, which is marketed not just as a high-end destination restaurant, but as a research/food lab that collaborates with local Indigenous communities as a way to "chronicle and revive ancient local ingredients and food practices that might otherwise be lost to time."[44] The images and rhetoric of "discovery" are unabashedly presented as part of the settler-colonial thrill of connection with new places and products that are now, literally, ripe for the plucking. For Martínez, this is a deeply emotional experience, another way for him to connect with his country: "It became an emotional, transformative experience to find ingredients in their native habitat. Seeing wild cacao beans, or Amazonian fish, eating fruit that had fallen into the water, was unbelievable."[45] This sentiment, and the centrality of Native products, is also evident in a description from the "research" section of Mater's website:

> Conveying the wonder of the discovery of new products in their natural habitat is impossible. However, at Central, thanks to Mater's foraging, it is possible to exhibit the wild beauty of roots, seeds, fruits, vines, tubers, and aromatic flowers that we gather along the way. And so, to satisfy the curiosity of restaurant visitors, we have the Mater Box, a type of glass case in which we display the discoveries of our journeys. We now have more than 150 products on exhibition, and we are convinced that the biodiversity of Peru will never leave us without new protagonists.

Note that the protagonists in Martínez's project are clearly Native products, not producers. These products—herbs, tubers, fungi, sea creatures—are then taken back to Central for their culinary experimental use. In presentation and content, these efforts to "exhibit wildness" harken back to long histories of botanical, geographic, and zoological exploration that accompanied earlier moments of colonial discovery, republican mapping, and eco-racial reconfiguration.

While Martínez remains the clear leader in this project, he often emphasizes the importance of collaborative work and the significance of his team, which expands beyond Central to Mater, and as I discuss later, Mil. But he likes keeping things in the family and accordingly asked his sister Malena, a physician by training, to join him in Peru and lead his research team. In *Chef's Table*, Nicholas Gill describes Malena as having a "science background; she brings this entire scientific method to all the ingredients of Peru that no kitchen elsewhere in Peru really has."[46] As head of Mater, Malena is tasked with hiring team members, planning expeditions, discovering new products, and bringing them back to Central (and now Mil) for documentation and experimentation. As she tells viewers of *Chef's Table*: "[W]e are focused on bringing all this stuff from different parts of Peru, and focused on doing identification of species. We are the research arm of Central."

Much like her brother, Malena seems to emphasize the importance of Indigenous knowledge. "Peruvian territory is very diverse, but we wouldn't be this biodiverse if it wasn't for people, if it wasn't for our cultures. There are communities in every part of Peru which have all this knowledge that we don't know about."[47] The next shot on *Chef's Table*, however, is of Malena working with others at Mater, noting the importance of identification and classification of various species of plants and telling someone to write out the names of plants in Quechua, noting that "Quechua is not a written language, so you need to sound it out, sense how to write it."[48] This is a particularly striking comment given the decades of work by Quechua, Peruvian, European, and American scholars on Quechua orthography and grammar, not to mention the importance of Quechua to Peruvian literary legend José María Arguedas, arguably the country's most important novelist.[49] It speaks clearly to who their audience is, and what they want to project: Central, Mater Iniciativa, and now Mil, as centers of exploration, discovery, and translation.

We could read Martínez and Mater as performing a kind of salvage anthropology with a culinary twist. And much like the coloniality of salvage anthropology—which assumed that as Native peoples would "vanish," Euro-American (primarily male) archaeologists were uniquely positioned to discover and preserve their Native "artifacts"—Martínez's approach centers the role of the explorer chef and his team in the efforts to discover, recover, and repurpose Native products. Indeed, Martínez is arguably less concerned with "preserving" than with mining the resources he finds and transforming them into products he can sell as authentic, though modern, cuisine. Salvage anthropologists were motivated not just by scholarly inquiry but also by entertainment and artistic pursuits as they responded to the interests of benefactors and a public curious to know more about "living people of the past," as Risling Baldy puts it.[50] Similarly for Martínez, "research" is intimately connected to his ability to appease the curiosity of his clients about not just the Indigenous products and ecosystems he serves them, but also those "living people of the past" who provide Martínez with such valuable "ancestral" knowledge.

An article in *KTCHN Rebel*, an online magazine for professional chefs, describes Martínez as "Indiana Jones with a chef's knife and a specimen container."[51] The article, tellingly titled "The New Incan Gold: Peruvian Cuisine," also describes Martínez's culinary work as "anthropology on a plate." This is, of course, a vulgar understanding of anthropology, but it nevertheless gestures toward the settler colonial foundations of the discipline. "Even today," the author writes, "certain parts of Peru are completely unknown to anyone but the indigenous tribes, so there are still more than a few blank spaces on the country's culinary map."[52] The coloniality of this view is unmistakable. One could argue that the author of this article has imposed her own perspective and does not in fact accurately represent Martínez's project. But let's take a look at the description of these expeditions on the Mater website.

The first thing that jumps out when you click on the Mater website's home page is the phrase, in large lettering, "*Afuera hay más*" ("Outside there is more").[53] The page shows Martínez, along with three other team members, standing somewhere in the high Andes, with a snow-capped mountain range in the background. Below the image is the following description: "Under the direction of Virgilio Martínez, a team of researchers travels across Peru collecting ingredients that grow on the banks of a river in the Amazon jungle, in the middle of the frozen Puna grasslands, or at more than 13,000 feet above sea level on a snow-covered mountaintop. The gastronomy of one of the four most megadiverse countries on the planet *demands* this type of expedition" (emphasis added). Note the language of what we might call compulsory settler colonial expansion: Peruvian gastronomy "demands this type of expedition." The "Indiana Jones" imagery of *KTCHN Rebel* might seem crude, but it is not far from the self-representation of the Mater researchers. Arguably, for Martínez, gastronomy is a new settler frontier, and his project exemplifies what Grey and Newman have called "culinary colonialism": "the extension of Settler jurisdiction over, and exploitation of Indigenous gastronomy."[54]

There is also a tension between the presentation of his culinary work as intellectually curious, respectful of, and grateful for Indigenous knowledge, and the neocolonial frame of discovery, exploration, and appropriation. All this makes Martínez's project more akin to extraction, arguably a part of what Macarena Gómez-Barris calls the "extractive zone": "The extractive view sees territories as commodities, rendering land as for the taking, while also devalorizing the hidden worlds that form the nexus of human and nonhuman multiplicity."[55] While she is thinking with and in different sites, such as Andean spiritual tourism, high-end gastronomy seems equally as extractive. Take the classification and display of products. Through Instagram photos, in Central's Caja Mater, on menus, and in his restaurants' decor, Martínez both centers *and* decontextualizes products in order to "re-contextualize them" and make them "known" to global elites through the culinary staging of ecosystems. This move evokes old histories of botanical expeditions and classificatory systems that were part of colonial histories of exploitation and dispossession and clearly linked to racial capitalist violence.[56] While some scholars argue that chefs have no choice but to exploit resources in order to stand out in an extremely competitive field (this is especially the case for chefs from the global South), this does not change the characterization of the structure and configuration of gastropolitics as violently colonial.[57] Indeed, if chefs have "no choice," that is even stronger evidence of Patrick Wolfe's familiar observation in which settler invasion is "a structure not an event."[58]

Martínez, and many on his team, would vigorously disagree with this reading. Since Mil's opening in particular, Martínez has noted that what sets this restaurant apart is the commitment to work with their Quechua-speaking neighbors in a "horizontal" way.[59] In interviews he speaks to concern for his Indigenous neighbors: "I'm considered a white guy [in Moray]. These people have been cheated for years. Their identity, their value, everything was trying to be erased."[60] As I would learn during a visit to Mil, this focus is largely thanks to Francesco D'Angelo, a Peruvian anthropologist hired by Mater to "strengthen the connection with its neighbors."[61]

But another way to read the impetus behind opening Mil is the desire to be close to particular products and the ability to access Indigenous knowledge about those products. Martínez can perform humility and appreciate the importance of working with communities, but disrupting neocolonial relations in Peru is not a driving factor for him. In other words, his public efforts to "save" Indigenous products (and producers?) from neglect do nothing to change the world structurally. Moreover, this new initiative is a bolder reflection of settler occupation. His obsession with Moray leads to staking a claim over this site, quite literally settling on territory that was once Indigenous land. While there may be moments of genuine connection between Martínez's team and their Indigenous neighbors, the chef's expansion into the Andes reflects an intensification of the coloniality of his culinary work.

"*DEL ENTORNO A LA MESA*": TOWARD A POLITICS OF EXTREME LOCALITY

Martínez opened Mil in 2018. Mil was the chef's "dream project," according to many with whom I have spoken. It was in many ways the culmination of that moment many years before when he first encountered the terraces at Moray and "knew" he had found his way to Peru and to a novel approach to gastronomy. While Central's menu was inspired by those terraces and the idea of verticality, Mil takes this "ecological" approach to a different level. As Martínez puts it: "Mil is not new like Central was. Here we talk about the unknown, in a very extreme way."[62] In other words, Mil offers the possibility of a deep dive into the biodiversity of Moray and its surroundings and easier access to those Native plants, tubers, and other "products" found at 3,680 meters above sea level. The restaurant serves dishes using only products found at this elevation and inspired by the traditions and histories of those products. In many ways, Martínez's project has a striking resemblance to the "New Nordic Manifesto," a document conceived of by Danish restaurateur Claus Meyer (cofounder, with René Redzepi, of the famed Noma) and University of Roskilde researcher and lecturer Jan Krag Jacobsen, that brought several Nordic chefs together around ten principles, at least three of which resonate deeply with Martínez's approach:

1. To base our cooking on ingredients and produce whose characteristics are particularly in our climates, landscapes and waters.

2. To promote Nordic products and the variety of Nordic producers, and to spread the word about their underlying cultures.

3. To develop potentially new applications of traditional Nordic food products.[63]

This is a movement proposing a radical sustainability that insists on using only ingredients from Nordic ecosystems. Much like some of these chefs who expect travelers to traverse long distances for a radically local and ecological culinary experience, Martínez invites diners from around the world to experience something "new" and "extreme." This is cuisine that is impossible to understand, Martínez might argue, without being there. "[We want] to give the diner a sense of time and place and people and view and landscape and produce," he tells *Eater* magazine. As he puts it, Mil "goes way beyond farm-to-table."[64] Francesco D'Angelo, who used to be the resident anthropologist at Mil and one of Mater Iniciativa's team members, puts it another way. As he told me during a conversation in October 2018, the move is now from "context (*entorno*) to table."[65]

Mil's opening coincided with Central's move to Barranco. While part of the reason for this move had to do with conflicts over the restaurant's location in Miraflores (located in a residential zone, Central was in violation of zoning laws), as I noted earlier the move was also an opportunity to refashion Central and foreground the role played by Mater Iniciativa. Mil is in some ways a more "extreme" (to use the chef's descriptor) reflection of Mater's place in Martínez's project. Mil houses Mater's Cusco office, though to call it an office feels inaccurate. The restaurant, designed by Lima-based Estudio Rafael Freyre, is supposed to reflect the cultural, historical, and ecological

FIGURE 4. Author dining at Mil, October 2018. Photograph by Jeff Olivet, reproduced with permission.

context of Moray. According to the designers, "the restaurant merges into Moray's natural, cultural and social setting organically and respectfully," and "ties into the local communities and brings continuity to the historical legacy of their traditions."[66]

When I walked into the restaurant, the first thing I saw was a wall of plant specimens, hanging upside down on nearly invisible wires, giving the effect of dried plants floating in midair. I then noticed the courtyard, a beautiful open space with a *queñua* tree in the center, an Andean tree that grows at high altitudes in Bolivia, Ecuador, and Peru, and that is threatened by habitat destruction. In addition to the dining space, the restaurant houses several research projects, including Mater and a food lab that experiments with local cacao, coffee, and macerated liquors. The dining area is a small but open space. The décor is minimalist and emphasizes the centrality of products—dried plant specimens were displayed on pages with brief annotations next to specimen jars filled with ocas, cacao, potatoes, and herbs, while another wall displayed a large, colorful *khipu*. The music was a hip, stylized "Andean" background music. Sitting at my table, tasting each dish, I looked out a window with a view that could be mistaken for a painting.

The restaurant's opening had been eagerly anticipated by foodies globally. Articles in sites such as *Eater*, *The New York Times*, and *The Guardian* all raved about Martínez's new venture, noting especially the restaurant's stunning location, its focus on context and local products, and the centrality of Mil's food lab.[67] Some articles also mention the restaurant's collaborative work with two neighboring communities—Mullak'as-Misminay and Kacllaraccay—noting that team members work side by side with communities, splitting the harvest in half.[68] When I visited the restaurant in October 2018, I too was struck by the breathtaking views of Moray and the surrounding Andean landscape. During my visit, I was fortunate to spend the day with D'Angelo, the Peruvian anthropologist who used to work closely with Martínez. He generously spent an entire day with me, talking with me for hours about his work with Martínez, with Mater, and most important, with families in Mullak'as-Misminay and Kacllaraccay. D'Angelo, a young, upper-class Limeño in his late twenties, has an interesting account of how he came to join the Mater team. As he told me, his mother saw the *Chef's Table* episode about Martínez and called her son to tell him about this work. D'Angelo was conducting fieldwork in Quechua communities in the area and called Malena Martínez to discuss the possibility of joining their team. Two days later, D'Angelo was hired.

On this cool spring day, I arrived just after 9:00 in the morning. Wearing jeans and a white T-shirt, and sporting boots from The North Face, a Columbia jacket, and long dreads, D'Angelo greeted me with a warm smile. Within minutes of our meeting he suggested we walk a short distance above the restaurant to find a place to sit and talk. As we walked—his small, white, friendly dog Oca Lucia leading the way—D'Angelo began to tell me about his work at Mil. Significantly, he began with a discussion of the consciousness-raising work he was doing (*concientización social*) with those working at Mil, including management, waiters, researchers, and others. As an anthropologist, he was hired to develop and sustain relationships with neighboring communities as part of the participatory project (*projecto participativo*) Mil and Mater hoped to develop with these communities. But as he described it, part of this work included working against the racism and prejudices that he found among those at Mil.

This is not surprising. The very idea of needing a resident anthropologist as part of the team at Mil signals the existence of a racialized "other." Indeed, in Peru and other countries with significant Indigenous populations, it is not unusual to find anthropologists working for private firms, like mining companies, oil companies, and others who seek to demonstrate their "corporate social responsibility."[69] Those anthropologists are hired to help improve relations with local communities and bridge the often vast cultural divide between company workers and local peoples. D'Angelo shared various anecdotes that confirmed this and reflected the huge gap he found between community members and many of those working at the restaurant. Moreover, he told me, "there is much talk about products, but no discussion about producers." His main concern, then, was to shift to a focus on community relationships and to find ways, as he told me, to "decolonize" those relationships.

One could argue that this is a lofty goal, and perhaps even an impossible one. The structure of the relationship is such that communities had little, if any, say in the development of Mil. When D'Angelo joined the team, Martínez's project was already in the works, though no one had bothered to let community leaders know. During our conversation, D'Angelo told me that the site where Mil now stands had been a vicuña farm before it was turned into a restaurant. That restaurant never really made a mark, he said, and was mostly rented out as a space for wealthy Limeños to host parties. The head of Sumac Tarpuy Qoyllor (the company that manages this land) wanted to avoid potential conflicts with communities over water consumption and land use, and Martínez agreed. So as Mil was being built, they chose to mislead people into thinking the old restaurant was being remodeled. What D'Angelo did not tell me until much later was that Sumac Tarpuy Qoyllor is owned by Eduardo Hochschild, Peruvian millionaire and chairman of Hochschild Mining, and that there are plans to continue expanding Mil by building a five-star hotel and "research center" next to the restaurant.

When D'Angelo joined the team, his first questions were about the restaurant's plans for working with community members from Mullak'as-Misminay and Kacllaraccay, and he quickly discovered there was no coherent approach. Malena suggested that he "go in" to communities with a representative from the company. D'Angelo agreed, but wanted to contact the community leaders to set up a meeting with them before arriving in the communities. When he asked for the cell numbers of the two community presidents, however, the representative's response was "those people don't have cell phones." This told D'Angelo all he needed to know. He was infuriated by such a dismissive, inaccurate, and racist attitude, and from that point on worked on his own to establish more equitable relations with both communities.

To his credit, D'Angelo was very clearly and genuinely committed to breaking down barriers between communities and folks at Mil and Mater, including Martínez and his sister. He told me about the moment when Martínez seemed to "get" what it meant to live and work with community members. "He said, 'oh, you mean be good neighbors,' and I knew he finally understood." While at Mil, D'Angelo's approach was relational, and he developed close relationships with particular families and individuals. He worked the fields alongside others from Mater and both communities; he worked closely with some families to develop new varieties of potatoes, beans, and other crops; and he supported the seed-saving work of one family in Kacllaraccay.[70] D'Angelo also confirmed that 50 percent of the potato harvest is for Mil, while the other 50 percent is for communities. However, that 50 percent is divided among all families in both communities, meaning that each family receives approximately three to four potatoes per harvest. When we spoke, D'Angelo was working on alternative approaches so families in both communities could benefit more fully from their connection to Mil.

I have no doubt that while he worked there, D'Angelo was aware of the power relations that are inevitably part of the dynamics at Mil. I remember a moment, when we had sat down to talk in the middle of a mountain trail, when he told me that the focus on the Moray terraces worried him. So often, he told me, people who visited Mil wanted to find the best views of the archaeological site. But in doing that, he said, you are quite literally giving your back to the communities. It was a powerful observation. And it was evident from my conversations with him (in person, via text, and online), and from watching him interact with families from Kacllaraccay and with researchers at Mater, that he is deeply invested in challenging histories of colonial domination and dispossession. But he is also invested in a particular kind of anthropology, one that while invoking decolonial possibilities, still reproduces colonial frameworks. Take for example a recent community study D'Angelo and others from Mater conducted in Kacllaraccay.[71] Researchers at Mater were interested in better understanding how food and work are perceived by community members. "We wanted to avoid creating unequal power dynamics, as it is the continual goal of Mil and Martínez to encourage the restaurant and community to work side by side. So we searched for investigative methods that would *decolonize* the research process, making it more about open dialogue, learning and knowledge sharing."[72] D'Angelo and his Mater colleagues, in collaboration with a National Geographic researcher, decided to use Photovoice, a research method that involves giving cameras to community members and asking them to take photos representing their understandings of food and work. The photographs were then used to "hold discussions including some open-ended questions to encourage the sharing of ideas and perspectives."[73]

The project reveals (or confirms) findings about the centrality of the *chakra*, or farming plot, to the community. It also reveals local ideas about what food actually gives you, such as "strength" (fava beans and chicha yes; pasta no), and what counts as "work" (working the chakra yes; tourism no). It concludes with the following observation: "Since collaborating with Mil, Kacllaraccay has been absorbed into a dynamic and ongoing journey in cultural exchange. Only time will tell what this means for perceived relationships between work and food, but it's certainly a unique experience for both one rural Peruvian community and a restaurant."[74] The lead author of the study, Rebecca Wolff, describes herself as working to "decolonize the research process." Yet, one might ask, what was the point of knowing about community members' ideas about work and food? How is this knowledge to be used? And how is this decolonial if outside researchers are still the ones determining the research questions and parameters, deciding what counts as research, and initiating the research process? Does the genuine effort to "learn from" community members mitigate the extractive and colonial dimension of social scientific research?[75]

D'Angelo told me another story about an encounter with the local community, when Mil invited community members to sample the tasting menu just before the restaurant's official opening. The memory that stood out to him from this encounter was having to take a tartare dish back to chef Pia León because a community member refused to eat raw meat, pointing to the divide and distance between them. But is this a moment of "sharing" and decolonial possibility, or is it giving the lie to the project? Despite good intentions, the structure is such that while D'Angelo and his colleagues' efforts are laudable, they don't change much. And is providing a high-end way for visitors to consume both the landscape and the local food, to borrow D'Angelo's excellent phrase, not another way of turning our backs on the community? By making this experience more beautiful and minimizing the power relations between business and community, is it not likely that this move represents an intensification of the coloniality embedded in Martínez's project? The description of Mil as a place where diners can come and eat and spend the day meditating or harvesting potatoes lines up with Victor Vich's analysis of a "magical, mystical" view of the Andes that works primarily to make it safe for global consumption.[76] Borrowing from David Harvey, Vich argues that in these touristic spaces, "we always see an 'aestheticized spatiality' in which, generally, all historical depth has been lost and it is impossible to find a narrative that would interpellate the visitors in any other manner."[77] Tradition becomes theater for the pleasure of outsiders. But such a judgment may be too harsh. Vich himself notes that we should not paint with too broad a brush; tourism can provide opportunities for local communities that should not be dismissed out of hand. "Like any other discursive machinery, tourism could produce a narrative of history that is more dignified and better conceived."[78] D'Angelo and Martínez would agree that this is precisely what Mil does by institutionalizing a space that will make community collaboration relevant to the work of tourism and gastronomy. In considering the tensions and opportunities of Martínez's updated encounter with "deep Peru," it is important to consider his representations of Indigenous knowledge.

KNOWLEDGE, INDIGENEITY, EXTRACTION

In countless articles, Martínez is described as applying "modern techniques to indigenous ingredients" or transforming unknown and unpalatable indigenous ingredients into cuisine that global elite food connoisseurs would appreciate.[79] However, Martínez has used a slightly different formulation, noting that he is in fact expanding European, North American, and Peruvian elite tastes to include Native products and knowledge. He describes his culinary approach not as one that appropriates Indigenous technologies and products, but as one that foregrounds *learning* from the landscapes and ecosystems and peoples of Peru. "We learn new ways of cooking and new technologies from our ancestors.... What we see in our roots is so modern."[80] The language is careful: we "learn," we don't extract; Indigenous traditions are modern. For Martínez, exploring new culinary landscapes and cooking ecosystems and crafting dishes that evoke specific altitudes necessitate a connection with "his roots," a rediscovery of Peru's lands and peoples, and a commitment to make deep Peru legible, desirable even, to elite Peruvians and foreigners alike.

At Central and Mil, Martínez uses only Peruvian ingredients, even though, as he notes, that makes the work harder for him and his team. "We have to work hard to make these obscure ingredients—things like *chaco clay* or *maca root*—seem as familiar in the restaurant as they were in their own ecosystem. Instead of shaving truffles, we shave *tunta*, a freeze-dried potato."[81] And as noted earlier, this emphasis on making the unknown, known, is crucial. "At Central," he tells viewers of *Chef's Table*, "we have a truly unique approach to our menu. We use 180 ingredients and probably 50% of them are unknown."[82] Nicholas Gill then adds: "Virgilio finds these things, like a tree bark with a resin in it; it is not even an ingredient; one village might use that thing for headaches or different medicinal uses; when Indigenous communities see that he is collecting these things to cook with, *they don't understand.*"[83] Martínez offers a similar take on his work to "discover" ingredients. During an interview in 2015, he traveled to Cusco with a writer for the *Wall Street Journal*, guided by Quechua women from the Acomayo community. "This is their annual walk to gather medicinal herbs," Martínez explained to the journalist. "The first time we came, they thought we were crazy. The idea of cooking with some of these ingredients doesn't make any sense to them. It would be like putting Xanax in a dish."[84] Gill adds that "Virgilio's cuisine is not always about cooking food that is tasty, sometimes there are dishes that are uncomfortable. But Virgilio feels it is important to have a taste of all these ingredients to understand these different regions of Peru."[85]

These descriptions foreground the product and almost trivialize Native knowledge. Indigenous peoples are presented as simple folk who "do not understand" what they have in front of them and what might be possible. But Martínez in fact foregrounds Native knowledge, though in somewhat problematic ways. "We always *take* something new from our trips; it isn't just trying to replicate one dish, one ecosystem, it is the whole idea of *replicating a way of thinking, a way of living, to understand their nature.*"[86] For Martínez, it would seem, Native knowledge is just as important as the product, if only because Indigenous producers are the ones who can share stories about particular products; they can offer insights into the product's culture and history (as descriptions on Central and Mater's websites attest). In a way, he is almost explicitly describing the "taking" of Native epistemologies and ontologies.

How should one read the aspiration to "replicate a way of thinking, a way of living"? For critical readers, the pretense of "replicating" a way of life raises serious concerns, and I return to those later. However, read generously, Martínez might be seen as exemplifying the kind of collaborative research that can be found in the works of anthropologists like Marisol de la Cadena that take seriously the importance of Indigenous ontologies and epistemologies.[87] Compare two passages. In the first, Martínez describes walking with his interlocutor Francisco Quico Mamani:

> As we walk up the mountain to look for herbs from the village of Chahuay, it appears in might rain. The clouds overhead are thick and gray. Francisco Quico Mamani begins blowing into the air. He huffs three times and then puffs three times to his right. Then he does the same to his left. He says it will help the rain stay away for a little while. I don't know if he actually believes

his huffing and puffing will stop the rain. Sometimes he says he is full of superpowers—and I generally trust him. I have to respect that his spiritual knowledge has value. To understand Andean cosmovision, I accept that Francisco's way of looking at the world may not always correlate with mine.[88]

Now consider de la Cadena's closing passage in a much-cited essay that takes seriously the agency of "earth-beings," like the Ausangate mountain as it is described in the Indigenous ontologies of her Quechua collaborator and teacher Nazario.

And although I would not be able to translate myself into Nazario's ontology, nor know with him that Ausangate's ire is dangerous, I would side with him because I want what he wants, to be considered on a par with the rest, to denounce the abandonment the state has relegated people like him—while at the same time threatening with assimilation—to denounce the mining ventures that do not care about local life; in a nutshell to defend in his way, in my way and in the way that may emerge as ours the place where Nazario lives.[89]

The striking similarity is perhaps not all that surprising, because Martínez knows his Andean anthropology. In the introduction to his cookbook, *Central*, he acknowledges his significant debt to John Murra's famous study of the importance of "verticality" in understanding the tremendous agricultural and social vitality of the Andean world. In Murra's famous description, the daunting Andean landscape made it difficult to see what locals always knew: that the vertical world was connected. Kinship and intentional agricultural strategies at different elevations forged connections between communities and between human and nonhuman kin like mountains and the land.[90]

Martínez has found a way to share this kind of relationality by adapting the Andean technology and practice of *huatia* to his urban kitchen. The huatia is an earth oven and is also the name of a traditional dish that involves cooking potatoes (and sometimes other tubers) in an earth oven. In most of the early documentaries and articles about Martínez, there is always a discussion of this Andean culinary technology. Martínez is shown visiting an Andean family and cooking huatia, always emphasizing that this tradition dates back to the Incas.[91] This is clearly an important component of his presentation of self and project.

During one interview, for example, Martínez takes a CNN reporter up to the Andean town of Acomayo in the department of Cusco. There he visits a family with whom he has developed a working relationship, and they begin the process of cooking huatia. As Martínez waits with others for the potatoes to cook, he tells the reporter that what he is hoping "to get out of this trip is to get to know a little more about this Andean vision, about the way the Andean people see the world."[92] Making sure to note that the Quechua farmers Martínez is with are "direct descendants of the Incas," the reporter then marvels at the chef's ability to transform this simple dish into the sophisticated version that appears on his menu at *Central*: "Virgilio uncovers the secret of the huatia; then this age-old dish is reimagined at the hands of the chef. In Virgilio's kitchen, the humble potato is elevated to an artful display, as the sliced tubers are topped with a crust of Andean herbs and a splash of kushuro sauce. In his desire to explore new culinary landscapes, Virgilio has rejuvenated an ancient recipe."[93] Martínez also speaks to the significance of the huatia, as dish and as method. "Huatia for us, as a technique, is very important to incorporate into the techniques we are using at *Central*. . . . We are not allowed to make a hole in the middle of the restaurant, but we can make our own little oven, we bring potatoes, herbs, the soil, tubers, rocks from the Andes."[94] Similarly, Gill comments on Virgilio's rendition of the huatia. "He brings the mountain back to the restaurant. The huatia gives this unique flavor to the potato. It is the essence of the land, you get a little bit of the earth inside of you; giving the diner that connection back to the land, it is something very beautiful."[95]

Very beautiful? On the plate, it is undoubtedly something to behold. However, what exactly is the connection to the land that is "given" to the diner? It says that this land, Indigenous land, is also yours. And it is yours to literally consume.

I talked with D'Angelo about the chef's obsession with the huatia, and he agreed. In fact, D'Angelo had quite a thoughtful critique of Martínez's project, the representations of Indigenous peoples as in the past, and the terms the chef used ("ancestral," "traditional") when talking about Indigenous knowledge. And this was a critique, he told me, that he had shared with Martínez. When he asked the chef why he was so focused on the huatia, Martínez responded that for him the huatia was significant because he saw it as the only moment when one does not need to go anywhere to eat and food does not need to travel. "You eat in the earth in the moment and that in itself is a celebration," he remembered Martínez saying. In an interview with *Eater* magazine, the chef also points to the importance of celebration: "*Huatia* is . . . a traditional preparation and method that means caring and celebration, and what we do is just transform the whole ceremony into something sweet, into one of the desserts [pointing to photographs included in the article]. We have two pictures: One is the sweet huatia that we serve in the dining room and the other one is the sweet huatia that we serve outdoors, just in front of the Moray ruins."[96]

The huatia, then, would seem to encapsulate the extreme locality that Martínez is trying to convey with Mil: eating in the earth, and perhaps eating the earth, is the celebration that is Mil, each of the menu's eight "moments" offering a taste of place, of context (*"del entorno a la mesa"*). "At Mil, first you touch the earth, and then you eat from it," he tells *Condé Nast Traveler* magazine.[97] This emphasis on the connection between taste and place, however, is less about terroir—the idea that particular foods are linked to and shaped by the environmental factors of a particular region—than about a romanticizing of dirt and earth.[98] This huatia-inspired experience is also, in some ways, a romanticizing of indigeneity precisely by placing Indigenous peoples closer to nature, closer to the earth and to dirt.[99] There is also something problematic about the idea of "transforming the whole ceremony" into dessert and serving it in front of the Moray ruins. Do community members have a say in these transformations?

I am reminded of a conversation I had with a Native activist and member of CHIRAPAQ, an Indigenous association in Peru that has been especially active in fighting in support of Native food sovereignty (and against the extractive dimensions of the gastronomic boom). This activist, whom I will call Jorge, shared his perspective about the appropriation and use of Native plants and animals that he saw as constitutive of the contemporary gastronomic revolution, noting in particular the violence involved in extracting specific beings from specific contexts. Jorge's concern can also be understood as one about relations and especially the ways in which colonialism entails the disruption of relations among humans, animals, plants, and other kin. Jorge, like other Native activists across the Americas, is working toward the restoration of good relations among kin.[100] In this context, the huatia-inspired dessert seems to me a step in the wrong direction. Perhaps the concern that arises first is that the huatia is considered a sacred ritual in many Andean communities, and it comes only in June, when the earth and grasses are dry enough to make this ritual possible. Like many Native rituals, there is a temporality to ceremony that is coordinated with the seasons. The temporality of this dessert responds to the rhythms of capital, markets, and the desire to consume something exotic.

CONCLUDING REFLECTIONS

A well-known Italian chef, in his endorsement of the book *Central*, notes that "[Martínez] is a chef who looks deeply into the unknown, into the forgotten and rejected to find a different way to embrace his culture."[101] Indeed, Martínez is seen by many as revindicating the nation through his work. An article in *El Comercio*, for example, described Martínez's participation at a culinary event in Mexico as one that "revindicated our products and paid homage to the *pacha mama* (mother earth) and her delicious fruits."[102] While one can be critical of this high-end homage to the *pachamama*, there is no doubt that this kind of discourse is preferable to the insulting dismissals of deceased president Alan García, who openly mocked Native peoples for believing in the sacredness of mountains and standing in the way of national development.[103] García also famously dismissed Indigenous people's objection to extractive industries in the Amazon as a syndrome of the "dog in the manger" who does not eat and does not let others eat.[104]

Martínez, however, has found that Indigenous peoples in fact hold the keys to what Peruvians (and everyone else) should eat and that partnership with them may lead to a deeper understanding of what Peru has to offer. This kind of collaborative partnership is what he is perhaps aspiring to with the work taking place at Mil. And this would seem to be mutually advantageous. Santiago Pillco, a community leader from Kacllaraccay, is quoted in *Bon Appétit*: "I want to share how I work with [the chefs at Mil] and then share the knowledge of those ingredients with the world. If we weren't sharing, we're losing our identity."[105] Pillco and his wife Seferina feature prominently in Mater's blog entries, where staff write about their experiences working with the neighboring communities. Some of these posts raise significant questions about the possibilities of collaboration, particularly between Western and Indigenous researchers, while others reflect more traditional approaches to "objective" ethnographic research and observation.[106] But even at their best, these efforts obscure the complexity of the sociality and politics of community and relations. For instance, it is primarily Pillco's family who are regularly featured in interviews and collaborations. Do other families refuse to be a part of these projects? What are the intra-communal tensions that emerge? As Native theorists and others have noted, the politics of inclusion and recognition can be powerful discursive forces that reinscribe colonial relations.[107]

In other words, such a progressive and beautiful reconciliation of elite cuisine, Indigenous knowledge, and national goals is certainly seductive and, in market terms, incredibly successful. Yet one wonders if this may in fact just be the latest, most ingenious form of neocolonial extraction. When talking with D'Angelo about the wall of dried plants you see when entering Mil, he told me: "[W]e have moved from botanical expeditions to ethnobotany. Now we ask people to tell us about each plant, their use. [W]e rely on Native knowledge." For him, this was a decolonial move. In my view, it is another example of the ways this project continues to extract Indigenous knowledge.[108] The appropriation of Indigenous knowledge remains at the center of the experience, or perhaps to put it more dramaturgically, Indigenous peoples, for the most part, remain backstage. The performance for which diners travel (sometimes thousands of miles) is to witness the mastery of Chef Virgilio Martínez and taste the magic he has extracted from the land.

In some ways, Martínez's vision and approach echo Acurio's beautiful fusion, but Acurio and Martínez theorize difference in particular ways. For Acurio, mixture creates something new; histories of colonial encounter and immigration transform a multiplicity of culinary traditions into one Peruvian cuisine. For Martínez, the emphasis is on the "real" Peru. This means foregrounding indigeneity, but he collapses indigeneity with wildness, biodiversity, and landscapes. With an ecological and aesthetic sensibility, he appreciates ingredients in their place—in their specific ecosystem and altitude—but remade, and presented as a literal taste of the nation, or of pieces of the nation.[109]

If Acurio's work is an updating of mestizaje or racial mixture, Martínez updates *indigenismo*, the artistic and political movement that celebrated the Native until that day, always lodged in the distant future, when the Native could speak for himself.[110] In other words, while Acurio emphasizes fusion and mixture, Martínez emphasizes an authentic, "ancestral," indigeneity, a key ingredient for Martínez but only as the authenticating anchor that allows him to mine Native knowledge and claim a link to Indigenous traditions through the presentation of Native peoples as "ancestors." If Indigenous peoples are in the city, they are always already representatives of ancestral tradition in the Andes, not on the coast. Never once does Martínez consider the Indigenous peoples who lived in Lima before the founding of the city in 1535. We could read Acurio's vision as one of transformation: moving Peru from the ugliness of racism and terror to a land of beautiful fusion and mixture. For Martínez, the work is about translation; he transposes Indigenous knowledge and ecosystems onto a plate and invites guests to literally consume Peru. Acurio's work with Indigenous producers—his ability to reframe, even beautify difference—was perhaps necessary to set the stage for Martínez, who can now invoke indigeneity, and Indigenous knowledge, as key to finding our authenticity, our identity. Indigenous peoples and ingredients are necessary to anchor and authenticate this new, modern, Peru, but they must be in their place.

Acurio's vision and message of a beautifully mixed nation, a nation for sale made ready through "very balanced, reflexive, and consensual" fusion, ignores (and in many ways reinscribes) the violence of "fusion," the sexual and racial violence of mestizaje. But Martínez's exploration and "discovery" of deep Peru is almost more insidious. The audacity of Martínez's claim to "replicate" Native understandings and ways of life is even bolder than the masters of twentieth-century indigenismo like Luis Valcarcel and Clorinda Matto de Turner, who also centered Cuzco in their imaginings. Martínez offers the seductive braiding of ecological, economic, and social causes with Native products and Indigenous knowledge. But what this belies, or perhaps hides in plain sight, is the clearly colonial act of ventriloquizing Indigenous voices, a hallmark of twentieth century forms of indigenismo. There is no question that Martínez is an artist and visionary, but his work is committed to an aesthetics that are his own and for a public that is unapologetically elite. His is the art of anti-politics, a move away from social issues and toward his own production. To the extent that he invites us to think about Indigenous peoples and knowledge, it is just enough for the diner not to think about the ongoing acts of extraction, dispossession, and erasure that continue in less picturesque contexts.

And yet. In "post-terror" times, doesn't a return to the aesthetics and "peaceful" work of indigenismo feel like progress? There is an understandable desire to tell a story about Peru that is not about violence. In addition, we should not minimize the benefits for young people training to be chefs, for Native producers and migrants who see entrepreneurial possibilities, the benefits, even, of what we might call Martínez's "radical locality," of valorizing Native epistemologies, of moving from "negative exoticism to positive exoticism."[111] As the vice president for an agricultural producers' association told me in 2015, "[W]e know [the way we are used] is messed up, but the boom offers us a space we can enter and manipulate for our own interests."

That said, Peru's contemporary national project, buoyed by its culinary success, reasserts and sustains a particular racial and gendered order of things. In the wake of the "disorder" produced by agrarian reform and the internal conflict of recent years, Acurio, Martínez, and others have brilliantly used gastropolitics as the way to reorder things. If mestizaje is an "all-inclusive ideology of exclusion," the Peruvian culinary project's emphasis on beautiful mixture and ethical alliances, on social inclusion and environmental conservation, in fact redraws social lines and reasserts hierarchies of exclusion that have historically marked Peru as a nation for the elite few.[112] Peruvian sociologist Raúl Matta notes that making Peruvian ingredients palatable necessitates the ability to "neutralize their unworthiness, their 'Indianness,' and their lower-class characteristics."[113] This attempt to "neutralize," repackage, and make Indianness consumable was especially evident at the culinary festival Mistura, to which I turn next.

"Gastronomy Is a Display Case"

AS IN EARLIER YEARS, Apega organized a training workshop during Mistura 2015 for the agricultural producers participating in the festival by selling their products at El Gran Mercado. This included producers from almost every region of the country. The workshop took place in the early morning, before the festival opened its doors. It was a cool spring day as producers arrived and settled into their seats in front of a large outdoor stage. After over an hour had passed, the workshop began with a performance by a clown. Much like one might do with children at a birthday party, the clown joked and laughed, eliciting audience participation. He performed for about twenty minutes, ending with a song called "el baile del gran vendedor" ("the dance of the great seller"). Taking over from the clown, a festival organizer whom I will call Carlos led the rest of the workshop. His focus as he addressed the approximately eighty men and women present was on three main points: the importance of presentation, cleanliness, and discipline. "Gastronomy is a display case," he began. "You need to make yourselves attractive so the consumer will fall in love." To do this, producers were told, it is necessary to bring to the surface "the magic of your origins" (*la magia de su origen*), and to offer "pretty, happy faces" (*rostros bonitos y sonrientes*) to consumers. As Carlos spoke, images of "happy faces"—all brown, all smiling widely, all wearing colorful hats—flashed on the screen behind him, clearly as examples of what to emulate. Carlos then talked about funds Apega had set aside to "beautify markets, produce stands, waiters; to beautify the presentation of the producer and the product."

Taking a break from speaking, Carlos then introduced an organization (created and supported by Apega) called BPM (Grupo Buenas Prácticas de Manipulación, or the Good Food-Handling Practices Group), which would teach them how to best present themselves as clean—how and why you use gloves, aprons, and hair nets, how and why you wash your hands—because, he said, "delicious and healthy food can only be possible with good and clean presentation of person and product."[1] Later, during an interview, he told me that the workshop's focus on hygiene was particularly important, as "we must teach them to be clean so they can have a healthy life, this is the mark of a healthy life." Finally, Carlos turned to the importance of rules and discipline. Transitioning from the previous discussions about presentation and cleanliness (and invoking religious doctrine), he reminded all present that being at Mistura was a great opportunity for them, but that they must remember that there were rules. In fact, he said, Ápega had a pamphlet that described the "Ten Commandments" for producers, commandments that would help them sell "better" at Mistura and other agricultural fairs. As one of the many festival workers handed out the small, colorful pamphlets, Carlos emphasized a few of those commandments: "always have happy, smiling faces," "always have good, clean presentation," and "always have orderly products and stands."

THREE

Staging Difference

THE GASTROPOLITICS OF INCLUSION
AND RECOGNITION

THE OLD WOMAN *made her way through the throngs of people, looking con-fused at times, but persistently calling out "Cuy! Rico cuy!" No one looked at her. All around, people moved happily from El Gran Mercado to food stands to beer gardens. They looked at their maps to decide where they might go next. They stood in line for the public bathrooms. They listened to musical performances or lectures about composting and the value of organic produce. Children ran past her, kicking up dirt and dust, almost knocking her down. I watched as she put down her basket to rearrange her* pollera *(traditional Andean skirt) and her hat. She picked up her basket, looked around as if looking for someone, and then a bit more loudly this time, called out once again, "Cuy! Rico Cuy!" She took one of the skewered fried guinea pigs out of the basket as she did, waving it around a little before putting it back in.*

Suddenly, as if out of nowhere, three security guards appeared. They were dressed in black and brown; pink and yellow tags indicating they were Mistura guards hung from their necks. They surrounded her, grabbed her by the arms, and almost lifted her off the ground. The woman looked more angry than scared. From where I was, I could not hear what they said to her, or what she replied. But I could see they wanted her out of the festival area, and they were taking her in the direction of one of many exits. Just as suddenly as the guards had appeared, two younger women arrived, waving their arms and yelling out. I had moved closer by then and I could make out a few words: "Huanta," "productora," "con nosotros" (Huanta, producer, with us). After a brief exchange, the guards let the woman go, and the two young women surrounded her, held her, and led her away from the guards and toward El Gran Mercado, where they disappeared into the maze of products and food stands.

Mistura, arguably the central stage for showcasing Peru's gastronomic revolution, began as a relatively small culinary festival in 2008 but grew quickly into the largest culinary festival in Latin America, with close to half a million visitors at the height of its existence.[1] Described as a celebration of Peru's culinary and cultural diversity, Mistura highlighted the gastronomic boom's emphasis on social inclusion, especially through alliances between chefs and producers.[2] While gastropolitical elites insist that Peru's culinary revolution promotes (among other things) racial healing through the recognition, celebration, and inclusion of previously marginalized populations, this chapter argues that this movement can be read instead as one that centers the production and promotion of a "civilized" subject: the agricultural producer.[3] If Mistura is the central symbol of the gastronomic revolution, the producer is its central figure, deployed strategically in particular contexts, spaces, and moments.

The attempted removal of the old woman with her cuyes offers a glimpse into the ways difference is sanitized and managed. The woman, selling cuy prepared in the traditional manner, disrupted Mistura's projection of an "orderly, clean, and beautiful" multiculturalism so carefully choreographed by festival organizers and gastropolitical elites. She, and the cuy, were entirely out of place. Like Mary Douglas's famous definition of dirt as "disorder" or "matter out of place," the woman and the cuy—skewered, with visible teeth, nails, and hair still present—were seen as dirty figures who did not belong and should be removed from the festival, from this so-called national celebration of diversity where, in Acurio's words, "no one is bothered by the other . . . and all embrace all."[4]

This is the familiar false universalism of liberal humanism and racial orders that speaks in a rights-bearing idiom but enables multiple exclusions, erasures, and forms of violence.[5] More specific to the ongoing formation of Andean colonial orders, the woman and her cuy figured a particular past, an agrarian one in which cuyes were raised in homes on dirt kitchen floors, not in industrial and (at least in theory) sterile confinement facilities; it invoked the "ugly, dirty, deep" Peru that gastropolitical elites have worked so hard to erase and refigure. Peru's gastropolitical project can be read as a contemporary manifestation of a long colonial history of attempts to sanitize, control, and civilize the Other. As Rudi Colloredo-Mansfeld argues, the creation of bourgeois subjectivities and modernities in the Andes has since the nineteenth century hinged on problems of hygiene.[6] Building on the insights of Michel Foucault and Ann Stoler, Colloredo-Mansfeld reminds us that "colonizers elevated hygiene into a gendered and racial 'micro site' of political control. It provided a context for appraising racial membership and designating 'character', 'good breeding', and proper rearing."[7]

As we will see, hygiene and concern over "dirty Indians" continue to preoccupy the designers of Mistura and the new Peruvian brand. Mistura's message of inclusion notwithstanding (*Mistura Somos Todos*), when festival organizers proclaim that "we are all Peru," it means both a particular "we" and also a particular "Peru." Resonating with the Habermasian notion of the public sphere, Mistura is often described as a space where the Peruvian collective can come together in a show of unity in diversity, where festival attendees and participants, despite differences, are all compatriots feeling pride in their culinary excellence, made possible precisely because of Peru's racial, cultural, and biological diversity. However, as Nancy Fraser has noted, this vision neglects the fact that real public spheres are often constituted by a "number of significant exclusions."[8] In other words, the Habermasian "bracketing" of social difference "usually works to the advantage of dominant groups in society and to the disadvantage of subordinates."[9] Indeed, Mistura supports producers who abide by certain expectations about presentation, behavior, and compliance, and who know their place in the hierarchies of emerging networks of local-global capital flows.

When I spoke with Carlos (the festival organizer mentioned in the interlude), he was very aware of the Andean woman trying to sell her cuyes. "She was selling her cuyes like a street vendor (*como ambulante*)!" he exclaimed. Carlos continued: "You can't do that; you can't sell out of place; you have to be in your place; the right place." The organizer was referring to the vendor stalls behind which each producer was expected to stand. He told me the incident demonstrated the work that still needs to be done to "train them," and that this was an example of how easily all the work they have done to promote Native products and to support producers can be undone. "We don't eat [the cuy] whole; certainly not with its head still on. People don't want to look at the face, especially tourists or Peruvians from a certain class. Her actions are taking us backwards."

For scholars of race and indigeneity in Latin America, this move is all too familiar. As many have observed, the deployment of multiculturalism (or *interculturalidad*) easily becomes another colonial tool for managing non-White bodies and spaces. The Other is included only as long as she does not

disrupt social and political orders. That is, certain cultural rights may be offi-
cialized and folkloric belonging may be celebrated, as long as subjects know
their place in the colonial-capitalist order.[10] Mistura, and the gastronomic
revolution it represents, can thus be read as a crucial component of what
Norbert Elias famously described as the civilizing process.[11] The Peruvian
brand, the marketing of nation, relies on the beautification of that nation,
and in elite terms this has everything to do with taste, with a particular
presentation of national culture (and cuisine), of that which authenticates,
and sets the terms for, difference.[12] Moreover, Carlos's comment connects to
racialized understandings of Indigenous and mestiza women as transgressive,
in particular those considered *cholas*, a derogatory term that as Weismantel
writes, "racializes produce vendors, turning attention away from the women's
occupation and onto their bodies, which it sexualizes in order to degrade."[13] It
evokes colonial geographies that are ostensibly very different from the performance space that is Mistura. Indigenous women and *cholas* in this formation
are figured as backward, dirty, ignorant.[14]

Mistura, then, is a key site for exploring the gastropolitical performance
of inclusion, one that is haunted by colonial legacies, as well as particular
Peruvian histories of agrarian reform and Indigenous labor.[15] As interviews
with gastropolitical elites and others showed, when Acurio says that Mistura is a space "where no one is *bothered* by the other" (emphasis added),
he is understood as speaking both to those who should be grateful for their
inclusion in the festival (such as Indigenous producers and festival attendees
from peri-urban areas of Lima) and to elite audiences in a challenge to racist
and exclusionary practices that have marginalized Indigenous and peasant
populations. While it may be the case that Acurio is addressing Peruvian
elites (indeed, he often speaks to the fact that Lima has "given its back" to
the countryside for too long), it is instructive to connect these comments to
his suggestion that the magic ingredient in Peruvian cuisine—"tolerance"—is
the product of "a dialogical and *respectful* encounter of all the races that gave
life to our culture."[16]

This is a reminder of the particular gastropolitical reading of colonialism
and race relations. Acurio's optimistic discourse of inclusion does the dirty
work of erasing (and simultaneously reinscribing) sexual, racial, and geno-
cidal violence from these historical narratives.[17] Such forgetting, as Renan
famously observed, is essential to nation-building projects.[18] "The act of forgetting, I would even say, historical error, is an essential factor in the creation
of a nation, which is why progress in historical studies often constitutes a

danger for nationality." He continues: "Indeed, historical enquiry brings back to light the deeds of violence that took place at the origin of all political formation."[19] One might add to Renan's observation that cultural analysis reveals that such violence not only occurs at the "origin" but rather is an ongoing part of the technology of reproducing the nation from one generation to the next.[20] In order to move Peru forward, in the dominant gastropolitical view, there is no place for "resentment." As I discuss in chapter 1, this formulation also confronts the ghost of Velasco and Peru's agrarian reform, as well as long histories of "the Indian problem."[21]

In what follows, I explore some of the ways we can read gastropolitics in Peru as a settler-colonial project invested in the elimination of "the Indian." Much like industrialization in Peru in the early 1900s was understood by elites as a project necessary for modernity, as "an embodied project of racial improvement" that "would bring about the elimination of the Indian," gastropolitics links the Peruvian nation's economic success to the re-placement of Indigenous peoples and the managing of Indigenous agricultural labor.[22] In his discussion of labor, race, and nation in Peru, Paulo Drinot argues that "the project of Peruvian nation-state formation . . . was and in many ways continues to be premised on the *overcoming* of indigeneity, that is to say on the de-Indianization of Peru."[23] In other words, the Peruvian nation is co-constitutive of Indigenous exclusion.

While gastropolitics in Peru today would seem to promote the *inclusion* of Indigenous Peruvians, with Drinot I argue that in fact this inclusionary promise is premised upon the exclusion of particular bodies and the disavowal of Indigenous vibrancy. Drinot notes that in Peru historically, "labor was commensurable with progress and indigeneity was commensurable with backwardness, [thus] it followed that labor was incommensurable with indigeneity."[24] While gastropolitics seemingly elevates the Indigenous producer and his labor as central to the success of the gastronomic revolution, the figure of the producer has been carefully crafted to promote what Anders Burman might call a "defanged" indigeneity: an image of docile, happy, and tolerant subjects.[25] We could argue that Acurio and Apega's work with producers is in fact an attempt to renarrate Native peoples as laborers. But I see instead a move to promote the labor of chefs as those with the vision and skill to transform the raw material products delivered by producers. Moreover, the gastropolitical move to transform Indigenous peoples into "productive" citizens is also linked to a desire for "returning" them to their appropriate place, and to "cleanse" Lima. As I discuss later, the celebration of producers is intimately linked with elite anxieties over racial contamination and hygiene. Put bluntly, this ostensible "centering" of producers is coterminous with what Wolfe referred to as the "logic of Native elimination" that characterizes settler colonialism.[26] In this case, the Native is not physically eliminated but rather erased through the work of cultural categories and representation. This is illustrated by the evolution of the Peruvian national holiday that, in Apega's formulation, has gone from the "Day of the Indian" to (with Velasco) the "Day of the Campesino" and now to the "Day of the Producer" (el Día del Agricultor). Note the shifting subject of celebration to a category— producer—that only has meaning in relation to markets and consumers.[27] Even when the imagery or folklore of Native peoples is deployed by slick marketing videos, Indigenous peoples are presented always in generic form, playing a role in a production that is not really their own.

PERFORMING INCLUSION

In a documentary about Mistura, Acurio tells viewers that "the word mistura means mixture, but Mistura [the festival] is a pretty mixture. Peruvian cuisine is a beautiful mixture."[28] For Acurio, Apega, and others, Mistura is a stage from which to display Peruvian diversity. It is also a site from which to showcase the "new Peru" and its inclusionary politics.[29] This message is evident in the many descriptions of Mistura on websites, in newspapers, on the radio, in magazines, and on television. It is also especially clear in a striking video trailer for Mistura 2015: *Mistura Somos Todos*.[30] Starting by emphasizing Peru's regional diversity ("*Los del centro . . . los de la costa, los de los Andes, los de la Amazonía*"), the narrator then moves on to name distinct Peruvian racial categories (*los cholos, los negros, los blancos, los colorados*) before moving on to some interesting racialized categorizations that reflect an odd blend of historical formations and more recent migrations from the Amazon and Andes to Lima: "those who migrate, the charapas, the Moche, the characatos, those who adopted this land as theirs" ("*los que migran, los charapas, los Moche, los characatos, los que adoptaron esta tierra como suya*"). The video then moves on to labor, including those who are considered productive neoliberal subjects: "those who produce, invent, contribute, export, farm, fish and harvest" ("*los que producen, los que inventan, los que aportan, los que exportan, los que crían, los que pescan . . . los que cosechan*"). Importantly in this context, the narrator also makes implicit reference to the much-celebrated chef-producer alliances:

those with "great knowledge" ("*los de mucho conocimiento*"), accompanied by an image of a White male chef, and those "worthy of acknowledgment" ("*y los dignos de reconocimiento*"), with images of Andean producers holding Rocoto de Oro awards, given to those who "labor to protect, harvest or disseminate information about" Peru's Native products.[31]

There is so much more, but this sampling of the "todos" in *Mistura Somos Todos* is more than enough to reveal who is included (and how) and who is excluded in the gastropolitical remaking of the nation. The images accompanying the racialized categories I have quoted here, for example, offer important clues about gastropolitical understandings of indigeneity. There is no mention of Aymara, Quechua, Shipibo-Conibo, or any other actually existing Indigenous peoples. Instead, indigeneity is represented by "los Moche," referencing the Moche pre-Columbian civilization who lived in what is now northern Peru, and included with an accompanying image of Moche ceramics. Apparently Indigenous peoples exist in the past, and what remains are archaeological artifacts. Contemporary indigeneity is perhaps signaled by the inclusion of *los charapas*, a derogatory term used by some in Peru to refer to people from the Amazon that, in the region of Loreto, means "turtle." The accompanying image here is of Amazonian women and men dressed in fetishized Indigenous clothes, made of feathers, beads, and animal skins, with a woman holding a snake.

There are other telling visual and narrative juxtapositions; "those who migrate" are Andean migrants, "those who adopted this land as theirs" are Asian migrants, and "the classic ones (*los clásicos*)" placed next to "the innovators (*los innovadores*)" is figured by an Afro-Peruvian woman, smiling and dressed as what in the United States could be an "Aunt Jemima" figure and in South America would be "La Negrita" or "Doña Pepa." Much as Aunt Jemima and similar representations figured an idealization of plantation life, or the "happy slave," this image too idealizes slavery in Peru and fixes Afro-Peruvians in particular spaces.[32]

Along with the minstrel-like figure of "the happy slave," Mistura (and gastropolitics more generally) promotes the fiction of "the happy Native," a version of what Silvia Rivera Cusicanqui has called "*el indio permitido,*" the authorized Indian.[33] As is by now well known, this term refers to the subject position that emerges in the context of neoliberal (or settler-colonial) recognition, when states "actively recognize and open space for... indigenous presence."[34] As I argue later in this chapter, however, "the authorized Indian" has been replaced by the figure of "the happy producer," a figure who

FIGURE 5. Screenshot from *Mistura Somos Todos*. Accessed June 19, 2019.

represents an authorized subject who bridges the feudal hacienda past and the neoliberal market future. As the interlude before this chapter shows, this subject is expected (and "trained") to be clean and docile, and to reflect Peruvian multicultural (or intercultural) diversity—Acurio's beautiful fusion—in appropriate ways.

As noted earlier, Apega was tasked with organizing Mistura and played a central role in linking the celebration of diversity to social inclusion. Following Acurio's "culinary ethics" (as seen in chapter 1), Apega was created in 2007 with a mission to "build bridges of harmony between our peoples by revaluing the role of the producer in the food chain." According to its website, Apega is the place "where chefs and peasants . . . are all equal; we want to cook the same thing: Peru's progress."[35] Apega's website describes Mistura almost in the language of Jürgen Habermas, in which "differences are left at the door"; for some, Mistura symbolizes the ideal Peru. Consider the words of Alexander Chiu Werner, a specialist in digital marketing writing in the pages of the business and economics daily *Gestión*, for whom Mistura stages a multisensorial version of the country, one that allows us to see, hear, and taste an "integrated" and "inclusive" Peru:

> Mistura is not a gastronomic festival to eat tasty dishes but rather a place in which you will live and taste for yourself the mixture that is Peru: from the agricultural worker of the farthest countryside to the cook who lives in the city. Mistura could be summarized as a space where you encounter the Peru that you want to see, feel and taste: an integrated Peru, inclusive, happy and proud. . . . [T]he consumers value a brand that satisfies you as a person, that teaches you and offers an emotional connection that goes beyond commercial exchange.[36]

To be clear, not everyone is as enamored with Mistura as these descriptions would suggest, and not everyone feels included. Critiques from journalists, chefs, food critics, and public intellectuals point to a politics of favoritism at Apega that excludes those who might offer alternative perspectives about how the festival should be run and who should participate.[37] When I asked several cab drivers about Mistura in 2015, all told me they thought it was great that I was attending the festival, but none had themselves attended. One young man in his late thirties told me that Mistura was not for "people like him." "The entrance price is too high [that year it cost 25 soles, or about 8 USD for a ticket]. And if you have a car," he told me, "you have to pay an additional 20 soles to park. Then you need to wait in line to pay for tickets to try food, and for what? So they can serve you like a cat [*para que te sirvan como gato*, meaning tiny portions]. And you don't go alone, so you have to pay for at least two people. And anyway, who has time to wait in line to spend money?" Another driver offered a similar answer, telling me that he had four kids, so taking them to Mistura was out of the question. Instead, he said, "it is much better to drive to Pachacamac [a district in southern Lima], and spend the day eating chicken and playing in the park."

Despite their criticisms, however, both of these men expressed their belief that Mistura mattered, that it was significant that tourists and important international chefs traveled to Peru to participate in the festival, and then they immediately moved on to praise Gastón Acurio and the work he had done to "elevate Peru." This is not experienced as a contradiction: Mistura can simultaneously be seen as exclusionary and positive. As in many unequal capitalist countries, the poor can celebrate and justify the privileges of the rich as they have embraced the ideological promise that one day, if they work hard enough, they too can have such luxuries. Other critiques, however, come from a different class position, and they are about Mistura becoming too "*popular*" or too "working-class." Such views belie Apega's claims of inclusion and Acurio's vision of a Peru "where none is bothered by the other."

When I traveled to Mistura again in 2016, my Uber driver had a very different reason for not attending Mistura. He positioned himself as a cultured, educated person ("*soy educado y tengo cultura*") and noted that driving for Uber was temporary, as he just needed some extra money for a home renovation project (also emphasizing that he was a homeowner). He told me he had attended Mistura since the beginning, in 2009, but that he no longer wanted to attend because there were now too many people "of the wrong kind, like from el Cono Norte [often read as a poor and peri-urban part of greater Lima]." He said that while it was laudable that festival organizers wanted to make Mistura a more inclusive space, lowering the entrance costs had "turned this prestigious culinary festival into a place where you now share space with just anyone (*ahora te topas con cualquiera*)." Carlos Galdós, a columnist for *El Comercio*, documents a similar sentiment. In a short essay on the "excuses" people give for not attending Mistura (excuses that, he argues, reflect the opinions of "those who are envious and want to fuck with our good times"), he writes that he heard "one of those women who think Peru is like her apartment building in San Isidro" complain about the long lines, suggesting that the price of food should be increased, otherwise "just anyone can buy it and then you have these interminable lines." Speaking specifically about standing in line to eat *chancho al palo* (pig cooked over wood fire), she noted that there should be a VIP line with VIP servings, and "for others, the remaining bones at working-class prices" (*para los demás los huesitos a precios populares*).[38]

Galdós ends his column with a plea to those who complain about Mistura: "Please stop fucking with Mistura, because what we wouldn't give for Peru to be like it: united, festive, proud of what is his, and without [inferiority or superiority] complexes."[39] While Galdós seems to be calling out the elite for exclusionary ideas and practices, his defense of Mistura reproduces the official, authorized, and exclusionary vision of inclusion, one predicated on tolerance, control, cleanliness, and all things being in their place.

SANITIZING DIFFERENCE

At Mistura one can find multiple food stands from a range of venues, from high-end restaurants to food trucks to *carretilleros* (street vendors). Visitors can taste artisanal beer made from quinoa, the latest pisco infusion, and some of the world's best coffee. And they can touch and taste and purchase fruits and tubers, honey and chocolate, quinoa and maca, directly from producers. There are also daily talks and workshops about composting, culinary innovation, and biodiversity, as well as cooking demonstrations by renowned chefs. But importantly, Mistura is the central site for foregrounding the role of producers and products, and the so-called chef-producer alliances, in Peru's gastronomic revolution. The producer is described as necessary for Peruvian gastronomy, as the "first link in the Peruvian food chain."[40] Acurio, Apega representatives, journalists, food critics, and others regularly note that without the labor of agricultural producers and the uniqueness of the products they offer, there would be no Peruvian gastronomy.[41]

Accordingly, the principal site at Mistura is El Gran Mercado, described as the *despensa nacional* (national pantry), a place where you can see and taste Native products—from potatoes, ajíes (chilis), and quinoa, to lesser known products such as *chalarina* (fruit from the North) and *babaco* (fruit from the Amazon). These are products that, in ways similar to representations of Peruvian producers, are described as natural, organic, healthy, colorful, and clean. In other words, they are suitable for consumption, for buying and taking home. Peruvians can thus perform their (gastro)nationalism by walking into a clean and colorful market and buying directly from producers. Apega foregrounds El Gran Mercado, with its more than one hundred food stands and over three hundred producers, as a place where the biological and cultural diversity of Peru is literally on display.[42] Also on display is Apega's support for producers, as the media are encouraged to feature particular producers and their products to help increase sales and to report on cooking presentations by famous chefs who use the products available at the market.

As others have noted, markets in the Andes are always already stages and involve performances in which vendors negotiate race, sex, gender, and class.[43] Moreover, as Jane Desmond reminds us, "the public display of [human and non-human] bodies and their materiality (how bodies look, what they do, where they do it, who watches, and under what conditions) are profoundly important in structuring identity categories and notions of subjectivity."[44] Indeed, El Gran Mercado is a crucial site for the gastropolitical performance of inclusion and diversity. It is a window into gastropolitical elite attempts at "cleansing" and reordering the city (Lima) and nation.

The celebration and inclusion of producers is shaped by particular ideas about social and racial hierarchies and a desire to "civilize." Producers are included in Mistura, but only if they adhere to strict rules and follow Apega's "ten commandments for improved selling." Moreover, producers are included in the festival *as producers*, a particular subject formation that projects a sanitized difference. If indigeneity is invoked at all, it is in the mention of "ancestral knowledge" and in the presentation of stylized and folkloric performances or dress. These are authorized subjects, subjects who agree to play by the rules, to smile, be friendly, and be helpful to customers, and who do not complain or demand or agitate. And they are subjects who know their place, in agricultural fields outside of Lima, and in city markets and agricultural fairs. Mariano Valderrama, former Apega executive director, writes that

"Mistura recognizes the small farmer as the first link in the gastronomic chain *and that is why* it has *El Gran Mercado*, a space that brings together producers from our various regions with their best products."[45] As we saw in the previous interlude, Apega offered workshops and other programs specifically designed to "train" producers, training that centered a specific presentation of otherness, one that hinges on hygiene and discipline. During an interview in 2015, Carlos (the festival organizer quoted earlier) told me these training workshops were a mandatory requirement to participate in Mistura. Moreover, he told me, producers had to participate in these workshops not only while working at the festival, but at least one additional time when they were offered in or near their province. If producers were interested in participating in the weekly *bioferias* managed by Apega, they had to attend an additional workshop at Apega's offices in Lima.

In 2012 I spoke with Valderrama and asked him questions about Apega's work and gastropolitics more generally. But Valderrama returned again and again to "the problem of hygiene" and to the importance of produce markets. He blamed municipalities for "not enforcing hygiene standards in markets," noting also that the "deplorable conditions in markets offer the wrong image of Peru to tourists."[46] Exalting the significance of tourism not only for Peru's economic development, but importantly, for the promotion of Marca Perú, Valderrama told me dirty markets (and presumably dirty vendors) were directly working against the Peruvian brand.[47] Tourists, he told me, should be able to "comfortably and hygienically stroll through colorful markets." "Unfortunately," he continued, "our most representative market, La Parada, is Calcutta." This is a striking remark, though not surprising when we consider that markets have been key sites in racial projects in the Andes.[48] "[P]roduce markets," writes Mary Weismantel,

> open up a space in the middle of urban life that is appealingly rustic and agricultural, but also dirty and dangerous. Its unruly appearance and organic nature offers an obvious contrast—even a welcome relief—from the concrete and steel grid that otherwise composes the cityscapes of Lima, La Paz, and Quito. But by the same token, the people and products of the market seem out of step with modern city life, an anachronism that is inevitably interpreted in racial terms... [These] "dirty Indians" ... are intruders and racial aliens who do not belong within the domain of all that is modern, civilized, and white.[49]

Indeed, "the produce market," she writes, "has long been perceived as a site where the city's racial defenses are especially vulnerable to attack."[50]

Moreover, she notes, "when politicians promise to 'clean up the markets,' they have no intention of providing the kinds of infrastructural development that would create healthier and more pleasant places to work and to shop."[51] She continues: "Rather, their rhetoric plays upon white fears, leading to demands that markets be controlled like other nonwhite parts of the nation: with violence, harassment, and intimidation. Race provides an alibi for the filth and crime that plagues the markets, making the problems seem to emanate not from political neglect of a vital sector of the economy, but rather from the innate unwholesomeness of those who work there."[52] Cleaning up markets, then, has been a part of Andean histories of racial cleansing and of "civilizing" and "modernizing" projects. Marisol de la Cadena eloquently describes sanitary campaigns in the city of Cusco in the 1920s that targeted markets as key sites for eradicating "the 'polluted' non-whites—Indians and *mestizas*—from places where contact between them and the *gente decente* was inevitable."[53] These campaigns reflected Indigenista bio-racial ideologies in Cusco that saw hybridity as impurity, immorality, and disease, and as such targeted mestizas, central actors in the Andean marketplace, as principal sites of this impurity. As she writes: "The cleansing of the marketplace was racialized. The meat, fruit, and vegetable stalls (owned by *mestizas*) were considered the filthiest.... City rulers were worried about the female vendors' appearance.... To the elite male authorities, the woolen skirt that *mestizas* proudly wore as a symbol of status, was a 'favorite nesting material for bugs and filth (*inmundicias*) of all sorts, and a permanent carrier of bacteria.' Instead of their usual dress, *mestizas* were to wear white, body-length aprons. This color would facilitate the supervision of their cleanliness."[54] There are echoes of these cleansing efforts from the 1920s in Apega's work with producers today at Mistura and elsewhere.

Thinking back to the woman and her cuy, forcibly lifted off the ground and about to be expelled from the festival, it is clear that certain bodies do not belong. As Mary Douglas has put it, "ordering involves rejecting inappropriate elements." Carlos, with whom I spoke about the woman, had also mentioned that she was "badly dressed" (*mal vestida*). When I pressed him on this, he responded that in order to participate in Mistura, producers needed to be clean and "appropriately dressed, with either clean costumes [*sic*], or white aprons, but definitely not with dirty polleras." "They have to learn," he told me. The reference to the woman's "dirty pollera" links directly to racialized associations between Indians, dirt, disease, and immorality.[55] Gastropolitical discourse is perhaps more subtle in its surveillance and management of racial difference than the indigenistas of the 1920s. On the other hand, the framing of Apega's work as one that supports the producer, works to uphold and value their labor, and works so that "the city will no longer give its back to the countryside," is even more insidious. Racial exclusions are no less real when they are euphemized by glossy marketing.

In 2016, Valderrama was still lamenting the "deficient conditions of produce markets," noting that Lima can't possibly aspire to become the gastronomic capital of Latin America if it doesn't have markets such as those found in Barcelona, Madrid, or Turín.[56] In a book about the future of Peruvian gastronomy, Valderrama offers an idealized vision of markets as "spaces of interaction between clients and *sus caseras*," where there exists a "special relation of trust that does not happen in supermarkets."[57] "*La casera* knows which products her clients enjoy . . . [and] her selection of fresh produce tends to be more careful than in modern commerce stores." He continues with a narrative tour of the architectural beauty of some of Peru's principal markets, all of them reflecting "European influence," some of them serving as sites for "galas for the highest authorities in the country."[58] These descriptions are akin to the idealized imaginary of (and nostalgia for) the old, White, and clean Lima discussed in chapter 1.

With these descriptions lodged firmly in the background, Valderrama then speaks to the sadness of the "deterioration suffered by traditional food markets during the last three decades," particularly in terms of infrastructure, water and sewage services, the "disorder in the location of food stands, and bad food handling practices."[59] Here, it is worth noting Valderrama's temporality. He laments the deterioration of the "last three decades," eliding the fact that markets have been a central site for elites and state agencies concerned with the "Indian problem" in Peru for at least the last century, and revealing a particular worry with recent migration into Lima, propelled by political violence and producing the so-called Andeanization (or *cholificación*) of the city.[60] In his autobiography, the Nobel prize–winning writer and conservative politician Mario Vargas Llosa captures this worry vividly: "The shantytowns and marginal districts . . . had crept across the deserts and mountains until they had turned into a gigantic belt of poverty and misery that had squeezed the old part of Lima more and more tightly."[61] As if it needed to be made more explicit, Robert Ellis notes in his analysis of Vargas Llosa's memoir that "the old part of Lima" refers to "white Lima," while the increasing population of migrants in the city reflects White fears of a menacing horde of brown bodies that will inevitably stain and despoil the capital.[62]

Valderrama closes the section of his book on markets with a call to "remodel certain emblematic markets and transform them into models and centers of tourist attraction" and to take "unpostponable measures to modernize markets, to order them and look after good food-handling practices."[63] For Valderrama (as for other gastropolitical elites), El Gran Mercado at Mistura is one step in this direction. Discussing the "limitations" of Peruvian markets, he writes that "*El Gran Mercado* at Mistura has been a space of exception (*espacio de excepción*)" where agricultural products are "revalued" and the regions' "best products" are showcased.[64] These exceptions, of course, reveal the general workings of racial orders in contemporary Peru.

As in other "spaces of exception"—in the sense that might be associated with Giorgio Agamben and others—security and surveillance are necessary tools. During Mistura (and throughout many of the weekly bioferias in Lima), Apega deploys "hygiene brigades" to ensure the cleanliness of food stands, eating areas, festival workers, and producers. The very name of these "hygiene brigades"—with its mix of biopolitical and military imagery—speaks volumes about the ways that these new spaces require significant investments in policing to make them "safe." They are also yet another example of the civilizing process that is a constituent part of the gastropolitical complex, one that creates a vision of Peru's future by sanitizing its feudal past.

DISCIPLINING SUBJECTS/STAGING THE REVOLUTION

At the end of Apega's workshop for producers, the one that began with a dancing and singing clown, Gastón Acurio took the stage and spoke to the producers present. This is how he began:

> First, I want to welcome you to Lima, the city that for centuries has turned its back on you, that for centuries did not know how to acknowledge that it was thanks to you that all our days were happy ones, because those dishes that our mothers prepared were possible only because of the marvelous ingredients that you provided, product of great effort, and from many early mornings when you woke up at dawn to produce. But it is never late and today we are here in the city that finally learned how to recognize, and thank you, for the work you all have done to bring joy to the cities of Peru and today, begin to bring joy to the cities of the world.

Acurio warmly welcomed producers to Lima. And this was not just a greeting referring to their specific trip to Mistura, but more generally, suggesting that they were now—*hoy día*—welcome in Lima, the city that for centuries had turned its back on them. Moreover, he told them the city was learning—finally, because it is never too late—to recognize and be grateful for their labor, without which Peru (and the world) would be deprived of the marvelous Peruvian ingredients that make cities happy. He went on to describe the current moment as one in which the world had "discovered that it is diverse and has learned to enjoy the marvels of cultural and biological diversity." This is why, he said, Peruvian cuisine and Peruvian products were now recognized around the world as "something different, something unique, that enters the hearts of people . . . , and make consumers in the city and the world fall in love with Peru." This was an opportunity, he told them, and it was important to take advantage of that opportunity by any means necessary.

Acurio continued by describing the "millions of consumers waiting to buy these new Peruvian products," who wanted to purchase these products by paying fair prices directly to producers, because they knew that these products would be "good for their bodies, good for their spirits, good for the environment, good for society." "These are the economic values of today," he told them, and they "benefit producers, they benefit a country like Peru, a region like ours; they benefit a world that is more fraternal, more solidary, more peaceful." This is why, he told them, producers needed to "prepare themselves, improve themselves, without fear," so they could sell more efficiently. This is also why, "we need to get used to mutually respecting each other and respecting the other is not pretending that others should understand us, but that we should understand them." He went on, noting that while producers might value all different kinds of potatoes—the big ones, the small ones, the imperfect ones, the ugly ones—they had to understand that there were consumers who wanted only the big ones, and so they needed to learn to respect that, and to price their products appropriately. At the same time, he continued, chefs needed to learn to appreciate diversity, to buy the entire harvest from producers, and to learn how to use different products. "Diversity is a challenge to creativity," he stated.

Acurio began his concluding remarks by emphasizing the importance of this "dialogue" between the producer, the consumer, and the chef, and noted that "the good news is that this is a magical dialogue, because everyone benefits." Chefs benefit from the challenge posed by new products and consumers benefit from eating these delicious culinary inventions. Producers, he told them, benefit because they know "the diversity of their harvest is valued, and they begin to learn too that there are minimum standards they need to comply with in order to build a solid and just commercial relationship." They benefit from the training they receive, from learning how to participate in the market; Mistura provides an opportunity to accumulate both economic and cultural capital. This is precisely one of the key dimensions of the "cunning" of recognition: "its intercalation of the politics of culture with the culture of capital."[65]

Acurio's emphasis on dialogue is not surprising. As Charles Hale reminds us, "neoliberal multiculturalism is more inclined to draw conflicting parties into dialogue and negotiation than to preemptively slam the door."[66] Also significant (and in line with Acurio's vision of Peruvian history as one of "consensual" and "tolerant" mixture) is the reframing of social relations as ones of "*magical* dialogue." As Jane Desmond notes in her discussion of cultural performance, "spectacle . . . replaces narrative, and with it the possibility of historical reflection. The social, political, and economic histories which brought performers and spectators together in the same space are either entirely absent, re-presented as nostalgia, or recoded as cultural or natural conservation."[67] In this case, violent histories of "discovery," dispossession, and marginalization are reframed as a dialogue that is equally beneficial for all those participating in it.

At this point, his voice increasing in tone and volume as he spoke, Acurio offered producers a powerful conclusion, eliciting whistles, strong applause, and a standing ovation from the crowd:

> Thus this is a virtuous circle in which chefs . . . finally have assumed our responsibility, understanding that we are in a privileged position . . . and because of that, because we are in magazines, and television, we have the obligation to become the ones who carry the voice of our agricultural brothers because they are far, working so that we may exist. We have the dream that one day in the near future, consumers will be able to celebrate the work of the small producer with the same emotion, energy, fervor and care as the work of the chefs. And just as there are guides and rankings for chefs, there will also be guides and rankings for producers, we form part of a chain in which all of us have equal importance. [Today] marks the start of a new phase in which we all must work together so that in a few years we . . . can say . . . that our products are all over the world . . . thanks to you. And you will see how your children will be people with more recognition, more prosperity, and your lands, your towns will be more recognized and loved by the city that finally gave you its eternal thanks.

Even with these words on a page, one can sense the emotional momentum that was so palpable in that space, the feeling of being seen, validated, and vindicated. It was the kind of energy that one finds at sporting events, campaign rallies, and perhaps even charismatic churches. But beyond the emotional energy, I was struck by the intricate tapestry Acurio was weaving, one that seemed to celebrate a glimmering future of equality and respect between the country and the city, but that nonetheless was as far from revolutionary as one could be. What he was celebrating was not some new transformation but rather the importance of citizens knowing their place. Acurio's civilizing project and vision for empowerment might seem to be at odds, but what his performance pulls off seamlessly is conveying a clear message about producers learning the rules of the game and knowing that if they follow them, the rewards for them and their children will be enormous. Left unspoken is what happens if producers dare not heed Acurio and Apega's advice.

It is important to remember that Acurio's speech came after a two-hour mandatory training workshop directed at producers, a workshop that began with a clown leading the group of men and women in calisthenics before launching into his "dance of the great seller." Once the clown left the stage, Carlos introduced the various regions of the country that were represented by producers participating at Mistura, then reminded those in attendance that they were not just representing their communities; they were representing a brand, Marca Perú. He addressed the importance of continuous training (*capacitación*) so producers could learn how best to "commercialize agro-food chains," "position their brand," and "sell to consumers." Every region should be linked to a particular product, he told them, which can then be promoted as part of the national brand. Tellingly, however, the rest of the workshop was not about marketing strategies or business plans or even specific forms of state support that could be offered to producers. It was focused on the "need to make [producers] more attractive so the consumer can fall in love." And as I noted earlier, this has everything to do with crafting a particular subject: the Peruvian producer, one who is clean, culturally authentic, well behaved, and happy. And he is also a man.

It is striking how, discursively at least, there is a shift from the figure of the market woman, who had been at the center of concerns for regional elites and a generation of anthropologists, to a new subject, the male producer of the modernizing rural countryside. The masculinization of modernity is, of course, an old idea. As María Josefina Saldaña-Portillo noted in her insightful reading of modernization theories of the Right and revolutionary visions of the Left, the subject of modernity is almost invariably masculine.[68] Arturo Escobar has come to a similar conclusion in examining the ways in which development, as a set of discourses, also produces an ethnocentric and andro-centric vision of the future.[69] For Escobar, this is one of the many effects of the disciplinary power that comes with development. If this is true, then Mistura is simply the latest instantiation of such disciplinary modalities.

In his address to the workshop's attendees, Acurio simply needed to refer to the importance of "training and improving yourselves," of "respecting the other," and of "learning how to understand what the other wants." If you want to sell your products, to benefit from this network of commercial exchange, Acurio was saying, you need to be open to new challenges and participate in the market appropriately. Still, the tone was laudatory and the sensibility one of humility, support, and social justice. This is a familiar version of justice, of course, one that in this context centers chefs, as according to Acurio they are the ones who have "the obligation to become spokespersons for our producer brothers." This can feel like a form of solidarity or even advocacy, and perhaps this was the spirit in which it was intended. Nevertheless, these comments can also be considered part of an old Andean tradition that Ecuadorian sociologist Andrés Guerrero called "ventriloquist representation," in which Indians are spoken for by traditional elites.[70] Landowners, political parties, local elites, and social scientists all profess to understand Indigenous needs and thus speak on behalf of "their" Indians. The voices of Acurio's brothers in the countryside remain distant here. There are others, of course, who do not share this view.

When I spoke with Carlos immediately after the workshop, he was gush-ing about Acurio's ability to "shatter frameworks" (*romper esquemas*). For Carlos, this was an entirely new approach to social inclusion. As we walked over to his office for our scheduled interview, he told me Acurio had just delivered a manifesto: "He has launched a manifesto, a framework for poli-cies that carries with it a revolution! (*"El ha lanzado un manifiesto, un marco de políticas, que trae consigo eso, una revolución!"*)

As we sat in his office, he leaned in and said, "You have to understand, he is a social innovator, he proposes new ways to see old problems." He continued: "For example, he says, you all are important; we are in a process of revalorizing your work, and you are the greatest exponents of cultural and biological diver-sity. But at the same time, he says 'we need entrepreneurs who know how to do business.' He makes them understand that it is not the case that I am going to accept anything that you want, they have to be serious. In other words, [Gastón] is a teacher: he explains possibilities but he also shows the *chicote*." At the mention of the *chicote*, a whip used for hitting and disciplining animals and people, like those who worked the fields of *hacendados* before agrarian reform, my face must have betrayed my thoughts. Carlos stopped talking, looked at me for several seconds, and then perhaps deciding that what my face registered was confusion, he explained, "the chicote is for hitting" ("*el chicote es para pegar*"). And then, restating this once more, he continued: "The chicote is an object for hitting. So [Gastón] says, 'I will buy from you but you must offer quality goods, you must be disciplined [*ordenados*] and comply with the deals you make.' If you don't, you can't participate. You can't benefit. In other words,' he is not the typical paternalist. It is not that typical paternalism that says sure, do what you want and I will help you. No, no no. This [the gastronomic revolution] is not a hand out (*asistencialismo*). He is a good *patrón*." A good patrón can mean a good boss, but it also evokes the image of the benevolent landlord who took care of his family, his lands, and his Indians. Once again, feudal, pre-agrarian reform tropes (*chicotes* and patrones) fold neatly into the neoliberal frameworks of the gastronomic revolution. In today's Peru, punishment for producers who do not comply with the gastronomic revolution's rules does not literally involve a whip, but it does mean exclusion from important market spaces, both at Mistura and the weekly bioferias.

At the workshop, Carlos gave the same message. He told those producers present that "if they behave well there are prizes, but if they behave badly (*si se portan mal*), there are penalties and punishments." This discourse is a familiar dimension of colonial projects, wherein racial taxonomies determine a subject's position in civilizational hierarchies, and those at the top hold not just political power but a "moral duty" to civilize and control unruly others. As Moore, Pandian, and Kosek have noted, "imperial projects of improvement [target] cultural characteristics, seeking their transformation through social and political technologies of rule."[71] In the Andean context, de la Cadena notes that in the mid-1900s, market women in Cusco who defied social rules and expectations were often fined, and she explains that these fines served an "educational purpose."[72] Of course, this kind of pedagogical project is inextricable from the histories of race, morality, and the formation of "proper" subjects in the long civilizing project that is Peru. If Lima is to welcome producers, to give its back to the countryside no longer, then Limeños (presumably *not* the majority of the city's inhabitants, who are migrants or the children of migrants) must "fall in love" with the producer and his products, and there should be a relationship of trust, much like Acurio's "relationship of mutual trust" or the one Valderrama waxed nostalgic about when discussing his idealized market and relations with his *caseras*. Apega's ten commandments reflect these ideals and expectations clearly.

FIGURES 6A and 6B. From Apega's pamphlet *The Ten Commandments for Improved Selling in Agricultural Fairs*. In the entire pamphlet, with the exception of one panel, all producers pictured are men. Photos by author.

All the components of the gastropolitical project's subject are on display: clean, smiling, friendly, trustworthy, and attentive. It is also clear what is to be avoided: anything that could be considered dirty, unsanitary, or untrustworthy. This combines old figures of the "dirty Indian" and the avaricious and shiftless market woman looking to take advantage of customers.

Once again, it is worth noting the importance given to appearance, cleanliness, and the projection of cultural authenticity. As we discussed the requirements for participating in Mistura, Carlos told me he wished the state could have a list of those producers who could be possible festival invitees, those who would have "a certain financial capacity so they can exchange goods, and appropriate attire."[73] These should be "people who have a certain quality, a presence, and who are pleasing, otherwise they show up but don't sell." He continued: "This is because they don't know how to treat the consumer, because the quality of their products is deficient, or because the people from the *Grupo Buenas Prácticas de Manipulación* sanction them because they don't use the appropriate attire, they come dirty. I just went to look around El Mercado and see. Many are well organized and dressed. But not all. Some of them are wearing civilian clothing, when they should all be wearing their regional costumes."

It is interesting to note the reference to "civilian clothing" in contrast to "regional costumes." Military discipline and order is part of this revolution, but it is a happy revolution, or at least it should look like one.[74] At the workshop, Carlos told the audience that "beautiful faces are ordered faces" (*"rostros bonitos son rostros ordenados"*). This connection between hygiene, beauty, order, and folklore is also evident in Apega's sixth commandment for producers: *"haga atractivo su puesto y la feria."* The figures in the image accompanying this commandment are not wearing their "civilian clothes" but are wearing their regional dress; ready for the expected cultural performance; and following all the rules connected to order, hygiene, and security. This also reflects the deliberate marketing of culture, albeit a particular, and "authentic," cultural representation.[75] At the workshop, Carlos told producers that as they are part of broader campaigns for Marca Perú, they must understand that Mistura and other agricultural fairs are also about selling culture. "We have to make ourselves beautiful because we are selling culture. Just as we celebrate it, we sell it so that the consumer can fall in love." As he said this, an image of Andean dancers in traditional dress performing at one of the bioferias flashed on the screen behind him.

During our interview, Carlos spoke to the importance of crafting a particular image of the producer, both for consumers (as a way to sell) and for producers (as a way to raise their self-esteem and revalorize their work and worth). And here, visual representation is crucial. "We have realized that the number of photographs we take of the agricultural producers is fundamental," he said. "It has created a beneficent, revalorized image of the faces that feed us. Therefore, they are no longer anonymous because there is someone on the other side of the camera saying, hey, this work is important." Untroubled by the fact that in actuality most of these photographs avoided naming the subjects photographed and thus were literally anonymous, he went on to describe the importance of understanding how to "transform diversity into an opportunity": "We must see diversity not as an obstacle, but as an opportunity. For example, people say, I want a chirimoya, but the chirimoya is ugly on the outside; it looks like a dragon with all its deformities. How do we transform that fruit, with all the obstacles it has, such as its ugly appearance. . . . [H]ow do we transform it into a possibility? It's like the producer. We can create pretty faces."

And as an example, he pointed to the various banners throughout Mistura with redeeming images of producers and rural families, all smiling, all wearing appropriate attire, and all in Andean fields. Apega's symbol (a red rocoto) was displayed prominently in the center of each banner, and below each image were phrases like "Peruvian agriculture: challenge and opportunity," and "Labor in the fields is savored at the table." The countryside and its inhabitants are redeemed (and consumed) in these images.[76] As the stewards of the nation's agricultural wealth, they literally carry Apega's seal of approval. They are the clean, smiling faces of Peru's gastronomic revolution.

CONCLUDING REFLECTIONS

This chapter has underlined the performative and dramaturgical dimensions of the culinary boom. As in theater, the staging of these gastropolitical performances is key. Everyone must know their place and their lines. Costumes and props must be just right, and the players must be aware of the gaze of the audience; aware, as Desmond puts it, that tourists (and in this case, Limeños who are there to experience a "different" Peru) have "purchase[d] the right to look."[77] I would add that in this case, they have also purchased the right to touch, taste, smell, and "feel" the other. As bell hooks might put it, in this context, "ethnicity becomes spice, seasoning that can liven up the dull dish that is mainstream white culture."[78]

Like other activities conducted under the tourists' gaze, "gastronomy is a display case," with many bodies on display.[79] There is great attention to detail in these performances, and listening to those managing them, it would seem that they are working well. Beyond cultural or even monetary success, however, these practices can also be considered "successful" in enacting the kind of colonial multiculturalism described by Elizabeth Povinelli:

> [M]ulticultural domination seems to work ... by inspiring subaltern and minority subjects to identify with the impossible object of an authentic self-identity; ... a domesticated nonconflictual "traditional" form of sociality and (inter)subjectivity. As the nation stretches out its hands. ... indigenous subjects are called on to perform an authentic difference in exchange for the good feelings of the nation and the reparative legislation of the state. But this call does not simply produce good theater, rather it inspires impossible desires: *to be* this impossible object and to transport its ancient prenational meanings and practices to the present in *whatever* language and moral framework prevails *at the time of enunciation*.[80]

The "staging of authenticity," then, is crucial not just as a mechanism to market culture and nation, but because it serves as "an ideological framing of history, nature, and tradition; a framing that has the power to reshape culture and nature to its own needs."[81] And as Desmond has argued, "[T]he physical presence of *some* bodies, not others ... functions as the ultimate grounding for these notions of the 'authentic.'"[82] Despite claims that Mistura is a horizontal space where all are equal, the bodies on display, and the performances they offer, suggest instead that this is a stage for the performance of social hierarchies as they should be. People "become signs of themselves"; they are in just the right place: smiling, clean, and compliant producers are in El Gran Mercado; performers dance in "appropriate" traditional Native dress; and famous chefs perform their craft and offer inspiring manifestos to adoring crowds.[83]

Despite claims of inclusion and equality, then, there is reason to be skeptical about just how much of that is being accomplished. Just after Acurio walked onto the stage to deliver his speech at the end of the producer-training workshop, two Andean producers, a man and woman, dressed in their "authentic" regional clothes, were hurried onto the stage with the great chef. They stood by his side as he spoke, as he answered questions, and as the crowd applauded, but they were never named and never spoke. The next morning, all of the major Peruvian newspapers carried the photograph of Acurio with these authorized figures, visually reflecting the chef's willingness to share the stage with Indigenous bodies. During my conversation with Carlos, he told me that one of Apega's slogans is that "diversity now has a first and last name." When I asked what he meant by that, he answered: "In other words, it isn't just saying that a Native potato comes from a particular community nine kilometers from the city of Puno where 90 families have lived for five centuries, but that the man who harvests those potatoes is called Moises Choque." He continued, telling me that restaurants in Lima now list the names of producers next to the products they sell. I have been to countless restaurants in Lima and have yet to see this, so I asked him for a list of those restaurants that showcase producers by name. He responded that maybe this was something chefs and others in support of Apega's vision were still aspiring to.

Perhaps. But here I want to return to Povinelli's point about the coloniality of multiculturalism and her argument that the performance of authenticity isn't just "good theater," but that it in fact "inspires impossible desires: *to be* this impossible object." In his work on development, agriculture, and the cultivation and care of the self in South India, Anand Pandian calls attention to development as "a matter of moral as well as material aspiration" in which the lived experience of subjects "reveals development as both a project of government and a work upon the self, an endeavor that seizes bodies and materials, but also desires, habits, and feelings."[84] Indeed, producers are more than mere props, and it would be inaccurate and even harmful to suggest that they are only the docile bodies required by the current regime of gastronomic governmentality. As always, the reality is more complicated and the agency of Indigenous peoples more intricate and nuanced than I have discussed thus far. What are some ways in which local producers navigate such "impossible desires," contest elite structures and discourses, and use them for their own projects and purposes? Can the valuing of products, of producers, offer tangible possibilities for change? For improved livelihoods? How do producers navigate the politics of recognition and inclusion that so often in fact reinforce neoliberal regimes and (settler) colonial domination? In the following chapters, I explore some of these tensions and consider the potential for a realigning of the "terms of recognition" as producers and others negotiate exclusionary terrain and create spaces of possibility.[85] While thus far I have explored the gastronomic boom "from above," the next section explores what I call narratives from the edge, narratives that open up alternative spaces within the gastropolitical frame, some enabled by this movement and others in contradistinction to it.

PART TWO

Narratives from the Edge

"Apega Needs Us to Look Pretty"

THE MORNING AFTER Apega's workshop for producers, I attended a workshop organized by the leadership of ANPE, one of the two producer organizations that had formed an alliance with Apega. The workshop took place in El Gran Mercado, next to several stands assigned to producers affiliated with ANPE. It was early in the morning, and as I walked through the market only a handful of producers were already there, preparing their stands and themselves for the day. I wasn't exactly sure where to find ANPE's stands, but then I heard voices and laughter and followed those sounds.

I arrived just as ANPE's president opened the workshop. He spoke briefly, reminding the dozen or so producers present about the purpose of this workshop, which was to practice the kind of self-presentation and approach to selling that Apega demanded. "Apega needs us to look pretty." He continued. "We need to change our look (*cambiar la cara*), offer a prettier face, smile, be polite, be clean. We need to convince the client, to flirt. But remember," he added, "what matters to us is selling. Think about who comes to Mistura, who these people are and what they expect. Sell them that but find a way to get our agro-ecological message across as you do." He went on to remind producers that if they didn't sell, they would not be able to cover the expenses already incurred during their trip to Lima and would not be able to return. He then reminded everyone that Apega deploys "secret evaluators" who pretend to be customers, "but really, they are checking up on us, watching us. Remember," he told them, "Mistura is for you to sell, not for you to walk around enjoying yourselves and drinking beer."

Producers then divided into groups to play out different scenarios. One of the young women I was standing next to during the president's comments smiled at me, grabbed my hand, and said "come with us. You can be one of our buyers." Over the next hour, we practiced various selling techniques, what to say and not to say. When ANPE leadership was near, producers practiced dutifully, always laughing and giving each other advice. But when leadership was out of earshot, producers relaxed, poked fun at each other, and spoke more freely. "Can you believe this is what we have to do?" asked the young woman who had invited me to join them. "We have to smile constantly. My face hurts at the end of the day." An older man, also in our group, nodded, adding that producers too should be able to enjoy strolling through Mistura. "I am up since 4:00 a.m. preparing for the day, setting up, then selling. Why can't I take a break and if I feel like it, enjoy a beer sitting by the ocean?"

FOUR

Gastropolitics Otherwise

STORIES IN AND OF THE VERNACULAR

vernacular—adjective

1. *(of language) spoken as one's mother tongue; not learned or imposed as a second language.*
   0.1 *(of speech or written works) using the mother tongue of a country or region. "vernacular literature"...*
2. *(of architecture) concerned with domestic and functional rather than public or monumental buildings. "vernacular buildings"*

Origin. Early 17th century from Latin vernaculus "domestic, native" (from verna "home-born slave") + -ar.[1]

THUS FAR IN THIS BOOK, what I have been calling "gastropolitics" has focused on top-down, elite-driven dynamics. Previous chapters have described how high-profile celebrity chefs, state officials, journalists, political elites, and wealthy tourists come together to make haute cuisine the latest way for the world to consume Peru. This framing of gastropolitics captures a crucial dimension of what is, in my view, a structure of extraction and accumulation. However, this characterization is perhaps too monolithic, as it overlooks the internal tensions and alternative spaces within the gastropolitical complex. If we are open to seeing differently, at the edges of the gastropolitical machinery of celebrity chefs and festivals, new possibilities emerge. Indeed, even within the workings of this structure, there are possibilities for surprising forms of agency and perhaps even resistance to the dominant logic of the current mode of culinary nationalism.

This chapter turns from monumental gastropolitics toward what we might call everyday or vernacular forms of gastropolitics. In doing this, I have been influenced by other scholars who theorize vernacular forms of political agency. For example, in his work on Indigenous local politics in northern Ecuador, Rudi Colloredo-Mansfeld develops the idea of "vernacular statecraft" to describe the use of the state's own "habits of governing" to promote Indigenous development and to organize uprisings against the state itself.[2] The utility of thinking in the vernacular lies not only in the linguistic ideas of everyday local communication but also in the architectural understanding of the vernacular, in which "builders imitate and appropriate standard elements of widely used design, adapting them for local conditions."[3]

In an attempt to get at some of these dynamics, this chapter explores the performative work of two cultural agents: an agricultural producer and a young chef, both of whom work from within the gastropolitical complex. In labeling both as performers, I don't mean to suggest that their expressions are not genuine. I simply want to signal that they are attentive to the ways in which they are seen. Thus, they also help us be attentive to other ways of seeing. Specifically, they help us move beyond the easy binary framing of "above" and "below," or the related opposition of hegemonic and counter-hegemonic. These actors complicate those stark separations. Even as their work seems to operate against the hegemonic forces of the complex, it is nevertheless still a kind of gastropolitics that upholds this state-led culinary project. If gastropolitics calls attention to difference in order to control it and make it safe, some of those working within the spaces of gastropolitics call attention to the boom's claims of social inclusion by both performing and critiquing that claim, moving between "hidden and public transcripts."[4] Or considering one more metaphor, we might see how these cultural agents, with roots in Andean and Indigenous worlds, occupy a kind of "third space" in the sense Kevin Bruyneel explores for Native nations navigating sovereignty in the United States.[5] In other words, this chapter offers an immanent critique of the boom and explores some unexpected opportunities that have been opened up by the tensions and contradictions within the gastropolitical apparatus.

"WE HAVE MADE OURSELVES VISIBLE":
NAVIGATING RESISTANCE AND COMPLIANCE

During one of my visits to Mistura, I spoke with a representative from the board of directors of the National Association of Ecological Producers of Peru (ANPE), a woman from Cusco whom I will call Aida.[6] We had coordinated our meeting over the phone as she was busy preparing for ANPE's participation at El Gran Mercado, so that conversation was brief. But I was struck by the way it ended. After I had introduced myself and we had quickly discussed logistics (where and when we would meet, for how long she could speak with me), Aida said, "[I]t's good that you are investigating the boom, and that you are a woman. Our voices are important." Before I could respond, she hung up.

Two days later, I met Aida at one of ANPE's produce stands in El Gran Mercado. We had not yet met in person, but as soon as she saw me approaching, she smiled widely and waved me over. "María Elena?" she asked, her warmth immediate, sincere. After introducing me to several of the producers setting up the stand in preparation for the day, she told them she was going to speak with me briefly (*por un ratito*) but would be back soon to help. We walked away from the market, toward the edges of the festival, and sat at a bench. We could smell the ocean from there, the sound of the waves a soothing backdrop to our conversation.

On the phone, I had told Aida that I was interested in the boom, and in particular, how the boom supported Indigenous producers like her. Was food in Peru a social weapon, and gastronomy the driver of a revolutionary movement focused on social inclusion, as so many proponents claim? As soon as we sat down to talk, she said, "I have been thinking about your question, and I think this boom, and this alliance between ANPE and Apega, has helped make us visible." Then she asked, "[A]re you taping this? You need to tape this." I told her I was and placed my phone closer to her, showing her the recording. She smiled, nodded, and then rephrased her point. "We have made ourselves visible (*nos hemos visibilizado*)." She continued:

> As I was saying, this union with Apega has helped us because it has made it easier to get to the consumer; it has helped consumers, and the country, finally recognize, in some way at least, the small-scale producer (*productor de agricultura familiar*). This is a basic point—without the producer gastronomy does not exist. But before we were not seen. Now, when Acurio talks, or Apega publishes articles about small scale agriculture and producers in *El Comercio*, people here (*la gente de aquí*), consumers, react. In some way, their consciousness is raised (*se concientizan*). We have made ourselves visible. And this is complemented by El Gran Mercado, where we have a space to make visible our biodiversity, the richness of our products. *We* have made ourselves visible. [Here, Aida moved from her refrain, *nos hemos visibilizado*, to emphasizing the agency of producers: *nosotros nos hemos visibilizado*.] But, in market terms, in national market terms, we can't say we are recognized. We still don't receive fair prices, even though they [Apega] talk about fair prices. If producers still can only receive two soles per kilo of native potatoes, then

consumers are not in fact more conscious (*no están tomando conciencia*). And the state still does not consider the small-scale producer; the state does not consider us human; a human group whom they can support, invest in. They don't help us develop our productive capacities.

There is so much to unpack in Aida's words. Her continuous refrain—"we have made ourselves visible"—signals her understanding of the significance of cultural agency and political recognition, of staking out a space that allows producers to be *seen*. During our conversation, Aida offered a nuanced engagement with the politics of visibility, expertly navigating the complexities of representation in the context of the boom and its hegemonic discourses and practices. She was very clearly aware of the persistent gaze she and other producers must contend with in order to participate in this culinary revolution. In other words, she knows others are watching, and that she must present herself and small-scale agricultural producers in specific ways and from within a specific frame.[7]

Aida's words resonate with Jorge Coronado's work on photography and agency in the Andes. While Coronado's focus is on the politics of self-representation among subaltern subjects in the southern Andes during the early to mid-twentieth century, his exploration of the ways Indigenous and mestizo men and women utilized photography to create visual documentations of their aspirations, of their personal engagements with modernity, resonates with Aida's insistence on voice. When she asked if I was recording, she was not just interested in my listening to her, but in my documenting her words and including them in this book. Coronado uses the term *self-fabrication* to describe the hidden agency in some of the photographs he encounters, in which racialized subjects are posing in ways that could be read as imitations of the observed behavior of dominant classes. Yet Coronado suggests that these photographs could be understood instead as acts of self-fabrication, attempts by miners, Indigenous women, and others to "codify and own the transformation they were experiencing."[8] In other words, these photographs, and the self-representations they reflect, can be read as agential cultural practices.

Similarly, Aida's discourse moved carefully but confidently between hegemonic and subaltern frames. Beginning by naming Apega and Acurio as allies, as supporting small-scale agriculture through work with both producers and urban consumers (*gente de aquí*), Aida was then able to emphasize the cultural and political agency of producers (*nos hemos visibilizado*), and then to highlighting the "we" in that formulation (nosotros *nos hemos visibilizado*). This subtle move was in fact significant in marking the difference between the performance of gratitude for Apega's inclusion of producers, for their "help" in making producers visible, and the signaling of Indigenous autonomy and ability to represent themselves. Even while working within dominant frames, Aida's words offer a different kind of performance of power, one that, as James Scott describes in his study of domination and resistance, "uncovers contradictions, tensions, and immanent possibilities."[9]

Even as Aida emphasized the newfound visibility of producers, she also expressed an acute awareness of the limits and complexity of recognition (even despite the boom's claims, producers still do not receive fair prices for their products) and of both the contemporary political context and the deep racial and colonial histories of Peru ("the state still does not consider the small-scale producer; the state does not consider us human"). This last point on histories of dehumanization (and I would add animalization) of Indigenous peoples could be read as a radical critique of the state, one that aligns with those more directly challenging the brutality of Peru's neoliberal project as evidenced by the continuous exploitation and extraction of Indigenous lands or the criminalization and murder of Indigenous environmental activists. But Aida moved this critique quickly and immediately to what amounts to a more compliant demand embedded precisely within neoliberal frameworks ("the state does not consider us a human group *whom they can support, invest in. They don't help us develop our productive capacities*). In some ways, this move placed Aida firmly within the frame of the "authorized Indian," a subject that, if supported by the state, might be content with enabling not just the status quo but continued repression against her "unruly Other."[10]

Put another way, however, as Scott has argued, "short of actual rebellion, powerless groups have . . . a self-interest in conspiring to reinforce hegemonic appearances."[11] The key word here is "appearances." What looks like conformity or complicity can in actuality be closer to subversion, albeit subtle. And it is in exploring these subtle cultural performances (discursive or otherwise) that move between hidden and public transcripts that we can begin to think with and about the spaces that open up when we move beyond seeing authorized or "unauthorized" subjects, or between resistance and compliance. Doris Sommer calls this the "wiggle room" offered by cultural agency, wiggle room that suggests a "preference for caginess over confrontation. The preference admits that opponents have greater weight and force, so that heroism is foolhardy and good sense demands creative options."[12] Indeed, she continues, "asymmetry is not news to the poor; their challenge is to make advantageous alliances even when equality doesn't enter into the bargain."[13]

This, I would argue, is precisely what Aida was trying to signal. ANPE's alliance with Apega works, even as it does not necessarily translate into material recognition for their labor, and even as it perpetuates particular histories of dehumanization and marginalization. We can read her conversation with me as a discursive act or performance, as an act of cultural agency, or of "self-fabrication." For Coronado, this kind of self-fabrication or self-representation might offer a mode of resistance or, importantly, a model for moving beyond resistance or survival to *resilience*, or what Anishinaabe scholar Gerald Vizenor has called *survivance*.[14] For Vizenor, "survivance is an active sense of presence, the continuance of Native stories, not a mere reaction, or a survivable name. Native survivance stories are renunciations of dominance, tragedy and victimry."[15] Shortly after Aida told me she thought the state could do more to invest in producers, she clarified that she was not talking about "handouts," and she was certainly not performing victimization:

> In this sense, there is still no real social inclusion, a real and concrete inclusion that supports small-scale agriculture. With this boom we have managed to make the producer visible, but the problem is that we are seen as clinging to our lands (*aferrados a nuestras tierras*), being almost part of our lands, and we can't move from there. They don't want us to move from there. But let me be clear. By support I mean professional development, financial investment, not *asistencialismo*. I don't like it when we victimize ourselves (*a mi no me gusta que nos victimizemos*). It enrages me, it makes me angry, when they call us "oh poor little ones" (*Me da rabia, me da colera, que nos digan "hay pobrecitas"*). I am disgusted when they call me poor, no, poor is the Devil, I say (*Me enchincha que me digan pobre, no, el pobre es el Diablo digo yo*).

Once again, Aida's powerful declarations offer important insights into the ways Indigenous producers grapple with their tenuous position in contemporary Peru. On the one hand, she astutely recognized that the marginal status of Indigenous producers is in fact central to Peru's gastropolitical project. Gastronomy can be a weapon of social inclusion only if producers continue to exist *as* Indigenous producers and as subjects in continuous need of state recognition and support. Moreover, she complicated the idea of visibility. Becoming visible, being finally recognized as crucial actors in the national stage, matters. But *how* they are seen, who controls the framing of the producer's image, matters just as much, if not more. On the other hand, her statements against *asistencialismo* aligned squarely within gastropolitics' neoliberal ideology. She still participated in, and at least performed support for, Peru's gastropolitical project, a project that, as we have seen in the previous chapters, is in many ways yet another example of the coloniality of power in Peru.

But this seemingly contradictory engagement with gastropolitics is in many ways not surprising. Coronado notes that resistance from alterity, or from "the outside," is not necessarily the place from where the "most power-ful forms of contestation" might reside.[16] "More than resistance and refusal," he writes, "the photographic practices that are deeply a part of subalterns' experience and negotiation of modernity are just that, a reflection of how tenaciously subaltern subjects enact strategies that allow them access to the fruits of modernity."[17] Aida was most certainly demanding consideration as a modern subject, one with equal access to technological innovation and professional development and equal ability for social advancement. To put it slightly differently, Aida's discursive performance could be read as toggling between self-fabrication and self-determination, enacting precisely the kind of "survivance story" Vizenor writes about. Aida's fiery rejection of being labeled poor or being seen as "stuck" to the land, and her self-presentation as a subject who can demand recognition and material support, speaks directly to the assertion of "Native presence" and the "renunciation of dominance" so central to Native survivance for Vizenor. She also can be read as perform-ing what Dakota Sioux historian Philip Deloria terms "counternarratives of Indian modernity," or "Indian stories about Indian encounters with and actions on a modern world."[18]

Along these lines, Aida's comments about Indigenous producers' con-nection to land are provocative and complex. Let's consider her words once again: "With this boom we have managed to make the producer visible, but the *problem* is that *we are seen as clinging* to our lands, being almost part of our lands, and we can't move from there. They don't want us to move from there" (emphasis added). Some might read here a surprising refusal of Indigenous relations to land, even a betrayal, perhaps, of Indigenous peoples throughout Peru resisting the continued invasion and destruction of their territories by mining, logging, industrial agricultural production, and other extractive industries. But an alternative reading uncovers a resistance to dominant and pervasive representations of "poor and dirty Indians," of histories of race, labor, and coloniality that anchor Indigenous peoples to land as subjugated workers. Aida was not diminishing the importance of Native lands to Native peoples; such a position would be profoundly self-defeating for someone whose work and life have been devoted to the livelihoods of agrarian Andean communities. Rather than denying the importance of Native roots in their lands, I understood Aida to be making a compelling claim about the equal importance of Native *routes*.

Andean peoples have long been in relation to lands, but not in any static or fixed way. Indeed, as John Murra's famous phrase the "vertical archipelago" made clear, the survival of Indigenous peoples in the Andes depended on mobility across various ecological zones.[19] In deploying the metaphor of the archipelago, Murra (perhaps unintentionally) drew up alternative geographies of indigeneity from seafaring peoples in Oceania, where Native peoples have developed sophisticated navigation technologies for moving across vast distances.[20] What Aida seemed to be really concerned about were efforts to limit and control Indigenous mobility. It was clear to me when we spoke that she was keenly aware of the ways in which gastropolitical representations sought to contain and constrain "the producer" through idealized visions of feudal orders, where Indigenous peoples labored on land controlled by White or mestizo landowners. As noted in chapter 3, in the gastropolitical imaginary Indigenous peoples are transformed into productive laborers, agricultural laborers who support, and in fact enable, the gastronomic revolution through the care and harvesting of Native products and their defense of Peru's biodiversity. But she knew this was still a project that enabled the appropriation of Indigenous labor and products.

Furthermore, when Aida stated "we can't move from there. They don't want us to move from there," she was not only referencing gastropolitical expectations about where Indigenous producers belong (and where they do not), but also the inability or unwillingness to imagine indigeneity otherwise. She was refusing, albeit in an entirely distinct context, what Deloria calls "reservation fixity."[21] Examining the willing participation of Native peoples in Wild West shows and in film companies in the late 1800s and early 1900s, Deloria writes: "Reservation regimes . . . meant to fix Indian subjects in place and make them visible through rolls, inspections, and institutional oversights. . . . In the midst of reservation fixity, the Wild West promised extraordinary mobility, and commentators have been right to point to it as a form of escape from agency surveillance."[22] Andean Peru, of course, has different histories and geographies from the North American "Wild West," but what connects settler colonial experiences across the hemisphere and the world are efforts to control Native bodies and dispossess Native lands. Aida was not saying that land does not matter. She was resisting neocolonial hierarchies that fix Indigenous peoples in a particular place and time. In demanding access to technological innovation, professional development, and calling for financial investment on the part of the state, she was perhaps also envisioning an alternative political arrangement that could include a revalorization of Indigenous relations to land and to networks of labor and kin that require mobility across archipelagos that are not only vertical, but also horizontal, and that connect Andean, Amazonian, and coastal spaces. Aida was making a powerful claim about Indigenous navigation of complex political and economic terrains, and she was doing so through what I understood as a skilled performance and storytelling, providing a political voice that she insisted be archived by my recorder and amplified by my writing.

Doris Sommer notes that "a focus on art reveals the charm of unpredictable moves as evidence of autonomous subjects, since a creative gesture literally becomes a per-sona; that is, a device to project the human voice."[23] The projection of voice, visibility, and strength was central to Aida's script. Hers was the performance of a gifted cultural agent, or as Macarena Gómez-Barris would perhaps call her, a "submerged theorist." In her exploration of what she calls "the extractive zone," or sites of rampant extractive capitalism, Gómez-Barris foregrounds such "submerged perspectives" as a way of "engaging the possibility of renewed perception."[24] In addition to documenting the advance of extractive capitalist power, she is interested in "analyzing the complexity of social ecologies and material alternatives" and of "pushing away from a paradigm of mere resistance into the more layered terrain of potential, moving within and beyond the extractive zone."[25] In avoiding terms like *compliance* and *resistance* and emphasizing instead the multilayered textures of engagement with and performance of power, Aida crafted an alternative (gastro) political narrative, one that perhaps offers the possibility of "renewed perception" or even of a rearticulation of the terms of recognition.

Midway through our conversation, Aida suddenly said, "[T]he [male] producer has been made visible, but the female producer has been made invisible (*se ha visibilizado al productor, pero a la productora se la ha invisibilizado*). I asked what she meant by that, and she emphasized her point: "There is no support for the true empowerment of women. They only offer gender workshops, but a workshop is not a solution. They think that because the workshops include 50% men and 50% women they are doing something; that if there is a male teacher, there should be a female teacher, and if there is male manager, there should be a female manager. But what does that mean? They give the woman a desk to sit in, and they give the man power. He makes the decisions. You understand."

That "you understand" landed squarely where she intended, noting that it was important that I, as a woman, write about the boom, about her and her work. Acutely aware of the complexity and challenges of gender politics at multiple levels, Aida continued, noting first the familiar conflict between (heterosexual) partners when women take on leadership roles or challenge patriarchal dynamics, before moving on to a critique of the state. "I have lived this very closely, seen women begin to awake and develop themselves as leaders, but that is when their partner resists, says we are abandoning our children. The husband wants a maid at home. Wants her to be available during the day, and the night, like a concubine. But we say, I am a mother, but also a woman . . . and by empowering myself, that is what will in fact help my children get ahead and do something for society." And she continued: "But as I was saying, at the level of the state, they don't understand women, they don't understand the female producer. I was just at a workshop on gender and climate change, but only the MIDIS [Ministry of Development and Social Inclusion] was there. Where were the ministries of education, health, agriculture? . . . These workshops don't help me. Instead, why doesn't the state give women the tools so they can work from within their own reality (*desde su propia realidad*)? That would be closer to social inclusion."

With these words Aida offered a forceful critique of gendered development politics and policies in Peru. Keenly aware of the many development initiatives in Peru that in fact perpetuate social hierarchies (rather than alleviating marginalization) and of the particularly disadvantaged location of women (especially Indigenous, migrant, and poor women), Aida's analysis resonated with academic critiques about the governmentality of development and the "management of poverty."[26] She was theorizing from experience, from life, as Dian Million might put it.[27] Her sophisticated analysis also included a critique of women, who she said were sometimes also "machistas" and even "enemies of our gender." She included herself in this, reminiscing about moments when she had placed her late husband's concerns over the needs of her compañeras. "We need to reflect, and as much as we possibly can, we need to be in solidarity with other women (*ser solidarias con otras mujeres*), support one another, and not just in the fields, but also in the city. This is how we make ourselves visible." In Aida's formulation, making oneself visible was intimately tied to empowerment on one's own terms, moving beyond generic workshops to more concrete technological support and to solidarity among women. Importantly, this included a recognition of women's mobility, and of Indigenous mobility, as we saw earlier. The reference to supporting women "also in the city" spoke to this and pointed to the recognition of the vulnerability of women in cities, particularly in the peri-urban regions of Lima.

Listening to the interview with Aida, I am struck again and again by the power of her critique and the astuteness of her performance as a producer working in alliance with Apega. She is certainly not the docile subject whom Apega, Acurio, and others see themselves "helping," nor does she embody the compliant figure of the producer projected by the gastronomic revolution's media machine. Aida is shaping the form that support takes, painstakingly crafting the contours of social inclusion, and of women's inclusion, as much as she is able to. In certain moments, and in certain ways, that translates into alliances with gastropolitical elites.

"LET'S EMBED SOME MESSAGES": THE FITFUL RISE OF PALMIRO OCAMPO

Aida's strategic engagements with power brought to mind other performances that navigate compliance and resistance, albeit from entirely distinct social locations. Such is the case, I argue, of Palmiro Ocampo, a young chef, entrepreneur, and social-environmental activist who both embodies the promises of gastropolitical inclusion and calls attention to the limits of that inclusion. Using social media, television, and culinary performance, Ocampo makes visible some of the contradictions of the gastronomic boom, even as he is held up by gastropolitical elites as an example of the promise of this revolution.

Ocampo is the son and grandson of Andean migrants. Ocampo's grandparents and their young son (Ocampo's father) migrated to Lima from Andahuaylas, a province in the region of Apurimac in the south-central highlands, and (along with Ayacucho) one of the regions hardest hit during the political violence of the 1980s and 1990s. Ocampo is a member of the Generación con Causa, the so-called fourth generation of chefs described as the new ambassadors of Peruvian cuisine, and the generation that would consolidate the revolution's third phase. As their web page—hosted on Marca Perú's official website and created with support from the *New York Times* T Brand Studio— states, "The generation with cause is represented by more than 50 young cooks from Lima and provinces whose mission is to continue consolidating the bases of Peruvian gastronomy. These young cooks will maintain the tradition of our cuisine, and will take that cuisine to higher levels, supported by their curiosity and creativity to surprise the world responsibly through

Peruvian flavors. These talents of Peruvian cuisine will actively participate in the different international presentations to represent Peru, and to make their gastronomic proposals known."[28]

This description foregrounds the familiar global marketing of Peruvian cuisine, but, aligning perfectly with the goals of the revolution's third phase, the website also describes Generación con Causa as a campaign that will "position Peru as a country that . . . is committed to the eradication of hunger, sustainability, innovation, and the wellbeing of our society." Ocampo and his fellow chefs, then, are deeply embedded in Peru's gastropolitical project. In fact, they are tasked with consolidating Acurio's revolution and expected to quite literally wear Marca Perú's imprint on their chef's coats.

However, reading Ocampo as a "submerged theorist" (like Aida) working within and beyond the belly of the gastropolitical beast offers a framework for thinking both about those messages embedded in his culinary perfor-mance *and* about the performances themselves. Understanding the limits to gastropolitical claims of social inclusion and sustainable development, Ocampo uses his newfound place as one of the soldiers of this revolution to work toward these claims while simultaneously calling attention to (and working to undo) the limits of the boom. Rather than operating solely in terms of the metrics of global restaurant rankings or commercial success, his work opens up alternative spaces for cultural and political engagement and possibility. These are small cracks, to be sure, but significant ones that call attention to the coloniality of the gastropolitical project and renarrate social relations in Peru.

To begin with, it is worth exploring the chef's professional trajectory and what it reveals about his social location. The slang term *cachuleo* in Peru is often used to describe moving back and forth from one job to another, doing what you can to make ends meet, and most commonly refers to someone, particularly from the middle or lower-middle classes, who needs to improvise, be astute about how best to achieve their goals. When I think of Ocampo's trajectory, that term comes to mind.

Even a brief biographical summary suggests a familiar Peruvian story of mobility, both in the sense of the importance of internal migration as a sur-vival strategy and in that of the progress over various generations from being seen as *provincianos* (from the provinces) to being recognized as successful and productive members of an emerging professional class. After spending years at a military boarding school, Ocampo was studying medicine when he decided to shift gears and study cooking at Le Cordon Bleu in Lima. In an interview with the young host of *Mujer Emprendedora*, a blog for young women who are interested in starting their own businesses, he shares his experiences.[29] "I saved money, and once I passed my exams I traveled to Spain to work, starting from the bottom, washing dishes, and eventually landing a job as sous-chef (second in command) at the famous *El Celler de Can Roca*." After his time abroad, he returned to Lima in the early 2000s to work at La Rosa Naútica (a famous upscale restaurant in Lima operating since the 1980s). Here, he pauses and tells the audience how important it is to work in other spaces before thinking of developing your own project, and tellingly, that one should gain this experience by using the resources of others: "You must gain experience with others' money, with other people's resources."

After his time at La Rosa Naútica, he paired up with a graphic designer friend and started work on a project focused on cooking technology, such as anti-stain aprons. Their start-up boasted a stand at Mistura for three years, but eventually the business failed. This was in part because he wanted to go back to cooking. Inspired by René Redzepi's approach to food and cooking, he traveled to Denmark and landed a job at Noma, at that time considered the best restaurant in the world, where he also spent time working at the Nordic Food Lab with others like Virgilio Martínez.[30] He returned to Peru after this experience, but once again, instead of opening his own restaurant like many of his fellow chefs, he instead began working as a culinary consultant before agreeing to join another chef as an associate in order to open their own restaurant. However, due to issues with the municipality, they were not able to get a license or open their restaurant.[31]

Throughout this time, Ocampo began teaching in some of Lima's cooking schools, where he started thinking more seriously about what he is now most known for: culinary recycling. As he has mentioned in several interviews, from the time he was a student in cooking schools he was struck by the inordinate amount of food waste generated in these spaces. Once he was teaching, he began to "play" with leftovers, creating dishes that utilized every part of the ingredients considered "waste." Slowly he developed "alternative syllabi" to teach students how to use these leftovers, and his students gave him a nickname: *el chef reciclador* (the recycling chef). But once he opened his own high-end restaurant in Lima (1087 Restaurante), he felt the tension between his desire to utilize the entirety of ingredients and the expectations of high-end cuisine. Suddenly he had to adhere to those same gastronomic standards of which he had become so critical. "What high-end chef, with a restaurant in [the upscale district of] San Isidro, would decide to destroy his career by cooking with waste? Limeños would think I was serving them trash. That idea, of utilizing every part of the product, had to remain buried forever," he tells the audience at a TEDxTukuy talk in Lima.[32]

This last point is interesting, and it speaks to Ocampo's social location. For him, the opportunity to open his own restaurant in a district as exclusive as San Isidro was a dream, one that he "gave his life to," and that happened because he had worked hard to gain an international reputation. But the decision to bury his concern over food waste would not last long. Shortly after Ocampo opened his restaurant, Apega asked him to serve as a guide for the British food activist Tristram Stuart, who was traveling to Peru to give a talk at Mistura. During his TEDxTukuy talk, and once again hinting at his place in Lima's social hierarchy, Ocampo tells the audience that he had served as a Mistura guide once before, and he loved it because "they give you a driver, per diem, access to any place you can imagine, and you can eat in Lima's best restaurants *for free*!" But Stuart did not want to eat at any of Lima's renowned restaurants. He told Ocampo that he needed to offset the carbon footprint he had amassed by flying to Peru from London. Instead, they spent three days collecting food from farms and restaurants that would otherwise have been thrown away, then used every bit of it to make enough food to feed two hundred youths from marginalized backgrounds. Ocampo then tells the audience that shortly after that experience, he read an interview in *El Comercio* with Stuart, in which the British activist talked about Ocampo's ability to transform waste into amazing high-end dishes. "When I saw this, I regained my confidence, and I felt empowered to take this concept to my restaurant." It is worth noting Ocampo's need to be recognized (or in Aida's terminology, to be made visible) in order to feel "empowered." Importantly, this recognition came in the form of a White British man (and an article in *El Comercio* that mentioned him by name).

Finally, then, Ocampo began to promote his philosophy of culinary recycling (which, as he told me in January 2020, quickly changed to culinary optimization, a more precise formulation of his approach), and began his anti-waste and anti-hunger work in earnest. Most significantly, he cofounded the nonprofit organization Ccori with his wife, Anyell San Miguel. Ccori (which means "gold" or "treasure" in Quechua) advances what Ocampo and San Miguel call *cocina* óptima. On the organization's Facebook page, Ccori is described as promoting "the sustainable optimization of foods in our society. Our objective is to transform Peru into a territory that optimizes its gastronomic richness from a socio-environmental approach." To Ocampo and San

Miguel, this means three things: (1) reducing malnutrition among Peruvian children ("by optimizing foods, we rescue vital nutrients that can support child development"), (2) eliminating food waste ("we can rescue beneficial nutrients for people and promote a sustainable and socio-environmental culture"), and (3) working with the female cooks of Peru ("through professional workshops we can empower female cooks and offer them tools and techniques that can aid in their and their family's development"). The organization also works with people in carceral spaces, with university students ("teaching them about culinary recycling and raising the social and environmental consciousness of those who will be future leaders"), and in particular with women who run *comedores populares* (communal kitchens) throughout Peru. Moving beyond the restaurant as a site of intervention, Ocampo underlines the pedagogical dimension of his work in an effort to change the way cooking is understood across Peru's social classes, or as he puts it, "bringing the techniques of high cuisine down to earth."[33]

However, even after boasting his own high-end restaurant, emerging as *el chef reciclador*, being one of the most prominent chefs who make up the Generación con Causa, and serving as director of Mistura in 2016, Ocampo has faced some significant challenges. His restaurant, for instance, closed for lack of economic resources. Another telling incident involved a recent venture, Huevón Lima, a *marca* or initiative that was featured as one of the stands at Mercado 28 in Miraflores. Mercado 28 is a gastronomic market that features fifteen to twenty "innovative proposals" by young entrepreneurs. Huevón Lima, Ocampo's proposal (along with two other chefs) was explicitly designed to move away from *alta cocina* or fine dining (which, he notes during the interview with *Mujer Emprendedora*, "is all the rage, but only 1% of the population can access"). "This is a rebellion against gastronomy," he tells viewers. Importantly, 70 percent of proceeds from Huevón Lima were donated to a community in Puno (in the southern Peruvian highlands) via Ccori and the NGO Action Against Hunger. But after less than a year, the small initiative failed, and as of this writing it appears to be permanently closed. This seems to be largely due to the chefs' inability to register their name after INDECOPI, the National Institute for the Defense of Free Competition and the Protection of Intellectual Property, charged them with "immorality": "The denomination 'Huevón' violates the moral values and principles that are imperative in order to preserve the social order that guarantees the wellbeing of society; . . . the denomination . . . constitutes an expression that violates the harmony and respect that must exist between people. . . . We warn that granting this trademark registration . . . would offend against morality and good manners."[34]

The word *huevón* in the name is key here, as it refers both to the predominance of eggs (*huevos*) in their menu, and to a slang term that crudely translates as "a man with large testicles." The term is often used colloquially to address a male friend or to refer to someone as lazy or dumb. Ostensibly, INDECOPI's objection had to do with the vulgarity of this term. In emphasizing morality, *buenas costumbres*, and social order, the state identified Ocampo's venture as going directly against the hegemonic understanding of gastronomy and gastropolitics as forces that *uphold* social orders, which are of course always gendered and racialized. The hypocrisy in the denial of Huevón's trademark makes this clear, since other ventures, such as Jorge Benavides's *La paisana Jacinta*, a television show in which Benavides performs demeaning and racist representations of Andean women in Redface, have no trouble receiving state approval.

As I researched this incident, however, I wondered if INDECOPI's decision was not also related to the chefs' use of Huevón's Facebook page as a platform for challenging social orders and calling on others to protest over recent corruption scandals. In a Facebook post, Ocampo and his fellow chefs urge people to join Huevón in marching in the streets to call for the resignation of Peruvian attorney general Pedro Chavarry, who eventually stepped down due to his poor handling of the Obredecht corruption scandal that has toppled a growing number of politicians across South America. Or perhaps INDECOPI was responding to the posting, also on Facebook, of a short video titled "Por qué?," in which the narrator, a young woman, says, "[W]hen we were children, we were told to wake up early, get good grades, to not speak back, to not ask why (*¿por qué?*); we were told to be good children," as images of White children praying show on the screen. Quickly, the video turns to defiant proclamations by women saying that no one should tell them where to work, how to dress, how to behave, or what words they can use.[35] Again, these are clear statements against heteronormative, patriarchal, and conservative religious frameworks. And these are radical moves in a country dominated by conservative (even authoritarian, I would say) forms of Catholicism, including the ultraconservative religious order Opus Dei that until recently controlled the Archdiocese of Lima. Ocampo does not simply represent a new generation of chefs. As we will see more clearly later in the chapter, he represents a particular approach to gastropolitical work that deliberately tries to undo some of the gendered and racialized orders in which gastropolitics is deeply embedded and invested in reproducing.

"FUCK PERFECTION!" RECLAIMING
GASTRONOMY, REFRAMING *LO ANDINO*

During his TEDxTukuy talk in Lima, Ocampo tells the audience that the French transformed eating into gastronomy (into "high-end cuisine, art, pleasure, and culture") and in doing this taught us about "the search for perfection." But what that search for perfection means, he says, is that "high-end cuisine has taught us to waste and contaminate." He offers the example of precision cuts, which he says are one of the first lessons any student learns in any culinary school around the world. In the search for the perfect, standardized cut, students and cooks will keep only those cuts that are "perfect," tossing the rest into the garbage. And he continues, "[T]he funny thing is that the ingredient with which we most often learn about these precision cuts, is the potato ... that Peruvian tuber that once helped combat hunger in Europe." Rather than the familiar gastropolitical *celebration* of the use of a Peruvian product throughout the world, of the global commodification of a particular product, Ocampo instead highlights the global *exploitation* of the potato, that Native product that Peruvian sociologist and cook Isabel Alvarez has poetically described as "the forgotten sister of Peru's favorite son [corn]."[36]

The centering of the potato—quintessential Peruvian product—in this story of gastronomy as "waste and contamination" matters. "How can we talk about the success of our gastronomy," he asks, "when half our population is malnourished and does not have access to nourishing foods?" Ocampo shows a potato on the screen behind him. The potato is peeled, mutilated by small holes made by a melon baller or similar culinary instrument. "This is what we throw away," he says, "in our search for perfection." Later, he returns to this and makes a powerful point: "The original meaning of gastronomy is the relations between human beings, culture, and foodways, in harmony with the environment. But the cuisine we prepare today is inconsistent with this definition. This is why we say *fuck perfection*! That perfection that seeks only the perfect product, that discriminates against the ingredient for being different ... and that seeks precision before optimization."

The culinary optimization (or the optimal use of products and ingredients in order to minimize food waste) he is talking about is a key dimension of his culinary philosophy, and the driving force behind Ccori. It would be possible to read this approach as yet another example of neoliberal extraction. Ocampo is maximizing the use of products, extracting and utilizing as much as possible from them, and along the way creating a culinary niche for himself (much like Martínez did using ecosystems), marking himself as distinct from other celebrity chefs. But a closer reading of Ocampo's work, not just through Ccori but through the reality television series he participates in, *Cocina con Causa* (which debuted in August 2017), complicates such a reading.

During one episode of the show, filmed in Andahuaylas (the land of his grandparents), Ocampo features an eighty-five-year old Indigenous campesino, Máximo Altamirano, who continues to labor regularly in the fields and who is presented as a model of strength and wisdom. Their discussion is fascinating for a number of reasons, such as the clear shift in discourse from concerns over food security to food sovereignty.[37] In a Facebook post written after the filming of that episode, Ocampo makes his commitments transparent. He begins by establishing his family's relation to Andahuaylas, noting that his grandparents migrated from that province to Lima. He continues, noting that he grew up learning much about Andahuaylas and Indigenous agricultural producers from his grandmother, but also from Máximo Altamirano, who he says is still proud of his son, Jorge Altamirano, who was killed during the recent *paro agrario* (an agrarian strike motivated by the increasing importation of foreign potatoes to Peru). "In my country, famous for being the country of the potato, they import so many foreign potatoes that our campesino brothers do not receive any justice. What are we waiting for? Do we want more blood to flow? Do we want more families to leave agriculture due to terror? If you want to learn more about the labor of campesinos . . . watch *Cocina con Causa*." He ends the post with a photo of him with his uncle Humberto in Andahuaylas, noting that it was taken after a day of work in the fields, once the filming of the episode was over.

The photograph serves to reconnect Ocampo to Andahuaylas, not just the land from where his grandparents migrated, but the land to which he is still connected through family and labor. It would not be a stretch to link the discussion of waste and the Peruvian potato during Ocampo's TEDxTukuy talk to the metaphorical throwing away of Peruvian Indigenous products and labor; to the violence of marginalization that keeps Native, migrant, and other poor bodies malnourished; and to the violence that kills for demanding the recognition and valorization of Indigenous labor. Significantly, the reference to terror here is not just the terror of the Shining Path but also the brutality of state violence against those who dare to protest.

In the TEDxTukuy talk, during episodes of *Cocina con Causa*, and in various interviews, Ocampo moves seamlessly back and forth between locating himself squarely within the gastronomic revolution and fiercely critiquing

FIGURE 7. Screenshot of Facebook post with photograph of Ocampo and his uncle in Andahuaylas on January 10, 2018. Accessed April 22, 2020. Reproduced with permission from Palmiro Ocampo.

that same revolution, implying that it does not go far enough. He deliberately uses gastronomy as a site from which to enact a particular politics, one that operates within the "wiggle room" between hidden and public transcripts. During the interview with *Mujer Emprendedora* he tells viewers that "gastronomy offers an opportunity to utilize cuisine as a platform for a much more substantive message than talking only about taste and refinement (*lo rico, lo fino*). Peruvians see gastronomy all day, every day. So let's embed some messages there, like promoting a cuisine that is zero food waste and that fights against hunger."[38]

His explicit and open discussion about embedding messages reminded me of the work of Peruvian political artists, and in particular the work of painter, architect, and silk-screen artist Alfredo Márquez. Years ago, in a summer program that I codirect on art and politics in Peru, our University of Washington students visited Márquez's studio. He noted that art often contains "hidden codes" that are for viewers to find and interpret. As illustrated in his collaboration with Angel Valdez, called *Caja Negra* (*Black Box,* like the flight recorders in airplanes), Márquez uses a remarkable variety of materials and images to create a neobaroque representation of Peru's political past and future.[39] As Márquez writes, his work employs a "strategy of sublimated sedimentation, that is to say that it is as if there were a series of accumulated strata in friction with each other that emerge and hide simultaneously."[40] The objective of the work, however, is not detachment from the world but engagement with it. As he suggests, his images "interact with a reality whose field of action is not limited to aesthetic experience but also meant for critical reflection and political action.[41] As Márquez puts it forcefully, "We are in a semiotic war more than an ideological one. My struggle is for a new visual language."[42]

I would suggest that we can conduct a similar reading of Ocampo's use of the culinary arts and communication technologies for embedding codes that are also in friction with the dominant ones of the gastronomic boom. We can think of the dishes Ocampo creates by using the entirety of products, sometimes by showcasing the parts of products that are most commonly discarded, as a form of culinary artistry that encodes a particular message about waste and environmental politics. Another text from which to explore these encoded messages is the television show, *Cocina con Causa*.

The show is coproduced by Peru TV and the United Nations World Food Program and supported by private funds in addition to technical support from various ministries, including the Ministry of Development and Social Inclusion, and the Ministries of Health, Culture, Energy and Mines, Agriculture, Foreign Trade and Tourism. It is described by its producers as a place where chefs from the Generación con Causa offer solutions to problems of nutrition. Featuring Ocampo and six of his fellow chefs, and working alongside families, nutritionists, and other medical "experts," the show's objective is to raise Peruvians' awareness about the significance of "proper nutrition for the development of people and communities."[43] This description might evoke familiar narratives of privileged young people "teaching" others how to eat, and in that way, it would align with Apega's civilizing project and its emphasis on training producers how to lead "clean and healthy lives." This is in fact what I expected when I began watching the show (many of the episodes are available on YouTube). But instead, I found a subtle but clear challenge to dominant and demeaning characterizations of subaltern subjects (Indigenous peoples, Andean migrants and their children, residents of marginalized peri-urban regions of Lima) and a reframing of gastropolitics as a site from which to challenge social hierarchies and enact *relational* dynamics.

The show's first episode, titled "El Despertar" (The awakening), aired in August 2017 and was focused on combating anemia in the highland region of Puno. But as the first episode in the series, it also served as an opportunity to introduce not only the television series, but also Ocampo, his message, and his work. He begins by positioning himself as a cook (*cocinero*) whose first contact with cuisine was through his grandmother, a woman from Andahuaylas who arrived in Lima with her husband and through much hard work established her own *verdulería* (fruit and vegetable stand) on the first floor of their house. He tells the audience that he grew up between her *verdulería* and the produce market where, as a boy, he played and helped his grandmother run her stand. He describes the joy he felt in the midst of the smells, sounds, and tastes of the market; all this shaped his love of food.

This is a significant point. Not only is he locating himself as the grandchild of Andean migrants, he is also revalorizing the intergenerational relations and cultural dynamics that include children playing and sometimes supporting the work of parents and grandparents, or even working in places like produce markets. By linking this experience to his current location as Peruvian chef and member of the Generación con Causa, he is not only validating it (he is not a chef *despite* his background, but *because* of it); he is pushing against civilizing and racialized discourses in Peru that commonly demonize poor Brown women as the primary agents of their children's exploitation. Assumptions about poor women who, because of economic need, lack of education, or cultural "backwardness," send their children to work and don't care for them properly, have long shaped moralizing state interventions into the lives of communities throughout Peru, and especially in many of the peri-urban regions of Lima.[44] Ocampo tackles this head on by insisting that Ccori's main partners are "the most important cooks in the country," the women who organize and sustain the comedores populares, thirty-two hundred of which are in Lima alone.[45] Ocampo and San Miguel have foregrounded the work these women do as one of the most important examples in Peru of working for communities and against hunger and waste, as women maximize their use of products in order to feed as many people as possible. They have also "rebranded" comedores populares as *cocinas bondadosas* or "kind kitchens," a move that serves to reframe the image of women in marginalized communities and the meaning of *popular* in Peru.

Ocampo also forcefully challenges stereotypes in *Cocina con Causa*'s second episode, titled "Mujeres de Hierro" (Women of iron), featuring women who work in the comedores populares of Ventanilla, a district in the province of Callao (which is part of the Lima metropolitan area and considered one of the most dangerous places in Peru). The episode focuses on anemia and the high incidence of iron deficiency in the region. It features the tremendous work of mothers and grandmothers in Ventanilla, not just fighting for their young children's nutrition but simultaneously feeding their communities through their creative work as cooks in the comedores populares of that region. The episode highlights a few community projects, such as an organic garden and a hydroponic garden project, along the way also showcasing the markets of that region as important spaces with a tremendous variety of nutritional foods. At one point, one of the mothers with whom Ocampo and fellow chef Fransua Robles are working asks: "What are we going to learn?" Ocampo and Robles respond that they are not there to teach, but to exchange ideas. They spend time with several women, their children, and their grandchildren, talking with them, learning about their food preferences and concerns, and eventually elaborating a few dishes using local ingredients rich in iron, but which look more like the kind of fast food kids are drawn to. (One of the young girls they interview had noted that she didn't like fish but loved burgers.) The dishes, which include a burger made with a blue fish called "bonito," are a hit. Toward the end of the episode, Robles emphasizes the importance of local and intergenerational knowledge, telling the audience that he and Ocampo simply followed the guidelines offered by women who are already doing so much.

"Mujeres de Hierro" is striking for several reasons. First, the representation of women in precarious urban spaces as caring, strong, and fierce protectors of family and communities is an important corrective to more common and damaging stereotypes. It is also a subtle critique of assumptions about the lives of migrants and their children; of the so-called *desborde popular* (popular overflow), as Peruvian anthropologist José Matos Mar famously described the influx and impact of Andean migration into Lima in the mid- to late 1900s. In addition to the depiction of women as kind, resourceful, and important (albeit neglected) historical actors in Peru, the young kids featured in the show are represented as joyful, playful, and serious about their studies.[46] Without diminishing the precarity in which they live, kids are represented *as kids*. One does not find in this episode the all-too-familiar depictions of thieving youth or caricatures of poor children (or poorly cared for children). Instead, one sees young people who are vibrant and full of hope, kids who have specific dreams, dreams that their mothers try to help them achieve, even in the midst of crushing poverty. Moreover, the positive representation of market spaces in Ventanilla, sites with "beautiful and nutritional produce, and an excellent variety of fish and other meats," contrasts starkly with Apega's insistence on the need to "cleanse" and "beautify" markets throughout Peru, a position that connects directly with the historic portrayal of markets as unclean spaces of disease and contamination. In other words, *Cocina con Causa* provides vivid examples of what we could call the audiovisual poetry of the vernacular, revealing the beauty and strength of ordinary life and the possibilities that emerge from the materials and ideas that surround people in their communities.

RECLAIMING AND REFRAMING INDIGENEITY

Many of the themes explored in the show are directly linked to Ocampo's life. I had a chance to speak with Ocampo in January 2020. We met in the lobby of his apartment building in Magdalena del Mar and took a cab from there to Lurín (in the outskirts of Lima) to visit two of the comedores working with Ccori. During the two-hour ride there, we talked about his life journey, his role in Generación con Causa and the gastronomic boom, and what led him to Ccori. We spent hours at two different sites in Lurín—talking with women at each comedor, listening in on a training workshop in one, and checking up on a recently built kitchen in another—and then spent another few hours making our way back to Magdalena, this time talking about life, children, food, and more.

Throughout our conversations, Ocampo confirmed many of my assumptions about his location and politics. At first, he simply described his work as a chef and food activist, linking his current work at Ccori with a concern about food waste and social justice. But as the cab made its way closer to Lurín, closer to the parts of Lima where his own family had migrated to from the Andes many years ago, he began to open up. He told me he had never felt he "belonged" in the world of high-end cuisine. At first, he said, he had "rejected his roots" in order to fit in and got caught up in the world of celebrity chefs ("I was set on becoming the best chef in Peru"). But slowly he made his way back. His father and grandmother figure powerfully in his story of return as examples of Andean migrants who maintained traditions of reciprocity and community solidarity. His father had studied medicine and offered free consultations in their home to those who could not afford medical care. "I grew up witness to that kind of community support," he told me.

His grandmother, too, was a model of Andean resilience and strength and serves as a crucial link to Andahuaylas and the Andes more generally. In the episode of *Cocina con Causa* filmed in Andahuaylas, Ocampo spends time in the market, tasting and smelling the various local fruits, tubers, and vegetables, and talking with some of the market women. He notes the significance of being there, of that sensorial experience, as it takes him back to his childhood and his grandmother, linking him to his roots and traditions. As we learn, the filming of this episode allowed him to travel to Andahuaylas for the first time and offered an emotional experience of "return," despite his not having physically been there until that moment. While not a direct example of the experiences of Andean migrants in Lima discussed by Indigenous Peruvian author Pedro Pablo Ccopa, Ocampo's expressions of nostalgia, brought on by smelling and tasting products native to his ancestral land, resonate deeply with Ccopa's discussion of the significance of food to memory and the sensorial and gustatory dimension of Andean migrants' experiences in Lima.[47]

Returning to his work as chef, Ocampo told me his commitment was now entirely with Ccori and the women with whom he and others from the organization work. He makes ends meet by consulting and cooking at several restaurants and is continuously searching for financial support to sustain his work with comedores. But as he put it, this is where his heart is. He realized this when a fellow chef told him that if he wanted to be a real chef, he should do this work as a hobby. "He told me those women would never learn how to use real culinary techniques; that I should not waste my time teaching them. This upset me and I took it personally." Then immediately he said, "I know it wasn't personal, but it hurt, because I could have been a kid eating at one of those comedores." This was his world too. This work *is* clearly personal and also speaks to a desire to reconnect—to reconnect with Andean traditions of solidarity and community, and importantly, with one of his Native languages, Quechua.

This recognition of his connection (and commitment) to Andean life and language is also increasingly political. In the first episode of *Cocina con Causa*, after he introduces himself and his work, Ocampo travels to Puno in Peru's southern highlands, the region in the country, we learn, that is most impacted by anemia. The episode features the struggles of a teacher trying to provide breakfast and lunch for her students, and of members from a community who work from what they have available to ensure their children are eating nourishing foods. He spends time learning from them about their efforts and creative approaches, noting along the way the fact that the most effective ways to address issues of malnutrition are usually found within cultural traditions. Without explicitly using the term *sovereignty*, he begins to make a case for Indigenous food sovereignty. This in itself is a shrewd move, as Ocampo seems acutely aware of the common assumption in Peru that the problem is the "cultural backwardness" or "stubbornness" of Indigenous peoples and the paternalistic belief that the answer lies in Indigenous peoples *changing* their cultural traditions in order to better feed themselves and their families. Malena Martínez, Virgilio Martínez's sister, displays this logic clearly in an interview about Ocampo. When the interviewer asks Malena what she thinks of Ocampo's goals (achieving o percent waste in his kitchen and using culinary optimization to eliminate extreme hunger in Peru by 2030), she replies that his goals might be too ambitious: "Feeding 240,000 malnourished kids will require more than the work of one cook. It demands government engagement on national, regional and local levels and across several agencies. *Not to mention the challenge of persuading communities rooted in tradition to modify their diets and cooking habits.*"[48] There is no question that this is an ambitious goal that goes beyond the capacity of any single chef. Nevertheless, Malena Martínez operates within a framing in which Native communities are the problem and outsiders carry the promise of solutions. It is outsiders who must "engage" and communities that must be "persuaded."

Ocampo, however, has a different location for agency. He foregrounds Indigenous culinary and cultural knowledge as the key to some of the most pressing nutritional concerns in the country. He also frequently comments on the culinary *creativity* of Indigenous peoples. They are not just consuming food for survival; theirs is a cuisine that emphasizes taste and creativity. Moreover, culinary traditions matter beyond "security." They carry important cultural, religious, and social significance, and nourish not just the individual body but also ancestral spirits.[49] Similarly, Indigenous parents, community leaders, elders, and others have sophisticated understandings of international discourses around hunger and malnutrition that position Indigenous children as victims and Indigenous communities as unable to address nutritional concerns without "outside" help and training. Ocampo, with other Peruvian scholars, pushes back against this by foregrounding Indigenous cultural and culinary knowledge.[50] The conversation Ocampo has on camera with Máximo Altamirano, the eighty-five-year old Quechua man from Andahuaylas who lost his son to state violence, is particularly striking in this regard. Ocampo begins that conversation by commenting on how strong and "fit" Altamirano looks, despite his age, and he asks what he eats in order to stay so strong.

Altamirano then offers a clear and concise response: he eats Indigenous foods, what he and his family harvest, and then determines what he can sell. Others, he says, will sell the best crops and then eat leftovers or use the money from the sale to buy nontraditional (and non-nutritional) products (such as pasta, sugar, and rice) in town markets. "You'll see those men walking all bent over like this," he says, offering a demonstration of the effect of malnourishment on the body. "That's not a way to eat properly."

This is a radical claim in the context of a revolution that centers producers because, in the dominant gastropolitical framing, they provide their best products to chefs and city dwellers. In this counternarrative, then, Indigenous producers are foregrounded by their decision to consume grains, tubers, legumes, fruits, and other products from their own harvest *first*, placing support for their ability to sell the remainder of their products in urban spaces second to their own nutrition. In other words, fighting against hunger and malnutrition includes supporting the ability of Indigenous communities to have more control over how to manage their own resources. Ccori is described as an organization committed to food security and socio-environmental cuisine, but Ocampo and San Miguel seem to be keenly aware of the distinction between food security and food sovereignty. They are also clear on their message. The first episode of *Cocina con Causa* ends with Ocampo stating: "[I]t isn't anemia that kills, it is indifference." As he says this, the scene is of him and other community members, men, women, and children, playing volleyball. These are not idealized Quechua "ancestors" wearing their best traditional attire and smiling at the camera. They are real flesh and blood human beings.

In his TEDxTukuy talk, Ocampo tells the audience that the onion makes him cry, but not because of the onion's sulfides or acids. The onion, he says, "was the first ingredient who whispered in my ear, and told me, 'Palmiro, I am not a part of your many recipes. I *am* the recipe.'" He continues, noting that sometimes we think ingredients are only a part of our recipes. "But what happens," he says, "if we begin to see differently, and if we shift just a little of the established order of things." Here, Ocampo talks about "decoding" the onion, the banana, the lime, and other ingredients, separating their various components and understanding what each of those components has to offer. He poetically describes what happens when you cook the cellulose of the onion, that thin gauzy film that covers each of the onion's layers. "Cooked slowly, at 80 degrees, in oil, it transforms into a crunchy crystal, and when it makes contact with our palate and the humidity of our mouth, it disappears, leaving the pleasing and delicious flavor of the onion." Describing the onion as someone who whispers in his ear connects to Indigenous understandings of more-than-human life. In the Andes in particular, Indigenous epistemologies point to the potato, for example, as a living, sentient being.[51] This adds another layer to Ocampo's discussion of the potato as a being that is mutilated, discriminated against, and discarded in the name of gastronomy, and helps bring to the surface his critique of gastronomy as violently wasteful.

Ocampo's emphasis on the onion as a being who speaks, as a being who helped him see and feel differently, and on the multilayered stories that each ingredient conveys, is similar to the work of ethnobotanist Robin Wall Kimmerer, member of the Potawatomi Nation and director of the Center for Native Peoples and the Environment at the State University of New York College of Environmental Science and Forestry. Kimmerer describes plants, rocks, and earth as elders who speak and to whom she listens carefully.[52] "The rocks are beyond slow," writes Kimmerer, "beyond strong, and yet yielding to a soft green breath as powerful as a glacier, the mosses wearing away their surfaces, grain by grain bringing them slowly back to sand. There is an ancient conversation going on between mosses and rocks, poetry to be sure. About light and shadow and the drift of continents."[53] The care with which Ocampo engages specific plants, fruits, and tubers, and the seriousness with which he listens to these products, resonates with Kimmerer's powerful and provocative prose. As I listened to Ocampo, I could not help but think back to Martínez's work via Mater Iniciativa. The contrast between their approaches and narratives is striking, with a focus on discovery, extraction, classification, and the decontextualized exhibition of "unknown" Native plants on the one hand, and Ocampo's "decoding" on the other, which recontextualizes the product, making the onion, the potato, the banana, and the lime whole again. In other words, these are not *just* ingredients. These are whole beings who speak, who whisper in our ears, if only we are willing to shift just a little of the established order of things.

CONCLUDING REFLECTIONS

In her work on the role of Native actors, directors, and spectators in both shaping and resisting representations of Native peoples in Hollywood and ethnographic films, Michelle Raheja (Seneca heritage) develops the concept of "visual sovereignty" as part of an "attempt to see an alternate vision of Native American representation and spectatorship as products of a complicated and sometimes discomfiting history with a vibrant, equally complex future rather than only as abject repositories of the victimized."[54] As she puts it, "Native American film, video-makers, and cultural artists are doing more than simply resisting and surviving, they are interrogating the powers of the state, providing nuanced and complex forms of self-representation, imagining a futurity that militates against the figure of the vanishing Indian, and engaging in visual sovereignty on virtual reservations of their own creation."[55]

For Raheja, visual sovereignty is a strategy, a "reading practice for thinking about the space between resistance and compliance wherein Indigenous filmmakers and actors revisit, contribute to, borrow from, critique, and reconfigure ethnographic film conventions, while at the same time operating within and stretching the boundaries created by these conventions."[56] In other words, visual sovereignty, as a "creative act of self-representation," "simultaneously addresses the settler population by creating self-representations that interact with older stereotypes but also, more importantly, connects film production to larger aesthetic practices" that strengthen traditional ("although by no means static") forms of sovereignty and cultural understanding.[57] Like visual sovereignty, food sovereignty in this context can be thought of as a strategy for navigating "the space between resistance and compliance" where producers and activist chefs can reimagine the conventions of the gastropolitical complex.[58] While Raheja is working in a North American context, her work resonates with insights across the Americas, including those of Vizenor, Coronado, and others like Aida and Ocampo, who call for frames that reject victimization and recognize a more complex engagement with power, one that doesn't necessarily "look like" resistance but in fact speaks back to power. These cultural and political theorists point us to more nuanced understandings of the lives of subjects who participate in structures of power, and who through their participation can subvert, reframe, or open up "alternate visions" (Raheja) or "the possibility of renewed perception" (Gómez-Barris), by shifting "just a little of the established order of things" (Ocampo). If we read Acurio, Apega, and other gastropolitical elites as staging difference, as setting the terms for and framing the possibilities of action, Aida and other producers are acutely aware of this staging and perform their subjectivity in part by navigating between expected projections of agricultural producers and pushing against those same expectations. Along the way, they carve out space for alternative political possibilities and thinking gastropolitics otherwise.[59]

As I was writing this chapter, I came across an Instagram post by Agroferias Campesinas—a bioferia that takes place every Sunday in Lima—that brought back Aida's critique about the boom's invisibilization of female producers.[60] The post was on the undervalued and unrecognized work rural women engage in and on the significance (and impact) of empowering female producers. It was also an opportunity to note the group's work with a sister organization in Bolivia, as was illustrated by the accompanying image of two women leaders in the market, vice presidents of the Peruvian and Bolivian producer organizations. What is striking about this post is that it reveals precisely the alternative space made possible through the kind of skilled negotiation and strategic alliance that Aida reflected in our conversation and in her work with Apega. Agroferias Campesinas, currently administered by a nonprofit organization of Indigenous producers, began as an initiative developed by Apega in 2012. Originally called Ferias Agropecuarias Mistura, its goal was to promote small-scale agriculture, showcase Peruvian biodiversity, and support agricultural producers through weekly bioferias that would ostensibly reproduce the experience of Mistura's Gran Mercado. A brief Apega video from 2014 about the bioferia that features interviews with producers and clients aligns beautifully with Apega's civilizing ideology, as consumers point to the "cleanliness, order, and cordial workers," and producers speak not only to their gratitude for being able to sell their products directly to consumers but also to what they have learned: "I have learned how to treat and engage directly with the consumer."[61] In January 2018, six years after the bioferia was inaugurated, producers took over its administration and changed its name to Agroferias Campesinas. As a key member in the producer-Apega alliance, ANPE, the organization of which Aida forms part, played a crucial role in this transition and continues to work closely with producers at Agroferias and elsewhere.[62]

In some ways, producers must still adhere to some of the familiar expectations about self-presentation in order to maintain their client base. Most of those who buy at the bioferia are familiar with the benefits of organic (and agro-ecological) products and affluent enough to be able (and willing) to pay higher prices for those products.[63] They also have their own ideas about who producers are, what they look like, and how they should behave. As in Raheja's notion of visual sovereignty, Peruvian producers negotiate old stereotypes as they strengthen their own livelihoods and self-determination. Indeed, producers are now able to use the market itself as well as their website and social media sites as texts from which to encode more specific messages,

messages that go beyond Apega's general celebration of small-scale agricultural labor. Their publicizing of the connection with Bolivian producers was particularly interesting, as it fostered the possibility of transnational solidarity, something Native activists have been doing for decades, challenging old geographies of belonging and generating new maps of Indigenous futurity.

From a different location, Palmiro Ocampo too is opening spaces that allow for alternate, vernacular visions of social relations in Peru. While he does not claim Indigenous heritage explicitly, he is connected to Andean peoples not only through kinship but also through his reliance on what are recognizably Andean forms of relationality and reciprocity, which guide his approach to culinary and environmental work. The emphasis in *Cocina con Causa* on *learning from and working with* communities, and on foregrounding local knowledge *as* knowledge in both Indigenous and precarious urban contexts, for instance, is akin to Cherokee scholar Clint Carroll's discussion about Indigenous pedagogy in the context of his work on land-based praxis and relationality in Oklahoma. During his work with Cherokee elders to develop a curriculum for a program focused on the relationship between health, land, and education, Carroll writes about the importance of incorporating alternative understandings of and approaches to teaching. An Indigenous pedagogy, he writes, "conveys both a sense of trusting receptiveness (as opposed to forceful instruction) and a hands-on, experiential element to learning."[64] Ocampo's insistence on telling viewers that chefs are "learning from," "collaborating with," and "offering support for" the various communities and individuals with whom they engage resonates with such an alternative pedagogical approach.[65]

Ocampo's is also a relational approach. As Gregory Cajete (Santa Clara Pueblo) writes, "[L]earning comes from being related, and being related brings learning. With this focus, we teach and learn in the context of relationships: kinship, community, and natural world."[66] Ocampo's desire to learn with men and women in Puno, with relatives in Andahuaylas, and with incarcerated women at the Penal Santa Monica in Lima; and his emphasis on the creativity, labor, and knowledge of Indigenous peoples in the Andes and mothers and grandmothers in Ventanilla—particularly in the context of Peru's highly racialized and unequal landscape—can be read as an approach that disrupts and subverts the dominant and hierarchical gastropolitical project, moving gastropolitics toward a more relational and community-based framing. Indeed, within a year of the inaugural episode of *Cocina con Causa*, the television program shifted in approach. The show no longer features Ocampo or any of the other chefs from the Generación con Causa as driving the story. As of this writing, each episode is focused entirely on showcasing community stories and strategies.

In June 2019, for instance, one episode featured a community in San Juan de Lurigancho, considered one of Lima's most dangerous districts. Rather than focus on the challenges of crime or the unquestionable violence represented by its infamous prison (el Penal de Lurigancho), the episode focuses on how "for more than four decades" community members have been "working in the name of their community's health, education, and professional development." The episode, titled "Parents Committed Since Forever and for Always" ("Padres Comprometidos Desde Siempre y Para Siempre") once again challenges preconceived notions about the people who reside in such spaces, highlighting their resilience and resourcefulness. Another episode, also from June 2019, features the work of a community organization in Piura (in the north of Peru) that developed a *radionovela* (a popular and long-standing Andean form of storytelling and knowledge production through local radio and in local languages) called *La Sangre Llama* (The llama's blood) to educate communities about the dangers of anemia.[67] The radionovela dramatizes the struggle of a mother whose daughter is anemic and how the preparation of a dish made from llama blood can help restore her daughter's health. Again, the focus is on what the community is already doing, not because of outside intervention, but because of their own activism, initiative, and creativity. As one of the community organizers notes, "[T]he idea comes from our people."

What emerges from the work of local communities, and individuals like Aida and Ocampo, is a view of the power of the gastropolitical vernacular. Working with and from local positions and relations, gastropolitics "from below" may not represent an outright refusal of the dominant framing of the gastronomic boom. Rather, by leaning into the celebration of Peruvian cuisine, these approaches represent opportunities to examine the work that has been taking place in communities before the boom even began. Against the story of heroic chefs who "discover" the local only to serve it to global elites, what this chapter has sought to document is that there are other stories in everyday places with everyday people. These (under)stories reveal gastropolitical possibilities that become more plural and transformative, especially if we see them from the perspectives of potatoes, onions, llamas, and even, as we see in the next chapters, guinea pigs.

Of Humor and Violence

NEWS REPORT, 2008. A young, manicured woman appears on the television screen, and with a smile begins to speak: "We are going to present to you a character now fashionable. The export boom in our country has showcased the guinea pig. This small rodent has been transformed into gastronomic patrimony, and every day there are more dishes created with its delicious meat. Can you imagine tasting an anticucho made from cuy? Or a cuy marinated in syrup from *nísperos* (Japanese loquats) and grapes?" As she continues to speak, images appear on the screen: people eating cuy at a festival, tourists (mostly female, white, and foreign) tasting this animal, some smiling and nodding, others shaking their heads ("it is a companion animal"), and others still cringing and noting that the cuy "is like a rat." Throughout this montage, other images flash in and out of focus on the screen: faces of guinea pigs, alive and adorable; then guinea pig carcasses; skinned cuyes roasting over coals; a skinned cuy head twirling on a plate. In the background, a punchy music plays, evoking laughter from the audience. Suddenly that music turns into an Andeanized version of "Camptown Races," a minstrel song about horse racing published in 1850 in the antebellum United States. At that moment a person (most likely a man) dressed in a cuy suit appears, dancing and jumping to the music. Just as suddenly, the music winds down and the news report turns to feature the importance of guinea pig production, its contribution to Peruvian exports, the different uses of guinea pig skin and fur, and the new dishes emerging in different parts of the country featuring the guinea pig in innovative ways that "hide" the animal but showcase regional creativity. You can taste these dishes paired with fine pisco from the south of Peru. A male producer then appears, holding a large guinea pig up to the camera, laughing while the animal squeals and scrambles to get away. The spot ends with images of skinned animals once again, and that skinned cuy head sitting in the middle of a plate, hollowed eyes looking out at the audience.[1]

I remember watching this and thinking about humor and laughter as strategies for making violence palatable. The use of nondiegetic minstrel music to accompany these images makes the point even more eerily disturbing.[2] It is likely the case that in Peru few people would be aware of the racial baggage that such a soundtrack carries, but the kinds of sonic and visual grammars it utilizes make sense in this moment of racial capitalism as much as they do in any other. The violence of production and inequality must be made not only tolerable but entertaining. Music that has an "old time" feel also suggests that these are traditional ingredients in modern forms. As I write now, more than ten years after this news report aired, I remember the words of a researcher during a one-day workshop on guinea pig production in 2016: "In order to succeed, we need to transform the cuy into an animal we eat with forks and knives, not with our hands. That is why we have partnered with Le Cordon Bleu in Lima." That the cuy had the potential to become a symbol of modernity and progress in Peru, that it could figure civilization, points to the power of this animal in this contemporary moment, or at least the possibility of power and profit projected onto its small body.

FIVE

Guinea Pig Matters

FIGURING RACE, SEX, AND NATION

IN A CRITICAL READING of Lucrecia Martel's film *Zama*, film studies scholar Rosalind Galt explores the significance of animals to what she calls Martel's "anticolonial aesthetics."[1] *Zama*, set in northern Argentina and Paraguay during the eighteenth century, tells the story of Don Diego de Zama, a mid-level colonial functionary born in South America, who has requested permission from the Spanish crown to leave his backwater post and return to his family. The request is denied, and Zama is left to roam his colonial outpost, bemoaning his fate even as he tries to assert power over those around him. The film is a critique of colonial violence, particularly that inflicted on Indigenous peoples and African slaves, but it also resists victimizing those marginalized subjects. For Galt, animals play a key role in the film's "radical reconfiguration of colonial space," and she spends time analyzing the inclusion of fish, dogs, and in particular, a llama.[2] The llama appears during an important scene in which Zama learns that his request to leave has been denied, even as others are able to return home. As Galt writes, "the moment appears tragic for Zama as hero, but it is fatally undercut by the appearance of a llama, which not only walks around photo-bombing (cine-bombing?) Zama throughout his humiliation, but also disrupts the scene aurally by neighing loudly." She continues:

> The llama thus teaches us how to read *Zama*'s spaces and its figures. It instructs us to pay attention to the background of the image, ... to the margins of the frame. ... Moreover, the llama teaches us that the purported main characters might not be the most important ones, and that we should reallocate our attention to those figures who might appear to be mere 'local color.'... Such recalibration of our attention turns, of course, on power: the llama directs us to the margins rather than the center of the image and to the soundscape beyond speech.[3]

Thinking with Galt and Martel's llama, in this chapter I explore the figure of the cuy, a figure that also usefully teaches us to "reallocate our attention." In Peru, guinea pigs are not only food animals. With a long history in the Andes, cuyes have been valued for their medicinal properties and utilized as shamanic diagnostic tools. More recently, the cuy—as figure and flesh— has been found in a wide variety of locations, including in advertising campaigns for a national bank, on the presidential campaign trail, as the protagonist of a popular comic strip, and as a valuable resource for Indigenous and migrant families seeking economic improvement. What can we learn by paying attention to this small Andean animal? What does thinking with the guinea pig tell us about the complicated stories of race, sex, and nation in Peru? What does turning our gaze toward the margins, and to those figures "who might appear to be mere local color," enable us to see? And perhaps in less ableist terms, what does it enable us to hear, feel, experience?[4] This chapter argues that if we take figuration seriously as a process that imbricates the semiotic and material, we can see just how much the cuy can teach us. While the cuy sometimes seems to be entirely symbolic, a figure that borders on the comical, it in fact figures an everyday materiality, such as the palpable violence, precarity, and racism experienced by migrants in urban communities. And while production (breeding, killing, skinning, packaging) might seem entirely like a material process, the beings and bodies at the center of cuy production figure particular gendered and racialized worlds, speaking powerfully to nation and modernity, difference and belonging.

LAUGHING LIKE A CUY

October 14, 2016. I arrived at Sinchi Roca Park in Comas to attend a cuy festival in honor of the National Day of the Guinea Pig, celebrated yearly (since 2013) on the second Friday of October. Comas is one of the poorest districts of Lima. It emerged as a pueblo joven *in the 1970s and is now a fast-growing residential community for working-class Peruvians.[5] The cuy festival had previously been held at the Campo de Marte, a large park in the metropolitan area of Lima next to Avenida de la Peruanidad (Peruvianness Avenue), but, as festival organizers told me, the celebration was moved to Comas in order to "be closer to those who know and appreciate cuyes, to the producers and consumers of this animal." On this first day of the three-day festival, I paid 3 soles (approximately 1 USD) to enter the park. After walking for about ten minutes through wide green spaces* and several playgrounds, I found my way to the festival. There was an interactive cuy farm where kids could touch and pick up guinea pigs while their parents spoke with festival workers about the business of cuy production. There were cuy producers and vendors showcasing their "specimens" and encouraging attendees to consider starting their own cuy business. There were a few stands with coffee, honey, chocolate, and quinoa for sale. But mostly there were food stands selling cuy. Cuy a la brasa *(grilled)*, cuy al chaufa *(a riff on* arroz chaufa, *a Peruvian-Chinese rice dish)*, cuy al cilindro *(cooked in a cylinder oven)*, cuy en caja china *(cooked in a "Chinese box," a portable oven)*. A few representatives from the Municipality of Lima *(from Economic Development Management)* were there to learn about emerging businesses that looked promising, and the local press was present to document and televise the possibilities of cuy production. Música criolla blared on the loud speakers, and festival workers periodically announced what was to come over the course of three days: live music performances by local bands, exhibitions of marinera *(a coastal Peruvian dance)* and caballos de paso *(Peruvian "dancing" horses)*, and "the largest cuy" contest. There was also a man in a large cuy suit *(ubiquitous at these kinds of events)* navigating the crowds and moving in and out of focus.

I walked by a large grill with skewers of cuy slowly turning as they roasted over coals. A reporter for a local television station, a tall, light-skinned Limeño, was speaking with the much darker and shorter young man in charge of watching over the cooking guinea pigs while his companion held a camera, taping the exchange. The reporter wanted to touch the cuyes as they roasted, but the young man shook his head and smiled. "No, you can't touch the cuy." The reporter insisted, and then laughing said, "I'll just touch it a little with my stick," waving a microphone he was using for interviews. At this, the young man said, "Okay, but only from behind." Delighted, the reporter then quipped, "but if it's male, won't he be angry?" The young man laughed, nervously looking at the camera, as the reporter looked intently into the camera, smiling before turning to the young man and saying, "You laugh like a cuy" (te ries como un cuy). As if on cue, the man in the cuy suit appeared at this exact moment, waving at the camera, and put his arm around the young man before moving toward the interactive farm.

FIGURATION AND THE GUINEA PIG

There is a fascinating figure in Peruvian popular culture called El Cuy. Drawn by Juan Acevedo, El Cuy is not just any cuy but the protagonist of an eponymous comic strip that first appeared in 1979 in a famous left-wing paper, *La Calle* (The street). This was a time of dictatorship in the country, when independent publications were prohibited. In other words, El Cuy was born a subversive, Andean, migrant figure. With the turn toward democracy, the emergence of Sendero, and the eventual return of authoritarian rule, El Cuy moved through various iterations and publications, but as Acevedo writes, "always on the side of social justice and freedom."[6] Most recently, El Cuy has his own blog and appears frequently in *El Comercio*.[7] In his discussion of the birth of El Cuy, Acevedo tells his readers that he wanted to "create a character that would represent Peruvianness (*lo peruano*)."[8] While this is a particular reading of Peruvianness—one squarely on the side of marginalized subjects, and representing a particular masculine and "popular" subjectivity—the equation of the cuy with Peru is significant.

Acevedo's work (not just El Cuy but various other projects) has been steeped in a nationalist imaginary of subaltern, working-class struggle. It is worth including a bit of dialogue between El Cuy and his street dog friend Humberto from the early 1980s to provide a flavor of this cuy's revolutionary imaginary. In the first strip, El Cuy complains about the problem that many people have in distinguishing cuyes from mice. His friend Humberto replies that this is understandable, as they look alike, to which the cuy responds with ideological clarity: "But we cuyes are workers. The mice are lumpen." One could say that the cuy metonymically stands in for Indigenous peoples, who in the revolutionary indigenista literature of José Carlos Mariátegui are cast as agents of history. Such a reading finds support in the following day's strip, in which Acevedo explores the "problem of the cuy" in clear reference to Mariátegui's famous 1928 essay, "The Problem of the Indian." El Cuy explains that the "problem of the cuyes is like that of the Chicanos and Blacks of North America. Or like that of all the Indians of the Americas or the Blacks of South Africa." Now, he continues, "we have stood up and said enough discrimination! And the empire of Mickey Mouse has begun to tremble."

Taken together, these strips provide a particular image of the cuy, qua cuy, not simply a metaphor but like other subaltern subjects, a productive agent of modernity and even anti-imperial struggle. This kind of revolutionary clarity will not last long, however. In the same month that these images appeared, Sendero Luminoso initiated its armed struggle by blowing up ballot boxes in the small Andean town of Chuschi. Over the next decade, as violence ensued between the state and leftist forces, poor people were especially vulnerable to the ferocity of violence that came from both Left and Right. *El Cuy* reflected

FIGURE 8. Comic strips from Juan Acevedo's *El Cuy*. These appeared in *El Diario de Marka* on April 28 and 29, 1980, respectively. Reproduced with permission from Juan Acevedo.

the changing political environment, with the main characters unsure of what to do in the face of increasing polarization; some are tortured, others are killed, and El Cuy is anxious about some of his offspring who are tempted by the call of armed struggle. This is not the place to explore the remarkably nuanced ways Acevedo dealt with these troubled times, but as we fast-forward to the "post-Sendero" moment of the gastronomic boom, what I would like to make clear is that the twenty-first-century figure of the cuy again reflects and helps constitute the horizons of possibilities for everyday people in the marginalized sectors of Peru.[9]

The guinea pig has been an important figure in the Andean world for centuries.[10] The animal was domesticated by Native peoples at least three thousand years ago in the Andean region of South America, and cuy remains can be found in archaeological sites and in colonial art across the region. A famous example is the painting of the Last Supper hanging in Cusco's cathedral, where cuy is the main dish. Recent efforts to intensify cuy production claim the animal as quintessentially Andean and recenter the Andes in the Peruvian national imaginary. Of course, long histories of interspecies relations make possible this reclaiming of the cuy in the first place. And yet these histories, these ongoing relations, are all but made invisible in the refiguring of the cuy in the current context of the gastronomic revolution. Tapping into anthropological discussions of *Perú profundo*, the Andean origins of the cuy authenticate guinea pig production efforts as a *Peruvian* endeavor and as part of the contemporary culinary nationalism that, similarly, uses indigeneity as an important anchor.[11] This is a move that both acknowledges and invisibilizes Indigenous labor with the cuy, a move that centers the past and extracts archaeological evidence to commodify and appropriate. Consider the following passage from a well-respected manual for cuy production: "The tremendous evidence found about the origins of the cuy in the Andes allows us to affirm, quite properly that the cuy is *our* animal. In other words, he is from the Andean regions of Peru, Ecuador, Bolivia and Colombia, and—*as he is ours*—he obliges us and commits us to not only improve his exploitation and quality, but also to create our own technology that deserves, in the future, our very best efforts."[12] Similarly, a website for a Bolivian project in cuy production and genetic improvement states: "The cuy was intensely consumed by the people of ancient Peru until the Spanish conquest tried to do away with our culinary tradition, and incorporated instead meat from cows, pigs, and sheep in our diet. Since then, in a process taking place over centuries, people began to see the cuy with different eyes. There are people today who are horrified to see this rodent, or a piece of the animal, on a plate. Without a doubt, these people know nothing about history, and even less about good food."[13]

Human dominion over guinea pigs is not only sanctioned by the familiar kind of theological arguments found in Genesis, but also by a sort of archaeonational logic that gives Andean nations the opportunity, perhaps even the obligation, to improve and exploit "our animal." Once again, we see the familiar idea of "time and the other": even as the cuy is rescued from the past and mobilized for the future, Indigenous peoples remain simply out of time; they, and their ongoing relations with the cuy, are nowhere in the contemporary linkages made between nation and national rodent.[14]

It is here that we can usefully point to Donna Haraway's idea that figuration "is about resetting the stage for possible pasts and futures."[15] The figure of the cuy makes possible a rearticulation of the past, of past laboring relations between "the people of ancient Peru" and this animal, in ways that skip over the present and instead offer new pathways toward modernity. But figuration, as I am using it here, is not simply a foregrounding of the figure and backgrounding of the flesh. Rather, drawing on Claudia Castañeda's work, I use figuration as a way to think about the articulations between "the semiotic and material" and, as Haraway suggests, between possible futures and pasts. These kinds of relations (semiotic, material, temporal) work to produce specific "figures" that necessarily bring forth connections to particular worlds. As Castañeda writes: "[F]iguration . . . makes it possible to describe in detail the process by which a concept or entity is given particular form—how it is figured—in ways that speak to the making of worlds. To use figuration as a descriptive tool is to unpack the domains of practice and significance that are built into each figure. A figure, from this point of view, is the simultaneously material and semiotic effect of specific practices."[16]

Castañeda's focus is on the figure of the child, a being who, she argues, is always in the making, always potentiality rather than actuality, a temporally ambiguous being that is full of futurity but clearly anchored in a genealogical past.[17] We can think of the cuy in similar ways. The cuy's power lies in its yet-to-be-ness, but also in its always already Peruvianness. In other words, the cuy is simultaneously a quintessential "national" animal, but as "he" becomes part of various modernizing projects, his body is literally modified by science and commerce in pursuit of various social goals. This is precisely the kind of figure that is needed in a postcrisis moment of nation building, something that can anchor the imagined community of Peru in a *longue durée* of being and belonging to a place and environment, but yet can also lend itself to the cosmopolitan and modern innovations of tomorrow. And yet it cannot be mere symbol but must also be edible flesh. As export commodity, high-end culinary ingredient, Andean body, and national symbol, the cuy is quite liter-ally on the move, even (especially) beyond its own death. In both a sacrificial and symbolic way, the cuy powers many practices and projects.

The figure of the guinea pig does great work—as symbol of economic pos-sibility, as Indigenous nature transformed into "modern," high-end cuisine—in reframing Peru, a society once on the brink of internal destruction, as a sovereign nation. This reframing is intimately linked to indigeneity and is inextricably tied to long histories of elite formulations of the "problem of the Indian" and the need for Indian pasts to authenticate Peruvian futures. Kate Soper tells us that "'nature' is the concept through which humanity thinks its difference and specificity."[18] Gastropolitics in Peru redraws naturalized racial hierarchies in novel and familiar ways; it can be understood only in the con-text of Peru's colonial legacies, where nature and indigeneity are coproduced. Native landscapes and peoples come together in the figure of the cuy, evoking worlds of "dirty, backward Indians" that must be cleansed, that is, distanced from their "natural" environments so that they can be brought into a modern and cosmopolitan nation anchored by romanticized, sanitized, or urbanized forms of indigeneity.

Consider a recent discussion about Acurio's famous dish, *el cuy pekinés* (Peking cuy). In an article in *The Guardian* about "Peru's fantastic food revolution," the author begins by noting that for most tourists, local Peruvian fare "used to mean roast guinea pig, nibbled en route to Machu Picchu."[19] He continues: "The idea of coming here specifically to eat would until recently have elicited bafflement, if not derision." And after describing the recent rise of Peru (and more specifically Lima) as the gastronomic capital of the Americas, the author ends his piece by telling his readers that if they are "set on eating guinea pig" they should "try the version at Astrid & Gastón, which the menu describes as having visited Beijing before travelling to Shanghai. *Rodent never tasted this good*" (emphasis added).[20] The transformation of cuy from a strictly Andean or Indigenous dish to a cosmopolitan variation that can appear in high-end restaurants (such as Acurio's Peking cuy) has been an issue of explicit discussion and debate. In earlier discussions about the development of cocina novoandina, the alpaca figured more prominently. Since the early 2000s, however, the cuy has risen to take its place as symbolic of the gastronomic revolution's emphasis on both fusion and authenticity, though always modified in ways designed to cleanse and disguise this small rodent.

Acurio puts the issue even more starkly. "I think *el cuy pekinés* helped extend the presence of cuy in Peruvian kitchens. It was a desperate attempt (*un grito desesperado*) to sever the cuy's head and paws because . . . exhibiting the head is an obstacle to its implantation." The newfound acceptance of the cuy on the menus of restaurants like his, he continues, is nothing less than the reversal of "centuries of the rejection of Andeans by the coast. That the cuy begins to be eaten on the coast is a way of embracing ourselves through the cuy." One can now see that "mestizaje is consolidating, the distances are shrinking and the fact that a restaurant like ours would not think of preparing a New Year's dinner without cuy is instructive." This change has been profound, and it has also been rapid. As Acurio concludes: "[I]f ten years ago you told me that we were going to serve cuy for New Years, I would have thought that I was on a hidden camera TV show."[21]

Acurio's comments make clear the way the labor of elite chefs is what makes cuy work in this context. Ignoring centuries of relations between Indigenous peoples and this Native animal, for Acurio it is his transformation of the cuy that "extends the animal's presence in Peruvian kitchens." Recalling

Castañeda's insights about the material and semiotic dimension of the figure, we see that the power of the figure lies in both what it makes possible and erases. As she notes, the "figure is a resource for wider cultural projects."[22] Here, the figure of the cuy evokes the authenticity of indigeneity, but it is important to note just how much labor goes into transforming and obscuring the cuy in ways that accord with lingering colonial notions of hygiene and the cosmopolitan aspirations of the gastronomic elite. The animal is appropriated by elite chefs who transform this otherwise dirty, Indian rodent into the key protagonist in tasting menus at high-end fusion restaurants. The cuy is essential for the transformation "from savage to sophisticated," but the animal must remain hidden.[23] This kind of sleight of hand, in which local Peruvian animals become magically transformed into cosmopolitan haute cuisine, is also simultaneously an act of Indigenous erasure. Any connection with actually existing Andean worlds is severed and disavowed. Stuart Hall puts it clearly: "One must start ... from the concrete historical 'work' which racism accomplishes under specific historical conditions—as a set of economic, political and ideological practices, of a distinctive kind, concretely articulated with other practices in a social formation."[24] These forms of power work as a complex of material and semiotic practices—in other words, as figuration.

The figure of the guinea pig is central to elite formulations of the labor involved in transforming Peru into a global commodity, into a sophisticated culinary destination. But this is work that centers the Andean animal only as it is sanitized and made palatable through the "labor of love" performed by chefs as they remake a rodent into airy cuy puffs, or as they "cook ecosystems." Put another way, gastropolitical elites put nature to work in ways that cleanse and erase the traces of Indigenous labor that made possible particular understandings of "nature" to begin with. As we saw in earlier chapters, elite chefs incorporate Native plants and animals in ways that render them into timeless nature, awaiting "discovery" and then transformation into beautiful food: tradition and modernity on a plate. This move also erases centuries of interspecies relations and labor; it could be read as a kind of struggle over whose labor can accrue value, or a colonial alchemy in which Indigenous dispossession and even disappearance creates the very conditions for capital accumulation.

For centuries guinea pigs have lived with Indigenous families, usually in the kitchen, sharing food and warmth and providing companionship. On special occasions—weddings, baptisms, the arrival of guests—cuyes are killed for food. This killing is usually done by women, and with care to avoid suffering (usually by breaking the neck). While there has been a move away from "familial production" toward the commercial production of cuyes (a move that in practice has meant placing guinea pigs outside the home, more selective breeding, and less consumption of cuy meat in favor of selling the animals at markets), this form of living with and killing cuyes still dominates the rural Andes. Without romanticizing women's roles in the care, breeding, and killing of cuyes, and heeding Tsing's warning that "home often sugarcoats captivity," this form of living with (and killing) the cuy is quite distinct from the more intensive cuy production in urban settings, often involving much different methods of killing (e.g., placing the animal upside down in a cone and slitting her throat, and sometimes electrocution).[25] By the time most chefs encounter the animal and begin their work to transform cuy into gourmet dishes, cuyes have been killed, gutted, and skinned.

There is a clear difference in the relation between human and guinea pig here, and as many Indigenous food activists note, this too is an important part of what they see as the violence of gastropolitics. Indeed, Indigenous activists often point to this as an ontological struggle, one that highlights the violence involved in extracting cuy (or other native plants and animals) from specific relations and refiguring the animal as fusion cuisine.[26] As one Indigenous activist told me in 2012, chefs and other proponents of the gastronomic boom "are tokenizing native products. The revalorization of Indigenous peoples is absent. For people in Lima involved with the boom, it is as if the products are simply 'there' to be taken, used, and exploited, but there is a lack of context and no attempt to understand them in history and tradition. The cuy, for example, must be prepared in the traditional manner, not using *caja china* or *cilindros*. La cocina novoandina may be creating new dishes, but they have nothing to do with us."

This critique also speaks to the distinction between traditional Andean forms of raising cuyes and new forms of production. Cuy producers frequently point to traditional Indigenous-cuy relations as one of the principal obstacles to expanding production. To move Indigenous families toward "modern" methods has meant the introduction of spatial separations between animals and humans, a move linked to familiar civilizing practices and discourses around hygiene and efficiency. For the purpose of the gastronomic boom, however, the transformation has involved moving cuy production out of the domestic sphere entirely, especially as cuy production emerges in the city as a way to fuel economic opportunities for working-class Peruvians, many of whom have themselves recently left the Andes. The cuy here is not simply "local flavor." The animal stands in for a modernizing story that begins with the domestication of an Andean rodent thousands of years ago and necessarily culminates by leaving Andean communities (where women's labor was central) for urban and industrial projects where men are now (mostly) in charge.

GUINEA PIG POWER

Feeling in Peru tells us that the cuy is Andean. Research tells us the cuy is coastal. He is Peruvian.

—CUY RESEARCHER

If there is a Ronald McDonald, there can be a Johnny McCuy.

—DIRECTOR OF A CUY PRODUCTION BUSINESS

Lilia Chauca, director of the Guinea Pig Project at the National Institute in Agrarian Innovation (INIA), wears her expertise lightly as she describes the state of the Peruvian guinea pig in her office in Lima. She is proud of the work she and her team have done in the "genetic improvement" of guinea pigs and in the development and intensification of cuy production. In 1968, with her husband, the late Marco Zaldívar, and with support from the International Development Research Centre in Canada, USAID, and the University of North Carolina, she established the Guinea Pig Project.[27] The project focused on teaching Indigenous peoples how to better manage their guinea pigs: how to pick which ones to eat, how to be more intentional and efficient about breeding. They also began developing specific breeds that would grow larger and more quickly, and females that could give birth to higher numbers of young in order to maximize productivity.

Zaldívar, Chauca's colleague and husband, was killed by Sendero while he was at one of their field sites in Ayacucho. Today, the INIA and the Guinea Pig Project are widely recognized as the most important sites for guinea pig research, breeding, and production in the country. The INIA is also recognized internationally, and its "Peruvian breed" (*raza peruana*) is sought out by producers and geneticists in Ecuador, Bolivia, and Colombia in an effort to "improve" their own cuy breeds. But as Chauca told me, it is only recently, in the context of the gastronomic revolution that has enveloped Peru, that the power of the guinea pig has become visible. "Now is our moment," she told me during an interview in 2012. "The guinea pig will save Peru."[28]

Indeed, a "guinea pig boom" (*boom del cuy*) has accompanied the Peruvian culinary boom. While supported by the state since the late 1960s, the *business* of cuy production has only taken off recently, and it is discursively linked to the gastronomic revolution. The celebration of Peruvian gastronomy and its emphasis on the promotion of *Peruvian* products offered Chauca (and others invested in cuy production) opportunities to promote and exploit this native animal. These efforts are in keeping with the forward-looking aspirations of the gastronomic boom: the hope of moving beyond precarity and toward the promise of seemingly more inclusive modes of modernity, cosmopolitanism, and development. Along these lines, the focus in cuy production has been primarily on developing cuy research and breeding (linked of course to the "development" of people, particularly Indigenous peoples). In practice, this has meant moving from *familial* production to small, medium, and large-scale *commercial* production. It has also meant moving from domestic spaces in which women were the protagonists toward commercial ventures dominated by men.[29]

As the guinea pig boom began in earnest (early to mid-2000s), the focus for many cuy breeders and producers was on export. As the head of one cuy business in Lima told me, there was particular excitement about the promise of what he termed "markets of nostalgia" (*mercados de añoranza*), referring to the large communities of Andean migrants who had left their countries (Peru, Ecuador, and Bolivia) and were now living in cities in the United States, Spain, and Japan.[30] While some producers do work with large companies to export their products, the primary focus of cuy production in Peru today is internal consumption. There are various reasons for this, such as the challenge of global consumption of the guinea pig, an animal who is seen not as a food animal but as a companion animal in many countries.[31] But an important reason for this shift has to do with the association between cuy production and both rural and urban development. During interviews with state and private producers, it became clear that only large companies with the financial means to pay for certification and navigate the bureaucratic processes required for export could participate in this market. Rural families or small cuy businesses are unable to compete. One cuy researcher put it starkly: "[E]xporting [cuy] hurts the country; it hurts Peruvians."[32] Unlike other products such as quinoa, it is hard to think about an organic fair-trade business for cuy (for example), given that most of those purchasing cuy abroad (Andean migrants) do not have the means to pay for the cost of business. Instead, most cuy producers have identified the national market as the most promising, particularly in the context of the gastronomic boom. And this has proven to be a smart move, as demand for cuy meat has soared in the country, and the small animal's meat is the most expensive in the nation.[33] This is the context in which one cuy business owner told me about his vision for a cuy-based fast-food chain: "If there is a Ronald McDonald," he told me, "there can be a Johnny McCuy."[34]

In some ways, the revalorization of native Peruvian products has reframed the association of the guinea pig with indigeneity. Rather than disparaging the animal because of its connection to Indigenous or poor migrant households, the cuy is now upheld as a quintessentially Peruvian animal, one that plays a crucial role in authenticating high-end fusion cuisine as *Peruvian* cuisine. Newspapers, Facebook posts, magazines, and blogs tout the health benefits of cuy meat (e.g., low in cholesterol, medicinal, even anticarcinogenic, properties), with some doctors even prescribing a daily dose of cuy soup to counteract chronic headaches and improve digestive health. This has led to an astounding surge in small cuy production businesses. Moreover, there are multiple seminars, workshops, and courses offered by universities, private companies, and state institutes (like the INIA) that train those interested in becoming cuy producers at small, medium, or large scales, and there are regular cuy producer conferences (regional, national, and international). And in 2013 the Ministry of Agriculture declared the National Day of the Guinea Pig in order to promote and increase cuy consumption in the country.

Narratives of cuy production, then, are framed within broader narratives of national pride and economic possibility. But they are also embedded in deep colonial histories of racial and economic exclusion. When Chauca says "the cuy will save Peru," what is the Peru she is talking about? And who are the Peruvians enabling this process? Writing in the early 1990s about ethnic identity and political participation in Peru, the late Peruvian scholar Carlos Ivan Degregori noted: "Those who at the beginning of this century appeared as strangers in their own country reclaimed space first through the struggle for land and the great migrations [to the city].... In Peru...the Andean/popular/provincial majorities have appropriated the concept of Peru and granted it a different meaning."[35]

Following Degregori, Victor Vich notes that in urban Peru there are unmistakable and innumerable forms of "popular agency" in which the poor are resignifying what "Peru" can mean. Vich's ethnographic exploration of street comedians (*cómicos ambulantes*) and their performances provides one useful path toward understanding urban subalternity as it tacks between precarity and resilience.[36] The performers Vich works with are all either Andean migrants or the children of migrants, navigating life at the margins of Lima, working to make themselves not only seen but seen as belonging. For example, faced with a reality in which migrants are perceived as out of place in the city, many of the *discursos* Vich analyzed—long speech performances full of slang and expletives and grotesque humor—emphasize the city (Lima) as a terrain of social struggle where previous qualities associated with rural life (such as physical strength and stamina) recede to the background and "new" character traits, such as *la habilidad y la maña* (ability and cunning), are instead central to surviving this social struggle. In this context, *la habilidad y la maña* become new forms of knowledge and identity that dissolve any supposed structural determinism. In other words, "If there exists a social structure that . . . can determine the making of subjects, thanks to ability and cunning these subjects begin to secure a small space to negotiate and transgress these conditions."[37]

The guinea pig boom may be another example of these forms of popular agency, both in terms of the material opportunities it offers and in the cultural work involved in generating multiple national projects and imaginaries. Here, the assertion in the epigraph to this section that "research tells us the cuy is coastal" and that "he is Peruvian" is of note. The cuy is not just an "Andean" animal who migrated to Lima, but a coastal animal taken to the Andes by pre-Incan peoples, who then returned "home" in the mid- to late 1900s. This researcher was specifically speaking about DNA research on pre-Columbian guinea pig remains that "proved" the animal was "Peruvian" (even though "Peru" did not yet exist).[38] But she was also making a point about belonging and recognition. As part of this discussion, she explicitly addressed ongoing "discrimination against the cuy, and the people who accompany the animal." "The cuy is not ugly," she continued. "He marks our biodiversity, our land, not only in the Andes, but also on the coast, since always." In this telling, Indigenous peoples have always belonged, in the Andes *and* on the coast. Indigenous migrants in Lima today, then, are in some ways reclaiming space, and the cuy is part of that claim. In other words, while cuy production can be understood as simply another example of a popular capitalist (and civilizational) project, one fitting well within the neoliberal and even colonial framing of the boom (given its emphasis on business, entrepreneurship, and development), we can also read cuy production as a subaltern project, one that repositions *lo popular* and the place of Andean migrants in particular.

One of the most visible guinea pig characters in Peru is the Peruvian bank's (Banco de Credito, or BCP) mascot, the "magic guinea pig," who champions popular capitalism and makes money appear for *cholo* entrepreneurs. This *cuy mágico* promises quick money and a Visa card for those who bank with BCP. He appears to struggling small business owners amid Andean flute music, dancing to the tune of his own song.[39] In different versions of the video and commercial, cuy mágico sings and dances, with a chicha sensibility (i.e., with a recognizably Andeanized urban flair), flanked by two voluptuous women dressed in very revealing cuy outfits. Other women—caricatures of Afro-Peruvian and Andean migrants—hold out bundles of money while screaming "money!" (*la plata!*) into the camera. The spot ends with the bank's motto: "Success is welcome" (*bienvenido el éxito*), and cuy mágico holding the magic Visa card up to the camera.

This is an extraordinary example of the contradictory deployment of the cuy. Here, imagined geographies of success are racialized and gendered in ways that mark clear limits to the upward mobility and entrepreneurship signaled by the economic support cuy mágico promises. Even as he sings about the capital needed for upward mobility, the cuy remains anchored to his Andean origins (as signaled by the Andean flute music) and to a particular social and cultural space. In the background, one can see recognizable images of the Andeanized urban cityscape: "chicha" posters (with their signature bright colors and distinctive fonts), local shops, and various faces and body types expected to occupy the working-class public spaces of greater metropolitan Lima. To appear in the wealthier parts of town, or with upper-class Limeños, would be to transgress economic and social boundaries very clearly delineated. In this reading then, the magic guinea pig figures a safe "other," the cholo entrepreneur who strives to succeed, but only within the limits accepted by Peruvian class norms; the guinea pig, seemingly "out of place" in urban Lima, is in fact happily holding his fellow subaltern subjects "in their place." This is also an example of the ways in which the guinea pig is linked to the perpetuation of elite visions and fantasies of the incorporation of the popular classes. "They" are given just enough access to capital (in the form of loans from private banks, of course) to operate their corner stores, juice stands, or micro-enterprises.

While Peru's economy is growing at a respectable rate, especially by current international standards, poverty and inequality still disproportionately affect Indigenous peoples and internal migrants. Socioeconomic inequality is a form of structural violence, a form less visible than the violence the country experienced in the 1980s and 1990s, and one that ads like the BCP cuy mágico seek to make even less visible. They instead reinforce the narrative of Peruvian success, a nation on the way up. Yet these stories of success are never innocent. With glittery complacency, they invite forgetting poverty and instead "welcome success." Thus, while the cuy is used often to symbolize progress, modernity, and even hope for a better future ("become a cuy producer and you can develop your own export business"), he also marks a particular—and limited—kind of social mobility for poor Peruvians.[40]

However, is there room for reading this ad against the grain, or for possibilities of cultural agency and resilience? El cuy mágico marks clear limits to social mobility that point to the endurance of hierarchies of power in Peru. But he also figures the recognition of choledad as central to the nation. For Aníbal Quijano, for instance, the cholo, their presence, and importantly the institutionalization of "the cholo" as a category, prefigured "a Peruvian destiny, distinct from the mere total 'assimilation' (*aculturación*) of the indigenous population in the context of Western creole culture (*cultural occidental criolla*)."[41] Similarly, in what is still the most influential work on the Andeanization of Lima, Peruvian anthropologist José Matos Mar provides a convincing case that migrants would be the key protagonists in the transformation of Peru, noting that the state would have to attend to their concerns and demands. Matos Mar and Quijano made these arguments from the perspective of social science and from the political left. But there are also neoliberal readings of this, and el cuy mágico could be read as a symbol of what conservative economist Hernando De Soto famously called, "the other path," that is, the efforts of the poor but entrepreneurial workers of urban Peru's informal sector to achieve economic prosperity.[42] As we saw in chapter 1, De Soto agreed with the understanding of Peru as an exclusionary and unequal country, but the answer for him did not lie in social protest or revolutionary action but rather in removing the legal and bureaucratic obstacles that stood in the way of the popular capitalism of Andean migrants. However, as Victor Vich insists:

> Theorizing informality in Peru should not be reduced to legal aspects, but rather understood as a phenomenon cut through with the effects of a modernization from the periphery, the dependent character of capitalism in Peru, and by complex sociocultural mechanisms inherited from different historical traditions. Informality is related to the Andeanization of the cities ..., with new kinds of social relations ... and with the structural violence brought by

the disparate development of markets and the lack of industrialization. The informal market, or the development of the small enterprise in Peru, is thus *a consequence of different modernization processes, but these are understood not as impulses external and alien to a reality described as "authentic" and "traditional," but rather as the attempts at renewal realized by the popular sectors in order to participate in the economic and cultural dimensions of which they have been historically excluded.*[43]

Following Vich, cuy production today operates as an additional form of cholo agency, of the kind of *habilidad* and *maña* that enables them not only to survive but to thrive. They are claiming space. While the cuy mágico can certainly be seen as an instrumentalized and caricatured version of popular identity, the surrounding cholo and chicha aesthetics serve as an indicator that the Andean world has left its mark on the coastal cityscape.

Similarly, returning to the cuy festival in Comas, we could read that space—and the cuy—as a "contact zone" or a terrain of struggle over recognition.[44] Rereading the encounter between the reporter and the festival worker in this context, we can expand the frame and see not just blatant racism (*"te ríes como un cuy"*), but also another example of Gerald Vizenor's survivance.[45] Much like Martel's llama, in this scene, the cuy (or the man in the cuy suit) helps us refocus our attention as he both marks and disrupts the reporter's racism.[46] He steps into the frame at a particular moment, putting his arm around the young worker and looking directly into the camera. Could we read these gestures as ones of solidarity? The reporter was clearly annoyed at having to cover this festival in Comas (as was evident throughout the day in multiple interactions with others), and he used humor as a strategy through which to reassert racial and gender hierarchies. But he *had* to be there, reporting on and documenting the phenomenon of cuy production in the city. The festival may have moved to Comas, but the cuy in this context figured the presence and resilience of Andean migrants in greater metropolitan Lima.

One might say that sometimes a man in a cuy suit is just a man in a cuy suit; that he is simply a funny prop, or "mere local color." But following Galt, and cultural studies scholar Steve Baker, I argue that we must not dismiss the "real" consequences of even the seemingly banal representation of animals. In thinking about dancing cuyes in bank commercials or a cuy mascot at a festival, we should "consider what such representations might reveal about attitudes both to animals and to other humans: in other words, to inquire into the consequences of their apparent inconsequentiality."[47]

In October 2016 I attended a day-long cuy production seminar at the INIA. These courses, offered since 2004, are aimed at the increasing numbers of working-class men and women in Lima who see in the cuy a means of support and the possibility of increased income. I arrived at the INIA early and was waiting by the guarded entrance gate with other men and women when a technician came to take us to the Cuy Project offices. On this day, the seminar began promptly at 8:30 in the morning. Most of the others present were young men, with only a handful of women in the group.[48] The technician lined us up in front of the small room where the seminar would take place (8:30 a.m.–5:30 p.m.). One by one we paid the seminar fee of 100 soles (approximately 33 USD) and received a packet with printouts of the Power-Point slides we would be viewing later that day. At the end of the seminar, participants received a certificate of participation and a CD with information from the lectures delivered that day. For an extra 5 soles (1.5 USD), one could also purchase a photocopy of a thin booklet on cuy production.

As is usually the case, the focus of the seminar was on the cuy as raw material for profit-seeking business. Speakers addressed cuy production, nutrition, reproduction, commercialization, and biosecurity. The workshop began with a lecture by a lead researcher I will call Veronica, who spoke about the history of the Cuy Project and the origins of the cuy, before noting the important work the INIA had done in moving guinea pig breeding in Peru from familial to commercial breeding, contributing greatly to the national economy along the way. "The guinea pig is only good for meat," she stated, and then asked the seminar participants if they knew Donald Duck's uncle, Scrooge McDuck (Rico McPato), "whose eyes turn into dollar signs when he sees potential for profit. *That* is cuy production." With an image of Scrooge McDuck on the PowerPoint slide behind her, Veronica continued her discussion by reminding her audience, made up of mostly men, that women have been central to cuy production. "Women saved the cuy," she stated, "because they took them to the kitchen." Veronica was referencing the traditional way that cuy husbandry, to use another curiously gendered term, relies largely on women who in Andean communities tend to care for cuyes, keep them in the home, and use them for food on special occasions. Veronica emphasized that in the move from (primarily) rural contexts of familial production to (increasingly) urban spaces of commercial production—a developmentalist move that the INIA is invested in—it was important to "disassociate the cuy from women, because men are the ones more interested in production."[49] "Women treat cuyes better," she noted, "but cuy production is about business and efficiency, not care, unless it is profitable (*rentable*)."[50] Gender ideologies are very much at work here, as discussions of efficiency and profit emphasize the importance of men in this moment, while essentialized understandings of women confine them to familiar contexts of domesticity, reproduction, and care.

While in retrospect it isn't surprising, on that day I was struck by how much of the discussion about production, profit, and business was entangled with ideologies of sex and gender. The discussions throughout that day and in other spaces for conversation about cuy production revealed the intimate linkages between development and gender, and more specifically, the masculinist dimension of development initiatives such as this one. Indeed, as Saldaña-Portillo has argued, "the discourse of development requires ... the subject to become an agent of transformation in his own right, one who is highly ethical, mobile, progressive, risk taking, and masculinist, regardless of whether the agent/object of a development strategy is a man or a woman, an adult or a child."[51] As feminist scholars have long noted, women also contribute to upholding patriarchy.[52] Sometimes this is quite explicit.

During a conference on cuy production in November 2016, a technician working with Antamina, one of the largest copper and zinc mining companies in the southern Peruvian highlands, told the large, mostly male, audience that its cuy project (part of the mine's corporate social responsibility initiatives) emphasized the importance of "bringing men in" and getting buy-in from communities, from families, and in particular, from husbands. "People still think cuyes are for women, but we need to change men's thinking, and move away from the prejudice of this, away from the idea that caring for the cuyes is women's work. We need to masculinize (*masculinizar*) cuy production, and move from the participation of women, to that of their male children, and eventually to the participation of the head of the household." The "head of the household" of course referred to the man in this context. In a similar vein, the INIA team, despite being led by a female researcher, provided innumerable examples of not only centering masculinist perspectives but also minimizing the suffering of female bodies.

During another lecture at the cuy production workshop, Veronica highlighted her team's efforts to synchronize cuy estrus so that all cuyes in one farm could give birth at the same time, thus streamlining cuy "harvest" and postpartum care.[53] She also proudly shared the work that went into lessening the time from birth to kill weight (from 120 to 56 days). And it was during this discussion about efficiency and reproduction that Veronica offered a striking comparison between female guinea pigs, herself, and her two daughters. She began by saying, "Look at me. I am short and chunky. One of my two daughters is also like me, short and prone to gaining weight." She then said that while we might think this means they eat a lot, in fact she and her daughter don't really eat much. Her second daughter, however, "is tall, skinny, and can eat all she wants and not gain weight. This is genetics," she said. She continued, "[I]f we were cuyes, my overweight daughter and I, we would have been chosen as breeders (*reproductoras*), because we don't consume much. This means we are low cost, but we still gain weight so we can give birth to higher numbers of young, and then have more meat once we are spent and ready for slaughter." She went on, "[M]y skinny daughter would have been sent to slaughter quickly, because she eats a lot—too much production cost—but does not gain weight. This is not efficient." In a strikingly effective performance, Veronica was figuratively serving up her body, and the bodies of her daughters, for consumption. In addition to the technical and scientific information she conveyed, Veronica's words also served to reinforce the heteronormative order in which women are controllable, consumable, and disposable.

In another fascinating if disturbing discussion about the importance of uniformity in cuy production, Veronica told the men and women at the workshop that efficient production meant cuy populations had to be homogenous. "In the military, the entire population is the same. They all must weigh the same and be equally tall. They don't let in short or fat men. Same with the cuy. They must all be the same size, weigh the same, have the same leg dimensions." And she continued, "[W]e want convex carcasses (*queremos carcasas convexas*). What kind of girl would you like? A girl with nothing in the front or back, or a convex one, with a curvy body? That is what we want with the cuy." Both the men and women in the room laughed heartily at this. Such humor certainly makes Veronica an effective teacher, but it also makes her part of the hegemonic masculinist ordering of the nation.

The way in which human bodies can stand in for cuy bodies might seem remarkable, but in fact practices and discourses of animal reproduction are always linked to gender ideologies and imaginaries about human bodies.[54] And as others have noted in scholarship on the violence of animal industries, humor—and very often sexualized humor—plays a significant role in uncovering these connections and masking unease around the violence of breeding.[55] It is also worth noting that, as Gillespie writes, "while female animals are more obviously subjects of gendered commodification and violence, male animals, too, experience a gendered appropriation of their lives and bodies."[56] This is certainly the case in the context of cuy production. Discussions about efficiency during this workshop and other lectures I attended had just as much to do with breeding female cuyes for maximal reproductive efficiency as it did with selecting the "best" male specimens. One producer's lecture at a conference was representative of this. With a slide of a cuy penis on the projector behind him, the producer discussed the importance of "a good working penis," noting that there are some males who do not work as they "should": "They don't work, they are worthless, or maybe they just don't like females. [Laughter and applause from the crowd.] You have to check the penis every month, measure the testicles, make sure they are working. If they are not, you must take them out of the reproductive space. Why should I let him rest? He has to work. If he doesn't, he is just wasting my money." This kind of "breeders only" comment reflects not just the familiar misogyny already noted, but also homophobia and particular ideas about masculinity.

In addition, much as Gillespie found for cows and bulls in the dairy industry, the male animal body is not only commodified but "simultaneously discursively employed to take responsibility for the sexual violence against the female body through the construction of the hypermasculine, virile *male*."[57] There was one discussion in particular during the INIA workshop that offers a telling example of just this kind of simultaneous discursive and material commodification and evokes precisely the kind of figurational politics Castañeda describes. The discussion was about the "postpartum estrus period," a period two to three hours after females give birth when they are once again able to be impregnated. Many producers take advantage of this period, a method called continuous or permanent mating (*empadre continuo*, or *empadre permanente*), described as providing no sexual rest for the female cuy.[58] During her lecture at the INIA workshop, Veronica put it this way: "[T]wo to three hours after giving birth, the female has another reproductive cycle, and the male can penetrate her once again. She sometimes does not want this, but she has no other choice (*no le queda otra*), and we need to take maximum advantage. Efficiency. Remember the eyes of Scrooge McDuck." As she spoke, the slide on the screen showed a cartoon image of a female cuy holding hands with a male cuy. With her other hand, she is swatting away her newborn baby, who is presumably in the way of her amorous liaison. The male cuy, who is holding a beer with his other hand, looks at her lasciviously, while a red heart over the female cuy's head signals she is in love (or at least willingly responsive to the male's desires).

Immediately after this comment, Veronica continued by reminding those of us in the workshop that the male cuy was the most important part of the reproductive space: "Remember, there are seven females and only one male in the *poza*. This is the male's harem [again, laughter]. He is the first to enter the *poza*, and he is the owner (*el dueño*). This is his territory. Once he is in, you slowly begin bringing in the females, two by two, until you have seven. You have to be creative, because the males will easily get bored with the females. They are just like men. They have to smell new things every so often; they have to smell new meat. So you need to move him once in a while to different *pozas* so he can smell new blood. This gives him energy. And then the females are happy too because they want a young stud, not an old man. This male works better if he is excited and energized, and that makes females happy."

"They are just like men." While one might have imagined such a statement to be the start of a critique of the familiar misogyny in so many places in the world, here it works to naturalize male dominance across human and nonhuman divides. Another technician at the INIA noted that guinea pigs will sometimes resist and refuse mating: "She does not always allow the male to mount her, unlike rabbits who are . . . crazy, like prostitutes, or like those women from the jungle (*como las de la selva*) who do not only consent to be mounted but in fact they are the ones seducing the male. The male is the one with no choice really, they put him to work all day long." Listening to this facile racism and misogyny was difficult for me, but in this masculinist space, it played all too well. There is no doubt that it was so effective because it reinforced the everyday misogyny found not only in daily conversation but also in the ideologies that validate violence—sexual and otherwise—against certain bodies. Policies across Latin America, from the criminalization of miscarriage in El Salvador (making headlines as I write this chapter in 2019), to the state-led forced sterilization of Indigenous women and men in Peru in the 1990s, show that this kind of violence operates at the intersections of race, class, and gender.

Here we might also consider the terminology that the INIA has used to discuss cuy breeding. In the 1970s, for example, the institute moved from what they called their "improved race" (*raza mejorada*) of cuyes to developing three different cuy "races": Peru, Inti, and Andina. (In Spanish "race" and "breed" are both signified by "raza"). In descriptions of each "race," gender and sexuality quickly come into play. Many within and outside the INIA recommend cuyes from *la raza Andina* for production as they are more "promiscuous" and have been bred to be more "reproductively efficient." This means they can reproduce more frequently, and deliver larger numbers of offspring, than cuyes from either the Peru or Inti "races." But even though Andinas would make better economic sense (given their reproductive efficiency), researchers at INIA often note that "no one wants them." "Everyone wants *la raza Peru*. No one wants *la Andina*. Not even *la Inti*. This is why we had to develop the 'interracial' lines, to improve certain qualities and expand the market." These interracial cuyes are cheaper than others, but as they are bred with cuyes from *la raza Peru* some people, especially those with less funds to invest in their business, are more open to buying them.

I found a similar sensibility at a cuy research and production institute in Bolivia. When I visited that institute, the head researcher there took me through their *galpones* and showed me the various *razas* they house, ranging from their "pure" *raza Peru* (gifts from the INIA), to *razas Auqui* and *Rosario* ("gifts from Ecuador" she told me), to their very own *raza Mejocuy* and other native Bolivian breeds. At one point, the researcher stopped to show me the various markings of each, saying that each cuy breed was like "human eco-types" (*eco-tipos humanos*). She explained, "[M]uch like people from different regions of Bolivia have different markings and characteristics, so do cuyes. In breeding, this is what we look for." There is of course a tremendous complexity to this process, and even some contradiction when one analyzes various cuy production manuals and breeding discourses, but the main point I want to make here is that breeding practices are intimately linked to racialized and sexualized bodies, both animal and human. They are also firmly embedded in the ongoing settler colonial project of civilization.[59]

It is hardly surprising, then, to hear how "cuy talk" is not only gendered but also racialized and connected to capitalist understandings of value. Consider, for example, the corporate social responsibility project of the Antamina mine. The technician at the cuy producer conference mentioned earlier discussed the importance of cuy production in "transforming Indigenous and rural peoples into productive citizens." In his telling, that transition entailed a transformation in the texture of care for the cuy, from its communal context in which the cuy is ritually and religiously important, to caring for "it" to the extent that its life is measured in profit. According to the technician, in the context of small-scale subsistence production, "if a cuy dies, it doesn't matter, they don't feel anything because you can just pick out another one. But as they begin to think about commercial gain, and attend training workshops, they begin to feel, they learn how to feel sadness for their cuyes." Here is the chronology of cuy production he presented to the audience:

- Stage 1: family production. Usually houses twenty to forty cuyes, and the animals live in the kitchen and feed from the family leftovers. Women are responsible for the animals' care, and they are consumed during special moments of celebration.
- Stage 2: "technified" family production. Includes approximately one hundred cuyes, in cages, but still connected to the home. Families begin to use "improved" males for breeding. The cuy is still used for household and community activities, but there is increased awareness of the potential of commercial use.
- Stage 3: commercial family production. This often involves work among several families in one community, and sometimes between communities. It involves between one hundred and five hundred cuyes. Communities now have better infrastructure, and cuyes are raised for the market. Community commitments are replaced by commercial ones. As the technician stated, "[I]n this stage, they need to leave their social commitments and dedicate themselves to commercial commitments. This is a hard choice, a tough change that involves looking toward other life options, improving their social condition."
- Stage 4: commercial production. Farms range from one to thirty thousand cuyes. The largest farms are in Ecuador, though some in Peru (in the southern coast) have reached ten thousand animals. The technician noted that this is the final stage in this evolutionary scheme, but that Peru is still far from achieving this goal. He also noted that in this moment, the previous stage of "the commercial family farm" is the most viable, and ended by noting that there was still much work to be done as there still is "too much family production" in the Peruvian countryside.

What is important about this scheme, for the purpose of this chapter, is not whether it "accurately" captures what is happening in Peru. Rather, it offers additional evidence of the civilizational work that comes with the gastronomic boom. In this increasingly rationalized mode of production, there is no space for social commitments like festivals and fiestas. The temporality is strictly that of cost-efficient industrial production. Virtually bringing E. P. Thompson to the Andes, this view suggests that modernity in Peru depends on the homogeneity of time, one governed not by religiosity or agricultural rhythms but by the homogenous time of market production.[60] Along with the discipline of time and work comes the discipline of affect. As guinea pig production gets urbanized and industrialized, it is increasingly characterized by the logics of efficiency and productivity, things that are associated with "men's work." And women are increasingly eclipsed in these modernizing visions, with rare cases like Chauca and Veronica representing those exceptions that prove the rule.

CONCLUDING REFLECTIONS

The story of the cuy in the Andes has often been narrated as one of early domestication thousands of years ago. Yet it might be better conceptualized as an ongoing and multidirectional story of humans and nonhumans acting upon each other. As Anna Tsing warns, however, we must be careful not to lose sight of the unequal power relations involved in these processes.[61] In particular, she writes, we must pay attention to the concepts of "home" and "civilization" in discussions of domestication. "Domestication is a feature of the political economy, not care, intelligence or survival."[62] Along similar lines, in their volume on multispecies domestication, Swanson, Lien, and Ween write that "domestication practices are *ordering devices* that often rank the civilized and the savage at the same time that they reconstitute temporal cycles and spatial choreographies. Ordering devices are effective political tools that often justify interventions in the name of progress, development, and/or modernity."[63] This is generative for thinking about cuy production in Peru today. The Antamina technician, for instance, explicitly framed cuy production as a disciplining and civilizing tool that teaches rural families how to "improve" their lives. And he is hardly alone. The modernizing chronology he presented, from family to industrial production, is ubiquitous, and one that INIA, the Agrarian University, private industries, and government entities also use. There are slight differences, with some producers seeing large-scale commercial farming (including export) as the goal and others (such as the INIA) focusing more on familial commercial production. But the direction of change is clear: from rural household economies to urban production at larger scales. In the view of the Antamina technician, this move is also one away from "asistencialismo," or paternalistic handouts (again, embedding this in a neoliberal frame). At the same time, and cutting against the emphasis of the autonomy or liberty of the new producer, knowledge-power relations are at work in this mission. As part of his lecture, for example, the company tech suggested that among the risks in learning new production techniques is "the risk of angering the *ingeniero* who helped you with training by not making the necessary changes to your life." The new producers can be on the road to being free market subjects, as long as they obey.

These civilizing, pedagogical projects are also part and parcel of the work of figuration, operating as Castañeda notes through a "constellation of practices, materialities, and knowledges."[64] The figure of the cuy in this process, removed from his "traditional" context in the Andes, now stands in for modernization. At the same time, however, he does not leave the Andes totally behind. For gastropolitical elites, the cuy figures Indigenous authenticity that is cleansed and transformed into global cosmopolitan cuisine. This signals that Peru has acquired the machinery of modernity with which we transform tradition and culture into commodities and futurity. For Chauca, Veronica, and other cuy researchers and producers, becoming modern subjects entails making the cuy visible, as a national symbol of modernity, of productive citizens, of civilization. They are claiming space. They are moving forward, not stuck in the past, and they (with the cuy) are saving Peru.

And yet the cuy is not only a figure. Writing about his work with botanists, geneticists, and others in Spain and Mexico engaged in cultivating biodiversity, John Hartigan discusses the importance of not losing sight of the more-than-human subjects we think with and write about.[65] He considers the openings—theoretical, methodological, and otherwise—made possible by engaging nonhumans (plants in his case) as ethnographic subjects in their own right and cautions against writing about nonhuman others, for example, as "mere screens on which racial projections are expressed."[66] Of course, Indigenous peoples in Peru and elsewhere have known this, and Native scholars and activists have been making this same point for many years.[67] In other words, the cuy is a living, sentient being, who experiences the processes I have described in this chapter in very particular ways. The cuy, like Martel's llama, also calls for our attention. In the next chapter, I begin to think of some ways we might listen "to the soundscape beyond speech."

Chemical Castration

THE VIDEO SHOWS three men and a young woman in a conference room in front of an audience. Two of the men are wearing white gloves, and one is holding a microphone, pointing to a white board and talking to the audience. The young woman remains in the background, looking in front of her but not participating. One of the men walks over to a small box on a chair and looks down toward it. I can't tell what he is thinking or feeling from the look on his face. He opens the top of the box, then closes it. As the man with the microphone approaches, the man by the box reaches in. The video cuts and we see only the two men and the woman holding something and hovering over it. Another man is erasing something on the white board while the man with the microphone continues to speak, but his attention is on what he and the others are holding. He examines what we will soon learn is a guinea pig. The woman watches without participating, and the man who had been near the box helps by holding the animal. The camera zooms in and we then see the cuy. He is held belly up, his head forcefully and tightly pulled backwards. In the background, the third man (who had been erasing the white board earlier) moves to a table behind them and opens what looks like a large, black medical bag, taking out instruments. The man with the microphone then begins to describe the process of chemical castration, pulling at the animal to expose his testicles. As the camera zooms in, we can detect a slight and subtle smile on the woman's face. As one of the men reaches for something, we see the cuy struggle, moving his paws and trying to pry his head from the man's grasp. The camera cuts again, and then we see the needle. The man with the microphone continues talking, describing what he is doing, as he impassively injects a chemical into one of the cuy's testicles. As he does this, the other man, who is holding the animal tightly, looks away with a grimace, but noticing the camera on him, offers an uneasy smile and then looks back toward the cuy. The animal continues to squirm and screeches. The man finishes one injection and moves on to the next. At this point, the woman very quickly dabs the area with a small gauze pad, and we see that she is now holding the microphone. Once the second injection is done, the camera zooms in on the cuy's inflamed testicles. We can see the animal breathing hard but no longer struggling. The man who had looked away then takes the cuy and puts him back in the box as the other man continues speaking to the audience.[1]

SIX

Death of a Guinea Pig

ON A WARM SUMMER DAY in 2012, I visited a commercial guinea pig farm north of Lima, Peru.[1] The visit was part of my research on the biopolitical dimensions of culinary nationalism, such as the intensification of cuy production and consumption discussed in chapter 5. There were approximately fifteen hundred cuyes at this farm, one of many cropping up throughout Peru, which consisted primarily of two *galpones* made out of corrugated tin.[2] The guinea pigs huddled close together and squealed anxiously as I walked into the *galpón* where they were housed. Most of these large and round cuyes were female, and many had just birthed or were about to give birth. In most cases, just two or three hours after giving birth, females would once again be impregnated, to take advantage of what breeders call the "postpartum estrus period."

I walked the rows of enclosures, looking closely at the pregnant animals. One cuy had just given birth and was repeatedly nudging a dead offspring, eventually giving up and moving on to clean the three others around her. Another round guinea pig was lying on her side, not moving much, and not looking well, so I called Walter over. Walter was the farm's owner and my guide during that afternoon. He looked at her, nodded, and said she was most likely dying of birthing complications. He leaned over, squeezed her, moved her around. She barely responded. Walter then picked her up and roughly tossed this pregnant, dying cuy out of the cage onto the dirt floor behind us. "She is almost gone. She will be dead by morning if not sooner," he said, placing a hand on my back and moving me away from that cage and toward another larger pen with dozens of very young cuyes huddling close together in the corner.

This chapter is a space to think with this individual guinea pig, to think through that encounter, which provoked in me a visceral questioning about the ethics and politics of multispecies ethnography. It also pushed me to consider what a "felt theory" of grief, following Dian Million, might offer in thinking about a politics of life. "A felt analysis," says Million, "is one that creates a context for a more complex 'telling'. . . [and insists on] the inclusion of our lived experience, rich with emotional knowledges, of what pain and grief and hope meant or mean now in our pasts and futures."[3] For me, the affective power of witnessing that moment is undeniable. After all, many years after that encounter, I continue to think and feel that particular moment. There was something about that experience that, as Naisargi Dave describes in her discussion of animal activism in India, called me into a sense of connection and responsibility. Dave writes about the intimacy of this kind of moment, because it "expands ordinary understandings of the self and its possible social relations."[4]

And yet I also worry about the limits of grief. What does my grieving for this guinea pig *do*? In this context, what are the politics of "feeling with animals," as geographer Kathryn Gillespie might say?[5] And what about Walter? Following Bhrigupati Singh and Dave, what would emerge in attending to the "everyday affects, the doubts and pleasures, cruelties and indifference expressed by our ethnographic interlocutors while witnessing or executing the death of animals"?[6] In these pages, then, I want to think about life through the multispecies (or multi-*being*) affective entanglements that make up this particular encounter with cuyes (and the humans) living, laboring, and dying in contemporary Peru.[7] Thinking with grief, I consider how these experiences of life, reproduction and death might inform discussions about multispecies ethnography and our responsibilities as ethnographers working with human and more than human others. What would it have meant, for instance, if I had responded not only to Walter (his hand moving me away from the dying animal), but also to the cuy's imminent death? I realize now that my grief was really about the way she died and the questions that raised about the way she lived. What can that cuy's death—or as Singh and Dave might put it, what could the mode and the mood of her dying—tell us about her life, about my life, about the knotted relations that are always already part of life itself? This chapter is a modest effort to theorize what grief has to offer to the practice of multispecies ethnography. Writing about the ethnographic encounter as one of tragedy and loss, I argue, might open up the productive possibilities of mourning and grief in connecting human and nonhuman worlds.

IT HAS TO BE DONE

It is a Friday in November (2016), and I'm at the auditorium of the Universidad Nacional Agraria in La Molina, a quiet middle- and middle-upper-class district in Lima. It is the first day of the national symposium, "Advances and Perspectives on Cuy Production," and the place is packed. Most of those in the auditorium are young men—university students, cuy producers, researchers—and of the fifteen or so featured speakers on this day, there is only one woman, a researcher from INIA. Discussions on this day range from a focus on genetic improvement and meat quality, to the most effective slaughter techniques and marketing strategies, to the historical and contemporary significance of the cuy in Peru and beyond. The INIA researcher's lecture moves familiarly through the beginning of the Cuy Project in the 1960s to the INIA's pioneering research on cuy genetics and its work with rural families in developing cuy production. At this point, she begins offering more details about the INIA's current research.

Researchers at the institute are working on manipulating muscle fibers in order to minimize fiber and increase the amount of cuy meat, and they are seeing some exciting results; they are working on further reducing the time between birth and kill-weight and are close to reducing this to fifty days. The goal is forty-five days. She then moves to a discussion about female cuyes and birthing. "You all want more and bigger babies, but imagine a woman weighing sixty pounds giving birth to a baby of thirty pounds." She continues. "We need to keep in mind the female's body, her breathing capacity, the size of her thorax. You want them to produce more milk, but we need to think also about mastitis. You men never think about this. The poor females have larger teats full of milk, but that means they are rubbing against the floor of their pozas, next to shit, getting infected. Do you treat this condition? No. You don't even notice. This is a problem." I am fascinated by her projection of blame—for "having" to manipulate cuy bodies for maximum production, for not caring properly for birthing mothers—onto the male producers present. And then she suddenly says , "and also, we need to start thinking about killing certain babies. We need to determine key qualities, such as size and strength, that we can use to know which ones to kill in order to maximize the survival rate of others. It breaks my heart (me parte el alma), but it has to be done."

Walter is the general manager of SuperCuy, a private guinea pig production company based in Lima.[8] As discussed in chapter 5, cuy production—the business of breeding, killing, and marketing guinea pigs for national and global consumption—has skyrocketed in Peru over the past few years. With the gastronomic revolution as background, demand for cuy meat has soared in the country, and increasing numbers of young men and women are trying their luck at starting their very own cuy business. This is the context in which Walter works. Walter self-identifies as mestizo. He was born in Lima, shortly after his parents migrated to the city from the Andes. At forty-six, he is proud of the fact that he has worked for most of his life to support his family, first his parents and siblings, now his wife and three children. About ten years ago he was struggling to find work when a friend told him about a cuy workshop. After attending the first lecture, he told me, he was hooked and decided to throw himself into the cuy business. He started in 2010 with a focus on large-scale export, but due to bureaucratic constraints, he shifted his focus to the promotion of cuy production and consumption within Peru. Walter regularly offers sessions for those eager to learn about the ins and outs of cuy business, and of course he owns his own breeder farm and sells guinea pigs to families, restaurants, and supermarkets in Lima. Like others involved in guinea pig production, Walter has produced countless YouTube videos discussing cuy production.

Walter is deeply invested in this business, and as I got to know him through conversations, encounters at festivals, and listening to interviews with him, I realized this was much more than just a business. His family has lived on the margins of Lima's sprawling metropolis for years, but through his business ("thanks to the cuy," he says), he is inching his way in. The time and resources he spends promoting the cuy as an animal of which Peruvians should be proud speak to broader concerns that betray a keen understanding of his own location in Peruvian racial hierarchies, hierarchies that link the cuy to particular bodies, rural spaces, and migrant neighborhoods in Lima. That said, let's return to Walter's business, and more specifically, to his breeding farm.

As he has told me many times, Walter's most valuable assets are the female bodies of the thousands of guinea pigs he owns. He earns at least three times as much from one *reproductora* than he does selling a male or "spent" female cuy for meat. "I care for them deeply. I love my little ladies," he told me during one lunch, his language of love and care seamlessly woven within a narrative of profit. It was at this lunch that Walter invited me to visit his farm. Access to these sites is not easy to obtain, so I was excited about this visit, and especially grateful to Walter for his openness and generosity.

It was a sweltering day in February 2012 when Walter picked me up at my grandmother's apartment in Lima. The door of his rusted red station wagon creaked when I opened it, and as I sat down on the scalding black leather seat, a blanket of heat and smoke engulfed me. As we drove north, Walter told me the farm was just a few months old. He had accumulated almost eight thousand *reproductoras* or female cuy "breeders" in another farm, but people broke in, destroyed that facility, and took his animals. "They left several hundred dead ones," he told me angrily, "and they left me lots of dead babies." He was quiet for several minutes. But then he added with a smile that he was determined to get back on track. He had been struggling financially, but he was convinced of the productive value of this business and excited about the possibilities.[9]

We arrived at Walter's farm at around three in the afternoon. The sun was strong and the air was thick. The one thing I have not yet mentioned is that I was seven months pregnant at the time. And in the stifling heat and humidity of this Lima summer, I was miserable. My feet and hands were swollen and sore, my throat cried out for constant hydration, and my back was in pain with the weight of new life in me. Maybe it was the physical discomfort, or the dryness of my throat, or the hyperawareness of life at that moment that made it so difficult to look at the fifteen hundred or so guinea pigs at Walter's farm. The guinea pigs were divided between two galpones, each with a double ceiling designed to help keep the heat at bay. Before stepping into each galpón, we had to put covers over our clothes, shoes, and hair and step on a white powdered substance to disinfect our covered feet.

As soon as we entered I heard cuyes scurrying, their high-pitched squealing piercing the air. Had Walter entered the galpón alone, the animals would not have scrambled to move away. Cuyes are social animals with a keen sense of smell and hearing who recognize and respond to their caretakers. They are easily stressed by disruptions, one reason a leading guinea pig researcher emphasizes the importance of delegating specific groups of cuyes to specific individual caretakers in order to avoid "unnecessary stress" that translates into a loss in profit.[10] I walked through the galpón, looking at the large and round cuyes. At first glance the animals looked fine, healthier and more alert than I thought would be the case given the stifling heat. But I noticed that the galpones did not include any water for the animals. When I asked about this,

Walter told me the animals got all the water they needed from the *forraje*, the roughage, they ate. I told him that what was left of the forraje in each of the dozens of enclosures seemed dry because of the heat, and he suggested we give them more. Walter took an armful of the rough branches leaning against the walls of the pen and handed them to me. The branches were heavy, jagged, and scratched my arms as I tried to place them gently on the ground around the cuyes, so as not to startle or hit the animals. I watched as Walter threw the branches at the cuyes, quickly and roughly. He laughed at my technique, saying that the way I was laying down the roughage would take all day and that there was no need to be so careful. The forraje does not hurt them, he said. "They are used to us throwing it at them." It was as I placed the forraje in each pen and looked more closely at the animals that I caught other details and noticed the guinea pig who would soon be tossed out onto the dirt floor.

And here is where I want to return to the question of grief, and of research with nonhuman others in specific contexts. In that moment, I tried not to betray my sadness. I tried to disconnect myself from Walter's roughness. I tried not to think about the guinea pig's wounded body, now lying alone, in the dusty, sweltering heat. I'm not sure what I could have done differently. Or rather, I'm not sure that anything would have changed had I done more than simply continue to walk, more than allow him to move me away from her. But I can't help but think back and attempt to theorize that moment of sadness, which I think is also one of shame—the shame of taking *his* side, of worrying about *my* research, about what would happen if I criticized his actions. Would doors close? Would my concern for this cuy raise questions that might imperil access to these kinds of spaces? In that moment, I felt my project, the so-called multispecies research I was conducting, was taking place at the expense of the animal.

KNOTTED ENCOUNTERS

As I worked through this encounter, I thought of Donna Haraway's work on companion species, connection and "response-ability." Following Haraway, I could think of these cuyes as "ordinary beings-in-encounter," that is, "meaning-making figures that gather up those who respond to them into unpredictable kinds of 'we.'"[11] But who exactly is gathered up in this unpredictable "we"? And what are the shifting contours and cartographies of that "we"? At what moments do I think of intimacy and connection with cuyes, and when do I connect mostly through betrayal? And anyway, is this about guinea *pigs*, or about a particular female guinea pig whom I happened to encounter when I, too, though in entirely distinct ways, was experiencing pregnancy?

Here I find it useful to think with Native scholars Kim TallBear (Sisseton Wahpeton Oyate), Daniel Heath Justice (Cherokee), and Dian Million (Athabascan) about the significance and specificity of *relations*.[12] As Million writes, "[W]e are living in a time when the most vulnerable die (this includes many, many life-forms), a worldwide experience that affects our vital relations with life itself. There is a struggle against the capitalization, the commoditization of life even as it is happening."[13] Relationality is central to considerations of human-animal entanglements.[14] Yet as these scholars all note, context matters. In Peru, the simple act of mentioning this multispecies connection as possibility—to think of the "we" made up of particular and individuated human-animal relations—is often seen as transgressive and inappropriate. To give one example, when I shared my distress over the death of this cuy with some women in my family, they became very angry and told me not to be ridiculous. In their view, referencing even the possibility of a connection to a pregnant (nonhuman) animal was insulting to women, and I shouldn't say such things. They are of course not alone in this view. There are many forces that keep us from voicing such thoughts, including those that operate in the everyday workings of anthropological research.

But this story is more complicated. Some in my family are also invested in the erasure of indigeneity from our history. For instance, I did not learn that my grandfather was a Quechua-speaking man from the southern Peruvian highlands until I was in my twenties. The refusal to acknowledge our Indigenous ancestry is a common story in Peru and elsewhere and is intimately linked to colonial histories of violence and dispossession. It is also linked to the disavowal of Indigenous epistemologies and ontologies that take seriously the sentience and political agency of more-than-human beings. While many of my Peruvian colleagues and interlocutors do take seriously the legacies of colonial violence that continue to shape the lives of a majority of Peruvians, they would not similarly worry about the lives of nonhuman animals or control over their bodies and beings, about the "overactive production" of animal life in the service of global capitalism.[15] Indeed, considering violence against animals in the context of ongoing dispossession and crushing human poverty can be read as enacting another kind of violence, evoking colonial ghosts. Long histories of racial violence, of the animalization of Native peoples, make this a particularly powerful concern in Peru. Indigenous peoples have long been seen as "just animals." During previous fieldwork I heard many Peruvian bureaucrats say that Indigenous peoples did not feel cold or pain in the same way they did, "because they are more like their animals," and Andean peoples have often been compared to alpacas and llamas.[16]

And yet it is perhaps all the more important that in this context, we call attention to the entanglements of human-animal violence. What happens when we refuse to see connections? Quite predictably, we miss the ways in which animality and racialization, nature and culture, have long mutually shaped each other. The same logics of classification and hierarchies of difference that govern human mastery over nonhumans are at work in projects of coloniality and racism.[17] Thinking of violence against humans and animals in critical juxtaposition and relation, and not in terms of moral or phenomenological equivalence, can move us from atomistic calculations to considerations of broader webs of life, kinds of relational ontologies that have long been part of the worldview of Native peoples throughout the Americas.

While for some in Peru, then, there is an incommensurability in thinking humans and animals together, for others it is a critical move toward alternative political projects. For example, José María Arguedas, Peru's most prominent novelist, known primarily for his important writings about cultural resilience and racial revolution, writes powerfully about the death of the Peruvian pelican in the coastal town of Chimbote. Arguedas describes the bodies of dying, mutilated birds on the beaches of Chimbote as a result of the pollution and toxic waste of multinational factories in that town.[18] Importantly, Arguedas makes a clear link between the suffering and death of these birds and the suffering of Indigenous peasants living in this town who "struggle for survival through desperate and creative means to overcome disease, hunger, despair and violence in the marginalized *barriadas* or slums of Chimbote, the discards of a frenetic and irresponsible industrialization."[19]

Thinking with grief, relations, and responsibility offers other ways to think about the complexities of care. For Walter, caring for his cuyes, and the profit extracted from their bodies, was intimately connected to caring for his family, including his ill and dying sister. I am interested in these entangled multispecies intimacies and ethics of care that so often include extraction, confinement, and killing.[20] Who counts as a subject? Who is made killable, or grievable?[21] Who lives, and how? These are all questions that take us back to material bodies. As I thought back to moving away from the cuy's dying body, my sense of connection to those other female bodies—also hot, also thirsty, also heavy—shattered in that moment of betrayal. I could not help but think about the abysmal difference between my pregnancy, full of futurity and potential, and their pregnancies, fueled by profit seeking and marked for death. And this feeling has haunted me. But could that moment, and its haunting, in fact open up possibilities for recentering and rethinking relations? Could grief highlight connections? A curiosity for better understanding the implications of not just how that cuy died, but how she lived? As I write now, I recall Veena Das reflecting on what it is "to hear the speech of the dying . . . , to desire to speak with the dead."[22] "In what way does one's ethnography contain the voices of the dead and what conflicts, cracks, and disarrays shape the way we (our interlocutors and us) are able to hear these voices?" she asks.[23] Can ethnography capture, or offer a means of listening to, the voices of dying (nonhuman) animals? And what about the *refusal* to listen? What could emerge from reading Walter's refusal to acknowledge—at least to me, in that moment—the guinea pig's suffering? Was I witnessing indifference? Cruelty? Perhaps this simply was another example of the "decidedly uninnocent" forms of relatedness, intimacy, and care that abound in our worlds and lives.[24]

I want to go back to that lunch, where Walter spoke to me about his work, his life, his love for his "little ladies." Walter told me he wanted me to eat his guinea pigs. So I did, knowing that this meal would be one more way in which I would be simultaneously connected to and disconnected from the lives and deaths that were under Walter's care. I would be literally consuming the objects of Walter's professed love, but I would also be asked not to think of these as dead animals. Walter ordered six elaborate dishes for us, all of them cuy based, and all of them centering the cuy unusually, though still "traditionally," evoking the new fusion movement sweeping the country.

After greeting the restaurant's owner, introducing me as "la doctora María Elena García de la Universidad de Washington" (as he would always introduce me), and chatting familiarly with our waitress, Walter motioned for me to sit down at a table next to the kitchen. He sat next to me, ordered some Inka Kola, and began telling me more about the work he is doing and the importance of promoting cuy both nationally and internationally. Walter was particularly proud of the work he and others did to establish the national day of the cuy. In literally putting the cuy on the national calendar, Walter brought this Andean animal into a tradition of nation-building gestures that includes the celebration of the Day of the Indian, later renamed as the Day of the Campesino. Moreover, the campaign to achieve official recognition of the significance of the guinea pig as a cultural and culinary icon in Peru went hand in hand with Walter's efforts to challenge the "persistent racist assumptions" (as he told me) that link eating cuy with indigeneity and poverty. He was very aware of, and extremely bothered by, depictions of cuyes as rats. "They only say cuyes are like rats because our people rely on them as an important food source. But things are changing and we will keep fighting for our cuy." This statement illustrates Walter's keen awareness of his own racial and social position in the country, an awareness that also links his life, and his future, to that of the cuy, one that intimately connects the deaths of these animals to the possibility of new lives, to the capacity to aspire.[25] As the son of poor Andean migrants who arrived in Lima searching for a better life, Walter has struggled financially for decades. His push to change attitudes is certainly driven by hopes of greater demand for his products, but it also reflects a sense of cultural struggle to reposition how people like him and his family are seen in Peru. As a working-class wing of the gastronomic boom, Walter wants to ride the cuy to great respectability, status, and a better livelihood.

The restaurant owner soon stopped by our table to check on our food. We both said all the dishes were delicious, though Walter noticed I was not eating much and exclaimed: "[G]ood thing I brought her here before going to the farm. She might not want to eat them at all after seeing *los animalitos*!" Once the owner left our table, I asked Walter if he ever felt conflicted, or attached to his cuyes, or to particular ones. He laughed and said no. But then he said he understood what I was talking about because like me, his children also worried about eating cuy; they too were sometimes "sentimental" and whenever they joined him at the farm and saw the cuyes, "especially the babies," they begged him not to kill them. Because of this Walter did not allow his children to have guinea pigs as pets, though they often asked. "I have had to explain to my children several times that cuyes are not pets, but food." More centrally for Walter, cuyes were his business. And he had been clear with his children that it was thanks to the cuy that they had food to eat, that they had been able to buy a computer and might be able to move to another more centrally located home in the near future. Or at least that was the case before his sister got sick. Once she was diagnosed with cancer, Walter spent most of what he had to care for her.

Our discussion about children and affective ties to animals seemed like a good opening for me to begin telling Walter about my interest in cuyes, beyond food and culture, especially as he had already compared me to his children, sentimentally (perhaps irrationally in his eyes) attached to *los animalitos*. I mentioned the field of animal studies and told him about some of the classes I had been teaching on interspecies relations. To my surprise he was fascinated by the idea of an interdisciplinary field in animal studies. He was thrilled, in fact, because as he told me, this connected us even more closely. He, too, had to delve into the field of animal behavior in order to know what was most efficient in terms of getting the most out of animals. For instance, he said, "[Y]ou need to know how many to put in one cage so they don't fight; how much food to have so they don't compete. Especially the male cuyes. They are like men: we fight over women and resources."

In line with discourses of cuy production at the INIA and elsewhere, Walter continued to reveal a gendered imaginary as he explained the complex nature of his work. There were precise calculations needed to determine how many females to place in the cage with one male. I was particularly interested in learning when and how often females were bred, so I asked. Walter replied with a fascinating, if disturbing, equivalency: "Waiting 5 days or [until the female guinea pig weighs approximately] 500 grams, would be like impregnating a 12-year-old girl. Waiting 10 days or 600 grams is like getting a 14-year-old pregnant. But waiting 20 days, or until they weigh 800 or 900 grams is like an 18-year-old being pregnant. We wait 21 days because then they are ready to be mothers."

Waiting twenty-one days, he told me, is also more cost efficient; at three weeks old, mothers are stronger, they have more offspring, and fewer of them die giving birth. This is a striking—even jarring—equivalence. But as I discuss in chapter 5, it is not an unusual dimension of practices of animal reproduction. What is also worth noting is the comfort with which Walter spoke of impregnating girls and women to me, a pregnant woman. But my pregnant body was somehow distinct from the pregnant twelve-, fourteen-, or eighteen-year old bodies he had in mind. The cultural capital and status that came with my US-based professional location created a comfortable distance between my pregnant Peruvian American body and the kinds of young women he may have been thinking about.

In my conversations with Walter I have been most struck by how technologies of violence and control deployed against female bodies are made invisible in part through discourses of care. Walter says he cares for his female guinea pigs. He does not extract as much use from their bodies as he could, and he lets female offspring remain with their mothers longer than many other breeders. This, for Walter, is directly linked to how long the animals might live (before they are spent and slaughtered). Naisargi Dave writes of the strange ways in which care for animals can seem more like its opposite: "Cow shelters in which a cow will spend her entire life tied on a short rope to a stake in the ground in the darkness of a shed, periodically milked. Of all the things I have seen, the one thing I wish I could unsee was that. Saved from slaughter, yes, but for what? For life itself. For profit. To perform one's humanity."[26]

Reading this description evoked Elizabeth Povinelli's "rotting worlds" in which life itself, it seems, is but a breath away from death.[27] Similarly for the guinea pigs in Walter's care, who are afforded perhaps some small kindnesses but are nevertheless subject to the sterile rationalities of the production manuals that guide his work. The (slow) death of the guinea pig is a necessary part in the life of his family. Dave writes: "Love is an injustice because when we love it is the one or ones who are special to us that we save."[28] For Dave, love individuates, chooses, makes the particular everything, and thus abandons all else. The clichéd idea that love conquers all may be an apt metaphor here, especially in postcolonial cities, increasingly sites of rampant global capital production that commodify, dismember, and consume bodies at alarming speeds and in ways that make this production invisible to most, even those at its center.[29]

LIFE WORLDS, DEATH WORLDS

In an essay on capitalist structural violence, Lauren Berlant develops the idea of "slow death" to think about what she calls "the phenomenon of mass physical attenuation under global/national regimes of capitalist structural subordination and governmentality."[30] Berlant is especially concerned with spaces in which experience is both extreme and ordinary, where the reproduction and extinguishing of life are difficult to distinguish. She writes: "[S]low death, or the structurally motivated attrition of persons notably because of their membership in certain populations, is neither a state of exception nor the opposite, mere banality, but a domain of revelation where an upsetting scene of living that has been muffled in ordinary consciousness is revealed to be interwoven with ordinary life after all, like ants revealed scurrying under a thoughtlessly lifted rock."[31]

Although Berlant does not extend the notion of slow death to include nonhuman others (aside from her metaphorical ants), I find her thinking provocative and useful. The lives of the guinea pigs at Walter's farm, and at the hundreds of farms emerging throughout the Andes (many of them aspiring toward more intensive agricultural models), are ones of slow death. Here, a guinea pig's existence is one of continuous and confined production of life as she moves toward death.

During our tour of his farm, I asked Walter about the rate of survival of his cuyes, and he said he had a very good one. He told me that less than 1 percent of his breeders die, probably meaning that they do not die while they remain "productive." Berlant reminds us of David Harvey's observation that in capitalist contexts health is defined by the ability to work, something that holds true across the species line.[32] This high survival rate was possible, Walter told me, because unlike many others (and as mentioned previously), he is careful about when to breed his cuyes. He explained: "Most breeders start breeding guinea pigs when they are only one or two weeks old. But that means removing the babies from the cages, which stresses the mothers and the babies, and leads to death. And many don't survive pregnancy when you breed them that early, and even if they do, they give birth to only one or two offspring and then they die."

I listened to Walter that day and felt his words in ways I had not previously experienced. Perhaps it was the impending experience of labor, the anxiety I had begun to feel, that enveloped my listening. Reading over his words again now that my child is eight years old, I can't help but read them through yet another layer of experiences: The physical exhaustion and trauma of thirty hours of labor, the weeks it took my body to recover, and the overwhelming love for this new person in our lives. But this love has been, for me, profoundly entangled with fear and haunted by the specter of death from the beginning. At thirty-eight weeks I had to be induced into labor because I had developed a rare liver condition that could lead to my child's death in utero just two weeks before his scheduled due date. Rushing to the hospital, full of adrenaline and expectation, his birth was already clouded by the possibility of his death. Thinking back to Walter's breeding practices, I can't help but wonder how guinea pigs experience them. Anxiety, fear, sadness. Those might have been the meanings behind the sounds of vocal mother-pup communication I heard. Such communication has been studied by many scientists, who confirm what we already knew: the mother-infant bond among cuyes is strong, infants call out in distress when separated from their mothers, and mothers show visible signs of grief and anxiety when separated from their pups.[33] And yet in that space, Walter and I were not trying to listen, just the opposite. Learned ignorance or evasion would be perhaps closer to the truth. There is need for more work to take up the task of finding new ways to hear and see. As Agustín Fuentes reminds us, "[W]e must retrain our gaze to include other beings, their diverse sets of physio-behavioral-ecological realities, as part of our questions about human beings with other beings."[34]

THE STRESS OF THE PAIN RUINS THE MEAT

Many of the cuy researchers and producers I met in Peru often referenced two people: Roberto Moncayo, a cuy producer in Ecuador known as having the largest cuy commercial farms in the world, and the director of a cuy production and research center in Bolivia whom I will call Claudia. I was interested in visiting the cuy institute in Bolivia because it had a close working relationship with Peruvian producers and with the INIA, and because I had heard they imported cuyes from the raza Peru in order to breed them with native Bolivian cuyes and then export those animals as Bolivian. They were also, according to several producers, still very interested in the super guinea pig (the genetically modified cuy that was often bred to be twenty times as large as a "normal" guinea pig), breeding them with Bolivian cuyes in order to export them to Europe as lab and fur animals. With all this in mind, I traveled to Bolivia in June 2018 to meet Claudia and learn more about the work at this institute. Much as producers had described, Claudia gushed about the "advances" coming out of Peru, particularly the INIA, and emphasized especially the superior qualities of the Peruvian cuy (el cuy peruano), meaning by this cuyes from the raza Peru. The institute did indeed use the Peruvian cuy "as a base" for its "interracial breeding experiments" (as she put it), but she also noted the importance of protecting the Native Bolivian cuy. She was proud of her institute's conservation efforts in this regard.

After talking for close to an hour, she leaned in toward me and said, "[W]e have been talking a lot about the genetic research we do here and our work with local communities, but what I am most excited to show you is our camal *(killing area). My friend Roberto [Moncayo] has been an amazing supporter, and he has taught me about the importance of "postproduction" (the process of killing and marketing). Efficiency is key, and technology is crucial. And he just gave us the most amazing gift: a peeling machine (*una maquina despeladora*). This has cut our peeling time from two minutes to ten seconds. Come! Let me show you." We walked through the institute offices, through the galpones full of cuyes, to the camal, where Moncayo's peeling machine stood in the center. She walked over to* *it, caressing the machine's side, and told me about the killing process. "We usually stun the animals with electricity before scalding them, but there is also a woman in town who can calm an animal by rubbing her fingers on its head. Then it is easy to cut their throat and bleed them before we scald them in water with lime (cal) to allow for the skin to soften. At this point we can use the peeling machine, and then we move to gutting, cleaning, and packaging."*

The emphasis on postproduction is an increasingly common one as businesses compete with each other and boasting the "best quality cuy" becomes ever more important for sales. Claudia's delight over Moncayo's gift was certainly related to a genuine appreciation for their collaboration and his support. But it was also appreciation for the ways this machine would aid in their production and postproduction of cuyes, as the sale of cuyes, both as breeders and as food, was one way the institute supported the research taking place there. This focus on postproduction also brought back a lecture at the conference where I had heard an INIA researcher talk about killing newborns. The talk, by an agronomist working on milk and meat production at the Agrarian University, was on the impact of postproduction on the quality of cuy meat. "You might have excellent production," he told the audience, "but if your postproduction techniques are not well conceived, you have failed." The agronomist was particularly fascinated with the use of electricity in the postproduction process. Noting "electronarcosis" (or electric stunning) as the preferred way to stun cuyes before killing them, he began describing the studies conducted at his lab. "We have worked extensively on this, conducting studies to see how much electric current is necessary to kill, to stun lightly, to stun appropriately. Sometimes if not done properly the electric current can cause males to ejaculate. And we have had cuyes wake up during scalding because they were not stunned enough. That is not good because the stress of the pain ruins the meat."

MULTISPECIES RESEARCH AND
METHODOLOGICAL ANXIETIES

In the late 1960s George Devereux wrote about the role of anxiety in shaping research.[35] He was especially interested in the anxiety provoked by certain data and the impact this affective engagement with research can have on the ethnographer and on the data. I found myself thinking about this as I reflected on this research trip. After visiting the breeder farm, during the drive back to my grandmother's apartment, Walter had invited me to participate in a guinea pig production workshop he was offering the weekend following my departure. "You should stay!" he exclaimed enthusiastically. "You could participate in the workshop. We have twenty people signed up, some coming from the south of Peru, and even some from Colombia. And the local news will be there."

I was scheduled to be on a plane that Saturday, flying back home. My first response to his invitation was a deep feeling of regret. Why couldn't I stay in Lima longer? Should I change my flight so that I could attend the workshop? This would certainly not be the last time Walter offered this kind of workshop (in fact he leads these sessions quite frequently), but the urge to be as "efficient" and "productive" as I could in that moment of fieldwork (given the impending birth of my child) was powerful. As I thought more about what participant observation might mean in this context, however, I began to worry. Walter had walked me through the different parts of the workshop. As a participant you learn how to pick the best "specimens." You learn to weigh them, brand them, what to feed them, how to house them. You also learn how to kill (or rather, you attempt to learn how to kill). And you practice by trying out several different kill methods (at least four), which include breaking the neck, slicing the throat while holding the animal at the same time, slicing the throat while the animal hangs upside down in a steel cone, and stunning before scalding to death.[36] Would I be capable of killing? And even if I chose not to participate but simply observed, would I be able to witness the suffering of so many animals being killed by unskilled hands? Was this part of the responsibility of choosing to conduct a multispecies ethnography? Or was this line of inquiry, my assumptions and presumptions about suffering and killing, foreclosing epistemological and methodological possibilities?

As a Peruvian woman and anthropologist, it has been a challenge to think about these difficult questions, for multiple reasons. But the concerns I explore here—about care and killing, life and death, race and settler colonialism, poverty and the nonhuman, and my own positionality as a Peruvian anthropologist based in the United States but committed to collaborative and decolonial frameworks—also pose a profound personal and intellectual challenge, because they take me back to my grandmother, the person who taught me so much in her kitchen and a woman who knew how to kill chickens and cuyes to feed her family when she lived in rural Peru, but who more recently enjoyed the convenience of supermarkets and delivery chicken in her home in urban Lima. As the smells and memories of my grandmother's kitchen became entangled with increasingly violent forms of industrial agriculture, I found myself wondering about the dark sides of love and the slow death that seems to envelop us all not only as people, but as animals caught in a political economy of living and dying.

Methodologically, how does ethnography change when it includes nonhuman others? How *should* it change? Along these lines, Alice Kuzniar asks "whether acknowledgement of empathic sensibilities might permit us to circumvent the condescension and cruelty that can often dominate relations with animals." She continues, "Mindful that we cannot fully eradicate the power relations that determine our dealings with the creatures dependent on our care, can we nonetheless try to rethink our attachment to it in terms of reciprocity and responsibility?"[37] But what does multispecies reciprocity and/or responsibility look like? What does collaborative research mean in this context?[38] This is tricky ethical territory. Anthropologists have a code of ethics with clear limits to participant observation. But multispecies research, if taken to mean that nonhuman lives matter beyond metaphor and symbolism, raises new questions about the intersection of ethics and methods. Is killing other-than-human animals, for example, an acceptable dimension of participant observation? What are the ethical implications of calls for "moving beyond human exceptionalism" and privileging multispecies analyses?[39] How can we move past human-centered understandings of hierarchies and lines separating the human from the animal, boundaries we reinforce daily even as we try to contest them?

As is by now well known, scholars in multiple fields are worrying with increasing specificity about how to apprehend ethnographically the vital presence of nonhuman actors, and many have cleared paths that lead us to more thoughtful ways to challenge human exceptionalism. I have in mind not only the contributions of multispecies ethnographers, historians, and literary scholars, but also work in "new materialisms," Indigenous metaphysics and theory, and recent work on the politics of seeing.[40] Some scholars insist that the value of multispecies work lies in the challenge it poses to naturalized distinctions between humans and other species.[41] As Emily Yates-Doerr puts it, "[T]he power of multispecies scholarship ... lies not in how it 'centers the animal' but in its challenge to conventional taxonomic formulations of classification and belonging."[42] The challenge I was experiencing was also a challenge to my understanding of ethical participant observation. How did the presence and suffering of guinea pigs affect the way that I could position myself in the ethnographic encounter?

To put it another way, when I enter Walter's farm, I must be Walter's friend, not the guinea pigs'. To understand the cuyes' fate, I cannot save them. Is this the tragedy of multispecies work? I think of colleagues like political scientist Timothy Pachirat, whose ethnography of violence and slaughter would not have been possible without his participation in the killing of thousands of animals, and of geographer Kathryn Gillespie, whose work on the gendered violence of dairy production provoked similar anxieties about the ethnographer's complicity in violence against nonhuman bodies.[43] But perhaps there is some hope that can be found in the echoes of these moments. In writing about the ethnographic encounter as one of tragedy and loss, we open up the productive possibilities that come with mourning and grieving.[44]

CONCLUDING REFLECTIONS

In the summer of 2018, the world was captivated by the remarkable story of a grieving orca mother, a twenty-year-old female whom scientists named Tahlequah, who had given birth to a female calf that died after thirty minutes. Tahlequah carried the body of her dead calf for seventeen days, what many called a "tour of grief," calling important attention to the complex emotional lives of nonhuman animals.[45] But Tahlequah's grief was recognizable in ways that the grief of other animals, such as cuyes, might not be. This is where the stories we tell, and the ways in which we tell them, matter. Thom Van Dooren invites us to tell "lively, fleshy stories" about multispecies entanglements because, he argues, they can "draw us into new kinds of relationships and, as a result, new accountabilities to others."[46]

In his affecting memoir *Eating Animals*, Jonathan Safran-Foer explores the terrain of shame. He expands on Walter Benjamin's and Franz Kafka's reflections on the link between eating animals, shame, and forgetting. He says: "[S]hame is the work of memory against forgetting. Shame is what we feel when we almost entirely—yet not entirely—forget social expectations and our obligations to others in favor of our immediate gratification."[47] He continues: "Silently the animal catches our glance. The animal looks at us, and whether we look away (from the animal, our plate, our concern, ourselves) or not, we are exposed. Whether we change our lives or do nothing, we have responded. To do nothing is to do something."[48]

I want to suggest that multispecies ethnographic research is necessarily, if only partially, an engagement with shame and against forgetting. But reflecting on research, writing, and producing multispecies ethnographies can be a way to remember, a way to conjure up the shame or grief of the ethnographic encounter as a pathway toward recalling and challenging violence. It can be a way to grieve for the other-than-human beings included in our work. Centering grief and rage as methodological inspiration and practice is not new in anthropological writing.[49] But with some important exceptions, it has thus far been primarily a human-centered endeavor. The anthropological turn to multispecies ethnography is an important corrective to this. Writing about the violence done to guinea pig bodies *as violence*, for instance, is a way to "do something," to grieve, to remember. In his essay on animals and precarious life, James Stanescu expands Giorgio Agamben's and Judith Butler's insights about bare and precarious lives to consider nonhuman animals.[50] He begins by describing the meat counter at his local grocery store, with people looking at cuts of meat and live lobsters, picking their dinner:

> And suddenly, the scene in front of you shifts. No longer are you seeing normal products of everyday existence. In front of you is the violent reality of animal flesh on display: the bones, fat, muscles, and tissue of beings who were once alive but who have been slaughtered for the parts of their body. This scene overtakes you, and suddenly you tear up. Grief, sadness, and shock overwhelms you, perhaps only for a second. And for a moment you mourn, you mourn for all the nameless animals in front of you.[51]

But immediately he notes that this mourning is all but unspeakable. Indeed, it is a reaction that for many, perhaps most, people is unintelligible and even laughable. For these reasons, Stanescu notes, "[M]ost of us work hard not to mourn. We refuse mourning in order to function, to get by. But that means most of us, even those of us who are absolutely committed to fighting for animals, regularly have to engage in disavowal."[52]

At their best, multispecies ethnography and animal studies can help us move from what Claire Kim calls the politics of disavowal to an ethics of avowal.[53] For my own work, I think back to the pregnant guinea pig Walter said would not survive her birthing complications and who was tossed onto the dirt to die, alone and forgotten. Writing about her and remembering her is perhaps a small gesture, but it is one way, the only way I have now, to refuse the idea that her life does not count, that hers is not a grievable life. This suggests that we need to find ways for anthropology to embrace and enact the poetic and political work of mourning, even while there may be limits. Walter Brueggemann's *Prophetic Imagination* offers a wonderful reminder that biblical prophets grieve on two levels: they grieve for the suffering of those they care for, and they grieve because the suffering that is so visible to them goes unseen by others. Because that pain goes unseen, Brueggemann notes, prophets must also be poets. The poetry of grief must conjure images and metaphors that are equal to the pain of disavowal and powerful enough to give public expression to that pain, illuminating the "real deathliness that hovers over and gnaws within us."[54] In the prophetic work of making pain public, new horizons of possibility emerge, or as Brueggemann puts it, "an embrace of ending permits beginning."[55]

One need not operate in the Judeo-Christian tradition to be open to these kinds of possibilities. Physicist and philosopher of science Karen Barad has made a similar call to be attentive to poetics, "as a mode of expression, not in order to move away from thinking rigorously but, on the contrary, to lure us toward the possibilities of engaging the force of imagination in its materiality."[56] Visual artist Chris Jordan provides a striking example of both Brueggeman's active mourning and Barad's poetic mode of expression in an arresting series of photographs and a film about the birdlife on Midway Island, an island that sits thousands of miles away from any human community and yet is still subject to the violence of human worlds.[57] Photographs of the decomposing bodies of albatrosses (along with many other species of birds, the sole inhabitants of that island) reveal stomachs full of plastic products. To make the tragedy even greater, many of the dead bodies are of albatrosses just days or weeks old. Jordan explains that the "chicks are fed lethal quantities of plastic by their parents, who mistake the floating trash for food as they forage over the vast polluted Pacific Ocean."[58]

As Jordan reflects on this work, he hopes that people might see these heartbreaking images as a kind of mirror. "Like the albatross, we first-world humans find ourselves lacking the ability to discern anymore what is nourishing from what is toxic to our lives and our spirits."[59] Jordan's work provides a complementary and perhaps even hopeful alternative view to the theoretical work on love provided by the theorists I have cited here. If the thick bonds of love are somehow linked to the reproduction of injustice in forgetting the many for the sake of the select few, Jordan suggests that there is hope in heartbreak. The heart, he told my students during a visit to my university, is a muscle, and like any muscle, it only gets thicker and stronger by breaking. I too hope that heartbreak may make us more open to more radically encompassing forms of justice that do not depend on the predictable collectivities of family, nation, race, or species, and leave room for the "unpredictable we" that crosses those lines. With Barad, I find solace that this kind of thinking "does not require anything like complete understanding (and might, in fact, necessitate the disruption of this very yearning)." Instead, as she concludes, "living compassionately requires recognizing and facing our responsibility to the infinitude of the other, welcoming the stranger whose very existence is the possibility of touching and being touched, who gifts us with both the ability to respond and the longing for justice-to-come."[60] Barad's graceful prose reminds us that our responsibility to the other, the very heart of the notion of justice, depends upon our very ability to respond.

In that spirit, I end with the words of Rocío Silva Santisteban, a Peruvian scholar who has brought a powerful ecofeminist sensibility to discussions of power and violence in Peru. She has published academic articles as well as opinion pieces in important Peruvian newspapers, but as Brueggeman, Barad, and others might have predicted, it is in her poetry that I find the most insight and power.[61] In one poem, "A Dog on the Tracks of the Metro," she describes a harrowing scene in which a dog, unaware of the dangers of public transportation, finds himself on the tracks of the metro. Awaiting the inevitable disaster or perhaps amused by the tail-wagging dog who was unaware of the scene he had created, she observes cutting through the anxiety of the onlookers a young girl with a pony tail, who hops down, saves the dog, and scrambles back onto the platform, without so much as a round of applause. She concludes her poem with questions that resonate deeply with my own:

¿Quién soy yo en esta escena?	Who am I in this scene?
¿Soy la víctima inocente sin salida	Am I the innocent victim trapped
que ladra y mueve la cola	barking and wagging her tail
irresponsable ante la muerte?	irresponsibly in the face of death?
¿Soy la joven que se lanza sobre los rieles	Am I the young woman leaping on the tracks
impelida por la vida a actuar de forma urgente	compelled by life to act urgently
sin respetar códigos o normas?	without concern for rules or norms?
¿O soy el que graba, acobardado, esperando	Or am I the one who cowardly records,

el impacto del tren contra ese cuerpo

para causar en las redes otro cierto
tipo de impacto?

¿Y quién eres tú que impasible

saboreas estas palabras
como si no fueran contigo?

awaiting the impact of train
and body

so that I can have another kind
of impact online?

And who are you, who
impassively

samples these words as if
they were not about you?

Epilogue

HUACAS RISING

AFTER OUR INITIAL DRINKS and appetizers on the terrace of Casa Moreyra, my dining companion and I were escorted to the main dining room at Astrid & Gastón, a warm but spacious room with gorgeous circular wooden tables, set just enough apart from each other to offer a semblance of privacy to diners. It was an unusually sunny day in June, and the light poured into what, really, felt like someone's living room. Our hostess sat us next to a striking and unusual painting called Story of the Fortunate Huaquero *(*historia del huaquero afortunado*), which struck me as an incredibly apt metaphor for gastropolitics in Peru.*

Huaqueros are looters, persons who clandestinely excavate archaeological sites in order to find pre-Hispanic artifacts to sell illegally, usually to foreign collectors. Huaca (or waca) means sacred in Quechua, and often refers to sacred objects and places. The painting depicts a figure at the top of a mound, with a clear path leading to a huaca, drawn as a simple white triangular outline (a shape often referencing the female gender) with a small, round face. The huaquero is fortunate, as he (huaqueros are usually represented as men) has found his treasure. It is late at night, the stars are shining and seem almost to lead the way. The black canvas and adobe red shadowing of the huaca (the site) provide the background to this story, quite familiar in Peru. To me, the painting spoke to the extractive dimension of this gastronomic revolution and the dishes Acurio, Martínez, and others are so skilled at preparing. It brought to mind the ongoing theft of Indigenous lands, sacred objects, and intellectual property. I wondered why they had chosen this particular painting. Was it mere coincidence that the huaca in the painting (both the site and the archaeological object) has the shape of a pyramid, much like the neighboring Huaca Huallamarca?

FIGURE 9. *historia del huaquero afortunado*, by Cuban artist José Bedia. This painting was on display in Astrid & Gastón during the author's visit in 2015. Image courtesy of Galería Enlace in Lima and reproduced with permission from the artist.

As I sat in front of that remarkable painting, I wondered if Acurio himself was not that *huaquero afortunado*, quite literally making a fortune from the sale of Peru's cultural riches. Of course, there is a clear difference. Huaqueros are considered criminals, tomb raiders, people who betray their country, selling national patrimony, selling history. Instead, the branding, marketing, and sale of Peru, so effusively promoted by gastropolitical elites and led by Acurio, is widely and loudly celebrated. Indeed, selling the nation is seen as the path to reasserting national sovereignty, to re-placing Peru. And it is the aesthetic and economic power of gastropolitics that is doing the quintessentially political work of legitimizing that which would otherwise be illegitimate. Despite claims of inclusion and reconciliation, does it not seem that we are once again in the field of multicultural neoliberalism, in which cultural diversity is celebrated so long as the workings of market liberalism are unencumbered?

Perhaps. But as I have tried to show in this book, beyond simply another example of the commodification of culture, gastropolitics in Peru reflects one moment in an older story of racial capitalism and settler colonialism. It relies on what Mark Rifkin has called settler temporality: a modernizing story that moves unidirectionally toward a form of prosperity that relies upon greater dispossession, capital accumulation, and Indigenous erasure.[1] Here, we might recall performance artist Elizabeth Lino's artistic rendition of Marca Perú, superimposed over the open pit mine that devoured her house and city. The bold and explicit link she makes between the violence of mining, tourism, and national branding offers a powerful critique of Peru's culinary revolution, and Peruvian gastropolitics, as a structure of accumulation and dispossession.

To put it more forcefully, if hegemonic gastropolitics is supposed to reflect the rebirth of Peru, Lino's critique shows us that it in fact signals death in (and produced by) the settler-colonial formation we now call Peru. Following K'iche' Maya activist and scholar Emil Keme, we can think of the gastro-political project that is "Peru" as yet one more "civilizational Eurocentric project" that "recycles colonialist logics" and where—with other nation-states in Latin America—the elimination of the Indian remains the organizing principle.[2] As Keme writes, the dispossession of Indigenous peoples is not in the past, nor has it been "resolved" by nation-states "through the adoption of 'multicultural' or 'intercultural' agendas. On the contrary, racism, xenophobia, heteronormative politics, and class oppressions maintain their force.... [And] those of us who resist extractivist economic policies continue to be viewed as a problem."[3]

Indeed, as we saw in the first part of this book, gastropolitics utilizes multiple strategies to restore racial orders, including (as Keme notes) through a politics of recognition and incorporation. Discussing the "advances" Apega had achieved in its work with producers, for example, Carlos (the Mistura organizer I write about in chapter 3) told me that "sometimes our producers are stubborn, but in general [they] are predisposed to improve. They leave aside critiques and complaints, which is already an extraordinary advance, and they become proactive (*se ponen propositivos*). That is what we need, not those who protest and see the ugly and negative in everything." When we spoke, antimining protests, many led by Indigenous activists, were regularly in the media.

Narratives that center Peruvian cuisine as the force leading to Peru's "second independence," as the culmination of centuries of "beautiful, tolerant, and consensual mixture" and "forbidden love," are not just attempts at making violent histories invisible. As a cultural, economic, and political project, gastropolitics rewrites these histories, depoliticizes them, and strives to reestablish racial and gendered orders. In renarrating the past by sanitizing and discarding specific histories of (for example) slavery, coloniality, and indentured servitude, gastropolitics in fact reimagines the past as a path toward crafting a Peruvian future. Take for example the first few lines of Peruvian poet and journalist Rodolfo Hinostroza's book, *Primicias de la Cocina Peruana. Primicias* means "first fruits" and refers to the link between those first fruits and their future potential. Hinostroza writes: "This is the story of a successful culinary mestizaje, of the peaceful encounter of two gastronomic universes, one European, the other American, to produce a delicious and properly Peruvian cuisine. It is the most successful synthesis of the Indian and Spanish created in America, with the happy contributions of the Arab and Black female cooks who came with the conquistadores.... This encounter led to a cuisine that is delicious and original, singular and succulent,... seductive and addictive, superior and distinct from all other cuisines of the region."[4] Note the language that describes the encounters of (at least) two worlds: peaceful, successful, happy, seductive. This is indeed a seductive framing that has shaped authorized state narratives about Peru as nation, people, and history, and has also obscured histories and futures of extractive capitalism and racial violence. Yet, as I also argue throughout this book, this hegemonic story is haunted by restless ghosts produced in large part by long histories of economic inequality. In particular, the ghosts of General Velasco Alvarado's agrarian revolution and Sendero Luminoso's violent Maoism refuse to let go. In trying to exorcise these ghosts, the gastronomic revolution has attempted to create its own utopic vision of neoliberal futurity. But like the optimistic periodization of the CVR and other efforts to narrate "postconflict" Peru, gastropolitics only serves to obscure what Jean Franco calls the "cruel modernities" that make up Abiayala (or the Americas) today.[5]

More to the point, one of the main arguments of this book is that we can and should read Peruvian gastropolitics as a settler colonial project of racial restoration and Indigenous erasure. Acurio's return to Casa Moreyra is emblematic of an attempt to imagine a future without a Velasquista past. In his role as the benevolent patrón who supports producers as they return to lands as laborers, but working for others, Acurio produces an image of a humane and multicultural capitalism, that is, without racialized rage or resentment. Perhaps even more striking is the example of Virgilio Martínez, a brilliant chef who seems deeply appreciative of the richness of Native landscapes and knowledges but is also literally occupying lands next to Moray. While some might argue that Martínez and his team work *with* Indigenous families, creating opportunities for improved livelihoods, to my mind the power relations at play in his project continue to reproduce agrarian hierarchies and relations. The aesthetic and culinary accomplishments of these chefs are notable, yet the very success of their projects reveals the challenge for Indigenous social movements and their allies to disrupt the reproduction of settler colonial logics and processes of accumulation and dispossession.

That said, we should continue to be attentive to the unexpected possibilities that emerge from the cracks of the cruel optimism of the present. Moreover, as Bolivian sociologist René Zavaleta has argued, the nation-state in the Andes is itself a product of the long struggle between the forces of colonialism and anticolonialism.[6] Some of these disruptions can be detected even within the gastropolitical machine. The stories we explored from Andean producers and chefs (like Aida and Ocampo in chapter 4) remind us that the cracks and contradictions of colonial structures have always been sites for the creation of counterhegemonic projects and new forms of agency.

Shifting our gaze to the new frontier of cuy production, we again find the colonial and capitalist work of dispossession and accumulation, in the ways theorized by Yellowknives Dene scholar Glen Coulthard.[7] In his insightful Indigenous updating of Marx, Coulthard notes that "primitive accumulation" was hardly just a starting point for capitalism but rather an enduring feature, one entangled with the workings of race and gender. Cuy production offers a glimpse of this phenomenon. Domesticated over centuries in the Andes, primarily through the labor and care of Quechua and Aymara women, cuyes are following the familiar script of modernization theory, moving to cities in industrialized settings now overwhelmingly controlled by men. This experience resonates with the findings of historian Frieda Knobloch in North America, where the modernization of agriculture also was a process to center the work of men and dispossess Native peoples from their lands.[8] And yet even here there are opportunities for rethinking agency and voice, in human and nonhuman forms. Seeing how marginalized Andean migrants place their hopes for inclusion on the success of cuy production or listening to how guinea pigs themselves experience these new intensive productive practices provides insights into human and other-than-human agency and mattering.

In a video performance art piece titled *Romería a Quiulacocha* (Funeral procession for the laguna of the seagulls), artist Elizabeth Lino, accompanied by a band, walks alongside local people and a priest in a march that has the feeling of a funeral procession.[9] She carries yellow flowers and arranges them tenderly next to the *laguna* that has ceased to be what it was. She ends the performance enveloped in yellow caution tape holding a sign that reads: "Enough with irresponsible mining and an absent state." This public event is simultaneously a wake and a crime scene. Like the open-pit mine itself, the *laguna* has become "a wound at the very center of the Peruvian map."[10] This performance resonates with Andean cosmologies that expand the limits of life. As Salas Carreño has noted, unlike underground mining that is understood as threatening the fertility of earth-beings, but not necessarily their existence, open-pit mines destroy earth-beings and extract resources from their corpses.[11] Lino's performance centers death and dispossession, all the while calling attention to alternative ways of being in relation with other-than-human kin. In other words, she calls attention to the coloniality of power in Peru and to thinking with "local terrains as sources of knowledge, vitality, and livability."[12]

Lino's work offers a provocation for considering other-than-human life, like cuyes, for including them in histories and politics as beings who labor, who feel, who communicate. It is also an important reminder that the violence of the boom goes beyond the human. What does Peruvian history look like if we take seriously the ghosts of more-than-human suffering? Like the guinea pig death that was rendered ungrievable in chapter 6, what do we do when faced with the spectralities of countless nonhuman lives that go uncounted in accounts of political violence and economic prosperity? For Avery Gordon, haunting evokes those moments when you lose your bearings, "when the over-and-done-with comes alive, when what's been in your blind spot comes into view. Haunting raises specters, and it alters the experience of being in time, the way we separate the past, the present, and the future."[13]

During my last research trip to Peru in January 2020, I found myself thinking back to the huaca, and not just the representation of the huaquero with which this epilogue began. On my last day in Lima, I visited the archaeological site known as the Huaca Huallamarca. This striking pyramidal mound is only a few blocks from Astrid & Gastón. Yet it also takes us to a moment long before the founding of Lima and Peru. Walking through the site one feels the incongruity of this pre-Columbian space surrounded by the opulence of one of Lima's more affluent neighborhoods. But as my friend and colleague, historian Adam Warren, reminded me, this may not be so incongruous. The Huaca serves as a tourist-friendly glimpse of cultural patrimony, a symbol of a modern nation-state that is able to display its Indigenous antiquity. With the argument of this book in mind, one could pessimistically think about this sacred space as yet one more way that settler colonialism operates as both a narrative structure and a structure of dispossession. And yet . . . at that moment, as I stood at the top of the site and looked out onto the city, I wondered, could the presence of this Huaca in fact not serve as a testament to the survivance of Native peoples?

The sign at the entrance to this site tells a brief story about the Huaca's origins and primary uses (from 200 BC to AD 200), its destruction during its use as a quarry for construction materials in the early 1900s, and its eventual restoration by a Peruvian archaeologist in the middle of the twentieth century. It depicts the lone Huaca in the midst of the city, surrounded by Lima's buildings and gray skies. Although it is quite different, this brought to mind the ways in which Chadwick Allen (Chickasaw ancestry) writes about the archaeological and historical representations of Serpent Mound in southwestern Ohio.[14] As in the case of Serpent Mound, this story, in the official version, is about death: the death of a site, of the peoples buried in the site when it was used as a cemetery, and the death of Indigenous peoples themselves, their traces left only as archaeological evidence of a time and life past. But as Allen also notes, following writer and activist Allison Hedge Coke's (Cherokee, Huron, Creek) reading of Serpent Mound, we could also think of the huaca as an "animate force in possession of its own voice" and of the "possibilities of [its] reclamation, restoration, and renewal."[15] "In Hedge Coke's vision," Allen continues, "however much earthworks may have been destroyed or degraded, . . . they remain vital and continue to embody knowledge."[16]

Serpent Mound, like the Huaca Huallamarca, could also be read as one more stop for tourists in Ohio. However, Native peoples, activists, and poets reenergize relations and listen to Serpent Mound, understand the mound and other earthworks as living beings. While the site and context I describe here are radically different, I still find it important to ask what it would mean for the Huaca Huallamarca to "embody knowledge." While I can't claim relation to this huaca, or to be able to hear the voices within or feel the knowledge it carries, I do know that as I stood there, I felt sadness, strength, resolution. And hope. I looked ahead to a few months later when I would return with my son, when I could offer him a different reading of this space, one that refused hegemonic narratives of Indigenous pasts and foregrounded instead Indigenous futures. Rather than seeing the Huaca in the midst of San Isidro as yet another example of indigeneity swallowed up by modernity, or as culture commodified, and following Palmiro Ocampo's invitation to shift just a little of the established order of things, perhaps we can see instead Indigenous vibrancy, a refusal to be consumed, a refusal to die on someone else's terms. With Aida, and many others, perhaps we can insist on visibility and resilience. Perhaps we can insist on life.

NOTES

PREFACE

1. Simpson (2014: 177). Reprinted with permission from Duke University Press.
2. King (2003: 9). Reprinted with permission from University of Minnesota Press.
3. "Documental Marca Perú 2011 (Versión Oficial de la Campaña Nacional)," posted on May 12, 2011, YouTube video, https://www.youtube.com/watch?v=8joXlwKMkrk.
4. "Peru Brand: A Symbol Linking All the Country," https://peru.info/en-us/brand-peru.
5. Unless otherwise noted, all translations are my own.
6. As I was finalizing book revisions, COVID-19 changed the world. Peru, like so many other places, has been severely affected by the pandemic, and its long-term impact on Peruvian gastronomy and tourism remains unclear.
7. See "The Generation with a Cause," Paid Post, *New York Times*, n.d., www.nytimes.com/paidpost/peru/the-generation-with-a-cause.html.
8. Quijano (2000). See also Lugones (2007) and Cusicanqui (1987).
9. Loichot (2013: 64).
10. Loichot (2013: 64).
11. Miranda (2013).
12. Miranda (2013: xvi).
13. Miranda (2013: xviii, xix).
14. Million (2014: 32).
15. Million (2009: 55).

INTRODUCTION

1. "The Generation with a Cause," Paid Post, *New York Times*, n.d., www.nytimes.com/paidpost/peru/the-generation-with-a-cause.html.

2. T Brand Studio (www.tbrandstudio.com) is the brand marketing unit of the *New York Times*.

3. "The World's 50 Best Restaurants," n.d., https://www.theworlds50best.com/. Nikkei cuisine holds an important place in Peru's culinary landscape and success. It is recognized as the first "brand" of Peruvian food to achieve global recognition, particularly through the culinary artistry of Nobu (Japanese chef Nobuyuki Matsuhisa). For more information see Acurio (2006), Balbi (1997), and Takenaka (2019).

4. In "The Generation with a Cause."

5. This contest was a private initiative organized by the New Open World Corporation; see New 7 Wonders, "Our Mission," n.d., https://about.new7wonders .com/our-mission/.

6. From Lino's site: *Miss Cerro de Pasco "La Ultima Reyna"*, video, n.d., https:// laultimareina.wordpress.com/miss-cerro-de-pasco-2/promocion-turistica. On her official sash, *reina* is misspelled as *reyna*, a mistake made by the tailor who made the sash for Lino. Rather than have another one made, she kept wearing that one proudly. Perhaps this is another way that she ironically calls attention to the contradictory nature of Peruvian triumphalism and its tendency to celebrate what is often clearly a mistake.

7. Lino's website: https://laultimareina.wordpress.com/.

8. Dajer (2015).

9. Quoted in Vich (2015b: 6).

10. Rodríguez-Ulloa (2013).

11. Vich (2015b: 11).

12. Vich (2015b: 11–12).

13. Vich (2015a).

14. For more on extraction in the Andes, see Bebbington (2009), Bebbington and Bury (2014), Gustafson (2020), and Li (2015).

15. Indeed, we might ask what gastropolitics looks like from, for example, the vantage point of students at the Pachacutec Institute of Culinary Arts, anti-GMO (genetically modified organism) activists, or kitchens in small restaurants in Arequipa, Iquitos, or Cajamarca. Similarly, stories featuring the perspectives of the late Afro-Peruvian chef Teresa Izquierdo, Chinese Peruvian chef Javier Wong, or Japanese Peruvian chef Mitsuharu Tsumura, might have brought to the fore alternative racial formations and histories. Future research should insist on decentering Lima (and the Andes) and attending to the multiple political, cultural, and affective layers that make up gastropolitics in Peru.

16. Berlant 2011 (cruel optimism).

17. CVR (2004). See also Degregori (2012), Del Pino and Yezer (2013), Denegri and Hibbett (2016), Gorriti (1999), Starn and La Serna (2019), and Stern (1998).

18. Wolfe (1998, 2006). See also Kauanui (2016).

19. Acurio (2018a). As others have noted with regard to male advocates of "slow food," "returning to the kitchen," and "cooking in the home," a critical feminist reading of Acurio's push for a return to home cooking would emphasize nostalgia for a heteronormative "past" that relied heavily on the labor of women.

20. Acurio (2018a). See also Acurio (2008).

21. Acurio (2018a). This is a telling gesture. Acurio seems to be reminding viewers that he, too, is a product of all the bloods, a mestizo embodying this Peruvian fusion. Even as he tries to decenter his elite whiteness, however, Acurio can't help but note his noble lineage: he is the son of an aristocratic mother and of a father who was not "just" from the Andes, but from Cusco and the Incas, a descendant of one of the largest empires in the history of the world.

22. Ahmed (2004).

23. Wade (2017: 1).

24. Appelbaum, Macpherson, and Rosemblatt (2003), Sanders (2014), Sanjinés (2004), Stepan (1991), Wade (2010, 2017), Wickstrom and Young (2014) (across the region). Cánepa (2003), De la Cadena (2000), and Portocarrero (2007, 2013) (in Peru more specifically).

25. Stutzman (1981: 45). But see Wade (2005).

26. De la Cadena (2001a).

27. Canessa (2008).

28. Cited in Markham (2010: 8). This description also resonates with discussions by guinea pig researchers and breeders about animal reproduction and birthing experiences. This is not surprising, as animal breeding practices have informed racialized and gendered ideologies about particular humans for centuries (Hartigan 2017; Ritvo 1997; Swanson, Lien, and Ween 2018).

29. Reproduced in Canessa (2012: 245).

30. Canessa (2012: 244).

31. For example, Lugones (2007), Smith (2005), Speed (2019), Stepan (1991), and Stephenson (1999).

32. Stepan (1991).

33. Miró Quesada Cisneros et al. (1992) and Vargas Llosa (1991).

34. Miró Quesada Cisneros (1992: 246).

35. Miró Quesada Cisneros (1992: 248).

36. Apega was a crucial promoter of Peru's gastronomic revolution. The organization officially disintegrated in 2019, after the death of Mariano Valderrama (one of its founders) and amid rumors of financial mismanagement.

37. Bernardo Roca Rey, a member of the elite Miró Quesada family, is a Peruvian entrepreneur and writer who owns *El Comercio* and was the president of Apega until the organization's disintegration.

38. Portocarrero (2007: 30).

39. Acurio's work with youth from marginal areas of Lima at his Pachacutec Cooking Institute is also often noted as an example of his work to improve the lives of poor Peruvians through education. Of course, "education" has played a crucial role in civilizing Native others in Peru and elsewhere (Child 1998; Child and Klopotek 2014; García 2005; Gustafson 2009; Luykx 1999).

40. Altamirano Rua and Altamirano Girao (2019).

41. Matos Mar (1984).

42. Brown (2006).

43. De Trazegnies (1992: 211).

44. De Trazegnies (1992: 211); emphasis added.

45. Elias (1994).

46. Generación con Causa, "Manifiesto," https://peru.info/es-pe/generacion concausa/manifiesto. Drafted by chef Palmiro Ocampo (whose work I discuss in chapter 4) in collaboration with Acurio and fellow chefs, this text offers a complex and multilayered representation of Peru's culinary revolution. While in many ways this document sustains the coloniality I argue is inherent in Peru's gastronomic revolution, it also opens up alternative readings of this movement and moment.

47. PDAC is described as "the leading convention for people, companies and organizations in, or connected with, mineral exploration" (www.pdac.ca/convention). The site also shows Peru as one of the official sponsors, along with some of the largest mining companies in the world. See Redacción Peru.com, "Canadá: Gastronomía peruana se lució en evento minero más importante del mundo," December 31, 1969 [*sic*], https://peru.com/estilo-de-vida/gastronomia/canada-gastronomia-peruana-se -lucio-evento-minero-mas-importantes-mundo-noticia-129383.

48. Galeano (1973).

49. While the term *nonhuman animal* is often used to mark the fact that humans are also animals, as others have argued, that formulation still centers humans and collapses multiple beings with distinct abilities and emotional lives (such as pigs, bears, whales, ants, dogs, and snakes) into the broad and flattening category of "animal" (see, e.g., de Waal 2017; Derrida 2002; von Uexküll 1957). In this book I try to refer to the specific animal I am speaking about whenever possible. However, for the sake of simplicity, I use either *animal* or *nonhuman animal* when speaking broadly. I also use "other-than-human" to indicate when I am writing about other-than-animal life.

50. See Healy (2001) and Markowitz (2012) for more on the politics and possibilities of the marketing and use of alpaca meat in the Andes.

51. Estes (2019), Justice (2014), and Womack (2013).

52. Acurio (2006), Lauer and Lauer (2006), Matta (2013, 2016a), and Roca Rey (1992).

53. A significant exception is El Señorío de Sulco, a restaurant headed by Isabel Alvarez (and now her son, Flavio Solorzano), which has showcased novoandina cuisine and served Indigenous and regional dishes with pride since the 1980s. As an important academic and writer in her own right, Alvarez has offered incisive critiques about the recentering of Lima and the elitism of the gastronomic revolution (2019).

54. Thanks to Adam Warren for this observation. Raúl Matta (2013: 10) similarly writes about Jaime Pesaque, chef and owner of Mayta restaurant in Lima, who developed a cuy dish in which the animal was deboned by applying the *sous vide* technique, an approach the chef termed an "overturn of tradition" (*un vuelco a la tradición*).

55. Méndez (1996). I was also concerned about the challenge of an ethnographic focus on nonhuman others, on the limits to "bringing the animal in," particularly

without the long-term immersion necessary for conducting sustained multispecies research.

56. While a handful of articles addressed Peru's culinary excellence prior to 2000, it was only at the beginning of this century that Peruvian cuisine began to appear on the global culinary scene (Lauer and Lauer 2006; Matta 2013).

57. Fraser (2006) and Sachs (2008).

58. Mistura began as a modest culinary festival in 2008, but with backing from Acurio and Apega, it grew quickly into the largest culinary festival in Latin America.

59. TallBear (2014: 3).

60. Greene (2006).

61. For example, Acurio recently praised my brother's efforts and his restaurant in a Facebook post. When my brother shared this post with me, I was ecstatic and beamed with pride. Despite my critiques of Acurio's discourse, I recognize the affective power and economic implications of such recognition.

62. Wolfe (2013: 2–3).

63. From the blurb of *The Settler Complex*, published as an edited book in 2016 by UCLA's American Indian Center. See also Rifkin (2014).

64. Melamed (2011).

65. As many critics have rightly noted, calls to move "beyond the human" often do not consider the fraught category of "human" and ignore the continued "animalization" of certain bodies and beings who remain at the edges of and below "Man" (Cattelino 2019; Jackson 2013, 2015; Livingston and Puar 2011; Wynter 2003).

66. Scott (1992).

INTERLUDE: HAUNTINGS

1. Portocarrero (2003: 229).

2. "'La revolución y la tierra' ya es el documental más visto de la historia del cine peruano," October 30, 2019, https://rpp.pe/cine/peru/la-revolucion-y-la-tierra-se -convirtio-en-el-documental-mas-visto-del-cine-peruano-noticia-1227088.

3. The museum's website: lum.cultura.pe.

4. The controversy over *Resistencia Visual* (Visual Resistance) at the LUM, an exhibit curated by visual anthropologist and artist Karen Bernedo in 2017, is a perfect example. See a short note about this at perusupportgroup.org.uk/2017 /08/controversy-at-the-memory-museum/. On the politics of institutionalizing memory see Drinot (2009), Feldman (2012, 2019), and Milton (2014, 2018).

5. Jorge Miyagui and Mauricio Delgado, personal communication with author in 2015; see also del Pino and Agüero (2014).

6. Del Pino and Yezer (2013), Drinot (2009), Falcón (2018), Milton (2014), and Rojas-Pérez (2017).

7. For more on Indigenous temporalities and Native struggles, see Hylton and Thomson (2007), Rifkin (2017), and Swenson and Roddick (2018).

1. Astrid & Gastón website: www.astridygaston.com.

2. "The World's 50 Best Restaurants," n.d., https://www.theworlds50best.com/.

3. This site is a testament to Indigenous histories in Lima prior to the city's founding, as well as their resilience in the face of dispossession and marginalization. There are dozens of *huacas* throughout the capital city, a reminder that Lima was built on top of and around these monuments. On the history of indigeneity in colonial Lima see Charney (2001) and Cogorno and Ortiz de Zevallos (2018).

4. In June 2015, when I visited Astrid & Gastón in its new location, diners had a choice between these two tasting menus. The restaurant has since changed to include an á la carte menu and one shorter tasting menu that changes seasonally.

5. Unlike Matta (2016a: 141), who distinguishes between what he sees as legitimately "Peruvian cuisine" and what he calls "fusion cuisine," I use the term *Peruvian cuisine* to refer to the recent emergence of Peruvian fusion cuisine, as well as more traditional dishes.

6. One story in *The Guardian* in 2014 described history in Lima as divided into two epochs: before Gastón and after Gastón. Nick Miroff, "Gastón Acurio, the Super Chef Who Put Peruvian Cuisine on the World Map," *The Guardian*, August 1, 2014, www.theguardian.com/lifeandstyle/2014/aug/01/gaston-acurio -celebrity-chef-peru.

7. In Medina, Acurio, and Adriá (2012: 15).

8. There is currently a campaign, for example, that calls for the celebration of Peru's "second independence" in July 2021 (Peru declared its independence from Spain on July 28, 1821) by, among other things, declaring Lima the gastronomic capital of the Americas (Apega 2015a). There are, of course, important critiques that speak directly to this issue, lamenting the recentering of Lima (Lauer 2019), and arguing that the boom should do more to foreground the importance of regional cuisine (Alvarez Novoa 2017b, 2019).

9. Veracini (2010) and Wolfe (1998).

10. Gunther (1992) and Parker (1998b). Those familiar with Peruvian history will be aware of the "myth of old Lima," an idealized representation of colonial Lima as a beautiful, clean, and prosperous city constructed by writers, singers, and public intellectuals (see, e.g., Pacheco Velez 1985 and Palma 1923). Among the fiercest critics of this myth is the Peruvian essayist, poet, and playwright Sebastián Salazar Bondy, who wrote his groundbreaking book, *Lima la horrible* (1964), during a context of increasing Andean migration to Lima.

11. Mayer (2009).

12. Before enrolling in Le Cordon Bleu, Acurio spent a couple of years studying at Vatel Madrid, Spain's most prestigious international hospitality school.

13. Gutsche is a renowned chef in her own right. She was named "Best Pastry Chef in Latin America" in 2015; see "Astrid Gutsche Wins the Award for Latin America's Best Pastry Chef, Sponsored by Cacao Barry," www.cacao-barry.com/en -US/astrid-gutsche-latin-americas-best-pastry-chef.

14. Rosenberg (2013: 22); emphasis in original.

15. In Medina, Acurio, and Adriá (2012: 32).

16. Acurio (2016a: 40).

17. Acurio (2016a: 41).

18. Quoted in Lauer (2012: 107).

19. The site was accessed on February 27, 2019.

20. *Viveza criolla*, translated as creole cleverness or cunning, is the idea that people move through the world trying to get away with as much as possible without having to work. It reflects the widely held notion that Peruvians are people who ignore rules and lack a sense of respect or responsibility for others or for their nation. This is, of course, racialized, and speaks to the civilizing dimension of this culinary movement.

21. Alvarez Novoa (1997, 2002, 2013, 2015, 2017a), Rodríguez Pastor (2000, 2007), and Olivas Weston (1996, 2001).

22. Such as La Rosa Náutica (www.larosanautica.com), El Señorío de Sulco (www.senoriodesulco.com), and José Antonio (www.joseantonio.com.pe/).

23. For a sense of the culinary and geographic range of Acurio's restaurants see the website: https://acuriorestaurantes.net/.

24. Cabellos (2009), Pérez (2011, 2014), and Santos (2012).

25. Acurio (2006, 2008, 2015, 2016a).

26. See Carrión (2006), Conaghan (2005), and Crabtree and Thomas (1998).

27. Arguedas (2001). On Arguedas see Melis (2011) and Pinilla (2005). On Toledo's mobilization of race, indigeneity, and a romanticized "Inca" tradition, see de la Cadena (2001b).

28. Vich (2007). This "magical, mystical" framing is also intimately linked to the commodification of indigeneity. One contemporary manifestation is the upsurge in New Age Andean spirituality tourism, what Gómez-Barris (2017) refers to as "new age settler colonialism," which has now expanded to include such things as "Inca weddings," in which couples can wed dressed up as "Incas," be pampered by Indigenous servants, and receive the blessings of *Apus* (mountains). See, for example, "The Romantic Andes: The Arac Masin, Inca Wedding," September 10, 2019, www .livinginperu.com/arac-masin/.

29. The national context is significant, but so is the global context. Having trained in Europe, Acurio would have been keenly aware of the increasingly powerful role of the celebrity chef (Matta 2019; Rousseau 2012). Indeed, he has relied on the support of a vast global network of chefs, with particularly close connections to Ferran Adriá, considered one of the best chefs in the world. This relationship is a central part of the documentary *Peru Sabe: Cuisine as an Agent of Social Change* (Santos 2012), and of a stunning volume, *eden.pe*, featuring writings by and interviews with Acurio and Adriá (Medina, Acurio, and Adriá 2012). More recently, Acurio has used this influence to expand conversations about the power of cuisine in enacting social and environmental change. He hosted the "Chefs' G9" meeting in Lima in 2011—a gathering of some of the world's leading chefs to discuss the role of chefs in the world and to draft what was named "the Lima declaration," a

"gastro-social manifesto" written in the form of a letter to "the chefs of tomorrow." The language of this document echoes many of Acurio's statements about ethics, aesthetics, and social development. Luciana Bianchi, "Chefs' G9: the 'Lima Declaration,'" Fine Dining Lovers, September 27, 2011, www.finedininglovers.com/blog /news-trends/chefs-g9-lima-declaration/.

30. *Guiso* is a stew; chicharrón is a dish of fried pork.

31. Sachs (2008).

32. Valderrama (2016:14).

33. *Anticuchos* are skewers made with marinated beef hearts.

34. Acurio in Pérez (2011).

35. See, for example, Cabellos (2009), Fan (2013), and Santos (2012).

36. For critical discussions of this video and Marca Perú, see Cánepa (2014, 2015), Matta (2014, 2017), and Palacios Sialer (2017).

37. Ají and rocoto are two different kinds of Peruvian chiles, and *picarones* are a typical Peruvian dessert, a kind of "donut" made with sweet potato and squash and served with a thick sweet syrup.

38. From Real Academia Española, *Diccionario de la lengua Española*, https:// dle.rae.es/?id=ANZfcNv.

39. This is also a familiar feature of the world of gastronomy. See, for example, Druckman (2010).

40. Roca Rey (2011: 12–13); emphasis added.

41. As in many parts of the world, certain fields of study are politicized in particular ways. In Peru, to study cultural anthropology was also to be perceived as belonging to the political Left. Given the context of that moment, my family's resistance to my work in the Andes was also linked to their concern over my physical safety. In this case, they saw my work as taking me into a racial, political, and social context that, for them, was unnecessarily risky.

42. Matos Mar (1984, 2004) and Degregori (1986).

43. Brooke (1989).

44. From PromPerú website: www.promperu.gob.pe. The point about sustainable and decentralized development is significant, as it is one of the principal dimensions of the gastropolitical story.

45. From Marca Perú website: https://peru.info/es-pe/marca-peru/campanas.

46. PromPerú (2006: 3).

47. Acurio (2016a).

48. García and Lucero (2008).

49. See Cánepa (2013) for more on nation branding in the Peruvian context.

50. Acurio (2016a: 15).

51. Acurio (2016a: 16).

52. Acurio (2016a: 17).

53. De Soto (1989). While the focus of the original text was on poverty and economic informality, the new and revised edition of De Soto's book emphasizes the links he sees between poverty and terrorism. The change in the book's subtitle is telling. The original text was titled (in English) *The Other Path: The Invisible*

Revolution in the Third World, while the revised edition is titled *The Other Path: The Economic Answer to Terrorism*. In this new edition (2002), De Soto has a new preface that makes connections between struggles against Sendero and the Taliban.

54. De Soto (2000: 169); see also 170–71.

55. Vasconcelos ([1925] 2007).

56. De la Cadena (2000, 2001a) and Portocarrero (2007).

57. Acurio (2015: 11).

58. This text, a large coffee-table book with spectacular photographs, offers a sweeping history of Peruvian cuisine, its principal ingredients, and its cultural influences. It also features Acurio prominently (the cover is a black-and-white photograph of his face), as well as plugging his principal restaurants by showcasing some of their recipes. The book, which was declared "Best Cookbook in the World" in 2008 by Gourmand World Cookbook Awards, was published by *El Comercio* and features a brief introduction by Bernardo Roca Rey, whose family owns the newspaper and who was president of Apega from 2010 until 2019. This itself is an illustration of some of the components of the gastropolitical complex.

59. Acurio (2008: 195).

60. Acurio (2015: 8–9).

61. Lauer and Lauer (2006: 16).

62. Acurio (2016a: 24–25).

63. Acurio in Cabellos (2009).

64. Apega replaced AGAPE, the Peruvian Association of Gastronomy, which was founded in the 1980s to explore the distinctiveness of Peruvian cuisine and promote its global export (Lauer and Lauer 2006; Matta 2013).

65. From www.apega.pe/nosotros/que-es-apega. The websites for Mistura and Apega were accessed prior to June 2019, when they were taken down. All quotes from these sites are recorded in my notes or captured in screenshots.

66. See Apega (2017a, 2017b, 2017c, 2017d), Ginocchio (2012), and Valderrama (2016).

67. Interview cited in García (2013).

68. Cabellos (2009).

69. Quijano (2000).

70. Caretas (2011).

71. Acurio (2009).

72. While the claim is that these young people are training to become chefs, it is increasingly clear that this training is also (perhaps especially) an effort to expand the labor force necessary for the ever-increasing list of high-end restaurants opening in Lima regularly. For a critical look at cooking schools in Peru, see Lasater-Wille (2015). For a scathing critique of labor practices in Peruvian restaurants, and of Acurio and Martínez's complicity, see Yun and Guzmán (2014).

73. Acurio (2015: 8).

74. Acurio (2016a: 69).

75. Acurio in Cabellos (2009).

76. Anderson (2016).

77. Appadurai (1981, 1988).

78. Cookbooks published in English: Acurio (2015) and Martínez (2015, 2016); with a Peruvian middle-class in mind: Acurio (2006, 2018b), Lauer and Lauer (2006), Lauer (2012), Misia Peta (2000); and "the time of fear": Mayer (1991) and Poole and Rénique (1992).

79. Acurio (2008, 2015), Lauer and Lauer (2006), Lauer (2012), and Valderrama (2016).

80. In 2007 the government declared Peruvian cuisine national heritage and worked toward its inclusion in UNESCO's list of intangible cultural heritage (Matta 2013). On the cultural, political, and economic dimensions of Peruvian cuisine as national heritage and intangible cultural heritage, see Matta (2016b) and Cox Hall (2019, 2020).

81. "Peru Unveils New 'Peru, the Richest Country in the World' Marketing Campaign at WTM 2017," Marketing Communication News, November 6, 2017, https://marcommnews.com/peru-unveils-new-peru-the-richest-country-in-the -world-marketing-campaign-at-wtm-2017/.

82. "Peru, the Richest country in the world," n.d., https://perutherichestcountry .peru.travel/en.

83. Apega (2015b).

84. Velasco's revolution was also known as "the Peruvian experiment" (McClintock and Lowenthal 2015) and "the peculiar revolution" (Hobsbawm 1971).

85. Aguirre and Drinot (2017: 2). That said, one of the most impactful episodes of violence in Peru happened under Velasco's rule in 1969, when students and their parents were massacred in Ayacucho (Huanta) when they dared protest against increasing student fees. Some argue that this massacre led to increased support for Sendero, as many of the student leaders killed had worked directly with Guzmán when he was a professor in Ayacucho.

86. "But rather shares": Pérez (2014); emphasis added. Similarly, Acurio often talks about "revolution as liberation," in ways strikingly similar to Velasco's rhetoric (see Aguirre 2017). As with all hegemonic processes, we see how the same political grammar repeats across the centuries in the service of different ideological projects. "Does not make demands": Lauer and Lauer (2006: 16).

87. Roca-Rey (2016).

88. Lauer and Lauer (2006: 16, 122). See also Lauer (2012).

89. Mayer (2009: 3). Velasco was deposed in 1975 due to increasing economic turmoil, unemployment, and political opposition. Military generals from the RGAF declared that Velasco's reforms had not achieved the ideals of the Peruvian revolution and appointed Francisco Morales Bermudez as president (1975–80). Moving away from Velasco's leftist approach, Morales Bermudez declared the "second phase" of the revolution, which would include a reversal of some of Velasco's policies and lead to democratic rule.

90. Portocarrero (2003: 231).

91. Mayer (2009: 3).

92. Mayer (2009: 241).

93. Mayer (2009: xviii).

94. Mayer (2009: 241).

95. Mayer (2009: xix).

96. Drinot (2017a).

97. Quoted in Drinot (2017a: 101).

98. In Drinot (2017a: 101–2).

99. In Drinot (2017a: 102).

100. In Drinot (2017a: 103).

101. In Drinot (2017a: 107).

102. Hirschman (1991).

103. Drinot (2017a: 103). See also Gandolfo (2009), Martuccelli (2015), Parker (1998a), and Protzel (2011).

104. Both in Drinot (2017a: 104).

105. For a fascinating historical analysis of Túpac Amaru's rebellion, see Walker (2014).

106. In Mayer (2009: 96–97).

107. Aguirre and Drinot (2017), Mayer (2009), and Portocarrero (2003).

108. In a telling reflection of the patriarchal nature of Peruvian society, the name Casa Moreyra comes from Luisa Paz Soldán's husband, Francisco Moreyra.

109. I wonder, also, about the personal dimension of this move. The Acurio family was one of many impacted by Velasco's reforms. The family owned half of Maras, a region in the Sacred Valley near the city of Cusco that is home to famous salt mines, and Moray, the archaeological site next to which Martínez built his latest restaurant, Mil. According to one of Acurio's cousins (with whom I spoke in January 2020), their grandmother was among the first to fight against the expropriation of their lands in court, and she was able to regain some of their territory.

110. Mayer (2009: 77).

111. Mayer (2009: 78).

112. See, for example, Garayar et al. (1997).

113. Quoted in Drinot (2017a: 97).

114. There are other examples of this recentering of Lima, such as Apega's "Lima Gastronómica" campaign (http://www.apega.pe/proyectos/lima-capital-gastronomica), and reclaiming the city's imagined history through its old recipe books (*recetarios*). Take one of the opening paragraphs of *Bitute: El sabor de Lima*: "[T]his book . . . is not only a tribute to the city, its old pleasures and to the people who with patience and love wrote down the recipes that brightened their homes in order to share them with us. This book is also a way of returning life to the past (*devolver vida al pasado*)" (Acurio and Masías 2016: 6).

115. See Astrid & Gastón, "The History of Casa Hacienda Moreyra," n.d., http://en.astridygaston.com/history/ (accessed February 22, 2019). Perhaps fittingly, the web design firm that created this site and those for many other elite restaurants in Peru is call Buendía, which translates simply as good day but can also be seen as an allusion to the Buendía family, the fictional founding family of Macondo made famous by Gabriel García Márquez in *One Hundred Years of Solitude* (García

Márquez 2006). That novel, like this house, is premised on a nonlinear sense of time, where the violence of colonial and modern periods is impossible to separate.

116. Altamirano and Altamirano (2019) also speak to what they call the "masculinization" of the gastronomic boom.

117. See Ballón (2014), Bueno-Hansen (2015), Ccopa (2016), Denegri and Hibbett (2016), Guerrero Espinoza (2014), Kovarik (2019), and Theidon (2014). Figures from the Ministry of Women and Vulnerable Populations (which tend to be conservative) note that approximately ten women are murdered every month in the country, and another twenty are victims of attempted femicide. Of the ten women killed, at least six are under the age of twenty (www.mimp.gob.pe).

118. Cipriani is also known for exclaiming, during the worst years of the war between the state and Sendero, that "human rights are bullshit" ("*los derechos humanos son una cojudez!*").

119. Prado (2016).

120. Santos (2012).

INTERLUDE: EATING THE NATION

1. Recipes reproduced from *Central* by Virgilio Martínez, under license from Phaidon Press Limited © 2016.

CHAPTER 2. COOKING ECOSYSTEMS

1. Jeter (2017).

2. See Orlove (1993) for a fascinating discussion of geographical representations of Peru in the late nineteenth and early twentieth centuries that not only created the category of "the highlands" but also linked Indians to highland Peru, while gradually erasing Indigenous peoples from representations of coastal and jungle regions.

3. See Cox Hall (2017), Pratt (2008), and Stepan (2001).

4. Jeter (2017).

5. Jeter (2017).

6. Murra (1975, 1985). See Babb (2020) for a discussion of the significance of Murra and verticality for thinking about race and gender in contemporary Peru.

7. Martínez (2016).

8. In addition to heading Mater, the chef's sister also manages all of his restaurants in Peru.

9. Abend (2018), Beggs (2019), Dixler Canavan (2018), Short (2018), and Kozolchyk (2018).

10. Fagioli (2012: 7).

11. Quoted in Valderrama (2016).

12. Janer (2007).

13. Martínez (2015: 10).

14. "Magnetic": Krader (2016); "chocolate-brown eyes": Bracken (2017).

15. Power (2016).

16. Gastón Acurio, review of *Central*, by Virgilio Martínez, at Phaidon, https://www.phaidon.com/store/food-cook/central-9780714872803/#tab-4.

17. Martínez (2016: 13).

18. Martínez (2016: 13).

19. Martínez (2016: 13). Note the implicit description of Lima as dirty and insecure "during that time," taking us back to gastropolitics as partly about "cleansing" the city.

20. Jeter (2017).

21. Between working in Peru for Acurio and chef Rafael Osterling, and working as executive chef of Astrid & Gastón in Colombia and Spain, Martínez traveled to Thailand and Singapore, where he says he was inspired by the cuisine's emphasis on local products. While staging at a Chinese restaurant in The Four Seasons in Singapore, he was impressed by the culinary ability of Chinese cooks and realized they were so skilled because "they had a lifetime immersed in [their] culture" (Martínez 2016: 14–15). This realization, he writes, had an important impact on him, as it was then that he began to think more deeply about Peru and its culinary heritage.

22. All quotations in this paragraph are from Jeter (2017). Martínez opened a second restaurant in London (LIMA Floral) in 2014.

23. Martínez (2015: 9).

24. Martínez (2015: 6).

25. Martínez (2016: 14).

26. Jeter (2017).

27. Jeter (2017).

28. There are also those who are increasingly spending extraordinary amounts of money to travel to "extreme" locations and experience culturally infused food; see Ligaya Mishan, "The World on a Plate, and the Business Behind It," New York Times, March 26, 2019, www.nytimes.com/2019/03/26/dining/food-tours.html.

29. Jeter (2017).

30. Indeed, during field research in Lima I met several people who had traveled to the capital to eat at Central, Maido, and Astrid & Gastón (the three Peruvian restaurants on the "50 Best" list at that time) and had no plans to travel beyond Lima.

31. Jeter (2017).

32. Jeter (2017).

33. Degregori (2000) and Mayer (1991); see also Bonfil Batalla (2010).

34. Quoted in CNN (2015).

35. Pratt (2008: 3).

36. "Latin America's Best Female Chef 2019," Latin America's 50 Best Restaurants, www.theworlds50best.com/latinamerica/en/Awards-Pages/best-female-chef.html.

37. Lieberman (2018).

38. Pratt (2008: 9). The websites for Central, Mil, and Mater were updated as I revised this book. The website quotes and images I analyze in this chapter refer to earlier versions, all accessed on or before April 2019.

39. Price (2018).

40. Lieberman (2018).

41. Price (2018).

42. Moseley-Williams (2018a).

43. Mater's website, now an important site for showcasing Martínez's culinary research, was also much less developed, until recently hosting only a blog. Moreover, at Mil, every meal begins with a tour of Mater Iniciativa's offices and research projects.

44. Kozolchyk (2018).

45. Martínez (2016: 21).

46. Jeter (2017).

47. Jeter (2017).

48. Jeter (2017).

49. Coronel-Molina (2008), Coronel-Molina et al. (2005), Godenzzi (1992), and Hornberger (1997). Significantly, Roxana Quispe Collante, a Quechua scholar of Peruvian and Latin American literature, recently (2019) defended her PhD thesis in Quechua at the Universidad de San Marcos, becoming the first person to do so. Her dissertation, on transfiguration and Quechua poetry, was also written entirely in Quechua.

50. Risling Baldy (2018).

51. Bertolt (2018).

52. Bertolt (2018).

53. While the Mater site no longer centers this image, the phrase "Afuera Hay Mas" remains a central guiding mantra. See also Martínez et al. (2019).

54. Grey and Newman (2018: 719).

55. Gómez-Barris (2017: 5).

56. On colonial expeditions and classification: López-Canales (2019), McDonell (2019), and Pratt (2008); racial capitalist violence: Bhattacharyya (2018), and Melamed (2011).

57. Matta (2019).

58. Wolfe (2006).

59. Beggs (2019: 101) and Dixler Canavan (2018).

60. Beggs (2019: 101).

61. Beggs (2019: 101.)

62. Dixler Canavan (2018).

63. Martínez is positioned squarely within global gastronomy circuits, and his work is clearly inspired by initiatives such as this one. He spent time at the New Nordic Lab (now the Nordic Food Lab) in Copenhagen, described as a space from where to explore the edible potential of the Nordic region. Martínez was listed as a collaborator on the Food Lab's recent volume *On Eating Insects* (2017), and you can also

see the Lab's influence in the exhibition of products at https://futureconsumerlab .ku.dk/lab-facilities/nordic-food-lab-archive/Nordic_Lab_FINAL_2020.pdf. For the complete manifesto and additional information about new Nordic cuisine, see Norden Co-operation, "The New Nordic Food Manifesto," www.norden.org/en /information/new-nordic-food-manifesto. For more on the "radical locality" of new Nordic cuisine, see Mead (2018). On the coloniality of the new Nordic, see Andreassen (2014). And for a discussion of links between Martínez and the new Nordic movement, see López-Canales (2019).

64. Dixler Canavan (2018).

65. D'Angelo stopped working at Mil in 2019.

66. Gibson (2019). Despite talk about the importance of context, D'Angelo told me the architectural firm had to bring *ichu*, the grass used to construct Mil's rooftop, from other parts of the Andes because it does not grow near Moray. This brings to mind the emphasis on "a Peruvian aesthetic" included in the recipe that uses quinoa included in the interlude, as well as the gastropolitical emphasis on "Peruvian authenticity," carefully choreographed and performed for the nation and world. See also García (2013).

67. Dixler Canavan (2018) and Kozolchyk (2018).

68. Abend (2018) and Beggs (2019).

69. Dolan and Rajak (2016).

70. Though this raises questions about intellectual property, as it remains unclear whether a family, the community, or Mil would "own" these new varieties.

71. Wolff et al. (2018).

72. D'Angelo, quoted in López-Canales (2019); emphasis added.

73. López-Canales (2019).

74. Wolff et al. (2018: 46).

75. Wolff might do well to read the many works of Native and other scholars who critique precisely these kinds of "decolonial" claims and who have offered numerous interventions on Indigenous and decolonial research methods and practices (e.g., Simpson 2007; Smith 1999; TallBear 2014; Tuck and Yang 2012; Wilson 2008).

76. Moseley-Williams (2018c).

77. Vich (2007: 8).

78. Vich (2007: 8); see also Babb (2010).

79. "Modern techniques to indigenous ingredients": CNN (2015). See also Matta (2016a).

80. CNN (2015).

81. Martínez (2016: 22).

82. Jeter (2017).

83. Jeter (2017); emphasis added.

84. Kahn (2015).

85. Jeter (2017).

86. Quoted in CNN (2015); emphasis added.

87. Others working in a similar "cosmopolitical" vein are Blaser (2010) and Di Giminiani (2018). (See also de la Cadena and Blaser 2018; Latour 2004; Stengers

2005). Connected to the "ontological turn" in anthropology (see, e.g., Descola 1996, 2006; Holbraad 2017; Kohn 2013; Viveiros de Castro 2004), these scholars explore the radical political possibilities opened up by more-than-human entanglements. While the emphasis on multiple worlds and world making (as opposed to thinking through cultural difference within one world) can be a powerful way to take Native epistemologies seriously (e.g., moving away from framings such as "they believe that"), there are also important critiques of such an approach, particularly when Indigenous voices, politics, and epistemologies are essentialized, romanticized, or erased altogether (Bessire and Bond 2014; Canessa 2017; Govindrajan 2018b; Graeber 2015; Todd 2016). The focus in much of this scholarship on the "incommensurability" of Indigenous peoples and politics in particular risks depoliticizing and essentializing Native political engagements and de-emphasizes the specificity of kin relations, place, and context (Carroll 2019; Todd 2016). Finally, it is worth noting that other scholars have made similar calls, in different contexts, for thinking with more-than-human life. Tsing, for example, rejected the distinction between material and semiotic in the "lived configuration of humans and nonhumans across a terrain" (2004: 172), and Chakrabarty argued for the historical translation of systems of thought in which "humans are not the only meaningful agents" (2000: 72).

88. Martínez (2016: 98).

89. De la Cadena (2010: 362).

90. Salas Carreño (2016, 2019) and Li (2013). See also Gose (2018) for a critical discussion of relations between mountains and humans in the Andes.

91. According to Rosario Olivas Weston, the name *huatia* comes from the verb *huatiyani* (or *watyay*). She relies on Jesuit priest and missionary Diego González Holguín's 1608 study of the Quechua language and states that the term meant "to roast in holes or earth ovens." When potatoes were cooked using this technique, the resulting dish was called *huatiya* (*watya*) or *huatiyascca* (*watyasqa*) (Olivas Weston 2001: 86).

92. CNN (2015).

93. CNN (2015).

94. Jeter (2017).

95. Jeter (2017).

96. Dixler Canavan (2018).

97. Moseley-Williams (2018c).

98. Although Martínez has certainly been heavily influenced by the concept of terroir, as reflected in an early (2016) pairing menu at Central titled *"terroir, lo que el suelo transmite"* ("terroir, what the earth transmits").

99. Orlove (1998); see also Colloredo-Mansfeld (1998).

100. Estes (2019), Kearns (2017), and TallBear (2014, 2019).

101. Massimo Bottura is the chef. You can find these and other reviews of *Central* and Martínez at https://www.phaidon.com/store/food-cook/central-978071 4872803/#tab-4.

102. *El Comercio* (2013).

103. "Alan Garcia presidente se burla de los APUS y como candidato los admira," posted by posted by Dennis Berrios on March 15, 2015, YouTube video, https://www.youtube.com/watch?v=WX1ZVkdDIWE.

104. García (2007). See also Larsen (2019).

105. Beggs (2019: 101).

106. Between Western and Indigenous researchers: Pompilj (2019); "objective" ethnographic research and observation: Nass (2018).

107. Alfred (2009), Burguete (2008), Byrd (2011), Coulthard (2014), and Hale (2008).

108. The recently published Mater catalog also contradicts this claim, as one of the editors explicitly locates this text in a long history and tradition of European botanical representation (Martínez et al. 2019). The author also notes that among the sensations the editors hope to provoke in readers with this text is nostalgia, a point that brings to mind Renato Rosaldo's discussion of imperialist nostalgia (1989b).

109. At Central's previous location in Miraflores, Martínez served many of his dishes on stunning ceramic plates that were even more striking as they were broken but positioned carefully by the wait staff seemingly in the process of coming back together. Perhaps this was a metaphor for a broken nation attempting to repair itself?

110. On Indigenismo and representation in the Andes, see Coronado (2009, 2018), de la Cadena (2000), García (2005), Moraña (1998), and Poole (1997).

111. Matta (2013: 7).

112. Stutzman (1981).

113. Matta (2013: 6).

INTERLUDE: "GASTRONOMY IS A DISPLAY CASE"

1. A more literal translation of the organization's name would be the Good Manipulation Practices Group.

CHAPTER 3. STAGING DIFFERENCE

1. Mistura was canceled unexpectedly in 2018. That year, Apega partnered with the Grupo Nexo Franquicia to create the "Mistura Franchise." According to Roca Rey, this would allow Apega to "export" Mistura, and Marca Perú, to the world (Melgarejo 2019). That plan backfired, leading to accusations of financial mismanagement that coincided with the death of Apega founding member Mariano Valderrama. By late 2019, Apega had disbanded, and Mistura seems to be over.

2. This refers to an alliance developed between Apega, Conveagro (National Convention of the Peruvian Agro or Convención Nacional del Agro Peruano; conveagro.org.pe), and ANPE (National Association of Ecological Producers or

Asociación Nacional de Productores Ecológicos; www.anpeperu.org). See Bohardt (2014), Ginnochio (2012), and Kollenda (2019).

3. While the emphasis is on the agricultural producer, artisanal fishermen are also upheld as key actors in Peru's gastronomic revolution.

4. Douglas ([1966] 2002); Acurio in Pérez (2011).

5. See, for example, Melamed (2011), Puar (2017), Reddy (2011), Weheliye (2014), and Wynter (2003).

6. Colloredo-Mansfeld (1998).

7. Colloredo-Mansfeld (1998: 187), citing Stoler (1995); see also Foucault (1990) and McClintock (1995).

8. Fraser (1990: 57).

9. Fraser (1990: 57).

10. Burman (2014), Hale (2004), Jackson (2019), Lucero (2013), Povinelli (2002), and Wade (2010).

11. Elias (1994).

12. Bourdieu (1984).

13. Weismantel (2001: xxvii).

14. Such representations remain all too alive in Peru, such as Peruvian comedian Jorge Benavides's character "La paisana Jacinta." For more on recent controversies over Benavides's television show and movie featuring this character, see Cánepa (2018), Wouters (2018), and Collyns (2014). In addition to performing in Redface, Benavides also performs in Blackface, playing the offensive character "El negro Mama" (Tegel 2013). It is worth noting that despite numerous criticisms and accusations of racism, Benavides continues to enjoy substantial support from Peruvians, who insist these are just "funny" representations. He also maintains Facebook pages for both "El negro Mama" (with over 8,000 followers) and "La paisana Jacinta" (with over 800,000 followers).

15. Aguirre and Drinot (2017), Drinot (2011), and Roca-Rey (2016).

16. Acurio (2012); emphasis added.

17. On this point, see also Melamed (2011) (for the United States) and Povinelli (2002) (for Australia).

18. Renan ([1882] 2018).

19. Renan ([1882] 2018: 251).

20. Reddy (2011).

21. Blanco (1972, 2007) and Mariátegui ([1928] 1994).

22. Drinot (2011: 3, 4).

23. Drinot (2011: 15); emphasis in original.

24. Drinot (2011: 13).

25. His labor: like many modernizing discourses, Peruvian gastropolitics betrays an androcentric bias. Burman (2014).

26. See also Loperena (2017) on settler violence in Honduras.

27. This is illustrated in APEGA Sociedad Peruana de Gastronomia, "Dia del Campesino," June 24, 2017, video posted on Facebook, www.facebook.com/apegate /videos/10155417520033879/.

28. Quoted in Pérez (2011).

29. Ginocchio (2012) and Valderrama (2016).

30. Nirvastudio, "*Mistura Somos Todos*: Mistura 2015," posted on July 21, 2015, YouTube video, www.youtube.com/watch?v=WjW26PdQDlU.

31. Once again, chefs are recognized for their *intellectual* labor, while producers are worthy of recognition for their work in the fields, sometimes linked to the "protection" of Peruvian biodiversity.

32. Wallace-Sanders (2009).

33. "The happy Native": Trask (1999); see also Desmond (1999). "*El indio permitido*": Cusicanqui (2007). See also Hale and Millamán (2006) and Hale (2004). Almost without exception, images of racialized others in *Mistura Somos Todos* (and in other visual representations of Mistura and Apega-sponsored agricultural fairs) show them smiling, laughing, and often dressed in ways that match up with idealized folkloric representations or racial tropes.

34. Hale and Millamán (2006: 284). For important variations on this theme, see Hale's argument about neoliberal multiculturalism (2002, 2005), Povinelli's "cunning of recognition" (2002), and Speed's formulation of the "settler-capitalist state" (2019).

35. Websites for Apega and Mistura were taken down in June 2019. These quotes are documented in the author's files.

36. Chiu Werner (2012).

37. Apega was well known as an institution that both provided opportunities and shut doors, depending on how well individuals aligned with its ideology. See Alvarez (2019), Lasater-Wille (2015), Masías (2016), and Medina (2014, 2016).

38. Galdós (2015: 58).

39. Galdós (2015: 58).

40. Valderrama (2016: 31).

41. Apega (2013), Ginocchio (2012), and Valderrama (2016).

42. Valderrama (2016).

43. Larson and Harris (1995) and Weismantel (2001: 133).

44. Desmond (1999: xiii).

45. Valderrama (2016: 31); emphasis added.

46. These and other quotes from my interview with Valderrama are cited in García (2013).

47. This comment brings to mind the familiar scapegoating of market women blamed for price gouging, among other "offenses" during difficult economic episodes in Peru's recent past (see Babb 1982, 1989; Seligmann 1989; de la Cadena 1996). Tellingly, the second of Apega's "ten commandments" for producers is "*Exhiba claramente los precios*" (clearly display all prices).

48. Cooking schools—particularly those training youth from marginalized areas of Lima—have also become important sites for the racialized deployment of ideologies about hygiene. They are increasingly significant spaces in the gastropolitical project to educate and "civilize" as they train the workforce necessary to sustain the gastronomic revolution's success (Lasater-Wille 2015).

49. Weismantel (2001: 19).

50. Weismantel (2001: 20).

51. Weismantel (2001: xxvii).

52. Weismantel (2001: xxvii).

53. De la Cadena (1996: 120–21).

54. De la Cadena (1996: 121). De la Cadena is quoting Luis Alberto Arguedas (1928) on "the sanitary needs of Cusco."

55. Colloredo-Mansfeld (1998), de la Cadena (2000), Orlove (1998), Weismantel (2001), and Weismantel and Eisenman (1998).

56. Valderrama (2016), 26 ("deficient conditions of produce markets") and 42 (found in Barcelona, Madrid, or Turín).

57. Valderrama (2016: 41). As Weismantel writes, "the Andean marketplace is sexed female" (2001: 46). But while markets are indeed often gendered female (as seen in Valderrama's centering of *las caseras*), Mistura's El Gran Mercado seems to center, or at least prominently display, male producers.

58. Valderrama (2016: 41).

59. Valderrama (2016: 41–42).

60. Of course, Andean migration to Lima predates the political violence of the 1980s and 1990s. For more on the "Andeanization" of Lima, see Guillermo Nugent's well-known publication, *El Laberinto de la Choledad* ([1992] 2014). See also Degregori (1986), Matos Mar (1984, 2004), and Martuccelli (2015).

61. Vargas Llosa (1993: 513).

62. Ellis (1998)

63. Valderrama (2016: 42–43). This emphasis on the "cleansing" and "beautification" of markets is similar to discussions about "cleaning up" certain streets and neighborhoods through the opening of particular kinds of restaurants and shops. These "cleaner" streets, markets, and neighborhoods have become central symbols of Marca Perú, of the new and improved nation. Relatedly, at Yuntémonos, the event marking the culinary revolution's "third phase," various speakers made a point to note when panels were beginning on time (or slightly early), stating that this punctuality was significant as it was an indicator of "our new Peru." See Consiglieri (2019) for more on the gastronomic boom and gentrification.

64. Valderrama (2016: 26).

65. Povinelli (2002: 17).

66. Hale (2004: 18).

67. Desmond (1999: xvi).

68. Saldaña-Portillo (2003).

69. Escobar (1995).

70. Guerrero (1997).

71. Moore, Pandian, and Kosek (2003: 19).

72. De la Cadena (1996: 128). See also Weismantel (2001: 38–40).

73. Participating in Mistura was costly for those without financial resources, and the selection process was complex. I spoke with various people about this

process, including Apega members and representatives from agro-ecological associations, and roughly, it seemed to go something like this: Apega determines how many slots there are for producers and communicates this number to the agricultural organizations with whom they work. It also reminds the organizations' leadership that producers must meet certain criteria. As the vice president of one of these organizations told me, "Apega demands that we comply with certain requirements, but especially, that we are clean, that we have a good presentation, and that we have a *registro sanitario* (a health register)." The organizations then determine the number of slots available and communicate with regional authorities, who determine who is eligible. Producers decide if they want to participate and let the organizations know. Once organizations have the names of producers, they create a spreadsheet with their recommendations, which they turn over to Apega. Apega looks over this document and makes the final determination. It reserves the right to replace producers on the list or deny participation to some. Producers must pay their own way if they choose to participate. One leader told me that several years ago the organization was able to cover travel expenses for producers, but as of 2015 that was no longer the case.

74. This sense of order is also evident in some restaurants. During dinner at Astrid & Gastón in 2017, a friend and I repeatedly heard young men in the open kitchen shouting "*oido!*" (heard!) in response to commands by chefs and waiters. Throughout our meal, we watched and listened as the men (I could see approximately fifteen cooks in the open kitchen and noticed only two women) worked furiously to get orders ready as efficiently as possible. Meanwhile, other men stood against the wall, arms crossed, military style. When we asked our waiter about the shouting, he said the exercise was designed to impose "order and discipline."

75. Comaroff and Comaroff (2009) and Desmond (1999).

76. And as Deborah Poole reminds us, visual images (and photographs in particular) have long played a significant role in shaping racial ideologies in the Andes (Poole 1997).

77. Desmond (1999: xiii).

78. hooks (1992: 21).

79. Desmond (1999). In many ways, Mistura could be read as part of a long history of the exhibition of human and nonhuman difference; another example of the kinds of human displays and performances at world's fairs and Wild West shows. Blanchard et al. (2009), Fusco and Heredia (1993), Griffiths (2002), and Redman (2009).

80. Povinelli (2002: 6); emphasis in original.

81. MacCannell (1992: 1).

82. Desmond (1999: xix).

83. Kirshenblatt-Gimblett (1991: 414). See also Kirshenblatt-Gimblett (1998) and MacCannell (1976).

84. Pandian (2009: 7).

85. Appadurai (2004).

1. Oxford Dictionaries, https://www.lexico.com/en/definition/vernacular.

2. Building on Colloredo-Mansfeld's concept of vernacular statecraft (2009) as well as Juliet Erazo's (2013) scholarship on the complex and contradictory work of "enacting" Indigenous sovereignty in the Ecuadorian Amazon, Manuela Picq also uses the idea of the "vernacular" and develops the concept of "vernacular sovereignty" to describe the political work of Kichwa women who engage strategically with international Indigenous rights norms and the Ecuadorian state in order to carve out local spaces of autonomy and self-determination (2018).

3. Colloredo-Mansfeld (2009: 17).

4. Scott (1992).

5. Bruyneel (2007).

6. ANPE website: www.anpeperu.org. See also Aponte (2013).

7. See Graham (2003, 2014) for terrific discussions of the politics of Indigenous performance. Aida's performance is also part of a long history of Indigenous women resisting imposed hierarchies and navigating politics through the production and consumption of food (e.g., Krögel 2010; Weismantel 1998).

8. Coronado (2018: 3).

9. Scott (1992: xii).

10. Hale (2004).

11. Scott (1992: xii).

12. Sommer (2006: 4–5).

13. Sommer (2006: 9).

14. Vizenor (1999, 2008). See also Hedge Coke (2007).

15. Vizenor (1999: vii).

16. Coronado (2018: 20).

17. Coronado (2018: 24).

18. Deloria (2004: 69, 68).

19. Murra (1975).

20. For a useful introduction to Native Pacific studies see Diaz and Kauanui (2001).

21. Deloria (2004: 69). We could also read Aida as performing an Indigenous politics of refusal, particularly the refusal of the coloniality of state recognition (Simpson 2007, 2014).

22. Deloria (2004: 69). See also Scarangella McNenly (2012). Deloria and others argue that Wild West shows offered a mobility lacking in sites such as the Chicago World's Fair of 1893 and other so-called human zoos that caged and surveilled Native peoples and other people of color considered "exotic" and "savage."

23. Sommer (2006: 13).

24. Gómez-Barris (2017: 1).

25. Gómez-Barris (2017: xv).

26. Escobar (1995), Li (2007), and Roy (2010). In the context of Aida's critique, ANPE's alliance with Apega can be read as an example of "conditional aid"

programs, such as Juntos (Together), a popular conditional cash transfer program developed under president Humala in 2006 that offers cash to poor mothers on the condition that they invest in the education and health of their children (Cookson 2018). In this case, in exchange for Apega's support, producers were expected to comply with its ten commandments, among other expectations.

27. Million (2014).

28. From Generación con Causa, https://peru.info/es-pe/generacionconcausa.

29. The interview is available at The Real Deal Blog, "Conversando con Emprendedores #4—Palmiro Ocampo, fundador de Huevón Lima & Ccori cocina óptima," posted on October 21, 2018, YouTube video, www.youtube.com/watch?v= lFNxwxaheow. *Mujer Emprendedora Peru* (blog), https://mujeremprendedoraperu .blogspot.com/.

30. Ocampo collaborated with Martínez on the Nordic Food Lab's production of *On Eating Insects* (Nordic Food Lab 2017), published by the high-end press Phaidon, a press that describes itself as "the premier global publisher of the creative arts" and one that works "with the world's most influential artists, chefs, writers and thinkers." Since then, Ocampo has published his own book on insects in Peru, *Delicious Peruvian Insects* or *Sabrosos Insectos Peruanos* (Ocampo 2019). It is worth noting the difference, however, separating Ocampo's publication—a relatively thin book published in Spanish and supported by the Peruvian state (via PromPerú and an initiative led by then vice president Mercedes Aráoz)—and the Nordic Food Lab's glossy publication, in addition to some of Acurio's (2008, 2015) and Martínez's (2015, 2016) publications, written in English and published by Phaidon. As Jack Goody has argued (1996), cookbooks can be read as representations of class and hierarchy.

31. Here we might notice the marked difference between Ocampo's inability to open a restaurant with a colleague due to licensing issues, and Virgilio Martínez's experience, in which he was able to keep his restaurant open *despite* licensing issues and conflict with the municipality of Miraflores.

32. TEDx Talks, "¿Se puede combatir el hambre desde la Alta Cocina?/Palmiro Ocampo/TEDxTukuy," posted on April 12, 2018, YouTube video, www.youtube .com/watch?v=-STVh2J_H84.

33. Quoted from TedX Talks, "¿Se puede combatir el hambre desde la Alta Cocina?"

34. This is an excerpt from INDECOPI's official document, posted on Huevón Lima's Facebook page.

35. Huevón Lima, December 21, 2018, video posted on Facebook, www.facebook .com/huevonlima/videos/1083596675146269/.

36. Alvarez (1997: 30–31). Alvarez is an outspoken activist in support of regional cuisines and Native products. See also Alvarez (2002, 2013, 2015, 2017a).

37. At the risk of simplifying a complex set of arguments about food security and sovereignty, generally speaking, *food security* refers to the availability and accessibility of nutritious food, while *food sovereignty* emphasizes community *control* over the production, consumption, and distribution of food. Though there is a lively

debate about the origins of this term (see, e.g., Agarwal 2014; Edelman 2014), *food sovereignty* is commonly attributed to the organization La Via Campesina, a transnational agrarian movement created by peasants' and farmers' organizations and Indigenous movements from the Americas, Africa, Asia, and Europe in the early 1990s, that advocates for sustainable, family farm–based, and culturally meaningful food production (though as Edelman [2014] notes, the term in Spanish, *soberanía alimentaria*, predates its English counterpart by several years and can be traced to a Mexican government food program). In recent years there has been a growing and vibrant discussion over food sovereignty, particularly in relation to Indigenous sovereignty, resurgence, and anticolonial struggles (e.g., Alfred 2005; Corntassel and Bryce 2012; Coté 2016; Daigle 2019; Figueroa 2015; Grey and Patel 2015; Gupta 2015; Huambachano 2015; Mihesuah and Hoover 2019; Simpson 2013).

38. Quote from "Conversando con Emprendedores #4."

39. This and other work can be seen on the virtual "micromuseo" at Micromuseo, "Lo impuro y lo contaminado," https://micromuseo.org.pe/rutas/loimpuro/revelaciones.html. For more on Márquez see Villar (2017, 2018).

40. Márquez (2011).

41. Márquez (2005).

42. Quoted in Villar (2018).

43. Generación con Causa, "Chefs de Generación con Causa dan soluciones a problemas de alimentación," https://peru.info/es-pe/generacionconcausa/noticias/det/chefs-de-generacion-con-causa-dan-soluciones-a-problemas-de-alimentacion.

44. Campoamor (2013, 2016). See also Alcalde (2010) and Taft (2019).

45. *Comedores populares* emerged in the late 1970s and were organized by women in marginalized areas of Peru. While often understood primarily as "survival organizations" (Wilson 2002), these communal culinary spaces can be read instead as sites of resilience and resistance, as women from comedores throughout Peru have developed strategic networks at local and national levels that enable demands against the state and support alliances with local and international NGOs (Hays-Mitchell 2002; Mortensen 2010; Mujica 1992, 1994; see also Boesten 2010 for a discussion of women and social policy in Peru in the 1990s, including the political complexities of comedores populares). María Elena Moyano is perhaps the most famous social activist in Peru who began her political activism from the kitchen of a comedor in Villa El Salvador. Moyano used her political organizing skills to challenge not just the state but the Shining Path, who eventually killed her and blew up her body in front of her children. For more on Moyano and on the political use of her image and memory, see Cozart (2012), Burt (2010), and Tupac (2000).

46. As Priti Ramamurthy has argued (2019), stories about friendship, love, and joy in the context of economic precariousness, migration, and peri-urban livelihoods offer a crucial complement (and corrective) to work that foregrounds only the suffering, despair, and violence experienced by marginalized populations.

47. Ccopa (2018).

48. Dall (2017); emphasis added. There is a moment in this episode when Ocampo seems also to be challenging Virgilio Martínez's sometimes exotifying

discourse, what we might call his "pachamamismo," particularly with respect to the huatia. As Ocampo tells viewers when several men from the community he is visiting in Puno begin to build a huatia, "[T]he huatia is nothing else than an oven made with stones and clay and where Peruvian potatoes are cooked and smoked." This statement, and Ocampo's materialist approach, contrasts starkly with Martínez's idealized representations of the huatia and reminded me of Million's important point about theory for Native peoples. "Theory," she writes, "is always practical first, rather than abstract" (Million 2014: 33).

49. Krögel (2010) and Sax (2011); see also Loichot (2013), especially chapter 3, for a discussion of food as resistance and cultural sustenance in a Caribbean diasporic context.

50. Del Pino et al. (2012).

51. Allen (2002: 146). See also Krögel (2010).

52. Kimmerer (2003).

53. Kimmerer (2003).

54. Raheja (2010: xi). For Raheja, visual sovereignty must be considered next to "redfacing, the process and politics of playing Indian;" and the "virtual reservation, the imagined and imaginative sites produced by the cinema" (xii).

55. Raheja (2010: 240).

56. Raheja (2010: 193).

57. Raheja (2010: 194, 19).

58. There were many other spaces where producers in particular attempted to "speak back" and assert alternative understandings of power, such as ANPE's workshop, described in the interlude, and Q&A sessions after important speeches, such as Acurio's at Mistura.

59. As Victor Vich also reminds us, "subalternity has been defined not as an ontological category but, rather, as a relational concept that consists of a performative act where subjects represent themselves by placing emphasis on the power relations in which they find themselves inscribed and connecting their individual lives with those of the group of which they feel they are a part" (2001: 51). See also Beverly (1999), Guha (1997), and Rodríguez (2001).

60. Agroferias Campesinas website: www.agroferiascampesinas.com. Bioferias are farmer's markets, usually promoting organic or ecological products. They are most successful in wealthy districts, where clients are affluent enough to purchase these products (Cody 2015).

61. Apega FAM, "Presentación de las Ferias Agropecuarias Mistura (FAM) de Apega," posted on October 23, 2014, YouTube video, www.youtube.com/watch?v=94vk5cEFVEM.

62. ANPE has also worked for years to petition the government for better food security laws and continues to work toward codifying Indigenous rights to food sovereignty (Murphy 2013).

63. While "organic" and "agro-ecological" entail similar values (e.g., "natural" and sustainable production, no use of pesticides, protection of biodiversity, environmentally responsible production, consideration of animal welfare), in Peru, the

distinction lies in the certification process. To be labeled organic, products must be officially certified by the state (via the Ministry of Agriculture and specifically SENASA, the National Service for Agrarian Health), and companies or producers who wish to be certified must follow the parameters laid out in Law 29196, the Law for the Promotion of Organic or Ecological Production. Agro-ecological producers who are not able to pay the fees associated with the complicated organic certification process usually participate in a relatively new process called the Participatory Guarantee System (Sistema de Garantía Participativa). According to a representative from ASPEC (the Peruvian Association of Consumers) who works on consumer protections with respect to food, this system involves working directly with producers and supporting community initiatives to shift toward organic or ecological production.

64. Carroll (2019: 4).

65. Ocampo's frequent use of Quechua is also notable, from the name of his organization (Ccori), to the title of the tasting menu at 1087 Restaurante ("Allin yuyaykuy allin mikuy," Bueno para pensar, Bueno para comer), to embedding *kausay* (life) in Generación con Causa's manifesto.

66. Cajete (2015: 197).

67. The double meaning of the title is of note, as it refers to the use of llama blood for local health but also can be translated as "the call of blood," perhaps itself a way of referencing the blood ties that connect the coast and highlands.

INTERLUDE: OF HUMOR AND VIOLENCE

1. "Los mejores videos sobre cuyes y caracoles," n.d., http://ricardo.bizhat.com /rmr-prigeds/videos-de-cuyes.htm.

2. In her searing account of cruelty and modernity in Latin America, Jean Franco also points to the particular role humor plays in undergirding violence, often reflecting the "casual but constant reinforcement of misogyny" (2013: 15).

CHAPTER 5. GUINEA PIG MATTERS

1. This chapter revisits and revises ideas advanced in a previously published essay (García 2019b).

2. Galt (2019: 3).

3. Galt (2019: 5–6).

4. Here I am thinking not just about the llama's neighing, but also about Laura Marks's provocative work on haptic visuality (2000) and Tina Campt's powerful work on the significance of "listening to images" (2017).

5. These "invasions" of unused land on the outskirts of Lima by rural migrants were renamed *pueblos jóvenes* (or young towns) by Velasco's revolutionary government. This shift in name entailed not just state recognition but also state support in the form of infrastructure and social programs.

6. Acevedo (n.d.).

7. El Cuy is gendered male, as is the case with various contemporary figurations of the cuy.

8. Acevedo (2008). In his blog, Acevedo recounts the origins of El Cuy, his enthusiasm about having created a character who could "represent Peruvian identitiy with tenderness," and the challenge he faced when realizing his enthusiasm for the cuy as symbol of Peruvianness was not shared by such important newspapers as *El Comercio* or *La Prensa*. From "Orígenes del Cuy (1)," *El Diario del Cuy* (blog), n.d., https://elcuy.wordpress.com/album/origenes-del-cuy-i/.

9. See Drinot (2017b) for more on El Cuy and the Left in Peru; see Foster (1989), Lent and Archambeault (2005), and Sagástegui (2009) for discussions about Acevedo's work. You can find El Cuy comic strips at "Orígenes del Cuy (VIII)," *El Diario del Cuy* (blog), n.d., https://elcuy.wordpress.com/album/origenes-del-cuy-viii/.

10. Archetti (1997), Morales (1995), and Yamamoto (2016).

11. Sulca (2016).

12. Rodríguez et al. (2009, 27); emphasis added.

13. Rico Numbela (2010).

14. Fabian (2002). This is often made explicit in discussions of production that take as a starting point the need to move from "familial production" (described as an "ancestral approach" to providing food security) toward a "modern" focus on commercial production, at small, medium, or large scales. During one discussion, a cuy researcher pointed to the global use of guinea pigs in development programs aimed at poverty alleviation and noted proudly that their institute offered support to these programs, sometimes providing them with cuy stock. Discussing one of these programs in Cameroon, he stated, "In Africa, they are now using cuyes like we were in the 1960s: for food security and poverty alleviation." In other words, those Indigenous families in Peru today who continue to live with cuyes and rely on these animals as part of food security strategies, or as important dimensions of enactments of food sovereignty, are figured as "living in the past," anachronisms in need of modernization.

15. Haraway (1992: 47).

16. Castañeda (2002: 3).

17. Castañeda (2002: 1).

18. Soper (1995: 155).

19. Tegel (2012).

20. *El cuy pekinés* was listed by the United Arab Emirates web journal *The National* as one of the "ten dishes to try before you die" (Matta 2016: 147): "Traditionally the 'cuy' was deep fried.... But, fortunately for pet lovers, Acurio... has disguised it here as Peking duck, serving it sliced up into chunks with a rocoto pepper hoisin sauce. Once it's wrapped up in a purple corn pancake, you won't even think about Fluffy." "In Pictures: 10 Dishes to Try before You Die," November 14, 2013, www.thenational.ae/lifestyle/food/in-pictures-10-dishes-to-try-before-you-die#1.

21. Quoted in Medina, Acurio, and Adriá (2012: 53). There is still much debate about the cuy's place in gastronomic circles. Take for example a discussion about

the most popular Peruvian dish, in which chefs debate the place of *lomo saltado* and *arroz con pollo*, before moving to the cuy (Lauer and Lauer 2006: 127–28, 176–77). Participants debate whether the cuy should be eaten fried or roasted but agree on the fact that while many won't include the animal on their menu, it has much potential, as long as it is prepared correctly (in a "refined" manner), without its head or feet, such as in a cuy lasagna. In another debate years later, Lauer asks participants their thoughts about "the dangerous cuy" (*el peligroso cuy*). This time Acurio notes that there is still much work to be done with this animal, that he doesn't see a future for it outside of Peru, and another participant agrees, telling Lauer that even though people have learned not to serve cuy with its head and feet, the animal is still seen as "a rat or a hamster, so people reject it. *Al cuy le falta manejo*" (2012: 121–22).

22. Castañeda (2002: 2).

23. This was a phrase I heard often during early field research, mostly from elite Limeños. An interview in *Gourmet* magazine with Chef Payet, one of Acurio's childhood friends, illustrates this nicely. As the interviewer writes: "For Payet, the flavors of these [novoandina] dishes heighten his sense of everything in Peru being familiar but entirely new. Fifteen years ago, when he left, no one dared to mix the various distinct cuisines in Peru. . . . *[L]imeños* disdained ingredients from the Andes, considering them peasant food. 'When I grew up, if you ate guinea pig you were a savage,' Payet says, biting into a leg of roasted organic guinea pig nestled in its bed of oca ravioli in a pecan sauce with Pisco" (Fraser 2006). Of course, part of the tourism experience for many travelers often includes the conspicuous consumption of "exotic" foods, and this is evident by the images that pop up with a simple Google search for "cuy (or guinea pig) Peru." See also Moseley-Williams (2014) for a high-end rendering of this.

24. Hall (1980: 338).

25. Tsing (2018: 232).

26. García (2013).

27. Morales (1995).

28. This interview is cited in García (2010, 2013).

29. This is why many NGOs are now hinging support for small-scale commercial production projects on women's empowerment, even though this often means "familial" empowerment (emphasizing "gender complementarity" or the inclusion of husbands and children in production). INIA's work with families upholds heteronormative development practices. One INIA researcher told me that while their work supported women, it was not about the empowerment of *women* per se, but rather supporting women so that they can take care of their families. Women, in this formulation, are always (or will become) wives and mothers.

30. During the early years of this move toward export markets, researchers bred what at least one producer called "super guinea pigs," animals sometimes twenty times larger than normal (García 2010). The assumption was that with more meat, these cuyes would be more desirable to migrants abroad. This backfired as, according to several producers, Andean migrants in cities from Queens to Paterson to Miami all preferred smaller animals. While the super guinea pig trend did not

last, this is a familiar move in animal agriculture, and one that may reappear in the case of the cuy. At least one cuy production and research center in Bolivia continues to explore ways to use these larger animals.

31. However, in the context of global development, cuyes are increasingly used in programs aimed at poverty alleviation, particularly in Africa and the Caribbean.

32. Despite this focus on internal consumption, companies that export cuy are doing well; the export of cuy meat has reached unprecedented levels in recent years. However, only large companies certified by Peru's National Service for Agrarian Health (SENASA) and with the means to compete can participate in the export economy. One can find frozen cuyes in markets from New Jersey to California, and some restaurants are now serving cuy as a special dish, though in some cases the cuyes used are bought live at pet stores.

33. Many have noted that current cuy production does not meet increasing demand for the animal's meat. This, as well as making cuy meat more affordable, is part of the push toward industrialization. Two recent reports, one from the CIP (Colegio de Ingenieros del Perú) and one from Peru's Ministry of Agriculture, offer interesting examples. See Colegio de Ingenierios del Perú, "Procesamiento e industrialización de la carne de cuy," posted on October 31, 2018, YouTube video, https://www.youtube.com/watch?v=g_Vc9QgH4aI; and Ministerio de Agricultura y Riego del Peru, "Carne de cuy combate la anemia," March 20, 2019, video posted on Facebook, https://www.facebook.com/watch/?v=387578405411674.

34. This producer was also very excited about the development of products such as "cuy jerky" and *cuy enlatado* (canned guinea pig). A more recent development in this vein is "guinea pig ice cream," developed in Ecuador and apparently quite popular (Castrodale 2019).

35. Degregori (1993: 129).

36. Vich (2001).

37. Vich (2001: 56).

38. This researcher's nationalist vision was clear, as she also discussed the work of some Chilean researchers who, she claimed, were trying to prove that the cuy originated in what is now Chile. As she put it during a production workshop in 2016: "We must verify that the cuy is Peruvian; we need to codify the real ancestry of the cuy and secure the apellation of origin."

39. "La Canción del Cuy Mágico (nueva canción)," posted on April 12, 2011, YouTube video, http://www.youtube.com/watch?feature=endscreen&v=g1uD3tOrIiU &NR=1.

40. This seems much like the limited possibilities for agricultural producers. It may be possible to improve rural livelihoods, but only up to a point. Producers can sell their products in the city, but they must return to their provincial fields to labor. And they will of course remain producers, allied with chefs, but rarely, if ever, themselves chefs.

41. Quijano (1980: 71). The term *cholo* is one used often to refer pejoratively to people of Andean ancestry living in the city of Lima or other large urban centers. In Peru, this racial category has been the subject of much scholarly debate. In addition

to the more recent contributions by Guillermo Nugent ([1992] 2014) and Matos Mar (2004), scholarly discussion about "choledad" goes back to the 1960s and 1970s, with most focusing on this subject's "in-between" state (see, e.g., Fuenzalida 1970; Mayer 1970; Quijano 1965). For Mayer, the cholo was an "*indio ex-campesino*," whereas for Quijano the cholo is a subject "in process": "[T]he process of cholificación implies the existence of a set of cultural elements and institutions that are in the process of formation and development, and that tend toward their institutionalization" (1980: 71). For Uriel García, the cholo was "the new Indian" who was oriented toward the future, as opposed to "the Indian" who would only look to the past (García 1973). The bank's choice of a cuy as a mascot speaks to this "in-between" state, as he is associated with rural peoples and their descendants in urban centers who are looking to the future (Degregori 1995). It is worth noting also that former Peruvian president Pedro Pablo Kuczynski (or PPK) decided on a cuy as his own mascot (known as PPCuy), a clear attempt to link this "modern" (and in Peru often read as White and "gringo") presidential candidate to his popular subjects, always racialized and situated in particular ways.

42. De Soto (1989).

43. Vich (2001: 55–56); emphasis added.

44. Pratt (2008).

45. Vizenor (2008).

46. And homophobia. Sexual humor in cuy production circles also often reflected heteronormative ideologies of gender and sexuality. For instance, during one cuy production workshop I participated in, a technician demonstrated how to tag cuyes in order to mark the animals' sex. Noting that male and female cuyes are tagged on different ears, the technician joked that they had to be careful to tag the "right" one on males so as to not insult the masculinity of male cuyes.

47. Baker (2001: 3).

48. There were thirty-seven of us, and only six women (including myself) in the group.

49. This does not mean the INIA does not support communities throughout rural Peru, but rather that its support is designed to move families toward commercial production, even if only at small scales. Technicians often talk about familial-commercial production (*crianza familiar-comercial*) as a midpoint and stepping-stone toward larger commercial enterprises.

50. The INIA's approach is more complicated than this calculation might reflect. While there is much talk about the importance of supporting and empowering women in communities, this vision of empowerment perpetuates heteronormative and patriarchal understandings of the role of women in society. As one technician told me, "[W]omen are empowered when they are better able to care for their families, support their husbands and provide for their children."

51. Saldaña-Portillo (2003: 9).

52. Blee (2002), Blee and McGee Deutsch (2012), Feitlowitz (2011), Power (1999), and Schreiber (2008).

53. There are similar efforts at work in US pork production (Blanchette 2020).

54. Adams ([1990] 2015, 2003), Davis (1995), Gillespie (2018), and Ritvo (1987, 1997).

55. Cassidy (2002), Gillespie (2013), and Blanchette (2020). Interestingly, many of these examples also reflect traces of animal agency and point to the recognition of this by researchers and producers. For example, there was one slide that explicitly addressed animal preferences: "What does the animal ask? Because animals also ask. He asks for good nutrition, a clean home, and that he be taken care of." But then there were other ways of describing animal preferences in the context of production: "The animal asks that he be demanded to produce without putting his life at risk."

56. Gillespie (2013: 5). There is much work on the gendered commodification of female animals in industrial animal agriculture, such as the genetic modification of cow bodies to maximize milk production; the captivity endured by "laying" hens, who sit in darkness without room to stretch out their wings or turn around; and the plight of sows who are forced into metal gestation crates for birthing and beyond. This commodification also includes continuous sexual violence against animal bodies, such as forced impregnation, as well as the continuous separation of mothers and their offspring, leading to significant emotional trauma. But male animals too are subjected to brutality in this industrial context, in which male chicks are killed immediately after birth, sometimes tossed into wood chippers while still alive; bulls are forcibly ejaculated to collect their semen (for artificial insemination), often by inserting electric prods into their anuses to shock the system; and male calves are turned into veal, tied in place and allowed extremely limited movement in order to keep their meat tender. See Adams and Donovan (1995), Gaard (1993, 2013), Gruen (2011), King (2017), Regan (2004), and Singer (2002).

57. Gillespie (2013: 5); emphasis in original.

58. This means she will be continuously impregnated during the course of one year. This usually leads to four or five births before the animal is "spent" and slaughtered.

59. On the linkages between breeding, race, species, and capital, see Anderson (2004), Franklin (2007), Hartigan (2017), Ritvo (1997), and Woods (2017).

60. Thompson (1967).

61. Tsing (2018).

62. Tsing (2018: 232).

63. Swanson, Lien, and Ween (2018: 22).

64. Castañeda (2002: 8).

65. Hartigan (2017)

66. Hartigan (2017: xvi).

67. TallBear (2011) and Womack (2013).

INTERLUDE: CHEMICAL CASTRATION

1. "Los mejores videos sobre cuyes y caracoles," n.d., http://ricardo.bizhat.com /rmr-prigeds/videos-de-cuyes.htm.

1. This chapter is a revised version of an article published in *Environmental Humanities* (García 2019a).

2. A *galpón* is a kind of warehouse of life where plants or animals are stored. In a different historical moment, it referred to the place used as slave quarters.

3. Million (2009: 54).

4. Dave (2014: 434).

5. Gillespie (2016).

6. Singh and Dave (2015: 233).

7. See Ogden, Hall, and Tanita (2013).

8. Walter and SuperCuy are both pseudonyms.

9. As Portocarrero has pointed out, the "obsession for economic success is [often] ... a response by subaltern (*popular*) subjects [in Peru] to marginalization and contempt" (2007: 32).

10. Stress has been known to lead to miscarriage and heart attacks in cuyes.

11. Haraway (2008: 5).

12. TallBear (2013, 2015), Justice (2014), and Million (2014).

13. Million (2014: 32).

14. See also Govindrajan (2018a).

15. Derrida (2002).

16. García and Lucero (2008).

17. Kim (2014).

18. Arguedas (1990).

19. Shea (2010: 2).

20. Govindrajan (2015), Hua and Ahuja (2013), Justice (2014), and Parreñas (2018).

21. Butler (2004).

22. Das (2012: 1).

23. Das (2012: 2).

24. Govindrajan (2018a) and Haraway (2016). E. B. White's 1948 essay, "Death of a Pig," also comes to mind here. In it, White describes his futile attempts at saving a sick pig, a pig who he was expecting to slaughter only a few months later. The essay is a rumination on the complexity of care, grief and loss: "When we slid the body into the grave, we both were shaken to the core. The loss we felt was not the loss of ham but the loss of pig. He had evidently become precious to me, not that he represented a distant nourishment in a hungry time, but that he had suffered in a suffering world."

25. Appadurai (2004).

26. Dave (2017: 48).

27. Povinelli (2006).

28. Dave (2016).

29. Pachirat (2011).

30. Berlant (2007: 754).

31. Berlant (2007: 761).

32. Berlant (2007: 754).

33. Kober et al. (2007). What I did not know until I read some of these studies is that this stress is communicated not only audibly, but also through scent and body language (Wagner 1976).

34. Fuentes (2010: 618–19).

35. Devereux (1967).

36. Walter lamented that due to lack of space and technological capacity, he could not include a fifth method: electrocution. The larger farms in Ecuador and southern Peru, he told me, are mechanizing death much like in the North. According to Walter, in those slaughter facilities guinea pigs are placed on a thin layer of water and electrocuted before scalding.

37. Kuzniar (2006: 3).

38. Govindrajan's work on interspecies relatedness in India is instructive. She demonstrates precisely what can emerge from an ethnographic practice that pays careful and continued attention to animals as subjects and to the complex relations between (individual) humans and animals that call one another forth in "response-ability."

39. Haraway (2008) and Kirksey and Helmreich (2010).

40. Contributions of scholars: A few examples from a growing literature: Blanchette (2020), Candea (2010), Dave (2014, 2016, 2017), Dransart (2013), Few and Tortorici (2013), Gillespie (2018), Govindrajan (2018a), Helmreich (2009), Kirksey (2014), Kohn (2013), Krebber and Roscher (2018), McHugh (2011), Nading (2014), Parreñas (2018), Tsing (2012), and Van Dooren, Kirksey, and Munster (2016); "new materialisms": Bennett (2010) and Chen (2012); Indigenous metaphysics and theory: Million (2014) and TallBear (2013); politics of seeing: Dutkiewicz (2018) and Pachirat (2011).

41. Dave (2016, 2017), Kirksey (2015), Kohn (2013), and Yates-Doerr (2015).

42. Yates-Doerr (2015: 310).

43. Pachirat (2011) and Gillespie (2016, 2018).

44. Desjarlais (2016), Gruen (2014a, 2014b), Stevenson (2014), and Van Dooren and Bird Rose (2013).

45. Yong (2018).

46. Van Dooren (2014: 9); see also McHugh (2019).

47. Safran-Foer (2009: 37).

48. Safran-Foer (2009: 38).

49. Rosaldo (2013, 1989a).

50. Stanescu (2011).

51. Stanescu (2011: 568).

52. Stanescu (2011: 568).

53. Kim (2014).

54. Brueggemann (2001: 50).

55. Brueggemann (2001: 60).

56. Barad (2012: 216).

57. The film, *Albatross*, is available at www.albatrossthefilm.com/.

58. In "Midway: Message from the Gyre (2009–Current)," Chris jordan Photographic Arts, http://www.chrisjordan.com/gallery/midway/#about.

59. "Midway."

60. Barad (2012: 219).

61. *Poemas de Rocío Silva Santisteban*, https://conlaa.com/poemas-de-rocio-silva-santisteban/

EPILOGUE

1. Rifkin (2017).

2. Keme (2018: 43).

3. Keme (2018: 56).

4. Hinostroza (2006: 9).

5. Franco (2013).

6. Zavaleta (1998).

7. Coulthard (2014).

8. Knobloch (1996).

9. La Ultima Reyna de Cerro de Pasco, "Romería a Quiulacocha (antes laguna,hoy poza de relaves mineros)", posted on July 30, 2012, YouTube video, https://www.youtube.com/watch?v=HxMXmx3HWYk.

10. Rodríguez-Ulloa (2013).

11. Salas Carreño (2016).

12. Gómez-Barris (2017: 1).

13. Gordon (2008: xvi).

14. Allen (2015).

15. Allen (2015: 395).

16. Allen (2015: 395).

REFERENCES

Abend, Lisa. 2018. "At Cusco's MIL, an Agricultural Exploration 500 Years in the Making." 12 Forward: The Now and Next in Gastronomy, May 22. https://12fwd.com/news/cusco-s-mil-discovers-what-the-inca-knew.

Acevedo, Juan. n.d. https://elcuy.wordpress.com/about/.

Acurio, Gastón. 2018a. "Can Home Cooking Change the World?" TED en Español en NYC, April. www.ted.com/talks/gaston_acurio_can_home_cooking_change_the_world?utm_source=tedcomshare&utm_medium=email&utm_campaign=tedspread#t-58443.

———. 2018b. *Bravazo! Más de 600 recetas para volver a cocinar en casa.* Miami, FL: Penguin Random House.

———. 2016a. *Sazón en Acción: Algunas recetas para el Perú que queremos.* Lima: Aerolíneas Editoriales, Mitin.

———. 2016b. "La Fragilidad." Facebook, October 22, 2016.

———. 2015. *Peru: The Cookbook.* London: Phaidon Press.

———. 2012. "Pasar al insulto es ir contra el espíritu de tolerancia." Interview, February 4, Peru16. https://issuu.com/diario16peru/docs/04-02-2012.

———. 2009. "Gastón Acurio: 'Cooking Is Combined with Moral Principles.'" The Power of Culture, March. www.powerofculture.nl/en/current/2009/march/gaston-acurio.

———. 2008. *500 Años de Fusión: La historia, los ingredientes y la nueva propuesta de la cocina peruana.* Lima: El Comercio.

———. 2006. *Las Cocinas del Perú.* Lima: El Comercio.

Acurio, Gastón, and Javier Masías. 2016. *Bitute: El Sabor de Lima.* Lima: Latino Publicaciones.

Adams, Carol. (1990) 2015. *The Sexual Politics of Meat: A Feminist-Vegetarian Critical Theory.* New York: Bloomsbury Academic.

———. 2003. *The Pornography of Meat.* New York: Continuum.

Adams, Carol, and Josephine Donovan, eds. 1995. *Animals and Women: Feminist Theoretical Explorations.* Durham, NC: Duke University Press.

Agarwal, Bina. 2014. "Food Sovereignty, Food Security and Democratic Choice: Critical Contradictions, Difficult Conciliations." *Journal of Peasant Studies* 41 (6): 1247–68.

Aguirre, Carlos. 2017. "The Second Liberation? Military Nationalism and the Sesquicentennial Commemoration of Peruvian Independence, 1821–1971." In *The Peculiar Revolution: Rethinking the Peruvian Experiment Under Military Rule*, edited by Carlos Aguirre and Paulo Drinot, 25–48. Austin: University of Texas Press.

Aguirre, Carlos, and Paulo Drinot. 2017. *The Peculiar Revolution: Rethinking the Peruvian Experiment under Military Rule*. Austin: University of Texas Press.

Ahmed, Sara. 2004. "Affective Economies." *Social Text* 22 (2): 117-39.

Alcalde, Cristina. 2010. *The Woman in the Violence: Gender, Poverty, and Resistance in Peru*. Nashville, TN: Vanderbilt University Press.

Alfred, Taiaiake. 2009. *Peace, Power, Righteousness: An Indigenous Manifesto*. Oxford: Oxford University Press.

———. 2005. *Wasáse: Indigenous Pathways of Action and Freedom*. Peterborough, ON: Broadview.

Allen, Catherine. 2002. *The Hold Life Has: Coca and Cultural Identity in an Andean Community*. Washington, DC: Smithsonian Books.

Allen, Chadwick. 2015. "Performing Serpent Mound: A Trans-Indigenous Meditation." *Theatre Journal* 67 (3): 391–411.

Andreassen, Rikke. 2014. "The Search for the White Nordic: Analysis of the Contemporary New Nordic Kitchen and Former Race Science." *Social Identities: Whiteness and Nation in the Nordic Countries* 20 (6): 438–51.

Altamirano Rua, Teófilo, and Eric Altamirano Girao. 2019. *La nueva cocina peruana: En la era del cambio climático, la contaminación ambiental, las migraciones y la masculinización*. Lima: CreaLibros.

Alvarez Novoa, Isabel. 2019. "El boom gastronómico peruano: Entre moda y promesas incumplidas; Entrevista a Isabel Álvarez." In "Gastro-politics: Culture, Identity and Culinary Politics in Peru." Special issue, *Anthropology of Food* 14.

———. 2017a. *Picanterías y chicherías del Perú. 2 Tomos, Patrimonio Cultural de la Nación*. Lima: Universidad de San Martín de Porres, Fondo Editorial.

———. 2017b. "La academia formal solo ve la parte bonita de la cocina." *Peru 21*, April 4. https://peru21.pe/cultura/academia-formal-ve-parte-bonita-cocina-73615.

———. 2015. *Las manos de mi madre*. Lima: Universidad de San Martín de Porres, Fondo Editorial.

———. 2013. *Reconociendo y revalorando las cocinas regionales del Peru*. Lima: Universidad de San Martín de Porres, Fondo Editorial.

———. 2002. *El Corregidor Mejía: Cocina y memoria del alma Limeña*. Lima: Universidad de San Martín de Porres, Escuela Profesional de Turismo y Hotelería.

———. 1997. *Huellas y sabores de Perú*. Lima: Universidad de San Martín de Porres, Fondo Editorial.

Anderson, Benedict. 2016. *Imagined Communities: Reflections on the Origin and Spread of Nationalism*. New York: Verso.

Anderson, Virginia DeJohn. 2004. *Creatures of Empire: How Domestic Animals Transformed Early America*. New York: Oxford University Press.

Apega. 2017a. *Mistura: Una marca que ha calado en el sentir de los peruanos*. Lima: Apega.

———. 2017b. *Innovación, tecnología, y nuevas oportunidades de negocios en la gastronomía*. Lima: Apega.

———. 2017c. *Revalorando el tesoro escondido*. Lima: Apega.

———. 2017d. *Cuál es el futuro de la gastronomía peruana?* Segunda Edición. Lima: Apega.

———. 2015a. "Lima: Capital gastronómica." www.apega.pe/lima-capital-gastronomica.

———. 2015b. *Gastronomía Peruana al 2021: Segunda independencia*. www.apega.pe /publicaciones/documentos-de-trabajo/gastronomia-peruana-al-2021---segunda -independencia.html.

———. 2013. *El Boom Gastronómico Peruano al 2013*. Lima: Apega.

Aponte, Walter Castro. 2013. *Non-Governmental Organizations and the Sustainability of Small and Medium-Sized Enterprises in Peru: An Analysis of Networks and Discourses*. Wageningen, Netherlands: Wageningen Academic Publishers.

Appadurai, Arjun. 2004. "The Capacity to Aspire: Culture and the Terms of Recognition." In *Culture and Public Action*, edited by Vijayendra Rao and Michael Walton, 59–84. Stanford, CA: Stanford University Press.

———. 1988. "How to Make a National Cuisine: Cookbooks in Contemporary India." *Comparative Studies in Society and History* 30 (1): 3–24.

———. 1981. "Gastro-Politics in Hindu South Asia." *American Ethnologist* 8 (3): 494–511

Appelbaum, Nancy, Anne Macpherson, and Karin Alejandra Rosemblatt. 2003. *Race and Nation in Modern Latin America*. Chapel Hill: University of North Carolina Press.

Archetti, Eduardo. 1997. *Guinea Pigs: Food, Symbol and Conflict of Knowledge in Ecuador*. New York: Bloomsbury.

Arguedas, José María. 2001. "Un Perú de todas las sangres.'" *El País*, July 28. https:// elpais.com/diario/2001/07/28/internacional/996271206_850215.html.

———. 1990. *El zorro de arriba y el zorro de abajo*. Pittsburgh: University of Pittsburgh Press.

———. 1964. *Todas las Sangres*. Buenos Aires: Editorial Losada.

Arguedas, Luis Alberto. 1928. "Las necesidades sanitarias del Cuzco." *Mundial Revista Semanal I Ilustrada*, December.

Babb, Florence. 2020. "'The Real Indigenous Are Higher Up': Locating Race and Gender in Andean Peru." *Latin American and Caribbean Ethnic Studies*, August 24. https://www.tandfonline.com/doi/full/10.1080/17442222.2020 .1809080.

———. 2018. *Women's Place in the Andes: Engaging Decolonial Feminist Anthropology*. Oakland: University of California Press.

———. 2010. *The Tourism Encounter: Fashioning Latin American Nations and Histories*. Stanford, CA: Stanford University Press.

————. 1989. *Between Field and Cooking Pot: The Political Economy of Marketwomen in Peru.* Austin: University of Texas Press.

————. 1982. "Economic Crisis and the Assault on Marketers in Peru." Women in International Development Working Papers. East Lansing: Michigan State University.

Baker, Steve. 2001. *Picturing the Beast: Animals, Identity, and Representation.* Urbana: University of Illinois Press.

Balbi, Mariella. 1997. *La cocina según Sato.* Lima: Universidad San Martín de Porres, Facultad de Turismo y Hotelería.

Ballón, Alejandra, ed. 2014. *Memorias del caso peruano de esterilización forzada.* Lima: Fondo Editorial de la Biblioteca Nacional del Perú.

Barad, Karen. 2012. "On Touching—The Inhuman That Therefore I Am." *Differences* 23 (3): 206–23.

Bebbington, Anthony. 2011. *Social Conflict, Economic Development and Extractive Industry: Evidence from South America.* London: Routledge.

————. 2009. "The New Extraction: Rewriting the Political Ecology of the Andes?" *NACLA Report on the Americas,* 42 (5): 12–20.

Bebbington, Anthony, and Jeffrey Bury. 2014. *Subterranean Struggles: New Dynamics of Mining, Oil, and Gas in Latin America.* Austin: University of Texas Press.

Beggs, Alex. 2019. "Where Potatoes Pass from the Ice to the Sun." *Bon Appétit,* April 30. https://www.bonappetit.com/story/mil-restaurant-peru.

Bennett, Jane. 2010. *Vibrant Matter: A Political Ecology of Things.* Durham, NC: Duke University Press.

Berlant, Lauren. 2011. *Cruel Optimism.* Durham, NC: Duke University Press.

————. 2007. "Slow Death (Sovereignty, Obesity and Lateral Agency)." *Critical Inquiry* 33 (4): 754–80.

Bertolt, Andrea. 2018. "The New Incan Gold—Peruvian Cuisine: From Blue Corn to Jungle Fish." KTCHN Rebel. https://www.ktchnrebel.com/peruvian-cuisine/.

Bessire, Lucas, and David Bond. 2014. "The Ontological Turn and the Deferral of Critique." *American Ethnologist* 41 (3): 440–56.

Beverly, John. 1999. *Subalternity and Representation: Arguments in Cultural Theory.* Durham, NC: Duke University Press.

Bhattacharyya, Gargi. 2018. *Rethinking Racial Capitalism: Questions of Reproduction and Survival.* London: Rowman & Littlefield International.

Blanchard, Pascal, et al. 2009. *Human Zoos: Science and Spectacle in the Age of Colonial Empires.* Liverpool, UK: Liverpool University Press.

Blanchette, Alexander. 2020. *Porkopolis: American Animality, Standardized Life, and the "Factory" Farm.* Durham, NC: Duke University Press.

Blanco, Hugo. 2007. "The 'Indian Problem' in Peru: From Mariátegui to Today." *Socialist Voice,* March 29. https://www.countercurrents.org/blanco290307.htm.

————. 1972. *Land or Death: The Peasant Struggle in Peru.* New York: Pathfinder Press.

Blaser, Mario. 2010. *Storytelling Globalization from the Chaco and Beyond.* Durham, NC: Duke University Press.

Blee, Kathleen. 2002. *Inside Organized Racism: Women in the Hate Movement.* Berkeley: University of California Press.

Blee, Kathleen, and Sandra McGee Deutsch. 2012. *Women of the Right: Comparisons and Interplay across Borders.* University Park: Pennsylvania State University Press.

Boesten, Jelke. 2010. *Intersecting Inequalities: Women and Social Policy in Peru, 1990–2000.* University Park: Pennsylvania State University Press.

Bohardt, Meghan. 2014. "Peru's 'Gastronomic Boom': Critical Perspectives on Elite Gastronomy and Social Food Justice." MA thesis, University of Illinois at Urbana-Champaign.

Bonfil Batalla, Guillermo. 2010. *Mexico Profundo: Reclaiming a Civilization.* Austin: University of Texas Press.

Bourdieu, Pierre. 1984. *Distinction: A Social Critique of the Judgement of Taste.* Cambridge, MA: Harvard University Press.

Bracken, Erica. 2017. "When the Best Chef in Latin America Came to Galway— An Interview with Virgilio Martínez." *The Taste.* https://thetaste.ie/wp /when-the-best-chef-in-latin-america-came-to-galway-an-interview-with-virgilio -Martínez/.

Brooke, James. 1989. "Peru's Guerrillas Become a Threat to the Capital." *New York Times,* June 12. www.nytimes.com/1989/06/12/world/peru-s-guerrillas-become -a-threat-to-the-capital.html.

Brown, Wendy. 2006. *Regulating Aversion: Tolerance in the Age of Identity and Empire.* Princeton, NJ: Princeton University Press.

Brueggemann, Walter. 2001. *The Prophetic Imagination.* Minneapolis, MN: Fortress Press.

Bruyneel, Kevin. 2007. *The Third Space of Sovereignty: The Postcolonial Politics of U.S.-Indigenous Relations.* Minneapolis: University of Minnesota Press.

Bueno-Hansen, Pascha. 2015. *Feminist and Human Rights Struggles in Peru.* Champaign: University of Illinois Press.

Burguete, Araceli. 2008. "Gobernar en la diversidad en tiempos de multiculturalismo en América Latina." In *Gobernar (en) La Diversidad: Experiencias Indígenas Desde América Latina. Hacia la Investigación de Co-Labor,* edited by Xochitl Leyva, Araceli Burguete, and Shannon Speed, 15–64. Mexico City: Publicaciones de la Casa Chata.

Burman, Anders. 2014. "'Now We Are Indígenas': Hegemony and Indigeneity in the Bolivian Andes." *Latin American and Caribbean Ethnic Studies* 9 (3): 247–71.

Burt, Jo-Marie. 2010. "Los usos y abusos de la memoria de María Elena Moyano." *A Contracorriente: Revista de Historia Social y Literatura en América Latina* 7 (2): 165–209.

Butler, Judith. 2004. *Precarious Life: The Powers of Mourning and Violence.* New York: Verso.

Byrd, Jodi. 2011. *The Transit of Empire: Indigenous Critiques of Colonialism.* Minneapolis: University of Minnesota Press.

Cabellos, Ernesto. 2009. *De ollas y sueños: Cooking up Dreams.* Lima: Guarango Cine y Video.

Cajete, Gregory. 2015. *Indigenous Community: Rekindling the Teachings of the Seventh Fire*. St. Paul, MN: Living Justice Press.

Campoamor, Leigh. 2016. "'Who Are You Calling Exploitative?' Defensive Motherhood, Child Labor, and Urban Poverty in Lima, Peru." *Journal of Latin American and Caribbean Anthropology* 21 (1): 151–72.

———. 2013. *Public Childhoods: Street Labor, Family, and the Politics of Progress in Peru*. PhD diss.,, Duke University.

Campt, Tina. 2017. *Listening to Images*. Durham, NC: Duke University Press.

Candea, Matei. 2010. "'I Fell in Love with Carlos the Meerkat': Engagement and Detachment in Human–Animal Relations." *American Ethnologist* 37 (2): 241–58.

Cánepa, Gisela. 2018. "La Paisana Jacinta: Para pensar la relación entre representación y discriminación racial." *Intercambio: Revista del Apostolado Social de la Compañía de Jesús en el Perú*, 41: 36–39. https://intercambio.pe/la-paisana-jacinta-pensar-la-relacion-representacion-discriminacion-racial/.

———. 2015. "MARCA PERU: Repertorios culturales e imágenes de peruanidad." In *VI Congreso Nacional de Investigaciones en Antropología Peruana*, 109–30. Puno: Universidad Nacional del Altiplano.

———. 2014. "Peruanos en Nebraska: Una propuesta de lectura crítica del spot publicitario de Marca Perú." In *Sensibilidad de frontera: Comunicación y voces populares*, edited by Abelardo Sanchez León, 207–35. Lima: Fondo Editorial, PUCP.

———. 2013. "Nation Branding: The Re-foundation of Community, Citizenship, and the State in the Context of Neoliberalism in Perú. *Medien Journal* 37 (3): 7–18.

———. 2003. "Geopolitics and Geopoetics of Identity: Migration, Ethnicity and Place in the Peruvian Imaginary; Fiestas and Devotional Dances in Cuzco and Lima." PhD thesis, University of Chicago.

Canessa, Andrew. 2017. Comment on *Earth Beings: Ecologies of Practice across Andean Worlds*, by Marisol de la Cadena. *HAU: Journal of Ethnographic Theory* 7 (2): 15–17.

———. 2012. *Intimate Indigeneities: Race, Sex, and History in the Small Spaces of Andean Life*. Durham, NC: Duke University Press.

———. 2008. "Sex and the Citizen: Barbies and Beauty Queens in the Age of Evo Morales." *Journal of Latin American Cultural Studies* 17 (1): 41–64.

Caretas. 2011. "Los Diez Mandamientos del Cocinero Peruano." *Caretas*, edición 2178, April 28.

Carrión, Julio, ed. 2006. *The Fujimori Legacy: The Rise of Electoral Authoritarianism in Peru*. University Park: Pennsylvania State University Press.

Carroll, Clint. 2019. "Land-Based Praxis, Affect, and Cosmopolitical Futures: Toward a Radically Relational Indigenous Political Ecology." Paper delivered at the Native American and Indigenous Studies Association Meeting, Aotearoa/New Zealand, June 26–29.

Cassidy, Rebecca. 2002. *The Sport of Kings: Kinship, Class and Thoroughbred Breeding in Newmarket*. Cambridge, UK: Cambridge University Press.

Castañeda, Claudia. 2002. *Figurations: Child, Bodies, Worlds*. Durham, NC: Duke University Press.

Castrodale, Jelisa. 2019. "Ecuadorean Ice Cream Vendor's New Best-Seller Is Made from Guinea Pigs." Vice. https://www.vice.com/en_us/article/ywaqek/ecuadorean -ice-cream-vendors-new-best-seller-is-made-from-guinea-pigs.

Cattelino, Jessica. 2019. "Post Which Human?" Paper delivered at Native American and Indigenous Studies Association Meeting, Aotearoa/New Zealand, June 24–26.

Ccopa, Pedro Pablo. 2018. *La Cocina de Acogida: Migrantes Andinos en Lima*. Memorias, sabores, y sentidos. Lima: Universidad San Martín de Porres.

———. 2016. "Memorias del Cuerpo: Género, raza y violencia sexual en el marco del conflict armado." In *Género y justicia: Estudios e investigaciones en el Perú e Iberoamérica*, edited by Marianella Ledesma Narváez: 237–54. Lima: Pontificia Universidad Católica del Peru.

Chakrabarty, Dipesh. 2000. *Provincializing Europe: Postcolonial Thought and Historical Difference*. Princeton, NJ: Princeton University Press.

Charney, Paul. 2001. *Indian Society in the Valley of Lima, Peru 1532–1824*. Lanham, MD: Rowman & Littlefield.

Chen, Mel. *Animacies: Biopolitics, Racial Mattering, and Queer Affect*. Durham, NC: Duke University Press, 2012.

Child, Brenda. 1998. *Boarding School Seasons: American Indian Families, 1900–1940*. Lincoln: University of Nebraska Press.

Child, Brenda, and Brian Klopotek, eds. 2014. *Indian Subjects: Hemispheric Perspectives on the History of Indigenous Education*. Santa Fe, NM: School for Advanced Research Press

Chiu Werner, Alexander. 2012. "La Marca Mistura." *Diario Gestión* (blog), August 27, https://gestion.pe/blog/anunciasluegoexistes/2012/08/la-marca-mistura.html.

[CNN]. 2015. "Part 1: Meet the Chef Taking Peruvian to New Heights." Culinary Journeys, December 1. https://www.youtube.com/watch?v=JwN9nXiHFhs.

Cody, Kevin. 2015. "'La misma realidad de cada lugar es diferente' ('The Same Reality of Each Place Is Different'): A Case Study of an Organic Farmers Market in Lima, Peru." *Journal of Agriculture, Food Systems, and Community Development* (March): 1–17.

Cogorno, Gilda, and Pilar Ortiz de Zevallos. 2018. *La Lima que Encontró Pizarro*. Lima: Taurus.

Colloredo-Mansfeld, Rudi. 2009. *Fighting Like a Community: Andean Civil Society in an Era of Indian Uprisings*. Chicago: University of Chicago Press.

———. 1998. "'Dirty Indians', Radical Indígenas, and the Political Economy of Social Difference in Modern Ecuador." *Bulletin of Latin American Research* 17 (2): 185–205.

Collyns, Dan. 2014. "Peru TV Slammed by UN as Racial Stereotypes Paraded for Cheap Laughs." *The Guardian*, September 3. www.theguardian.com/global -development/2014/sep/03/peru-tv-racial-stereotypes-paisana-jacinta.

Comaroff, John, and Jean Comaroff. 2009. *Ethnicity, Inc.* Chicago: University of Chicago Press.

Comisión de la Verdad y Reconciliación (CVR). 2004. *Hatun Willakuy: Versión Abreviada Del Informe Final De La Comisión De La Verdad y Reconciliación, Perú.* Lima: Corporación Gráfica.

Conaghan, Catherine. 2005. *Fujimori's Peru: Deception in the Public Sphere.* Pittsburgh, PA: University of Pittsburgh Press.

Consiglieri, Natalia. 2019. "Integradora y excluyente: El rol de la gastronomía en la Urbanización Santa Cruz (Lima, Perú)." *Anthropology of Food* 14. https://journals.openedition.org/aof/.

Cookson, Tara Patricia. 2018. *Unjust Conditions: Women's Work and the Hidden Cost of Cash Transfer Programs.* Oakland: University of California Press.

Corntassel, Jeff, and Cheryl Bryce. 2012. "Practicing Sustainable Self-Determination: Indigenous Approaches to Cultural Restoration and Revitalization." *Brown Journal of World Affairs* 18 (2): 151–62.

Coronado, Jorge. 2018. *Portraits in the Andes: Photography and Agency, 1900–1950.* Pittsburgh, PA: University of Pittsburgh Press.

———. 2009. *The Andes Imagined: Indigenismo, Society, and Modernity.* Pittsburgh, PA: University of Pittsburgh Press.

Coronel-Molina, Serafín. 2008. "Inventing Tawantinsuyu and qhapaq simi: Language Ideologies of the High Academy of the Quechua Language in Cusco, Peru." In "Indigenous Encounters in Peru." Special issue, *Latin American and Caribbean Ethnic Studies* 3 (3): 319–40.

Coronel-Molina, Serafín, et al., eds. 2005. *Lenguas e Identidades en los Andes: Perspectivas Ideológicas y Culturales.* Quito: Abya-Yala.

Coté, Charlotte. 2016. "'Indigenizing' Food Sovereignty. Revitalizing Indigenous Food Practices and Ecological Knowledges in Canada and the United States." *Humanities* 5 (3): 57.

Coulthard, Glen. 2014. *Red Skin, White Masks: Rejecting the Colonial Politics of Recognition.* Minneapolis: University of Minnesota Press.

Cox Hall, Amy. 2020. "Cooking Up Heritage: Culinary Adventures of Peru's Past." *Bulletin of Spanish Studies* 97 (4): 593–613. doi:10.1080/14753820.2020.1699364.

———. 2019. "Heritage Prospecting and the Past as Future(s) in Peru." *Journal of Latin American and Caribbean Anthropology* 24 (2): 331–50.

———. 2017. *Framing a Lost City: Science, Photography, and the Making of Machu Picchu.* Austin: University of Texas Press.

Cozart, Daniel. 2012. "La Madre Coraje y sus enlaces: Remembering María Elena Moyano." *Latin Americanist* 56 (2): 119–36.

Crabtree, John, and Jim Thomas. 1998. *Fujimori's Peru: The Political Economy.* London: Institute of Latin American Studies.

Cusicanqui, Silvia Rivera. 2007. "Everything Is Up for Discussion: A 40th Anniversary Conversation with Silvia Rivera Cusicanqui." By Linda Farthing. *NACLA Report on the Americas* 40 (4): 4–9.

———. 1987. *"Oppressed but Not Defeated": Peasant Struggles among the Aymara and Qhechwa in Bolivia, 1900–1980.* Geneva: United Nations Research Institute for Social Development.

Daigle, Michelle. 2019. "Tracing the Terrain of Indigenous Food *Sovereignties*." *Journal of Peasant Studies* 46 (2): 297–315.

Dajer, Tony. 2015. "High in the Andes, a Mine Eats a 400-Year-Old City." *National Geographic*, December 5. https://news.nationalgeographic.com/2015/12/151202 -Cerro-de-Pasco-Peru-Volcan-mine-eats-city-environment/.

Dall, Nick. 2017. "The Peruvian Chef Daring to Serve Recycled Food—and End Hunger Nationwide." OZY, July 31. www.ozy.com/rising-stars/the-peruvian-chef -daring-to-serve-recycled-food-and-end-hunger-nationwide/79698.

Das, Veena. 2012. "Death and the Recreation of Life." Paper delivered at the American Anthropological Association Meeting, San Francisco, November 15–18.

Dave, Naisargi. 2017. "Something, Everything, Nothing; or Cows, Dogs, and Maggots." *Social Text* 35 (1): 37–57.

———. 2016. "Love and Other Injustices: On Indifference to Difference." Durham, NC: Franklin Humanities Institute, Duke University.

———. 2014. "Witness: Humans, Animals and the Politics of Becoming." *Cultural Anthropology* 29 (3): 433–56.

Davis, Karen. 1995. "Thinking Like a Chicken: Farm Animals and the Feminine Connection." In *Animals and Women: Feminist Theoretical Explorations*, edited by Carol J. Adams and Josephine Donovan, 192–212. Durham, NC: Duke University Press.

De la Cadena, Marisol. 2015. *Earth Beings: Ecologies of Practice across Andean Worlds*. Durham, NC: Duke University Press.

———. 2010. "Indigenous Cosmopolitics in the Andes: Conceptual Reflections Beyond 'Politics.'" *Cultural Anthropology* 25 (2): 334–70.

———. 2001a. "Reconstructing Race: Racism, Culture, and Mestizaje in Latin America." *NACLA Report on the Americas* 34 (6): 16–23.

———. 2001b. "The Marketing of El Cholo Toledo." *NACLA Report on the Americas* 34 (6): 20–21.

———. 2000. *Indigenous Mestizos: The Politics of Race and Culture in Cuzco, Peru, 1919–1991*. Durham, NC: Duke University Press.

———. 1996. "The Political Tensions of Representations and Misrepresentations: Intellectuals and Mestizas in Cusco (1919–1990)." *Journal of Latin American Anthropology* 2 (1): 112–47.

De la Cadena, Marisol, and Mario Blaser, eds. 2018. *A World of Many Worlds*. Durham, NC: Duke University Press.

De Soto, Hernando. 2002. *The Other Path: The Economic Answer to Terrorism*. New York City: Basic Books.

———. 2000. *The Mystery of Capital: Why Capitalism Triumphs in the West and Fails Everywhere Else*. New York: Basic Books.

———. 1989. *El otro Sendero: La revolución informal*. Lima: Instituto Libertad y Democracia.

De Trazegnies, Fernando. 1992. "Violencia y Modernización en el Peru." In *500 años después: El nuevo rostro del Peru*, 209–23. Lima: Nuevas Ideas S. R. L.

De Waal, Franz. 2017. *Are We Smart Enough to Know How Smart Animals Are?* New York: Norton.

Degregori, Carlos Iván. 2012. *How Difficult It Is to Be God: Shining Path's Politics of War in Peru, 1980–1999*. Madison: University of Wisconsin Press.

——. 2000. *No hay pais mas diverso: Compendio de antropologia peruana*. Lima: Red Para El Desarrollo De Las Ciencias Sociales en El Peru.

——. 1995. "El estudio del otro: Cambios en los análisis de la etnicidad en el Perú." In *Peru 1964–1994: Economía, Sociedad y política*, edited by Julio Cotler and Agusto Alvarez Rodrich, 303–32. Lima: IEP.

——. 1993. "Identidad étnica, movimientos sociales y participación política en el Perú." In *Democracia, etnicidad y violencia política en los países andinos*, edited by Alberto Adrianzén, Jean-Michel Blanquer, Ricardo Calla Ortega, et al., 113–33. Lima: Institut français d'études andines.

——. 1986. "Del mito del Inkarry al mito del progreso." *Socialismo y Participación* 36: 49–56.

Del Pino, Ponciano, and José Carlos Agüero. 2014. *Cada uno, un lugar de memoria: Fundamentos conceptuales del Lugar de la Memoria, la Tolerancia y la Inclusión Social*. Lima: LUM.

Del Pino, Ponciano, and Caroline Yezer. 2013. *Las formas del recuerdo: Etnografías de la violencia política en el Perú*. Lima: IEP–IFEA.

Del Pino, Ponciano, et al. 2012. *Repensar la desnutrición: Infancia, alimentación y cultura en Ayacucho, Perú*. Lima: Instituto de Estudios Peruanos.

Deloria, Philip. 2004. *Indians in Unexpected Places*. Lawrence: University Press of Kansas.

Denegri, Francesca, and Alexandra Hibbet. 2016. *Dando cuenta: Estudios sobre el testimonio de la violencia política en el Perú (1980–2000)*. Lima: Fondo Editorial de la PUCP.

Derrida, Jacques. 2002. "The Animal That Therefore I Am (More to Follow)." Translated by David Wills. *Critical Inquiry* 28 (2, Winter): 369–418.

Descola, Philippe. 2006. "Beyond Nature and Culture." *Proceedings of the British Academy* 139: 137–55.

——. 1996. *In the Society of Nature: A Native Ecology of Amazonia*. Translated by Nora Scott. New York: Cambridge University Press.

Desjarlais, Robert. 2016. *Subject to Death: Life and Loss in a Buddhist World*. Chicago: University of Chicago Press.

Desmond, Jane. 1999. *Staging Tourism: Bodies on Display from Waikiki to Sea World*. Chicago: University of Chicago Press.

Devereux, George. 1967. *From Anxiety to Method in the Behavioral Sciences*. Boston: Mouton.

Di Giminiani, Piergiorgio. 2018. *Sentient Lands: Indigeneity, Property, and Political Imagination in Neoliberal Chile*. Tucson: University of Arizona Press.

Diaz, Vicente, and J. Kehaulani Kauanui. 2001. "Native Pacific Cultural Studies on the Edge." *Contemporary Pacific* 13 (2): 315–42.

Dixler Canavan, Hilary. 2018. "Feast Your Eyes on Mil, Virgilio Martínez's Groundbreaking New Restaurant." *Eater Magazine*, February 21. www.eater.com/2018

/2/21/17033912/mil-virgilio-Martínez-cusco-peru-menu-reservations-photos
-moray-ruins.

Dolan, Catherine, and Dinah Rajak. 2016. *The Anthropology of Corporate Social Responsibility*. New York: Berghahn Books.

Douglas, Mary. (1966) 2002. *Purity and Danger*. New York: Routledge.

Dransart, Penelope, ed. 2013. *Living Beings: Perspectives on Interspecies Engagements*. London: Bloomsbury.

Drinot, Paulo. 2017a. "Remembering Velasco: Contested Memories of the Revolutionary Government of the Armed Forces." In *The Peculiar Revolution: Rethinking the Peruvian Experiment under Military Rule*, edited by Carlos Aguirre and Paulo Drinot, 95–119. Austin: University of Texas Press.

———. 2017b. "Cyber-Cuy: Remembering and Forgetting the Peruvian Left." In *Comics & Memory in Latin America*, edited by Jorge Catalá Carrasco, Paulo Drinot, and James Scorer, 138–65. Pittsburgh, PA: University of Pittsburgh Press.

———. 2011. *The Allure of Labor: Workers, Race, and the Making of the Peruvian State*. Durham, NC: Duke University Press.

———. 2009. "For Whom the Eye Cries: Memory, Monumentality, and the Ontologies of Violence in Peru." *Journal of Latin American Cultural Studies* 18 (1): 15–32.

Druckman, Charlotte. 2010. "Why Are There No Great Women Chefs?" *Gastronomica: The Journal of Critical Food Studies* 10 (1): 24–31.

Dutkiewicz, Jan. 2018. "Transparency and the Factory Farm: Agritourism and Counter-Activism at Fair Oaks Farms." *Gastronomica: The Journal of Critical Food Studies* 18 (2): 19–32.

Edelman, Marc. 2014. "Food Sovereignty: Forgotten Genealogies and Future Regulatory Challenges." *Journal of Peasant Studies* 41 (6): 959–78.

El Comercio. 2013. "Virgilio Martínez Reivindicó Nuestra Tierra." May 23. https://elcomercio.pe/gastronomia/peruana/virgilio-martinez-reivindico-nuestra-tierra-cumbre-culinaria-mesamerica-noticia-1580154/?outputType=lite.

Elias, Norbert. 1994. *The Civilizing Process: The History of Manners and State Formation and Civilization*. Oxford: Blackwell.

Ellis, Robert. 1998, "The Inscription of Masculinity and Whiteness in the Autobiography of Mario Vargas Llosa." *Bulletin of Latin American Research* 17 (2): 223–36.

Erazo, Juliet. 2013. *Governing Indigenous Territories: Enacting Sovereignty in the Ecuadorian Amazon*. Durham, NC: Duke University Press.

Escobar, Arturo. 1995. *Encountering Development: the making and unmaking of the Third World*. Princeton, NJ: Princeton University Press.

Estes, Nick. 2019. *Our History Is the Future: Standing Rock Versus the Dakota Access Pipeline, and the Long Tradition of Indigenous Resistance*. New York: Verso.

Fabian, Johannes. 2002. *Time and the Other: How Anthropology Makes Its Object*. New York: Columbia University Press.

Fagioli, Marco. 2012. "Henri Matisse, il Primitivismo e l'arte moderna." *Critica d'Arte* 1 (51–52): 7–40.

Falcón, Sylvanna. 2018. "Intersectionality and the Arts: Counterpublic Memory-Making in Postconflict Peru." *International Journal of Transitional Justice* 12: 26–44.

Fan, Judith. 2013. "Can Ideas about Food Inspire Real Social Change? The Case of Peruvian Gastronomy." *Gastronomica: The Journal of Critical Food Studies* 13 (2, Summer): 29–40.

Feitlowitz, Marguerite. 2011. *A Lexicon of Terror*. Oxford: Oxford University Press.

Feldman, Joseph. 2019. "Memory as Persuasion: Historical Discourse and Moral Messages at Peru's Place of Memory, Tolerance, and Social Inclusion." *Museums and Sites of Persuasion: Politics, Memory and Human Rights*, edited by Joyce Apsel and Amy Sodaro, 133–49. London: Routledge.

———. 2012. "Exhibiting Conflict: History and Politics at the Museo de la Memoria de ANFASEP in Ayacucho, Peru." *Anthropological Quarterly* 85 (2): 487–518.

Few, Martha, and Zeb Tortorici. 2013. *Centering Animals in Latin American History*. Durham, NC: Duke University Press.

Figueroa, Meleiza. 2015. "Food Sovereignty in Everyday Life: Toward a People-Centered Approach to Food Systems." *Globalizations* 12 (4): 498–512.

Foster, David William. 1989. *From Mafalda to los Supermachos: Latin American Graphic Humor as Popular Culture*. Boulder, CO: Lynne Rienner.

Foucault, Michel. 1990. *The History of Sexuality*. Vol. 1. New York: Vintage Books.

Franco, Jean. 2013. *Cruel Modernity*. Durham, NC: Duke University Press.

Franklin, Sarah. 2007. *Dolly Mixtures: The Remaking of Genealogy*. Durham, NC: Duke University Press.

Fraser, Laura. 2006. "Next Stop Lima." *Gourmet*, August. www.gourmet.com /magazine/2000s/2006/08/nextstoplima.

Fraser, Nancy. 1990. "Rethinking the Public Sphere: A Contribution to the Critique of Actually Existing Democracy." *Social Text* 25 (26): 56–80.

Fuentes, Agustín. 2010. "Naturalcultural Encounters in Bali: Monkeys, Temples, Tourists, and Ethnoprimatology." *Cultural Anthropology* 25 (4): 600–624.

Fuenzalida, Fernando. 1970. "Poder, raza y etnia en el Perú contemporáneo." In *El Indio y el Poder en el Peru*, 15–87. Peru problema, no 4. Lima: Instituto de Estudios Peruanos.

Fusco, Coco, and Paula Heredia, dirs. 1993. *The Couple in the Cage: A Guatinaui Odyssey*. Daisy Wright Authentic Documentary Productions.

Gaard, Greta. 2013. "Toward a Feminist Postcolonial Milk Studies." *American Quarterly* 65 (3): 595–618.

———. 1993. *Ecofeminism: Women, Animals, Nature*. Philadelphia, PA: Temple University Press.

Galdós, Carlos. 2015. "No Voy a Mistura porque . . . Las excusas de los que quieren bajarle la llanta al festival." *Somos, El Comercio*, September 12, 58.

Galeano, Eduardo. 1973. *Open Veins of Latin America: Five Centuries of the Pillage of a Continent*. New York: Monthly Review Press.

Galt, Rosalind. 2019. "Learning from a Llama, and Other Fishy Tales: Anticolonial Aesthetics in Lucrecia Martel's *Zama*." *Cine-Files* 14 (Spring). http://www .thecine-files.com/galt/.

Gandolfo, Daniella. 2009. *The City at Its Limits: Taboo, Transgression, and Urban Renewal in Lima*. Chicago: University of Chicago Press.

Garayar, Carlos, et al. 1997. *La Hacienda en el Perú: Historia y Leyenda*. Lima: Ediciones Peisa, Banco Latino.

García, Alan. 2007. "El síndrome del perro del hortelano." *El Comercio*, October 28. https://archivo.elcomercio.pe/edicionimpresa/html/2007-10-28/el_sindrome _del_perro_del_hort.html.

García, María Elena. 2019a. "Death of a Guinea Pig: Grief and the Limits of Multispecies Ethnography in Peru." *Environmental Humanities* 11 (2): 351–72.

———. 2019b. "How Guinea Pigs Work: Figurations and Gastro-politics in Peru." In *How Nature Works: Rethinking Labor on a Troubled Planet*, edited by Sarah Besky and Alex Blanchette, 131–48. Santa Fe, NM: School for Advanced Research Press.

———. 2013. "The Taste of Conquest: Colonialism, Cosmopolitics, and the Dark Side of Peru's Gastronomic Boom." *Journal of Latin American and Caribbean Anthropology* 18 (3): 505–24.

———. 2010. "Super Guinea Pigs?" *Anthropology Now* 2 (2, September): 22–32.

———. 2005. *Making Indigenous Citizens: Identity, Development, and Multicultural Activism in Peru*. Stanford, CA: Stanford University Press.

García, María Elena, and José Antonio Lucero. 2008. "Exceptional Others: Politicians, Rottweilers, and Alterity in the 2006 Peruvian Elections." In "Indigenous Encounters: Race, Place, and Gender in Contemporary Peru." Special issue, *Latin American and Caribbean Ethnic Studies* 3 (3, November): 253–70.

García, Uriel. 1973. *El nuevo Indio*. Lima: Editorial Universo.

García Márquez, Gabriel. 2006. *One Hundred Years of Solitude*. New York: Harper Perennial Modern Classics.

Gibson, Eleanor. 2019. "Fraying Grass Roof Tops Mil Centro Restaurant in Peru's Historical Sacred Valley." De Zeen, January 10. https://www.dezeen.com/2019 /01/10/mil-centro-estudio-rafael-freyre-sacred-valley-peru/.

Gillespie, Kathryn. 2018. *The Cow with Ear Tag #1389*. Chicago: University of Chicago Press.

———. 2016. "Witnessing Animal Others: Bearing Witness, Grief, and the Political Function of Emotion." *Hypatia* 31 (3): 572–88.

———. 2013. "Sexualized Violence and the Gendered Commodification of the Animal Body in Pacific Northwest US Dairy Production." *Gender, Place & Culture: A Journal of Feminist Geography* 21 (10): 1321–37. doi:10.1080/0966369X.2013.832665.

Ginocchio Balcázar, Luis. 2012. *Pequeña agricultura y gastronomía: Oportunidades y desafíos*. Lima: Apega.

Godenzzi, Juan Carlos, ed. 1992. *El Quechua en debate: Ideología, normalización y enseñanza*. Cusco: Centro de Estudios Andinos "Bartolomé de las Casas."

Gómez-Barris, Macarena. 2017. *The Extractive Zone: Social Ecologies and Decolonial Perspectives*. Durham, NC: Duke University Press.

Goody, Jack. 1996. *Cooking, Cuisine and Class: A Study in Comparative Sociology*. Cambridge, UK: Cambridge University Press.

Gordon, Avery. 2008. *Ghostly Matters: Haunting and the Sociological Imagination.* Minneapolis: University of Minnesota Press.

Gorriti, Gustavo.1999. *The Shining Path: A History of the Millenarian War in Peru.* Chapel Hill: University of North Carolina Press.

Gose, Peter. 2018. "The Semi-social Mountain: Metapersonhood and Political Ontology in the Andes." *HAU: Journal of Ethnographic Theory* 8 (3): 488–505.

Govindrajan, Radhika. 2018a. *Animal Intimacies: Interspecies Relatedness in India's Central Himalayas.* Chicago: University of Chicago Press.

———. 2018b. "More-Than-Human-Democracy: On the Political Lives of Cows, Rivers, and Mountains in India." Paper delivered at the Simpson Center for the Humanities Society of Scholars Fellows Program, University of Washington, November 28.

———. 2015. "'The Goat That Died for Family': Animal Sacrifice and Interspecies Kinship in India's Central Himalayas." *American Ethnologist* 42 (3): 504–19.

Graeber, David. 2015. "Radical Alterity Is Just Another Way of Saying 'Reality': A Reply to Eduardo Viveiros De Castro." *HAU: Journal of Ethnographic Theory* 5 (2): 41.

Graham, Laura. 2014. *Performing Indigeneity: Global Histories and Contemporary Experiences.* Lincoln: University of Nebraska Press.

———. 2003. "How Should an Indian Speak: Amazonian Indians and the Symbolic Politics of Language in the Global Public Sphere." In *Indigenous Movements, Self-Representation, and the State in Latin America,* edited by Kay Warren and Jean Jackson, 181–228. Austin: University of Texas Press.

Greene, Shane. 2006. "Getting over the Andes: The Geo-Eco-Politics of Indigenous Movements in Peru's Twenty-First Century Inca Empire." *Journal of Latin American Studies* 38 (2): 327–54.

Grey, Sam, and Lenore Newman. 2018. "Beyond Culinary Colonialism: Indigenous Food Sovereignty, Liberal Multiculturalism, and the Control of Gastronomic Capital." *Agriculture and Human Values* 35 (3): 717–30.

Grey, Sam, and Raj Patel. 2015. "Food Sovereignty as Decolonization: Some Contributions from Indigenous Movements to Food System and Development Politics." *Agriculture and Human Values* 32 (3): 431–44.

Griffiths, Alison. 2002. *Wondrous Difference: Cinema, Anthropology, and Turn-of-the-Century Visual Culture.* New York: Columbia University Press.

Gruen, Lori. 2014a. *Entangled Empathy: An Alternative Ethic for Our Relationships with Animals.* New York: Lantern Books.

———. 2014b. "Facing Death and Practicing Grief." In *Ecofeminism,* edited by Carol J. Adams and Lori Gruen, 127–41. New York: Bloomsbury.

———. 2011. *Ethics and Animals: An Introduction.* New York: Cambridge University Press.

Guerrero, Andres. 1997. "The Construction of a Ventriloquist's Image: Liberal Discourse and the 'Miserable Indian Race' in Late 19th-Century Ecuador." *Journal of Latin American Studies* (29) 3: 555–90.

Guerrero Espinoza, Ana María. 2014. *Lo inescuchable: Reflexiones sobre practicas en salud mental a partir de la violencia sexual durante el conflict armado interno.* Lima: Centro de Estudios y Publicaciones.

Guha, Ranajit. 1997. *Subaltern Studies: Writings on South Asian History and Society.* Vol. 1. Oxford: Oxford University Press.

Gunther, Juan. 1992. "Las Ciudades Hablan." In *500 años después: El nuevo rostro del Peru*, 57–71. Lima: Nuevas Ideas S. R. L.

Gupta, Clare. 2015. "Return to Freedom: Anti-GMO aloha ʻĀina Activism on Molokai as an Expression of Place-Based Food Sovereignty." *Globalizations* 12 (4): 529–44.

Gustafson, Bret. 2020. *Bolivia in the Age of Gas.* Durham, NC: Duke University Press.

———. 2009. *New Languages of the State: Indigenous Resurgence and the Politics of Knowledge in Bolivia.* Durham, NC: Duke University Press

Hale, Charles. 2008. "En contra del reconocimiento? Gobierno plural y análisis social ante la diferencia cultural." In *Gobernar (en) La Diversidad: Experiencias Indígenas Desde América Latina. Hacia la Investigación de Co-Labor*, edited by Xochitl Leyva, Araceli Burguete, and Shannon Speed, 515–24. Mexico City: Publicaciones de la Casa Chata.

———. 2005. "Neoliberal Multiculturalism: The Remaking of Cultural Rights and Racial Dominance in Central America." *Political and Legal Anthropology Review* 28 (1): 10–28.

———. 2004. "Rethinking Indigenous Politics in the Era of the ʻIndio Permitido.'" *NACLA: Report on the Americas* 38 (2): 16–21.

———. 2002. "Does Multiculturalism Menace? Governance, Cultural Rights and the Politics of Identity in Guatemala." *Journal of Latin American Studies* 34 (3): 485–524.

Hale, Charles, and Rosamel Millamán. 2006. "Cultural Agency and Political Struggle in the Era of the *Indio Permitido.*" In *Cultural Agency in the Americas*, edited by Doris Sommer, 281–304. Durham, NC: Duke University Press.

Hall, Stuart. 1980. "Race, Articulation, and Societies Structured in Dominance." In *Sociological Theories: Racism and Colonialism*, 305–45. Paris: UNESCO.

Haraway, Donna. 2016. *Staying with the Trouble: Making Kin in the Chthulucene.* Durham, NC: Duke University Press.

———. 2008. *When Species Meet.* Minneapolis: University of Minnesota Press.

———. 1992. "Ecce Homo, Ain't (Ar'n't) I a Woman, and Inappropriate/d Others: The Human in a Post-Humanist Landscape." In *Feminists Theorize the Political*, edited by J. Butler and J. W. Scott, 86–100. London: Routledge.

Hartigan, John. 2017. *Care of the Species: Races of Corn and the Science of Plant Biodiversity.* Minnesota: University of Minnesota Press.

Harvey, David. 2000. *Spaces of Hope.* Berkeley: University of California Press.

Hays-Mitchell, Maureen. 2002. "Resisting Austerity: A Gendered Perspective on Neo-liberal Restructuring in Peru." *Gender & Development* 10 (3): 71–81.

Healy, Kevin. 2001. *Llamas, Weavings, and Organic Chocolate: Multicultural Grassroots Development in the Andes and Amazon of Bolivia*. Notre Dame, IN: University of Notre Dame Press.

Hedge Coke, Allison Adelle. 2007. *Blood Run*. Cromer, UK: Salt Publishing.

Helmreich, Stefan. 2009. *Alien Ocean: Anthropological Voyages in Microbial Seas*. Berkeley: University of California Press.

Hinostroza, Rodolfo. 2006. *Primicias de cocina Peruana*. León, Spain: Everest.

Hirschman, Albert. 1991. *The Rhetoric of Reaction: Perversity, Futility, Jeopardy*. Cambridge, UK: Harvard University Press.

Hobsbawm, Eric. 1971. "Peru: The 'Peculiar' Revolution." *New York Review of Books*, December 16.

Holbraad, Martin. 2017. *The Ontological Turn: An Anthropological Exposition*. Cambridge, UK: Cambridge University Press

hooks, bell. 1992. "Eating the Other: Desire and Resistance." In *Black Looks: Race and Representation*, 21–39. Boston: South End Press.

Hornberger, Nancy, ed. 1997. *Indigenous Literacies in the Americas: Language Planning from the Bottom Up*. New York: Mouton de Gruyter.

Hua, Julietta, and Neel Ahuja. 2013. "Chimpanzee Sanctuary: 'Surplus' Life and the Politics of Transspecies Care." *American Quarterly* 65 (3): 619–37.

Huambachano, Mariaelena. 2015. "Food Security and Indigenous Peoples Knowledge: El Buen Vivir – Sumaq Kawsay in Peru and Tē Atānoho, New Zealand, Māori-New Zealand." *Food Studies: An Interdisciplinary Journal* 5 (3): 33–47.

Hylton, Forrest, and Sinclair Thomson. 2007. *Revolutionary Horizons: Past and Present in Bolivian Politics*. New York: Verso.

Jackson, Zakiyyah Iman. 2015. "Outer Worlds: The Persistence of Race in Movement 'Beyond the Human.'" *Gay and Lesbian Quarterly (GLQ)* 21: 215–18.

———. 2013. "Animal: New Directions in the Theorization of Race and Posthumanism." *Feminist Studies* 39 (3): 669–85.

Jackson, Jean. 2019. *Managing Multiculturalism: Indigeneity and the Struggle for Rights in Colombia*. Stanford, CA: Stanford University Press.

Janer, Zilkia. 2007. "(In)Edible Nature: New World Food and Coloniality." *Cultural Studies* 21 (2–3): 385–405.

Jeter, Clay, dir. 2017. *Chef's Table*. Season 3, episode 6, "Virgilio Martínez." Released February 17, 2017, on Netflix. www.netflix.com/title/80007945.

Justice, Daniel Heath. 2014. "Why We Eat Our Relatives: The Predation Perplex of Other-Than-Human Kinship." Talk delivered at the University of Washington, November 13.

Kahn, Howie. 2015. "Chef Virgilio Martínez Takes Peruvian Cuisine to New Heights." *Wall Street Journal*, March 4. www.wsj.com/articles/chef-virgilio-martinez-takes-peruvian-cuisine-to-new-heights-1425485872.

Kauanui, J. Kehaulani. 2016. "'A Structure, Not an Event': Settler Colonialism and Enduring Indigeneity." *Lateral: Journal of the Cultural Studies Association* 5 (1). https://csalateral.org/issue/5-1/forum-alt-humanities-settler-colonialism-enduring-indigeneity-kauanui/.

Kearns, Faith. 2017. "Water Is life, Relationality, and Tribal Sovereignty: An Interview with Melanie K. Yazzie." *The Confluence* (blog), October 24. https://ucanr.edu/blogs/blogcore/postdetail.cfm?postnum=25499.

Keme, Emil. 2018. "For Abiayala to Live, the Americas Must Die: Toward a Transhemispheric Indigeneity." *Native American and Indigenous Studies* 5 (1): 42–65.

Kim, Claire. 2014. *Dangerous Crossings: Race, Species and Nature in a Multicultural Age*. Cambridge, UK: Cambridge University Press.

Kimmerer, Robin Wall. 2003. *Gathering Moss: A Natural and Cultural History of Mosses*. Corvallis: Oregon State University Press.

King, Barbara. 2017. *Personalities on the Plate: The Lives and Minds of Animals We Eat*. Chicago: University of Chicago Press.

King, Thomas. 2003. *The Truth about Stories: A Native Narrative*. Minneapolis: University of Minnesota Press.

Kirksey, Eben. 2015. "The Multispecies Salon: An Interview with Giovanni Aloi and Maddi Boyd." *Antennae* 32: 8–12.

———. *The Multispecies Salon*. Durham, NC: Duke University Press, 2014.

Kirksey, Eben, and Stefan Helmreich. 2010. "The Emergence of Multispecies Ethnography." *Cultural Anthropology* 25 (4): 545–76.

Kirshenblatt-Gimblett, Barbara. 1998. *Destination Culture: Tourism, Museums, and Heritage*. Berkeley: University of California Press.

———. 1991. "Objects of Ethnography." In *Exhibiting Cultures: The Poetics and Politics of Museum Display*, edited by Ivan Karp and Steven D. Lavine, 386–443. Washington, DC: Smithsonian Institution.

Knobloch, Frieda. 1996. *The Culture of Wilderness: Agriculture as Colonization in the American West*. Chapel Hill: University of North Carolina Press.

Kober, Melanie et al. 2007. "Vocal Mother-Pup Communication in Guinea Pigs: Effects of Call Familiarity and Female Reproductive State." *Animal Behaviour* 73 (5): 917–25.

Kohn, Eduardo. 2013. *How Forests Think: Toward an Anthropology Beyond the Human*. Berkeley: University of California Press.

Kollenda, Heidi. 2019. "From Farm to Table: Productive Alliances as a Pathway to Inclusive Development in Peru." *Anthropology of Food* 14. https://journals.openedition.org/aof/9992.

Kovarik, Jacquelyn. 2019. "Silenced No More in Peru." *NACLA Report on the Americas* 51 (3): 217–22.

Kozolchyk, Abbie. 2018. "A Peruvian Chef Who Conquered the World Scales Higher Heights." *New York Times*, March 24. www.nytimes.com/2018/03/24/travel/mil-restaurant-review-peru-virgilio-Martínez.html.

Krader, Kate. 2016. "Latin America's Best Chef Will Open a Restaurant at the Top of the World." Bloomberg News, October 19. www.bloomberg.com/news/articles/2016-10-19/latin-america-s-best-chef-will-open-a-restaurant-at-the-top-of-the-world.

Krebber, André, and Mieke Roscher. 2018. *Animal Biography: Re-framing Animal Lives*. Palgrave Studies in Animals and Literature. Cham, Switzerland: Springer Nature.

Krögel, Alison. 2010. *Food, Power, and Resistance in the Andes: Exploring Quechua Verbal and Visual Narratives*. Lanham, MD: Lexington Books.

Kuzniar, Alice. 2006. *Melancholia's Dog: Reflections of Our Animal Kinship*. Chicago: University of Chicago Press.

Larsen, Peter Billie. 2019. "'The Dog in the Manger': Neoliberal Slogans at War in the Peruvian Amazon." In *Slogans: Subjection, Subversion, and the Politics of Neoliberalism*, edited by Nicolette Makovicky, Anne-Christine Trémon, and Sheyla S. Zandonai, 101–21. London: Routledge.

Larson, Brooke, and Olivia Harris, eds. 1995. *Ethnicity, Markets, and Migration in the Andes: At the Crossroads of History and Anthropology*. Durham, NC: Duke University Press.

Lasater-Wille, Amy. 2015. "The Taste of Distinction: Culinary Education and the Production of Social Difference in Lima, Peru." PhD diss., New York University.

Latour, Bruno. 2004. "Whose Cosmos, Which Cosmopolitics? Comments on the Peace Terms of Ulrich Beck." *Common Knowledge* 10 (3, Fall): 450–62.

Lauer, Mirko. 2019. "La revolución gastronómica peruana: Una celebración de 'lo nacional.'" Entrevista a Mirko Lauer. In "Gastro-politics: Culture, Identity and Culinary Politics in Peru." Special issue, *Anthropology of Food* 14.

———. 2012. *La Olla de Cristal: Mirando el future de la cocina peruana*. Lima: Universidad de San Martín de Porres, Fondo Editorial.

Lauer, Mirko, and Vera Lauer. 2006. *La Revolución Gastronómica Peruana*. Lima: Universidad de San Martín de Porres, Escuela Profesional de Turismo y Hotelería.

Lent, John, and Teresa Archambeault. 2005. "Conversations with Three Peruvian Cartoonists." In *Cartooning in Latin America*, edited by John Lent, 321–32. New York: Hampton Press.

Li, Fabiana. 2015. *Unearthing Conflict: Corporate Mining, Activism, and Expertise in Peru*. Durham, NC: Duke University Press.

———. 2013. "Relating Divergent Worlds: Mines, Aquifers and Sacred Mountains in Peru." *Anthropologica* 55: 399–411.

Li, Tania Murray. 2007. *The Will to Improve: Governmentality, Development, and the Practice of Politics*. Durham, NC: Duke University Press.

Lieberman, Sara. 2018. "Award-Winning Peruvian Chef Pia León on Her New Restaurant, Kjolle." *Condé Nast Traveler*, November 2. www.cntraveler.com/story /award-winning-peruvian-chef-pia-leon-on-restaurant-kjolle.

Livingston, Julie, and Jasbir Puar. 2011. "Interspecies." *Social Text* 29 (1): 3–14.

Loichot, Valérie. 2013. *The Tropics Bite Back: Culinary Coups in Caribbean Literature*. Minneapolis: University of Minnesota Press.

Loperena, Christopher. 2017. "Settler Violence? Race and Emergent Frontiers of Progress in Honduras." *American Quarterly* 69 (4): 801–7.

López-Canales, Jorge. 2019. "Peru on a Plate: Coloniality and Modernity in Peru's High-End Cuisine." *Anthropology of Food* 14. https://journals.openedition.org /aof/10138.

Lucero, José Antonio. 2013. "Ambivalent Multiculturalisms: Perversity, Futility, and Jeopardy in Latin America." In *Latin America's Multicultural Movements: The*

Struggle Between Communitarianism, Autonomy, and Human Rights, edited by Todd Eisenstadt et al., 18–39. Oxford: Oxford University Press.

Lugones, Maria. 2007. "Heterosexualism and the Colonial/Modern Gender System." *Hypatia* 22 (1): 186–219.

Luykx, Aurolyn. 1999. *The Citizen Factory: Schooling and Cultural Production in Bolivia*. Albany: State University of New York Press.

MacCannell, Dean. 1992. *Empty Meeting Grounds: The Tourist Papers*. London: Routledge.

———. 1976. *The Tourist: A New Theory of the Leisure Class*. New York: Schocken Books.

Mariátegui, José Carlos. (1928) 1994. *Siete ensayos de interpretación de la realidad peruana*. Lima: Biblioteca Amauta.

Markham, Clements. 2010. *The Letters of Amerigo Vespucci and Other Documents Illustrative of His Career*. London: Routledge.

Markowitz, Lisa. 2012. "Highland Haute Cuisine: The Transformation of Alpaca Meat." In *Reimagining Marginalized Foods: Global Processes, Local Places*. Tucson: University of Arizona Press.

Marks, Laura. 2000. *The Skin of the Film: Intercultural Cinema, Embodiment, and the Senses*. Durham, NC: Duke University Press.

Márquez, Alfredo. 2011. "Revolución Cultural y Orgía Creativa: El Taller NN (1988–1991)." Entrevista a Alfredo Márquez by Miguel A. López. *Tercero Text*, no. 2 (June): https://criticalatinoamericana.files.wordpress.com/2012/04/tercer-texto_lopez_marquez.pdf.

———. 2005. "Memoria de Inkarri." In *Inkarri Vestigio Barroco: Catálogo de la exposición*, edited by Alfredo Márquez et al. Lima: Centro Cultural de España.

Martínez, Malena, Virgilio Martínez, and Carlos Eduardo Vargas Tagle, eds. 2019. *Mater Catálogo: 30 especies para Central*. Lima: Edítalo SAC.

Martínez, Virgilio. 2016. *Central*. London: Phaidon.

———. 2015. *Lima the Cookbook: Peruvian Home Cooking*. London: Phaidon.

Martuccelli, Danilo. 2015. *Lima y sus arenas: Poderes sociales y jerarquías culturales*. Lima: Biblioteca Nacional del Perú.

Masías, Javier. 2016. "Mistura, la muerte lenta." *Correo*, September 18: https://diariocorreo.pe/opinion/mistura-la-muerte-lenta-699108/.

Matos Mar, José. 2004. *Desborde popular y crisis del estado: Veinte años después*. Lima: Fondo Editorial del Congreso del Perú.

———. 1984. *Desborde popular y crisis del estado: El nuevo rostro del Peru en la década de 1980*. Lima: IEP.

Matta, Raúl. 2019. "Celebrity Chefs and the Limits of Playing Politics from the Kitchen." In *Cooking Media and Mediatized Food: Exploring Globalized Eating Cultures*, edited by Jorg Dürrschmidt and York Kautt, 183–201. Houndmills, Basingstoke, UK: Palgrave Macmillan.

———. 2017. "Unveiling the Neoliberal Taste: Peru's Media Representation as a Food Nation." In *Taste, Power, Tradition: Geographical Indications as Cultural*

Property, edited by Sarah May et al., 103–17. Göttingen, Germany: Universitäts-verlag Göttingen.

———. 2016a. "Recipes for Crossing Boundaries: Peruvian Fusion." In *Cooking Technology: Transformations in Culinary Practice in Mexico and Latin America*, edited by Steffan Igor Ayora-Diaz, 139–52. New York: Bloomsbury.

———. 2016b. "Food Incursions into Global Heritage: Peruvian Cuisine's Slippery Road to UNESCO." *Social Anthropology* 24 (3): 338–52.

———. 2014. "República gastronómica y país de cocineros: Comida, política, medios y una nueva idea de nación para el Perú." *Revista Colombiana de Antropología* 50 (2): 15–40.

———. 2013. "Valuing Native Eating: The Modern Roots of Peruvian Food Heri-tage." *Anthropology of Food* S8. https://journals.openedition.org/aof/7361.

———. 2011. "Posibilidades y límites del desarrollo en el patrimonio inmaterial: El caso de la cocina peruana." *Apuntes. Revista de Estudios sobre Patrimonio Cultural* 24 (2): 196–207.

Mayer, Enrique. 2009. *Ugly Stories of the Peruvian Agrarian Reform*. Durham, NC: Duke University Press.

———. 1991. "Peru in Deep Trouble: Mario Vargas Llosa's 'Inquest in the Andes' Reexamined." *Cultural Anthropology* 6 (4): 466–504.

———. 1970. "Mestizo e indio: El contexto social de las relaciones interétnicas." In *El Indio y el poder en el Peru*, 88–152. *Peru problema*, no 4. Lima: Instituto de Estudios Peruanos.

McClintock, Anne. 1995. *Imperial Leather: Race, Gender, and Sexuality in the Colo-nial Contest*. New York: Routledge.

McClintock, Cynthia, and Abraham Lowenthal. 2015. *The Peruvian Experiment Reconsidered*. Princeton, NJ: Princeton University Press.

McDonell, Emma. 2019. "Creating the Culinary Frontier: A Critical Examination of Peruvian Chefs' Narratives of Lost/Discovered Foods." *Anthropology of Food* 14. https://journals.openedition.org/aof/10183.

McHugh, Susan. 2019. *Love in a Time of Slaughters: Human-Animal Stories against Genocide and Extinction*. University Park: Pennsylvania State University Press.

———. 2011. *Animal Stories: Narrating across Species Lines*. Minneapolis: University of Minnesota Press.

Mead, Rebecca. 2018. "Meal Ticket." *New Yorker* 94 (17): 46–55.

Medina, Ignacio. 2016. "La agonía de una gran feria." *El País*, September 9. https://elpais.com/elpais/2016/09/09/estilo/1473382437_263206.html.

———. 2014. *Mamá, yo no quiero ser Gastón*. Lima: Editorial Planeta Perú.

Medina, Ignacio, Gastón Acurio, and Ferran Adriá. 2012. *edén.pe: 21 revelaciones para el mundo*. Lima: Latino Publicaciones.

Melamed, Jodi. 2011. *Represent and Destroy: Rationalizing Violence in the New Racial Capitalism*. Minneapolis: University of Minnesota Press.

Melgarejo, Víctor. 2019. "Apega: 'Mistura 2019 Será Fuera de Lima.'" *Gestión*, January 14.

Melis, Antonio, ed. 2011. *José María Arguedas: Poética de un Demonio Feliz*. Lima: Fondo Editorial del Congreso del Perú.

Méndez, Cecilia. 1996. "Incas Si, Indios No: Notes on Peruvian Creole Nationalism and Its Contemporary Crisis." *Journal of Latin American Studies* 28 (1): 197–225.

Mihesuah, Devon, and Elizabeth Hoover, eds. 2019. *Indigenous Food Sovereignty in the United States: Restoring Cultural Knowledge, Protecting Environments, and Regaining Health.* Norman: University of Oklahoma Press.

Million, Dian. 2014. "There Is a River in Me: Theory from Life." In *Theorizing Native Studies*, edited by Audra Simpson and Andrea Smith, 31–43. Durham, NC: Duke University Press.

———. 2009. "Felt Theory: An Indigenous Feminist Approach to Affect and History." *Wicazo Sa Review* 24 (2): 53–76.

Milton, Cynthia. 2018. *Conflicted Memory: Military Cultural Interventions and the Human Rights Era in Peru.* Madison: University of Wisconsin Press.

———. 2014. *Art From a Fractured Past: Memory and Truth-Telling in Post-Shining Path Peru.* Durham, NC: Duke University Press.

Miranda, Deborah. 2013. *Bad Indians: A Tribal Memoir.* Berkeley: Heydey.

Miró Quesada, Francisco. 2004. "*Desborde popular y crisis de Estado*: Comentarios a un libro de José Matos Mar." In *Desborde popular y crisis del Estado: Veinte años después*, 152–58. Lima: Fondo Editorial del Congreso del Perú.

Miró Quesada Cisneros, Alejandro. 1992. "El Viaje de Colón Continua." *500 años después: El nuevo rostro del Peru*, 245–62. Lima: Nuevas Ideas S. R. L.

Miró Quesada Cisneros, Alejandro, et al., eds. 1992. *500 años después: El nuevo rostro del Peru.* Lima: Nuevas Ideas S. R. L.

Misia Peta. 2000. *Nueva Cocina Peruana.* Lima: Editorial Mercurio.

Moore, Donald, Anand Pandian, and Jake Kosek. 2003. "Introduction. The Cultural Politics of Race and Nature: Terrains of Power and Practice." In *Race, Nature, and the Politics of Difference*, edited by Donald S. Moore, Jake Kosek, and Anand Pandian, 1–70. Durham, NC: Duke University Press.

Morales, Edmundo. 1995. *The Guinea Pig: Healing, Food, and Ritual in the Andes.* Tucson: University of Arizona Press.

Moraña, Mabel, ed. 1998. *Indigenismo hacia el fin del milenio: Homenaje a Antonio Cornejo-Polar.* Pittsburgh, PA: Biblioteca de América.

Moreton-Robinson, Aileen. 2015. *The White Possessive: Property, Power, and Indigenous Sovereignty.* Minneapolis: University of Minnesota Press.

Mortensen, Amy. 2010. "Everyday Politics and the Absent Presence of the State in Lima, Peru." PhD diss.,, University of North Carolina at Chapel Hill.

Moseley-Williams, Sorrel. 2018a. "Everything You Need to Know about Pía León's New Restaurant Kjolle." The World's 50 Best Restaurants. www.theworlds50best.com/blog/News/everything-you-need-to-know-pia-leon-kjolle-restaurant.html.

———. 2018b. "How Virgilio Martínez and Pía León Are Changing the Culinary Landscape with New Restaurant Mil." The World's 50 Best Restaurants, June 28. www.theworlds50best.com/blog/News/virgilio-Martínez-pia-leon-changing-culinary-landscape-new-restaurant-mil.html.

——. 2018c. "Is This the Ultimate Destination Restaurant?" *Condé Nast Traveler*, n.d. https://www.cntraveller.com/gallery/mil-peru.

——. 2014. "The One Dish to Try in Peru Is . . . Guinea Pig." *Condé Nast Traveler*, September 25. www.cntraveler.com/stories/2014-09-25/the-one-dish-to-try-in-peru-is-guinea-pig.

Mujica, María-Elena. 1994. "Meals, Solidarity, and Empowerment: Communal Kitchens in Lima, Peru." Working Paper, Michigan State University, Office of Women in International Development, vol. 246.

——. 1992. "Women's Grassroots Organizations: Communal Kitchens in Lima, Peru." PhD diss., University of Iowa.

Murphy, Annie. 2013. "Peru Says No to GMO." *Christian Science Monitor*, April 25. www.csmonitor.com/World/Americas/2013/0425/Peru-says-no-to-GMO.

Murra, John. 1985. "'El Archipielago Vertical' Revisited." In *Andean Ecology and Civilization*, edited by S. Masuda, I. Shimada, and C. Morris, 3–13. Tokyo: University of Tokyo Press.

——. 1975. *Formaciones económicas y políticas del mundo andino*. Lima: Instituto de Estudios Peruanos.

Nading, Alex. 2014. *Mosquito Trails: Ecology, Health, and the Politics of Entanglement*. Berkeley: University of California Press.

Nass, Jesper. 2018. "Food: Experience, Culture and Performance." *Mater Iniciativa* (blog). https://www.blogmateriniciativa.com/post/food-experience-culture-and-performance.

Nordic Food Lab. 2017. *On Eating Insects: Essays, Stories and Recipes*. London: Phaidon.

Nugent, Guillermo. (1992) 2014. *El Laberinto de la Choledad: Páginas para Entender la Desigualdad*. Lima: Universidad Peruana de Ciencias Aplicadas.

Ocampo, Palmiro, Rosario Rojas, and Michel Sauvain. 2019. Sabrosos *Insectos Peruanos: Del Alimento Tradicional a la Innovación Gastronómica*. ISSUU, June 23. https://issuu.com/nhidalgov86/docs/pdf_issue_compressed.

Ogden, Laura, Billy Hall, and Kimiko Tanita. 2013. "Animals, Plants, People, and Things: A Review of Multispecies Ethnography." *Environment and Society: Advances in Research* 4: 5–24.

Olivas Weston, Rosario. 2001. *La cocina de los incas: Costumbres gastronómicas y técnicas culinarias*. Lima: Universidad de San Martin de Porres, Escuela Profesional de Turismo y Hotelería.

——, ed. 1996. *Cultura, Identidad, y Cocina en el Peru*. Lima: Universidad de San Martin de Porres, Escuela Profesional de Turismo y Hotelería.

Orlove, Benjamin. 1998. "Down to Earth: Race and Substance in the Andes." *Bulletin of Latin American Research* 17 (2): 207–22.

——. 1993. "Putting Race in Its Place: Order in Colonial and Postcolonial Geography." *Social Research* 60 (2): 301–36.

Pacheco Velez, Cesar. 1985. *Memoria y Utopía de la Vieja Lima*. Lima: Universidad del Pacífico.

Pachirat, Timothy. 2011. *Every Twelve Seconds: Industrialized Slaughter and the Politics of Life*. New Haven, CT: Yale University Press.

Palacios Sialer, Moshe. 2017. "Marca Perú: Perú Nebraska, subjetividad neoliberal y nueva narrativa nacional." MA thesis, Pontificia Universidad Católica del Perú.

Palma, Ricardo. 1923. *Tradiciones Peruanas*. Madrid: Calpe.

Pandian, Anand. 2009. *Crooked Stalks: Cultivating Virtue in South India*. Durham, NC: Duke University Press.

Parker, David. 1998a. *The Idea of the Middle Class: White-Collar Workers and Peruvian Society, 1900–1950*. University Park: Pennsylvania State University Press.

———. 1998b. "Civilizing the City of Kings: Hygiene and Housing in Lima, Peru." In *Cities of Hope: People, Protests, and Progress in Urbanizing Latin America, 1870–1930*. Boulder, CO: Westview Press.

Parreñas, Juno. 2018. *Decolonizing Extinction: The Work of Care in Orangutan Rehabilitation*. Durham, NC: Duke University Press.

Pérez, Patricia. 2014 *Buscando a Gastón*. Lima: Chiwake Films.

———. 2011. *Mistura: The Power of Food*. Lima: Chiwake Films.

Pettijohn, Terry. 1979. "Attachment and Separation Distress in the Infant Guinea Pig." *Developmental Psychobiology* 12 (1): 73–81.

Picq, Manuela Lavinas. 2018. *Vernacular Sovereignties: Indigenous Women Challenging World Politics*. Tucson: University of Arizona Press.

Pinilla, Carmen María, ed. 2005. *Arguedas y El Perú de Hoy*. Lima: SUR Casa de Estudios del Socialismo.

Pompilj, Giulia. 2019. "Los Colores del Apu Wañinmarcca." *Mater Iniciativa* (blog). www.blogmateriniciativa.com/post/los-colores-del-apu-wa%C3%B1inmarcca.

Poole, Deborah. 1997. *Vision, Race, and Modernity: A Visual Economy of the Andean Image World*. Princeton, NJ: Princeton University Press.

Poole, Deborah, and Gerardo Rénique. 1992. *Peru: Time of Fear*. London: Latin America Bureau.

Portocarrero, Gonzalo, ed. 2013. *Sombras coloniales y globalización en el Perú de hoy*. Lima: Fondo Editorial, Pontificia Universidad Católica del Perú, Universidad del Pacífico and IEP.

———. 2007. *Racismo y Mestizaje y otros ensayos*. Lima: Fondo Editorial del Congreso del Perú.

———. 2003. "Memorias del Velasquismo." In *Batallas por la memoria: Antagonismos de la promesa peruana*, edited by Marita Hamann et al., 229–56. Lima: Red para el Desarrollo de las Ciencias Sociales en el Perú.

Povinelli, Elizabeth. 2006. *The Empire of Love: Toward a Theory of Intimacy, Genealogy and Carnality*. Durham, NC: Duke University Press.

———. 2002. *The Cunning of Recognition: Indigenous Alterities and the Making of Australian Multiculturalism*. Durham, NC: Duke University Press.

Power, Gina. 2016. "In Heaven: The Tasting Menu at Central in Lima." *Food & Travel Blog.* http://gina-power.com/central-restaurant-lima-peru/.

Power, Margaret. 1999. "Women on the Right." *NACLA Report on the Americas* 32 (6): 24–26.

Prado, Manuel. 2016. "Califican de insultantes las delcaraciones de Cipriani sobre las mujeres y el abuso sexual." *La Mula*, July 30.

Pratt, Mary Louise. 2008. *Imperial Eyes: Travel Writing and Transculturation.* London: Routledge.

Price, Laura. 2018. "'Now It's My Turn'—Pía León Steps into the Spotlight with Kjolle." The World's 50 Best Restaurants. www.theworlds5obest.com/blog/News /pia-leon-best-female-chef-steps-into-spotlight-kjolle.html.

PromPeru. 2017. "The Generation with a Cause." *New York Times*, Paid Post, n.d. www.nytimes.com/paidpost/peru/thgeneration-with-a-cause.html?tbs_nyt= 2017-june-nytsocial_facebook-organic&cpv_dsm_id=9548558.

———. 2006. "Memoria 2001—2006: Comisión de Promoción del Perú— PROMPERU Gerencia de Planificación, Presupuesto y Desarrollo," 1–24.

Protzel, Javier. 2011. *Lima imaginada.* Lima: Universidad de Lima, Fondo Editorial.

Puar, Jasbir. 2017. *The Right to Maim: Debility, Capacity, Disability.* Durham, NC: Duke University Press.

Quijano, Anibal. 2000. "Coloniality of Power, Eurocentrism, and Latin America." *Nepantla: Views from the South* 1 (3): 533–80.

———. 1980. *Dominación y cultura: Lo cholo y el conflicto cultural en el Perú.* Lima: Mosca Azul Editores.

———. 1965. "El movimiento campesino en el Perú y sus líderes." *América Latina* 3 (4): 43–64.

Raheja, Michelle. 2010. *Reservation Reelism: Redfacing, Visual Sovereignty, and Representations of Native Americans in Film.* Lincoln: University of Nebraska Press.

Ramamurthy, Priti. 2019. "The Country and the City: Poetic Lives in India's Informal Economy." Presentation delivered at the Simpson Center for the Humanities, University of Washington, October 16.

Redman, Samuel. 2009. "Remembering Exhibitions on Race in the 20th-century United States." *American Anthropologist* 111 (4): 517–18.

Reddy, Chandan. 2011. *Freedom with Violence: Race, Sexuality, and the US State.* Durham, NC: Duke University Press.

Regan, Tom. 2004. *Empty Cages: Facing the Challenge of Animal Rights.* Lanham, MD: Rowman & Littlefield.

Renan, Ernest. (1882) 2018. "What Is a Nation? (*Qu'est-ce Qu'une Nation?* 1882)." In *What Is a Nation? and Other Political Writings*, edited and translated by M. F. N. Giglioli, 247–63. New York: Columbia University Press.

Rico Numbela, Elizabeth. 2010. "Conozca al Centro "Mejocuy" de Bolivia," January 6. http://ricardo.bizhat.com/rmr-prigeds/cadena-del-cuy.htm.

Rifkin, Mark. 2017. *Beyond Settler Time: Temporal Sovereignty and Indigenous Self-Determination.* Durham, NC: Duke University Press.

———. 2014. *Settler Common Sense: Queerness and Everyday Colonialism in the American Renaissance.* Minneapolis: University of Minnesota Press.

Risling Baldy, Cutcha. 2018. *We Are Dancing for You: Native Feminisms and the Revitalization of Women's Coming-of-Age Ceremonies.* Seattle: University of Washington Press.

Ritvo, Harriet. 1997. *The Platypus and the Mermaid and Other Figments of the Classifying Imagination.* Cambridge, MA: Harvard University Press.

———. 1987. *The Animal Estate: The English and Other Creatures in the Victorian Age*. Cambridge, MA: Harvard University Press.

Roca Rey, Bernardo. 2011. "La niña de sus ojos: El mundo posa la vista sobre nuestra gastronomía en busca de inspiración." In *Perú en Boca del Mundo: El Triunfo de Nuestra Cocina en Madrid Fusión*, 11–13. Lima: Editorial Planeta Perú.

———. 1992. "El Gusto Compartido." In *500 años después: El nuevo rostro del Peru*, 177–89. Lima: Nuevas Ideas S. R. L.

Roca-Rey, Christabelle. 2016. *La propaganda visual durante el gobierno de Juan Velasco Alvarado (1968–1975)*. Lima: IEP.

Rodríguez, Ileana Yamileth, ed. 2001. *The Latin American Subaltern Studies Reader*. Durham, NC: Duke University Press.

Rodríguez, Luis Aliaga, et al. 2009. *Producción de cuyes*. Lima: Fondo Editorial UCSS.

Rodríguez Pastor, Humberto. 2007. *La vida en el entorno del tamal peruano*. Lima: Fondo Editorial de la Universidad San Martín de Porres.

———. 2000. *Herederos del Dragón*. Lima: Fondo Editorial del Congreso del Perú.

Rodríguez-Ulloa, Olga. 2013. "La Última Reyna-Miss Cerro de Pasco: Performance y contaminación." *e-misférica* 10 (2). http://hemisphericinstitute.org/hemi/en/e-misferica-102/rodriguezulloa.

Rojas-Perez, Isaías. 2017. *Mourning Remains: State Atrocity, Exhumations, and Governing the Disappeared in Peru's Postwar Andes*. Stanford, CA: Stanford University Press.

Rosaldo, Renato. 2013. *The Day of Shelly's Death: The Poetry and Ethnography of Grief*. Durham, NC: Duke University Press.

———. 1989a. "Grief and a Headhunter's Rage." In *Culture & Truth: The Remaking of Social Analysis*, 1–11. Boston: Beacon Press.

———. 1989b. "Imperialist Nostalgia." *Representations* 26 (Spring): 107–22.

Rosenberg, Robin. 2013. "We Need a Hero: Superhero Origin Stories Inspire Us to Cope with Adversity (Capes Are Optional)." *Smithsonian* 43 (10, February): 22.

Rousseau, Signe. 2012. *Food Media: Celebrity Chefs and the Politics of Everyday Interference*. London: Berg Publishers.

Roy, Ananya. 2010. *Poverty Capital: Microfinance and the Making of Development*. New York: Routledge.

Sachs, Adam. 2008. "Peru's World-Class Cuisine." *Food & Wine*, November, 40–49. www.foodandwine.com/articles/perus-world-class-cuisine.

Safran-Foer, Jonathan. 2009. *Eating Animals*. New York City: Back Bay Books.

Sagástegui, Carla. 2009. "Acevedo and His Predecessors." In *Redrawing the Nation: National Identity in Latin/o American Comics*, edited by Hector Fernández L'Hoeste and Juan Poblete, 131–50. New York: Palgrave Macmillan.

Salas Carreño, Guillermo. 2019. *Lugares parientes: Comida, cohabitación y mundos andinos*. Lima: Pontificia Universidad Católica del Perú, Fondo Editorial.

———. 2016. "Places Are Kin: Food, Cohabitation, and Sociality in the Southern Peruvian Andes." *Anthropological Quarterly* 89 (3): 813–40.

Salazar Bondy, Sebastián. 1964. *Lima la horrible*. Lima: Ediciones PEISA.

Saldaña-Portillo, María Josefina. 2003. *The Revolutionary Imagination in the Americas and the Age of Development*. Durham, NC: Duke University Press.

Sanders, James. 2014. *The Vanguard of the Atlantic World: Creating Modernity, Nation, and Democracy in Nineteenth-Century Latin America*. Durham, NC: Duke University Press.

Sanjinés, Javier. 2004. *Mestizaje Upside-Down: Aesthetic Politics in Modern Bolivia*. Pittsburgh, PA: University of Pittsburgh Press.

Santos, Jesús. 2012. *Perú Sabe: Cuisine as an Agent of Social Change*. New York: Media Networks.

Sax, Marieka. 2011. *An Ethnography of Feeding, Perception, and Place in the Peruvian Andes*. New York: Edwin Mellen.

Scarangella McNenly, Linda. 2012. *Native Performers in Wild West Shows: From Buffalo Bill to Euro Disney*. Norman: University of Oklahoma Press.

Schreiber, Ronnee. 2008. *Righting Feminism: Conservative Women and American Politics*. New York: Oxford University Press.

Scott, James. 1992. *Domination and the Arts of Resistance: Hidden Transcripts*. New Haven, CT: Yale University Press.

Seligmann, Linda. 1995. *Between Reform and Revolution: Political Struggles in the Peruvian Andes, 1969–1991*. Stanford, CA: Stanford University Press.

———. 1989. "To Be in Between: The Cholas as Market Women." *Comparative Studies in Society and History* 31 (4): 694–721.

Shea, Maureen. 2010. "José María Arguedas' Sacred Link to the Animal in *El zorro de arriba y el zorro de abajo*." Paper presented at the Annual Meeting of the Latin American Studies Association, Toronto, October 7.

Short, Steven. 2018. "Locally Grown: Peruvian Chef Virgilio Martínez'ss New Restaurant." Luxury Defined, Christie's International Real Estate, November 14. www.christiesrealestate.com/blog/putting-local-first-peruvian-chef-virgilio-Martínezs-new-project/.

Simpson, Audra. 2014. *Mohawk Interruptus: Political Life Across the Borders of Settler States*. Durham, NC: Duke University Press.

———. 2007. "On Ethnographic Refusal: Indigeneity, 'Voice' and Colonial Citizenship." *Junctures* (9, December): 67–80.

Simpson, Leanne. 2013. *Dancing on Our Turtle's Back: Stories of Nishnaabeg Re-creation, Resurgence, and a New Emergence*. Winnipeg, MB: Arbeiter Ring Publishing.

Singer, Peter. 2002. *Animal Liberation*. New York: Ecco.

Singh, Bhrigupati, and Naisargi Dave. 2015. "On the Killing and Killability of Animals: Nonmoral Thoughts for the Anthropology of Ethics." *Comparative Studies of South Asia, Africa and the Middle East* 35 (2): 232–45.

Smith, Andrea. 2005. *Conquest: Sexual Violence and American Indian Genocide*. Durham, NC: Duke University Press.

Smith, Linda Tuhiwai. 1999. *Decolonizing Methodologies: Research and Indigenous Peoples*. London: Zed Books.

Sommer, Doris. 2006. "Introduction: Wiggle Room." In *Cultural Agency in the Americas*, edited by Doris Sommer, 1–28. Durham, NC: Duke University Press.

Soper, Kate. 1995. *What Is Nature?* Cambridge, UK: Blackwell Publishers.

Speed, Shannon. 2019. *Incarcerated Stories: Indigenous Women Migrants and Violence in the Settler-Capitalist State.* Chapel Hill: University of North Carolina Press.

Stanescu, James. 2011. "Species Trouble: Judith Butler, Mourning, and the Precarious Lives of Animals." *Hypatia* 27 (3): 567–82.

Starn, Orin, and Miguel La Serna. 2019. *The Shining Path: Love, Madness, and Revolution in the Andes.* New York: W. W. Norton.

Stengers, Isabelle. 2005. "The Cosmopolitical Proposal." In *Making Things Public: Atmospheres of Democracy,* edited by B. Latour and P. Weibel, 994–1003. Cambridge, MA: MIT Press.

Stepan, Nancy Leys. 2001. *Picturing Tropical Nature.* Ithaca, NY: Cornell University Press.

———. 1991. *The Hour of Eugenics: Race, Gender, and Nation in Latin America.* Ithaca, NY: Cornell University Press.

Stephenson, Marcia. 1999. *Gender and Modernity in Andean Bolivia.* Austin: University of Texas Press.

Stern, Steve, ed. 1998. *Shining and Other Paths: War and Society in Peru, 1980–1995.* Durham, NC: Duke University Press.

Stevenson, Lisa. 2014. *Life Beside Itself: Imagining Care in the Canadian Arctic.* Berkeley: University of California Press.

Stoler, Ann. 1995. *Race and the Education of Desire: Foucault's History of Sexuality and the Colonial Order of Things.* Durham, NC: Duke University Press.

Stutzman, Ronald. 1981. "El mestizaje: An All-Inclusive Ideology of Exclusion." In *Cultural Transformations and Ethnicity in Modern Ecuador,* edited by Norm E. Whitten Jr., 45–94. Urbana: University of Illinois Press.

Sulca, Rosalyn. 2016. "Cuy, alimento ancestral aliado de la salud." *RPP Noticias,* October 14. https://vital.rpp.pe/expertos/por-que-el-cuy-es-un-alimento-ancestral-que-sigue-vigente-noticia-1002430.

Swanson, Heather Anne, Marianne Elisabeth Lien, and Gro B. Ween. 2018. *Domestication Gone Wild: Politics and Practices of Multispecies Relations.* Durham, NC: Duke University Press.

Swenson, Edward, and Andrew Roddick. 2018. *Constructions of Time and History in the Pre-Columbian Andes.* Boulder: University Press of Colorado Press.

Taft, Jessica. 2019. *The Kids Are in Charge: Activism and Power in Peru's Movement of Working Children.* New York: New York University Press.

Takenaka, Ayumi. 2019. "'Nikkei Food' for Whom? Gastro-Politics and Culinary Representation in Peru." *Anthropology of Food* 14. https://journals.openedition.org/aof/10065.

TallBear, Kim. 2019. "Why Is Sex a 'Thing'? Making Good Relations for a Decolonial World." Lecture presented at the University of Washington, Seattle, April 24.

———. 2015. "Dossier: Theorizing Queer Inhumanisms: An Indigenous Reflection on Working Beyond the Human/Not Human." *GLQ: A Journal of Lesbian and Gay Studies* 21 (2–3): 230–35.

———. 2014. "Standing with and Speaking as Faith: A Feminist-Indigenous Approach to Inquiry." *Journal of Research Practice* 10 (2): 1–7.

———. 2013. "An Indigenous Approach to Critical Animal Studies, Interspecies Thinking, and the New Materialisms." Paper delivered at the University of Washington, May 24.

———. 2011. "Why Interspecies Thinking Needs Indigenous Standpoints." *Fieldsights*, November 18. https://culanth.org/fieldsights/why-interspecies-thinking-needs-indigenous-standpoints.

Tegel, Simeon. 2013. "Peru's Blackface 'Negro Mama' Continues to Offend." The World, December 21. www.pri.org/stories/2013-12-21/peru-s-blackface-negro-mama-continues-offend.

———. 2012. "Peru's Fantastic Food Revolution." *The Guardian*, September 21.

Theidon, Kimberly. 2014. *Intimate Enemies: Violence and Reconciliation in Peru.* Philadelphia: University of Pennsylvania Press.

Thompson, E. P. 1967. "Time, Work-Discipline, and Industrial Capitalism." *Past & Present*, no. 38: 56–97.

Todd, Zoe. 2016. "An Indigenous Feminist's Take on the Ontological Turn: Ontology Is Just Another Word for Colonialism." *Journal of Historical Sociology* 29 (1): 4–22.

Trask, Haunani-Kay. 1999. *From a Native Daughter: Colonialism and Sovereignty in Hawai'i.* Honolulu: University of Hawai'i Press.

Tsing, Anna. 2018. "Nine Provocations for the Study of Domestication." In *Domestication Gone Wild: Politics and Practices of Multispecies Relations*, edited by Heather Anne Swanson, Marianne Elisabeth Lien, and Gro B. Ween, 231–51. Durham, NC: Duke University Press.

———. 2012. "Unruly Edges: Mushrooms as Companion Species." *Environmental Humanities* 1: 141–54.

———. 2004. *Friction: An Ethnography of Global Connection.* Princeton, NJ: Princeton University Press.

Tuck, Eve, and K. Wayne Yang. 2012. "Decolonization Is Not a Metaphor." *Decolonization: Indigeneity, Education & Society* 1 (1): 1–40.

Tupac, Diana M., ed. 2000. *The Autobiography of María Elena Moyano: The Life and Death of a Peruvian Activist.* Gainesville: University Press of Florida.

Valderrama, Mariano. 2016. *Cuál es el futuro de la gastronomía peruana?* Lima: Apega.

Van Dooren, Thom. 2014. *Flight Ways: Life and Loss at the Edge of Extinction.* New York: Columbia University Press.

Van Dooren, Thom, and Deborah Bird Rose. 2013. "Keeping Faith with Death: Mourning and De-extinction." Presentation delivered at "Dangerous Ideas in Zoology," the 2013 forum of the Royal Zoological Society of New South Wales.

Van Dooren, Thom, Eben Kirksey, and Ursula Münster. 2016. "Multispecies Studies: Cultivating Arts of Attentiveness." *Environmental Humanities* 8 (1): 1–23.

Vargas Llosa, Mario. 1993. *El Pez en el Agua: Memorias.* Barcelona: Seix Barral.

———. 1991. "Questions of Conquest: What Columbus Wrought, and What He Did Not." *Harper's Magazine* 281 (1687): 45–54.

Vasconcelos, José. (1925) 2007. *La raza cósmica*. México: Porrua.

Veracini, Lorenzo. 2010. *Settler Colonialism: A Theoretical Overview*. London: Palgrave Macmillan.

Vich, Victor. 2015a. *Poéticas del Duelo: Ensayos sobre arte, memoria y violencia política en el Perú*. Lima: IEP.

———. 2015b. "No se trata de oponerse a la minería; más bien, se trata de identificarse con ella: El cuerpo de una Reyna de belleza en Cerro de Pasco." Lecture, Casa Pausa, Lima, Peru, June 17.

———. 2007. "Magical, Mystical: 'The Royal Tour' of Alejandro Toledo." *Journal of Latin American Cultural Studies* 16 (1): 1–10.

———. 2001. *El discurso de la calle*. Lima: Red para el Desarrollo de las Ciencias Sociales en el Perú.

Villar, Alfredo. 2018. "Alfredo Márquez: La imaginación militante." *El Comercio*, April 8. https://elcomercio.pe/eldominical/alfredo-marquez-imaginacion-militante-noticia-510101.

———. 2017. "Estrategias neobarrocas en 'La Pachakuti' de Alfredo Márquez." *Panambí: Revista de investigaciones artísticas* (5, December). https://revistas.uv.cl/index.php/Panambi/article/view/1040/1134.

Viveiros de Castro, Eduardo. 2004. "Exchanging Perspectives: The Transformation of Objects into Subjects in Amerindian Ontologies." *Common Knowledge* 10 (3): 463–84.

Vizenor, Gerald. 2008. *Survivance: Narratives of Native Presence*. Lincoln: University of Nebraska Press.

———. 1999. *Manifest Manners: Narratives on Post-Indian Survivance*. Lincoln: University of Nebraska Press.

Von Uexküll, Jakob. 1957. "A Stroll Through the Worlds of Animals and Men: A Picture Book of Invisible Worlds." In *Instinctive Behavior: The Development of a Modern Concept*, translated and edited by Claire H. Schiller, 5–80. New York: International Universities Press.

Wade, Peter. 2017. *Degrees of Mixture, Degrees of Freedom: Genomics, Multiculturalism, and Race in Latin America*. Durham, NC: Duke University Press

———. 2010. *Race and Ethnicity in Latin America*. 2nd ed. London: Pluto Press.

———. 2005. "Rethinking 'Mestizaje': Ideology and Lived Experience." *Journal of Latin American Studies* 37 (2): 239–57.

Wagner, Joseph. 1976. *The Biology of the Guinea Pig*. New York: Academic Press.

Walker, Charles. 2014. *The Tupac Amaru Rebellion*. Cambridge, MA: Harvard University Press.

Wallace-Sanders, Kimberly. 2009. *Mammy: A Century of Race, Gender, and Southern Memory*. Michigan: University of Michigan Press.

Weheliye, Alexander. 2014. *Habeas Viscus: Racializing Assemblages, Biopolitics, and Black Feminist Theories of the Human*. Durham, NC: Duke University Press.

Weismantel, Mary. 2001. *Cholas and Pishtacos: Stories of Race and Sex in the Andes.* Chicago: University of Chicago Press.

———. 1998. *Food, Gender, and Poverty in the Ecuadorian Andes.* Long Grove, IL: Waveland Press.

Weismantel, Mary, and Stephen Eisenman. 1998. "Race in the Andes: Global Movements and Popular Ontologies." *Bulletin of Latin American Research* 17 (2): 121–42.

White, E. B. 1948. "Death of a Pig." *Atlantic*, January. www.theatlantic.com/magazine/archive/1948/01/death-pig/309203/.

Wickstrom, Stefanie, and Philip D. Young, eds. 2014. *Mestizaje and Globalization: Transformations of Identity and Power.* Tucson: University of Arizona Press.

Wilson, Dana. 2002. "Starting with Stomachs: In Lima's Most Impoverished Neighbourhoods, Communal Kitchens Are Survival Oorganizations." *Alternatives Journal* 28 (2): 30–31.

Wilson, Shawn. 2008. *Research Is Ceremony: Indigenous Research Methods.* Black Point, NS: Fernwood Publishing.

Wolfe, Patrick. 2013. "The Settler Complex: An Introduction." *Settler Colonialism and Native Alternatives in Global Context, American Indian Culture and Research Journal* 37 (2): 1–22.

———. 2006. "Settler Colonialism and the Elimination of the Native." *Journal of Genocide Research* 8 (4): 387–409.

———. 1998. *Settler Colonialism and the Transformation of Anthropology: The Politics and Poetics of an Ethnographic Event.* New York: Continuum.

Wolff, Rebecca, et al. 2018. "Understanding the Meaning of Food and Work Through Community Photography in Peru." *Langscape Magazine*, Winter, 46–50.

Womack, Craig. 2013. "There Is No Respectful Way to Kill an Animal." *Studies in American Indian Literatures* 25 (4): 11–27.

Woods, Rebecca. 2017. *The Herds Shot Round the World: Native Breeds and the British Empire, 1800–1900.* Chapel Hill: University of North Carolina Press.

Wouters, Kwinten. 2018. "The Paisana Jacinta Controversy Continues to Divide Peruvians." *Peru Reports*, January 9. https://perureports.com/paisana-jacinta-controversy-continues-divide-peruvians/6553/.

Wynter, Sylvia. 2003. "Unsettling the Coloniality of Being/Power/Truth/Freedom: Towards the Human, after Man, Its Overrepresentation—An Argument." *CR: The New Centennial Review* 3 (3): 257–337.

Yamamoto, Dorothy. 2016. *Guinea Pig.* New York: Reaktion Books.

Yates-Doerr, Emily. 2015. "Does Meat Come from Animals? A Multispecies Approach to Classification and Belonging in Highland Guatemala." *American Ethnologist* 42 (2): 309–23.

Yong, Ed. 2018. "What a Grieving Orca Tells Us." *Atlantic*, August 14.

Yun, Hanguk, and Alejandro Guzmán. 2014. "Gastón Acurio: 'Si hay un problema de explotación'" and "Los Hombres Invisibles de Central." *Carta Abierta* 5, 12/2014–2/2015: 20–47.

Zavaleta Mercado, René. 1998. *50 Años De Historia.* Primera reimpressión de la primera ed. Cochabamba, Bolivia: Editorial Los Amigos del Libro.

INDEX

Italicized page numbers refer to illustrations.

anthropology, 75, 80–83, 224n41, 231–32n87

anticucho, 34, 156, 224n33

anxiety, 19, 198, 200–203, 206

Apega (Peruvian Society of Gastronomy): civilizing ideology of, 93–94, 109, 147, 153; elite ideology of, 9, 219n37; and gender roles, *115*; and Mistura, 102, 221n58; organization of, 16, 42–43, 102, 233n1; ten commandments of, 114–17

Appadurai, Arjun, 45

appropriation: of Indigenous knowledge and culture, xiv, 16, 63, 76, 88, 90; of Indigenous labor and bodies, 63, 90, 132, 173

Aráoz, Mercedes, 239n30

Arguedas, José María, 33, 75, 193

Arguedas, Luis Alberto, 107, 236n54

ASPEC (Peruvian Association of Consumers), 241–42n63

Astrid & Gastón, 7, 15, 26–31, 45, 53–54, 57, 209–10, 237n74

Ausangate mountain, 86

authenticity, 2, 16, 61–62, 68, 98, 118–19, 183

Aventura Culinaria, 31, 33

Ayacucho (Huanta) massacre (1969), 226n85

Aymara people and language, 25, 101, 213

babaco, 105

Bad Indians (Miranda), xv

Baker, Steve, 174

Baldy, Risling, 75

bananas, 150–51

Barad, Karen, 205–6

BCP (Banco de Crédito), 172

Bedia, José, 209–10

Benavides, Jorge, 140, 234n14

Benjamin, Walter, 203

Berlant, Lauren, 197–98

Bernedo, Karen, 221n4

Berrios, Dennis, 233n103

biodiversity: and cuy, 171; and gastronomic revolution, 2, 46, 132; and Indigenous producers, 235n31; and Mistura, 104, 127, 153; and Virgilio Martínez, 62, 64, 74–75, 77–78, 90

bioferias, 106, 109, 114, 116, 153–54, 241n60

Bitute: El sabor de Lima (Acurio and Masías), 227n114

Blackface, 234n14. *See also* race and racism

Bon Appétit, 16, 89

Bottura, Massimo, 88, 232n101

Brown, Wendy, 11–12

Brueggemann, Walter, 204–5

Bruyneel, Kevin, 126

Burman, Anders, 99

Butler, Judith, 204

Cabellos, Ernesto, 43

cacao, 74, 79

cachuleo, 136

Caja Negra (*Black Box*), 143–44

Cajete, Gregory, 154

Calle, La, 161

cama indecente, la del amor prohibido, La, 7

camal (killing area), 199–200

Campt, Tina, 242n4

"Camptown Races" (Foster), 156

Canessa, Andrew, 8

capitalism: colonial settler and racial, 18–19, 50–51, 76, 98, 103, 157, 210, 212–13; extractive, 133, 212–13; popular appeal of, 171–74, 180; and slow death, 192, 197–98

Carlos (Mistura festival organizer), 93–94, 97–98, 106–7, 112–17, 211

Carroll, Clint, 154

Casa Moreyra, 26, 28, 53–55, 57, 209, 212, 227n108

Castañeda, Claudia, 163–64, 166, 178, 183

Catholic Church, 26, 56, 140, 228n118

Catholic University of Peru (Pontificia Universidad Católica del Perú), 28

causa, 1, 12–13. See also *Cocina con Causa*; Generación con Causa

causas cinco razas, Las, 40–41

Ccopa, Pedro Pablo, 148

Ccori, 138–39, 141–42, 145, 147, 150

Central, 1–2, 60–62, 64, 66–67, 69, 72–78, 87, 233n109

Central (Martínez), 86

Cerro de Pasco, 2–4, 13–14

ceviche, 2, 33, 64

chaco clay, 84

chakra, 83

Murra, John, 61, 86, 132
Museo de la Nación (Museum of the Nation), 24
Mystery of Capital, The (De Soto), 39–40

Nazario (Quechua collaborator with de la Cadena), 86
Nazca Lines, 33
Negrita, La, 101–2
negro Mama, El, 234n14
neoliberalism: and gastronomic revolution, 32, 39–40, 48–49, 114, 129–30, 171–73, 182–83, 212; ideas of, 48–53; and Indigenous people, 100–102; and multiculturalism, 111, 210–12
"New Incan Gold: Peruvian Cuisine, The" (*KTCHN Rebel*), 75–76
Newman, Lenore, 76
new materialisms, 202
"New Nordic Manifesto" (2004), 78
newworlder.com, 67
New World Review, 67
Nikkei cuisine, 218n3
#NiUnaMenos, 56
Nobu (Nobuyuki Matsuhisa), 218n3
Noma, 78, 137
Nordic Food Lab, 137, 230n63
novoandina cuisine, 9, 15, 45, 165, 167, 220n53, 244n23
Nugent, Guillermo, 245–46n41

obesity, 2, 46
oca, 79, 244n23
Ocampo, Humberto, 142, *143*
Ocampo, Palmiro: and environment, 135–36, 138–39, 141, 144, 150, 154; and food waste, 137–43, 147–49, 151; and gastronomic revolution, 136–40, 142–47, 152, 213, 215, 220n46; on huatia, 240–41n46; and Indigenous knowledge and creativity, 142, 149–50, 242n65; life and career, 135–40, *143*, 147–51; TEDxTukuy talk, 138, 142, 150–51
Olivas Weston, Rosario, 232n91
On Eating Insects: Essays, Stories and Recipes (Nordic Food Lab), 230n63, 239n30
One Hundred Years of Solitude (García Márquez), 227n115

onions, xiii, 150–51, 155
Open Veins of Latin America: Five Centuries of the Pillage of a Continent (Galeano), 14
optimization of food, 137–42, 149. *See also* food waste
Opus Dei, 56, 140. *See also* Catholic Church
organic production: bioferias and, 153, 241n60; and cuy, 169–70, 244n23; Mistura and, 105–6, 195; Palmiro Ocampo and, 146; use of term, 241n63. *See also* food production
Orlove, Benjamin, 228n2
Ortiz de Zevallos, Felipe, 38
Osterling, Rafael, 45, 229n21
Other Path, The (de Soto), 39

Pachacutec Institute of Culinary Arts, 44, 218n15, 219n39
pachamama, 89
Pachirat, Timothy, 203
paisana Jacinta, La, 140, 234n14
Pandian, Anand, 114, 119
Participatory Guarantee System (Sistema de Garantía Participativa), 241–42n63
pasta, 83, 150
Payet, Guillermo, 244n23
Paz Soldán family, 26, 53
PDAC (Prospectors & Developers Association of Canada), 13
peeling machine (una maquina despeladora), 199–200
pelican, 193
Penal de Lurigancho, 155
Peru, Nebraska, xi–xii, 28, 34
"Peru, the richest country in the world," (PromPerú), 46–47
Peru 21, 38
Peru Sabe: Cuisine as an Agent of Social Change (2012), 223n29
Peru: The Cookbook (Acurio), 41
Peru TV, 144
Pesaque, Jaime, 220n54
Photovoice, 82
picarones, 34–35, 224n37
Picq, Manuela, 238n2
Pillco, Santiago, 89
Pillco, Seferina, 89
Pineau, Giséle, xiii

CALIFORNIA STUDIES IN FOOD AND CULTURE

Darra Goldstein, Editor

Founded in 1893,
UNIVERSITY OF CALIFORNIA PRESS
publishes bold, progressive books and journals
on topics in the arts, humanities, social sciences,
and natural sciences—with a focus on social
justice issues—that inspire thought and action
among readers worldwide.

The UC PRESS FOUNDATION
raises funds to uphold the press's vital role
as an independent, nonprofit publisher, and
receives philanthropic support from a wide
range of individuals and institutions—and from
committed readers like you. To learn more, visit
ucpress.edu/supportus.